College & University Budgeting

COLLEGE & UNIVERSITY
BUDGETING

○

An Introduction for Faculty and Academic Administrators

RICHARD J. MEISINGER, JR.
LEROY W. DUBECK

©1984 by the National Association of
  College and University Business Officers
One Dupont Circle
Washington, DC 20036

Library of Congress Cataloging in Publication Data

Meisinger, Richard J., 1945–
    College & university budgeting.

    Bibliography: p.
    1. Universities and colleges—United States—
Finance.   2. Universities and colleges—United
States—Business management.   I. Dubeck, Leroy W.,
1939–   . II. Title.   III. Title: College and
university budgeting.
LB2342.M43   1984   378′.02′0973   84-25583
ISBN 0-915164-22-1

Contents

Foreword

The American Association of University Professors and the National Association of College and University Business Officers had discussed for some time the need to provide a handbook for faculty members elected to budget committees and in other ways involved in the budget process. Both organizations have long shared a commitment to involving faculty in understanding the finances of the university and in decisions about the allocation of resources. In 1980 a jointly prepared proposal was funded by the Exxon Education Foundation. Thanks to the generosity of Exxon, we are now able to share with you this introduction to college and university budgeting.

The handbook is directed to two audiences: first, faculty members who are interested in participating in university and college budgeting; and second, academic administrators whose background is in disciplines other than economics and accounting and who are placed in the position of having to lead the budgeting process in departments, divisions, or universities as a whole. We believe the needs of both constituencies are similar and that this handbook is a resource not previously available.

It is imperative that all members of the university community understand the critical role of budgeting in communicating institutional priorities. Since many of the academic policy decisions of the 1980s have been and will continue to be strongly influenced by budget decisions, collegial decision making must be informed by a broad understanding of institutional finances and fiscal issues. Few committee responsibilities can compare in importance with service on a budget committee, and faculty serving on such bodies will doubtless wish to acquire an understanding of the budget process at their institution. In the future some faculty and all academic administrators will be more actively involved in influencing budget choices; those persons will need not only to understand generally but also to approach budget problems at the more sophisticated level discussed herein.

A task force composed of representatives of NACUBO and AAUP oversaw development of this handbook. In order to improve the book's usefulness, the task force attempted to make the text more descriptive than prescriptive. When the authors have considered them applicable, policies and practices encouraged by AAUP and NACUBO are reported. However, the handbook represents the views of its authors and is not a policy statement of AAUP or NACUBO.

D. F. FINN
IRVING J. SPITZBERG, JR.

Acknowledgments

While preparing this book, we received the support of a number of individuals without whose interest our work would have suffered. We are indebted to these persons.

Stephen D. Campbell, then director of NACUBO's Financial Management Center, developed the original proposal for this book and coordinated the project through its first phases. His successor at NACUBO, James A. Hyatt, ably continued in the role as project coordinator. Irving J. Spitzberg, Jr., then general secretary of AAUP, strongly supported the concept of a joint AAUP-NACUBO approach to the preparation of this book. D. F. Finn, then executive vice president of NACUBO, generously offered encouragement in the belief that better understanding of the budget process and of the faculty's role in it would benefit every institution.

Funds for this project were provided by the Exxon Education Foundation.

A key role in the conceptualizing and preparation of this book was played by an advisory panel composed of AAUP and NACUBO representatives: David J. Berg, University of Minnesota; Claude Campbell, City University of New York; Donald C. Cell, Cornell College; Elmer Jagow, Hiram College; Mary M. Lai, Long Island University; and Jon C. Liebman, University of Illinois, Urbana-Champaign. These individuals generously gave considerable time to reviewing the book in its many stages.

Early drafts of this book were reviewed by a number of our colleagues and many suggestions were received for improvement of the manuscript. In particular, we wish to thank the following persons for stimulating our thinking: Frederick R. Ford, Purdue University; W. C. Freeman, The Texas A & M University System; Lyman A. Glenny, University of California, Berkeley; Marilyn McCoy, University of Colorado; James R. Mingle, Southern Regional Education Board; Louis W. Moelchert, Jr., University of Richmond; Anthony W. Morgan, University of Utah; Michael L. Shattock, University of Warwick; Paul Strohm, Indiana University; Aaron Wildavsky, University of California, Berkeley; and Robert O. Berdahl, Stewart L. Edelstein, Allen Schick, Frank A. Schmidtlein, and Charles F. Sturtz, University of Maryland, College Park. Also, Ralph S. Brown, Jr., Yale University, discussed with us the AAUP definitions of financial exigency, and Ilona Turrisi, Florida State University, provided some case materials for departmental budgeting.

We are also indebted to Marjorie Huseman and Virginia Obermeier for typing and proofreading many drafts of this book.

Preface

Once upon a time at a large city zoo a recently arrived lion cub was placed in a cage next to a grizzled old-timer of a lion. The first evening the zookeeper came by at feeding time with his food wagon and tossed the old lion a huge piece of sirloin steak. The old lion began to gnaw at the steak with relish. Then the zookeeper tossed a pile of hay into the lion cub's cage and rolled the food wagon away. The young lion looked at the pile of hay for a moment, looked at the steak on the floor of the old lion's cage, and called after the zookeeper, "There's been some mistake here!" But by this time the zookeeper was out of hearing range. The old lion looked across his cage at the cub and said, "Pipe down, kid!"

The next evening at feeding time the zookeeper again tossed the old lion a piece of sirloin steak and gave the lion cub a pile of hay. This time the lion cub began to rattle on the bars of his cage with a piece of chain to get the attention of the zookeeper. He also shouted, "Come back here! There's been some terrible mistake! I don't want hay!" The zookeeper either ignored him or didn't hear him. The old lion looked up from his sirloin steak and said, "Pipe down, kid! And stop complaining!"

The third evening at feeding time the zookeeper again tossed the old lion a sirloin steak and gave the lion cub a pile of hay. The lion cub was beside himself with rage, storming around his cage and pounding on the bars with the piece of chain. He also bellowed, "I can't live on hay! I need red meat!" The zookeeper paid no attention to him, but the old lion wandered over to the cub's cage and asked, "Hey, kid, what's bothering you?" The young lion said, "There's been some terrible mistake. I'm a young, virile cub and I need red meat to keep my body going. Instead, they give the steak to *you,* an old-timer in his declining years. They give me nothing but hay. There's been some mistake here." The old lion smiled and shook his head sagely. "Kid, there's been no mistake here. It's just that you're being carried on the budget as a zebra."

The budgets of institutions of higher education can be every bit as puzzling to the uninitiated as the zoo's budget was to the lion cub. The purpose of this volume is to remove some of the mystery behind the budget process in public and independent institutions of higher education. The primary audience for this primer is composed of new academic administrators and faculty members who seek a more active role in campus governance and therefore need a greater knowledge of administrative processes, particularly in the area of budgets and budgeting. The book should also be useful to seasoned campus financial and academic officers who wish to be sensitized to the faculty role in the budget process.

Readers should gain sufficient understanding of the budget process to enable them to phrase academic questions in terms of budgets and the budget process and to become more constructive and knowledgeable participants in the budget process. This increased sophistication should lead to improved communications among participants in the budget process and should reduce frustration. The handbook should also enable faculty participants to better identify the issues with significant budget consequences and therefore to influence the budget process and its outcomes.

The handbook has two parts. The first is designed to provide a general grounding in budget theory and practice for the person newly assigned to a budget committee or placed in an academic administrative role. It will help readers to understand the framework within which university and college budgeting occurs and to become familiar with the terminology and the important issues. The more experienced budget committee member and academic administrator will find the second part full of technical information that should permit them to participate more effectively in the budgeting process.

Chapter 1 is an introduction to budgets and the budget process, with a brief explanation of why budgeting is an important element of policy making. The chapter answers a number of basic questions frequently asked by those unfamiliar with budgeting: What is a budget? Is a budget more than a thick, incomprehensible document? Why do budgeting? What, in a technical sense, comprises a budget?

Chapter 2 discusses the broader economic and political environment of budgeting and describes the framework for the budget process both on and off the campus. In this chapter the various sources of funds for both public and independent institutions are identified. Answers are sought for the following questions about the effect of political and economic factors on institutional budgets: For what goods and services do institutions expend their resources? Do the costs of these goods and services increase faster for higher education than for other sectors of the economy? What specific social and political factors, such as demographics and federal legislation, directly influence institutional budgets? How do states and local governments differ with respect to wealth, willingness to tax wealth, and the proportion of taxes directed to higher education? To what extent do public and independent institutions differ in their sources of revenues?

Chapter 3 identifies factors that distinguish the budget process of one institution from that of another. The concept of roles is discussed to provide a simple framework for understanding budget behavior at various levels of the budget process. To illustrate the complexity and overlap of budget cycles, multiyear summaries of the budget process in different types of institutions are presented. Finally, the principal actors are identified and the chronology of the budget process discussed for public and independent institutions.

The chapter seeks to answer the following questions: How does an institution's character shape the budget process? How can faculty and administrators participate more actively in the budget process? How do the roles of participants in the budget process affect the expectations of the participants? Why are budgets largely set two years ahead? To what extent is participation in the budget process constrained by the schedule of budget development? At what stages of the budget process is participation by faculty more likely? What do decision makers consider when they prepare and review budgets?

Chapter 4 describes how participants can influence the budget process. Questions are suggested for testing the assumptions underlying the process in a particular institution. Separate sections are devoted to institutional character and environmental factors, the structure and timing of the budget process, academic and administrative policies and procedures, revenue sources, the relationship of the capital budget to the annual operating budget, and the hidden costs of policy decisions. Some of the major policy issues confronting public institutions and state officials are identified. Finally, there is a brief discussion of how analytical tools and financial reporting can be used by participants to alter budget outcomes. The chapter attempts to answer questions frequently raised by faculty and administrators at the department and college levels: How are faculty salary adjustment pools determined each year? How is faculty workload commonly measured? How are budget allocations made among departments or colleges?

Chapter 5 examines sources of flexibility in the budget process. Flexibility and the ability to maneuver within a system of constraints are viewed as necessary for effective management. In many ways flexibility is the central concept in budgeting. Several constraints experienced by budgeters are identified and certain strategies suggested for increasing flexibility. Questions frequently raised by department chairpersons, deans, and faculty are addressed: Why is it important to conform to cumbersome institutional accounting procedures? What effect does collective bargaining have on the budget process? How can more resources be obtained for a particular department or college?

Chapter 6 discusses the sensitive issue of budget planning for reallocation and retrenchment. The least disruptive reallocation and retrenchment strategies tend to be those implemented in anticipation of fiscal stringency or of a need to reorder institutional priorities. In the midst of a financial crisis the range of options and the flexibility available to an institution tend to be limited. The experiences of participants in several institutions that have suffered fiscal reversals or major changes in priorities are cited to identify the major considerations in these situations. Also, several short-term, intermediate-term, and long-term strategies for coping with retrenchment and reallocation are identified. These strategies are applicable to both public and independent institutions.

Part 2 (chapters 7–14) describes certain basic technical tools used in the budget process.

Chapter 7 is an extensive introduction to fund accounting. The financial condition of a hypothetical institution is traced throughout the chapter. From this material the reader should begin to appreciate the complexity of even the smallest institution's financial framework and the need for a systematic monitoring of income and expenditures. The chapter will be of particular interest to faculty and administrators in independent institutions.

Chapter 8 summarizes the characteristics of several different approaches to budgeting: incremental budgeting; planning, programming, and budgeting systems (PPBS); zero-base budgeting; performance budgeting; formula budgeting; and cost-center budgeting. These approaches are not necessarily mutually exclusive; rather, they emphasize different aspects of the budget process.

Chapter 9 summarizes some of the primary policy issues in the area of endowment management. The emphasis in this chapter is not on particular strategies but on questions about spending strategies and the direction of endowment investment.

Chapter 10 outlines the procedures for cost analysis, a tool often used as the basis for decisions on the internal allocation of resources. A simple example illustrates the development of program and discipline cost data. The chapter also discusses some of the pros and cons of using comparative cost data, particularly across institutions.

Chapter 11 explains the instructional workload matrix, which displays the relationship between disciplines and student degree programs. The matrix for an institution represents the cumulative impact of individual student major profiles on student credit hour distribution.

Chapter 12 provides the briefest of introductions to enrollment forecasting. The technical bases for forecasting are discussed to demonstrate that projections are products more of science than of art. This chapter identifies factors that influence enrollment projections and distinguishes between those over which the institution has some control and those over which it has little control.

Chapter 13 discusses the nature of indirect costs associated with sponsored programs. What many faculty and administrators view as an arbitrary tax on sponsored activities is shown to have a solid basis in cost accounting.

For the reader who is more mathematically inclined, chapter 14 introduces a range of mathematical models that have been used in budgeting. This chapter demonstrates that although some institutions, including Stanford University, have adopted sophisticated modeling techniques, it is quite possible to enhance an institution's analytical capability through the use of relatively simple models.

This volume is not intended to be a comprehensive discussion of financing and budgeting in public and independent institutions of higher education. Participants in the budget process who do not have primary responsibility for budgeting generally have limited time to devote to the process. It seems reasonable to expect them to focus on the policy issues arising from the budget process rather than to immerse themselves in technical detail. As participants become more familiar and more comfortable with the process, however, they probably will begin to delve more into the technical aspects.

It is not possible here to do justice to the unique character of each of the nation's 3,000 institutions of higher education and the effect of that character on the budget process at each institution. Also, it is difficult to distinguish adequately between the public and independent sectors. Many institutions have strong traditions that account for enormous differences in the ways faculty and administrators participate in the budget process. Accordingly, this introduction to the process must be interpreted by the reader in the context of his or her own institution's unique character.

Part 1
The Budget Process

1 / Introduction

Budgets often seem on first impression to be thick documents composed of incomprehensible lists of names, salaries, and objects of expenditure such as equipment, supplies, communications, and travel, all categorized by certain organizational subdivisions or functions of the institution. The same impression holds that this document is designed by, and prepared for, a small number of technicians who communicate only among themselves and who have value frameworks much different from those of faculty and academic administrators. Accordingly, the budget is seen as an accountant's delight and a layman's nightmare, and, like institutional purchasing and accounting systems and physical plant activities, is a necessary part of day-to-day functioning that is too boring to engage the interest of most faculty and administrators. This all-too-common perception of the budget as something static and mechanical is shortsighted and highly inaccurate. In fact, the budget has a number of roles that have significant daily impact on institutional life. (See appendix 2 for the detailed description of institutional budgeting from *College & University Business Administration*.)

Clearly, budgets would be unnecessary if sufficient resources were available to satisfy the needs of everyone in the institution. And just as clearly, resources will always be insufficient to meet existing demands. Therefore,

3

a budget becomes a mechanism for setting priorities for institutional activities. After alternative expenditure plans are deliberated, the budget summarizes which activities will be supported within resource constraints. If additional resources become available, it will be possible to engage in more activities or to support the activities high on the priority list in grander fashion; if fewer resources become available, it will be necessary to engage in fewer activities or to reduce support for activities low on the priority list.

Similarly, a budget is a plan of action for the institution. The budget represents a list of proposed activities with price tags attached. As the budget cycle progresses, the nature of the activities may be altered and the estimates of expenditures may be changed, but the budget still provides the overall direction for the institution. The budget also provides coherence in an aggregate sense to a number of relatively interdependent activities, from the operation of academic departments to administrative support services and research programs.

If the budget is a plan of action, it is also a form of contract. In the public arena a state government appropriates funds for institutions with the expectation that the institutions will provide certain instructional, research, and public services. In both public and independent institutions, academic departments are allocated a share of the available resources with the understanding that faculty will teach a specified schedule of courses, counsel students, perform some department-sponsored research, and engage in public service. On the other hand, academic and support departments within the institution expect to be funded at certain levels in return for the services they provide. The budget is a summary of commitments made by both the funding agency and the recipient of those funds. From this implicit contractual understanding inherent in the budget arises a concern for accountability.

The budget can be viewed as a control mechanism. The flow of resources to activities is regulated in accordance with institutional objectives. Once resources have been allocated, their expenditure can be monitored and checked for conformity with plans and expectations. To ensure accountability, operating units whose expenditures deviate from the plan can be asked to justify the differences. If the deviations are significant but appropriate, they might be signals to modify the budget plan during the next budget cycle.

As a network of communication the budget is often the best way for an operating unit, department, or institution to express its objectives and to identify the resources needed to meet those objectives. This is timely and efficient in that most budget requests are reviewed at roughly the same time so that judgments can be made about competing activities. Also, decisions about how many resources a unit or institution is to receive are a form of communication as to how the activities of that unit or institution are valued by decision makers at higher levels. Changes in the budget from one cycle to another also communicate information about changes in priorities among activities supported by the budget and about changes in the availability of resources. These changes are especially important in that the budget is, among other things, an accumulation of historical obligations. Within a budget cycle the monitoring of expenditure patterns provides information about deviations from the expenditure plan and gives an indirect indication of how the institution and its operating units are adapting to unanticipated changes in their environment.

Above all, the budget is a political thing. It reflects the outcome of a series of negotiations over what activities should be funded and at what levels. To create the budget, a number of bargains must be struck and a number of trade-offs made. Participants in budgeting assert their leadership and influence to bring about changes in the distribution of resources. Also, there are always two or three budget cycles under consideration at any time. The results of negotiations over the budget for one annual or biennial cycle have an effect on the negotiations over the budgets of other cycles. As in any negotiation, the demands of one side are never completely satisfied. However, through the negotiation process the participants can effectively communicate their demands for services and their resource needs. Out of this process, too, should come a better understanding of the other activities competing for the same scarce resources. Negotiations over resources can be acrimonious, but if structured properly they should lead to consensus-building either within the institution or between the institution and its funding sources.

BUDGETING AS A PROCESS

As soon as a budget document rolls off the printing presses the commitments in it will have changed. Because the budget is an attempt to plan expenditures and forecast income and because such plans and forecasts cannot anticipate all future events, the budget generally undergoes revision as it is implemented. Thus, budgeting is a process that does not end with the assembly of a budget volume.

The single most important determinant of the budget for a given cycle is the budget for the previous cycle. Budgets represent a consolidation of decisions made earlier about the institution or its operating units and tend to be altered incrementally to reflect marginal changes in the complexion of the institution from one budget cycle to another. The budget for a particular budget cycle portrays an institution of a certain size, with a certain distribution of faculty salaries and ages and tenure statuses, with a certain student body of a given geographical distribution and academic and extracurricular interests, with a certain location, with a certain mission, and, in general, with a certain institutional "character." Because the nature of the institution changes, albeit slowly, the composition of its budget must change, too.

Budgets are designed to anticipate as much as possible any fluctuations in the institution's fiscal fortune so that faculty and administrators are not surprised by surpluses and deficits. At the same time, the budget must be flexible enough to allow institutional officials to respond to changes in the environment.

In summary, a budget is never "still." Thus, budgeting should be viewed as a dynamic consensus-building process that involves all the key decision makers in an institution or state.

WHY DO BUDGETING?

Budgeting as we know it is a relatively recent practice begun in the late nineteenth century. For centuries before, a budget was nothing more than a leather pouch in which the king or government official kept the receipts of taxation or the spoils of war or other sources of revenue, and from which he withdrew funds for his expenditures. The budget evolved into an expenditure plan as organizational life grew more complex and it became necessary to anticipate the future cost of operations and to compare those costs with expected revenues. The budget became a method for dealing with present and future problems in an organized fashion and for reducing uncertainty.

Institutions of higher education have extremely complex fiscal underpinnings. At Stanford University, for example, there are approximately 8,000 income accounts, most of them restricted to specific purposes (e.g., research grants and contracts can be applied only toward the project for which they are awarded; gifts earmarked for a particular function can be used only for that purpose; and revenue from the purchase of time on an institution's nuclear reactor must be used to operate and maintain the facility). The budget process becomes the means for planning and tracking revenues and expenditures so that resources can be used most effectively to meet the institution's educational goals as well as to comply with contracts that limit the use of the income. The management of resources serves at least two important functions. First, it satisfies the accountability requirement that unrestricted funds be spent properly according to the institution's legal framework and goals. In this sense the budget serves as a control mechanism. An underlying issue is the delicate balance between accountability to the source of income and institutional autonomy and academic freedom. Second, it recognizes that there is a direct dependence of several activities on certain restricted or designated funds. Under these circumstances administrators and faculty must realize that as funds decrease or disappear, the activities supported by these funds must be curtailed or eliminated.

Budgeting as a process of negotiation is also a means of deciding "fair shares," an ambiguous but important notion indicating how operating units or institutions stand relative to one another in the distribution of resources. Thus, the term does not necessarily imply a proportional distribution of increases or decreases in resources. No participants in the budget process ever receive as many resources as they could possibly use, but they are generally satisfied with their allocation if they perceive that relative to other participants they are treated equitably. If the reasons for the unequal distribution of resources are known and generally accepted, participants will tend to perceive that they have received fair shares of the resource pool. The extent to which participants believe that they have received fair shares is also a measure of the perceived legitimacy of the process through which resources are allocated and, more broadly, of the whole decision-making process within the institution or state.

The preparation of a budget should be viewed as an opportunity for individuals and agencies with a commitment to the institution to examine the institution's programs and activities. Although the operations of the institution are continuous, they can be rechanneled through changes in the budget. Because of the direct relationship between program operations and resources, the review of program priorities must be translated at some point into the language of dollars. Thus, fiscal decisions have academic implications, just as academic decisions have fiscal implications.

WHAT COMPRISES A BUDGET?

In any institution of higher education there are generally several different kinds of budgets in operation concurrently. Faculty and administrators at the departmental level may be affected directly by only some of these budgets that together comprise the institution's total budget. The following are the different components.

Operating budgets
Capital budgets
Restricted budgets
Auxiliary enterprise budgets
Hospital operations budgets
Service center budgets

The above may be characterized differently at many institutions. The broadest and most frequently encountered designations are the operating budget and the capital budget. The other components listed may be subsets of these but are discussed separately here because of their unique characteristics. (See chapter 7 for a detailed discussion of fund accounting.)

The operating budget generally includes all of the regular unrestricted income available to the institution plus those restricted funds (e.g., endowed professorships and sponsored programs) that are earmarked for instructional activities and departmental support. Activities included in the operating budget are the basic expenses of departments, schools, and colleges; student services; libraries; administration; campus operations and maintenance (i.e., facilities operation); development; and the unrestricted portion of endowment income, gifts, and student aid. Although the operating budget is interconnected with the other budgets and is therefore not independent, it is usually viewed as the core budget. Because the operating budget includes all unrestricted income, it is the budget most responsive to decisions about changes in program priorities.

The capital budget generally covers expenditures for major facilities construction or renovation. There is an obvious but often overlooked relationship between the capital budget and the operating budget: as new facilities are placed in operation, funds are required to equip, heat, light, and maintain them. Renovated facilities may be less expensive to heat and maintain. These factors must be anticipated when developing the capital budget and must be incorporated in the appropriate operating budget.

Restricted budgets usually encompass federally sponsored research grants and contracts, nongovernmental grants, certain endowment and gift income, and student aid from external sources. One example of the linkage between the operating budget and the restricted budgets is the relationship of the instructional program to sponsored research programs, which provide support for graduate students involved in research. Funding for the direct costs of research contracts and grants is restricted revenue, whereas reimbursement for indirect costs (i.e., overhead) is unrestricted revenue. An important aspect of much restricted income is its limited duration. Thus, the restricted portion of the institution's total budget is often subject to greater uncertainty than other portions of the budget.

Auxiliary enterprises are those activities that support the institution but that are financially self-contained and specific enough to be managed as separate budget items. Furthermore, each auxiliary enterprise has a source of income derived from students and, in some cases, the public. Examples of such activities are residence and dining halls, student union retail activities, intercollegiate athletics, bookstores, and college or university presses.

Normally, auxiliary enterprise funds can be transferred to education and general funds. However, there are several caveats. Some states prohibit these transfers in public institutions. Also, there may be unexpected tax implications. Furthermore, it is important that all costs, including depreciation, be moved to auxiliary enterprise accounts before any surplus is tranferred out.

Another type of auxiliary enterprise is a teaching hospital affiliated with an institution. The hospital operating budget encompasses the noninstructional components of the operations of the teaching hospital, to the extent that the instructional and noninstructional costs of medical or health services training can be separately identified.

Service centers are units in the institution that are established primarily to provide services within the institution and that receive most or all of their income from internal sources. These units include central word processing facilities, campus stores, photography and reproduction, and physical plant shops. Units treated as service centers have their own internal budgets but are not included in the institution's total budget because they charge other offices and departments within the institution for their services. From an accounting perspective these transactions are, for the most part, internal transfers of funds.

Subsequent chapters will focus mainly on the operating budget. Other portions of the institution's total budget will be discussed as they intersect the operating budget.

FOR FURTHER READING

An excellent introduction to budgeting is Aaron Wildavsky's *The Politics of the Budgetary Process,* 3rd ed. (Boston: Little, Brown & Co., 1979). Although this book focuses on budgeting at the federal level, the principles apply to budgeting in all settings. This book is essential reading for those who wish to become active participants in the budgetary process.

J. Kent Caruthers and Melvin Orwig provide a good overview of budgeting as it relates to higher education in *Budgeting in Higher Education,* AAHE/ERIC Higher Education Research Report no. 3 (Washington, D.C.: American Association for Higher Education, 1979). A well-written introduction to college and university financial matters is *Colleges and Money: A Faculty Guide to Academic Economics,* prepared by the *Change* Panel on Academic Economics (New York: Change Magazine and Educational Change, 1976).

2 / The Economic and Political Environment

Preparation and implementation of an institution's budget are as dependent on the general economic and political environment within which the institution exists as on the particular character of the institution itself. Most of these external forces are beyond the control of individual institutions or even the national higher education community. Accordingly, institutional budget planning must anticipate changes in economic and political conditions that may influence the income available to the institution and the costs that the institution may have to bear. Unless the institution's budget can withstand outside strains continually, the institution cannot survive.

NATIONAL ECONOMIC AND POLITICAL FACTORS

Higher education was a $70 billion business in 1981–1982, comparable in magnitude to agriculture's contribution to the Gross National Product and equal to that of the automobile industry, the communications industry, or the petroleum processing industry. In fall 1983 more than 12.3 million individuals enrolled in full-time and part-time degree programs. Off-campus extension, noncredit continuing education, and community service programs reached another 20 million individuals. Colleges and universities

11

now perform more than 50 percent of the basic research and 15 percent of the applied research conducted in the United States. They employ nearly 1.9 million people: 793,000 faculty, 280,000 managerial personnel, and 791,000 nonprofessional staff. Institutions of higher education employ one-quarter of the nation's scientists and engineers (Association Council for Policy Analysis and Research, 1981; private correspondence, Stephen D. Campbell).

An enterprise as large as higher education is affected by the same economic and political pressures that affect other major activities in this country. Some of the most significant pressures are long-term: (1) personnel costs, especially in an industry as labor-intensive as higher education; (2) the costs of plant maintenance; (3) the prices of purchased goods and services; (4) and the costs of complying with federal regulations and mandated social programs. Other pressures have been added recently: (1) the decline in the size of the traditional college-age population; and (2) reduced federal aid and state support as policy makers seek to control deficits produced by the recession.

PERSONNEL COSTS

By far the largest portion of higher education costs is faculty and staff compensation. Based on fiscal year 1972 data, salaries, wages, and benefits are estimated to account for 82 percent of educational and general expenditures (see figure 1) (Halstead, 1978, 5, 6; Halstead, 1983b, 52). The labor-intensive nature of higher education poses real problems for budget planners. The principal difficulty is that higher education, as a professional industry, is beset by slow gains in productivity. Increased productivity here is defined as an increase in the value of services without a concomitant increase in costs to the consumer of those services. Some service industries such as banks and insurance companies have, through the introduction of computer technologies, increased their productivity so as to allow for significant increases in salaries and wages without increasing the cost of services. In higher education, however, as in most professional industries, it appears more difficult to increase productivity by introducing new technologies. A true gain in productivity requires that the quality of the service be at least maintained. Thus, larger classes will not increase an instructor's productivity if the instruction becomes less effective.

Howard Bowen (1983, 21) has noted that "faculty compensation is less than half the total outlays for personnel and only a quarter of all expenditures." This computation uses as its base all institutional expenditures, including auxiliary enterprises. If one limits the base to educational and general expenditures, which exclude capital expenditures and auxiliary enterprises, faculty compensation generally ranges from 40 to 55 percent of expenditures. In the final analysis, faculty compensation accounts for a significant fraction of an institution's budget and represents the largest portion of total employee compensation.

In an earlier work Bowen (1980, 30–31) points to three characteristics that separate service industries from other sectors of the economy. First, many are based on an intellectual foundation requiring many employees to have exceptional skills that can be obtained only through years of rigorous training and experience. Second, they are tradition-bound in part because they are responsible for maintaining and furthering the intellectual and cultural values and development of this country. Third, most service industries require that their professionals be physically present to their clients. This requirement for personal communication in the delivery of services places limits on the scale of operations. However, in higher education several technologies, including television, computers, and films, have been available. Taking advantage of a gifted lecturer through telecasts or use of computer-assisted learning may represent a true increase in productivity. Perhaps such technologies would have had a more significant effect on productivity had faculty and administrators not resisted their wider use.

Because such a large proportion of the costs in a labor-intensive industry are personnel-related, the only way to achieve significant economies through nontechnological means is to control expenditures for salaries and wages. These economics usually require that, in the face of steady or declining budgets, salaries and wages or the number of employees be reduced. Institutions that anticipate financial difficulties and plan accordingly probably will have more options available and have less traumatic experiences than institutions that do not have a firm grasp of their financial condition (see chapter 6). Reducing faculty and staff affects morale sharply if it is done over a very short period of time. Also, rapid reductions are difficult to accomplish without major distortions because of tenure and longer-term contracts. Allowing attrition through resignation, retirement, and death is perhaps the most humane form of action, but during the 1980s this strategy will not suffice for many institutions. Faculty and staff mobility probably will be limited during the decade because of a relatively static job market, and the demographic bulge of faculty and staff in their late thirties and early forties promises fewer reductions because of retirement or death.

The relationship of the Consumer Price Index to faculty and staff salaries during the 1970s and early 1980s and projections of economic conditions for the balance of the 1980s indicate that faculty and staff compensation policies will be a major consideration of budgeters during the next decade. As shown in figure 2, since 1976–77 faculty salaries have not kept pace with either the Consumer Price Index or the salaries and wages of nonagricultural employees. Moreover, the gap between faculty salaries and the Consumer Price Index has increased over that period. Since 1970 faculty base salaries have declined in buying power by 20 percent. Additionally, faculty salaries have lost more ground than those in other professions in government and industry (Association Council for Policy Analysis and Research, 1981; private correspondence, Stephen D. Campbell). In the short term the salary differential should not prevent institutions from filling vacancies. Except for a small number of fields such as engineering, computer science, and business, many staff members do not move rapidly in and out of the educational labor market and are slow to respond to changes in compensation.

Even in the short run, however, it will be difficult to attract into expanding fields young people who are also in demand in industry and government and to retain the most able individuals in all fields. In the long run, the gap between academic and nonacademic salaries must be closed through some combination of a decrease in the supply of entrants competing for positions and an increase in demand, if the overall quality of faculty and staff is to be maintained. This may necessitate some hard choices among important values. The virtue of across-the-board salary increases is that they help maintain the real income of the entire group. At the same time, when funds are not available to meet the market for those who are in demand, the quality of the faculty and staff will tend to suffer.

COSTS OF PLANT MAINTENANCE

During the 1960s and early 1970s many colleges and universities enlarged their physical plants to accommodate increased student enrollments. Because these facilities were new or recently renovated, they did not require significant expenditures for maintenance during the past decade. However, many of these new facilities are now requiring substantial investments for upkeep as major building systems begin to wear out. Unfortunately, many institutional budgeters have become accustomed to allocating an insufficient share of budgets to plant maintenance, and the sudden demand for increased maintenance expenditures is beginning to strain institutional budgets. A major part of the shock comes from the inflated cost of replacement systems and renovation construction.

Even institutions that have not made major additions to their physical plants during the past two decades have tended to balance budgets by skimping on plant maintenance. Facilities that are not regularly and adequately maintained deteriorate more quickly than those that are cared for. Many institutions, especially those in the public sector with restricted accounting procedures, not only defer maintenance for too long a period but also do not set aside a portion of annual operating expenses to create a reserve for depreciation. By not adequately anticipating the future costs of depreciation and obsolescence, budgeters leave their institutions vulnerable to budget shocks when suddenly unavoidable renovation costs beyond ordinary maintenance are incurred. Ideally, from 1 to 3 percent of an in-

stitution's budget should be reserved for equipment and facilities maintenance (Jenny et al., 1981).

PRICES OF PURCHASED GOODS AND SERVICES

To measure the average changes in prices for a "market basket" (fixed
in terms of amount and quality) of goods and services purchased by colleges and universities through current fund educational and general expenditures, a Higher Education Price Index (HEPI) was developed. Updated
annually, the HEPI is based on the salaries of faculty and staff, the prices
of contracted services such as data processing, communications, and transportation, and the prices for supplies and materials, equipment, books and
periodicals, and utilities (Halstead, 1978). The various items priced are
weighted in the HEPI according to their relative importance in the current
fund educational and general budget, as estimated from national averages.

It is often argued that the prices of goods and services that colleges and
universities buy increase faster than the general price level in the economy.
However, when one compares the HEPI with the U.S. Bureau of Labor
Statistics Producer Price Index (formerly called the Wholesale Price
Index), one finds that the changes in indexes are nearly the same. Between
1966–67 and 1982–83 the HEPI rose from 100 to 308.8 while the Producer Price Index rose from 100 to 302.5. Between 1969–70 and 1979–80
the change in indexes was almost identical (Bowen, 1980, 111). Thus,
higher education has not been at a great disadvantage relative to other sectors of the economy in terms of the pressures placed on it by inflation.
However, in terms of the ability of the educational industry to maintain
sufficient flexibility to respond to these demands, it can be argued that a
distinct disadvantage does exist.

Comparing the HEPI and the Producer Price Index hides some of the effects of inflation on colleges and universities. For the last decade institutions of higher education have been meeting the rapid increases in the cost
of utilities, books and periodicals, supplies, and employee benefits by
holding down salary increases or eliminating faculty and staff positions.
Although energy costs, for example, have quadrupled since the 1973
OPEC oil embargo, they are still a relatively small part of an institution's
total operating budget when compared with faculty and staff salary costs
(see figure 1). Some colleges and universities have been able to balance
projected utility bills with only minor restrictions on salary increases. But
if this practice continues, the salary structure at those institutions will be
seriously eroded.

Most institutional budgets cannot withstand major fluctuations caused by
enormous jumps in the prices of goods and services. Many reductions can
be achieved at little or no cost, but significant reductions in fuel bills, for
example, often can be realized only through major renovations that en-

hance energy efficiency or through the use of computers to monitor and control utility consumption. For many institutions the cost of major energy conservation plans exceeds the amount of capital funds available to make the modifications.

During the past decade the largest increases in expenditures have been in noneducational and general activities, auxiliary enterprises, and hospitals, activities not reflected in the HEPI (Lingenfelter and Beets, 1980, 15). And in the 1980s colleges and universities may suddenly be faced with the cost of replacing expensive instructional and research equipment purchased during the expansion years of the 1960s and 1970s. Unless institutions have set aside depreciation reserves with which to purchase replacement equipment, the purchases will have to be made from the current operating budget. Most institutional budgets cannot readily absorb the shock of such expenditures.

COSTS OF FEDERAL REGULATION AND SOCIAL PROGRAMS*

A portion of the costs of doing business in any industry can be attributed to the responses to informal social pressures and government mandates in a number of areas: personal security, work standards, personal opportunity, participation and due process, public information, and environmental protection. Colleges and universities experience costs associated with these universal pressures and with several peculiar to higher education: emancipation of youth, federal grants and contracts, teaching hospitals and clinics, and tax reform. Federal regulations and mandated social programs touch all aspects of colleges and universities, from athletics to the care of laboratory animals.

It is difficult to isolate the fiscal impact of externally imposed regulations and guidelines. First, colleges and universities may be sympathetic to the objectives of many of the programs and would want to implement the programs in some form on their own initiative. Second, many of the costs of implementation cannot be separated from the routine operations of the institution (Lingenfelter and Beets, 1980, 21).

In assessing the impact of federal regulation and social pressures, several factors should be considered. First, the adoption of programs could result in either increased *or* decreased costs. For example, introducing a staff development program may lead to greater employee morale and productivity and hence decreased operating costs. Second, the costs of socially imposed programs should be considered in two parts: (1) costs of actual program operations, and (2) costs associated with compliance or the reporting of information. Much of the present concern about increases in institutional

---

*The section under this heading is adapted from Bowen (1980, 76–100).

operating costs arises more from inefficiencies in the way the programs are implemented or information is provided than from actual operations. For example, a frequent complaint is that affirmative action reporting requirements are too detailed, thereby imposing additional regulation. Third, the costs of socially imposed programs should be analyzed over a specific period of time. Some programs require the one-time expenditure of large sums of money that, if amortized over time, would not be significant on an annual basis. Fourth, the implementation of some social programs may not lead to higher aggregate expenditures but to a redistribution of expenditures among the various activities included in the budget. The net effect is a reduction in the priority of some activities and thus in the amount of funding for them. For example, resources once earmarked for additional library acquisitions might be directed to implementing affirmative action programs.

Overall, profit-making enterprises probably have an advantage in dealing with socially imposed costs. In the for-profit sector it is easier to pass on to the consumer (through higher prices) the costs of implementing these programs. Colleges and universities must rely on additional funding from legislatures and donors and increases in tuition and fees. (Legislatures are sometimes sympathetic to the fact that institutions incur additional costs in implementing programs but may be unwilling to increase taxes or cut other programs to compensate.) Increased costs that cannot be supported from these sources must be absorbed in the form of reduced instructional, research, and service programs.

The following list summarizes some of the specific mandates and requirements of the various social programs and provides a sense of their complexity.

Personal security. The federal regulations and legislation include: the Social Security Act of 1935, as amended (retirement pensions, survivors' insurance, disability insurance, unemployment compensation, health insurance); the Occupational Safety and Health Act of 1970 (OSHA); the Employment Retirement Income Security Act of 1974 (ERISA); and legislation on radiation safety and the protection of human and animal subjects used in research and teaching.

Work standards. The major pieces of legislation are: the National Labor Relations Act of 1935, which covers the rules of collective bargaining and employee organization; the Fair Labor Standards Act of 1938, which establishes minimum wages, maximum work hours, and overtime compensation; and the Equal Pay Act of 1963, which requires that employees doing similar work must receive equal pay regardless of the employee's sex.

Personal opportunity. In the area of affirmative action the federal regulations and legislation include: Executive Order 11246 of 1965, as amended in 1967, which prohibits discrimination on the basis of sex; the Employment Act of 1967, which prohibits discrimination on the basis of age; Title VII of the Civil Rights Act of 1964, as amended by the Equal Employment Opportunity Act of 1972, which prohibits discrimination on the basis of sex, race, creed, or national origin; Title IX of the Educational Amendments of 1972, which prohibits discrimination on the basis of sex in educational policies, facilities, programs, and employment practices; student financial aid programs, some of which require institutional contributions or impose significant administrative burdens; Internal Revenue Service regulations concerning discrimination in employment and student admissions; and various judicial decisions.

Participation, openness, due process, and privacy. The guiding legislation includes: the First Amendment of the Constitution; the National Labor Relations Act of 1935; and the Family Educational Rights and Privacy Act of 1974 (the Buckley Amendment), which deals with the management of records and the release of information.

Public information. Requests for information occur primarily in five areas: consumer protection, fund raising, enforcement of government programs, general statistical needs of society, and general public demands for accountability. Examples include: the need to clear with the Office of Management and Budget (OMB) questionnaires on federal grants; the financial, faculty-effort, and staff-effort reporting requirements of OMB Circular A-21; audit reports on student aid; and the annual data reporting requirements of the Higher Education General Information Survey (HEGIS).

Environmental protection. Colleges and universities are increasingly affected by pollution control requirements, restrictions on research involving radiation or recombinant DNA, and, especially in urban settings, crime, vandalism, and the problems of neighborhood deterioration.

Emancipation of youth. The constitutional amendment lowering the age of majority to eighteen has had a visible impact in three areas: (1) it has altered significantly the nature of student services such as residence and dining facilities; (2) because more students declare themselves "independent" of their families and are less dependent on their families for financial support, they place greater demands on student aid programs; and (3) instate and out-of-state student tuition and student aid differentials are undermined when emancipated students establish residence where they attend college.

Shared costs in federal grants and contracts. Colleges and universities tend to absorb some of the costs associated with conducting research generated by federal grants and contracts in that overhead reimbursement generally does not cover all indirect costs associated with conducting research and certain granting agencies specifically require the sharing of direct costs (see chapter 13).

Special costs of teaching hospitals and clinics. Teaching hospitals and clinics are subject to restrictions and guidelines governing patient care review, accreditation and licensure, accounting procedures, use of drugs and blood, use of radiation, and use of human and animal subjects for research.

Tax reform. Some of higher education's traditional tax-exempt privileges are being eliminated. Philanthropy has been hindered by changes in the general tax laws for individuals and corporations as less credit is allowed for donations and gifts. Also, the Internal Revenue Service has increased its scrutiny of the operations of nonprofit organizations in the effort to discover taxable income.

DECLINE IN SIZE OF TRADITIONAL COLLEGE-AGE POPULATION

The demographic profile of the United States will profoundly affect institutions of higher education in the next decade. During the 1980s there will be a decline of 15 percent (4.4 million individuals) in the traditional college-age population. By 1988 most institutions in this country will have felt the impact of this downturn (Glenny, 1980, 374).

Several factors compound the problems created by a diminished clientele base. First, the college attendance rate of persons age 18 to 24 actually declined during the period 1969 to 1978 (since then the rate has leveled). There is nothing to indicate that this decline will be reversed in the near future. Second, the career decisions of minority youth, who represent an increasing proportion of those age 18 to 24, will greatly affect the demographic profiles of colleges. Third, it seems unlikely that adults entering college will make up for the loss in the 18-to-24 age group, in part because there are a growing number of opportunities for instruction and training in business, industry, and government that will attract potential adult college students. In fact, post-high school educational opportunities offered by social, religious, civic, and nonprofit organizations and by business, industry, and government are expanding more rapidly than any group of opportunities except those offered by community colleges (Glenny, 1980, 374–378). Fourth, to maintain a given full-time equivalent enrollment requires many more part-time than full-time students. Institutions that have traditionally catered to full-time students in the 18-to-24 age group will find it difficult to change character rapidly enough to accommodate an older, part-time clientele.

The impact of demographics by region and type of institution may differ significantly from the aggregate picture. Also, it is important to distinguish between demographic data, which reflect existing conditions, and enrollment projections, which are based on certain assumptions (see chapter 12).

As a result of this changing demographic profile, most colleges and universities will engage in intense competition for students during the next 10 to 15 years. Institutions should expect their advertising, promotional, and recruiting costs to increase markedly. To be more attractive to potential students, institutions will probably have to offer more financial aid. Academic programs for which there is strong student demand will have to be expanded, and some academic programs will have to be changed to make them more attractive. Similarly, to accommodate the adult learner offerings will have to be scheduled at convenient times and locations. Public institutions may have to seek a larger proportion of out-of-state students.

CHANGES IN FEDERAL FUNDING PHILOSOPHY

The manner in which the federal government funds social programs in general, and higher education in particular, will greatly affect the revenues of colleges and universities during the next decade. Whatever strategies are employed, it appears that fewer federal dollars will be directed toward higher education because of deep-rooted changes in funding philosophy and growing competition from other sectors of government.

Being raised in the reexamination of the federal role in higher education are the questions of who benefits from and who should pay for higher education. More and more policy makers believe that the balance of benefits has shifted from society to the individual. Some of these policy makers have come to believe that the current system of higher education is over-built. A major aspect of the debate over who should pay for higher education is deciding the proper balance between the federal and state and local governments.

Before World War II the states were largely responsible for public subsidies to public higher education in the form of low tuition. Few public funds were directed to independent institutions in the form of institutional aid. After World War II the federal government became a more important participant in financing higher education. The G.I. Bill of Rights of 1944 provided massive sums of money to institutions as well as students. Both public and independent institutions benefited from this law. The balance was altered, however, in the early 1950s when the Korean conflict G.I. Bill awarded funds for college directly to the veteran without an institutional aid component. The federal government broadened its support of higher education in 1958 with passage of the National Defense Education Act. This law provided funds to institutions as well as students, especially students at the graduate level. During the late 1950s and 1960s the federal government provided considerable funds for buildings and facilities, libraries, and research and training. Direct aid to institutions peaked in 1965–66 and declined thereafter as the federal involvement in higher education began to focus on student aid. The 1972 Amendments to the Higher Education Act of 1965 established the policy of basing federal student assistance programs on need (Benezet, 1976).

Federal monies to public and independent colleges and universities awarded in the form of grants and contracts for research development and training are of the same order of magnitude as student aid funding. The federal government has attempted to maintain in its funding a delicate balance between the public and independent sectors by avowedly favoring neither.

In the early 1980s a reevaluation of the federal government's role in supporting higher education began. (An example is the removal of educational survivor benefits from social security.) During the previous three decades the nation's focus had moved from mass to universal higher education. The philosophy guiding federal support for this transition was based on increasing the access to higher education largely by promoting student aid. Over this period the emphasis on aid to economically disadvantaged individuals was broadened to include students of the middle class. One of the foundations of the federal government's generous support of higher education had been higher education's role as the primary means of social mobility. Over the last 30 years, however, the character of higher education has changed markedly. The community college movement, for example, has greatly expanded the access to some form of college experience. Also, college student bodies are no longer composed exclusively of full-time students in the 18-to-21 age group. More part-time students and adult learners are seeking college training while they support families and maintain jobs. More individuals are returning to college for recertification or to upgrade their professional skills or to embark on training for new careers.

The working out of a new relationship between the federal government and higher education for the 1980s will probably shift the burden of support away from the federal level. The states and the individual consumers of higher education will likely be asked to bear more of the costs. Business and industry and the nonprofit research organizations may be expected to take on more of the burden of basic and applied research.

STATE AND LOCAL ECONOMIC AND POLITICAL FACTORS

State and local governments are the single most important source of financial support of higher education in the United States. Of the $65.6 billion in current funds received by all public and independent colleges and universities in fiscal year 1981, $21.9 billion (33.4 percent) came from state and local government appropriations and grants and contracts. Other major revenue sources were tuition and fees ($13.8 billion) and federal appropriations and grants and contracts ($9.7 billion). The remainder came from auxiliary enterprises, institutional sources such as endowment income and sales and services of educational activities, and private gifts (National Center for Education Statistics, 1983).

State and local economic and political factors should have a significant impact on the fiscal fortunes of individual institutions. For example, the cost of energy and labor is generally cheaper in the Sunbelt than in the Northeast. The cost of housing is generally higher in metropolitan areas than in rural areas and becomes a factor in establishing the salary structure for faculty and staff. Also, state and local regulations often parallel federal programs in areas such as workers' compensation, building and safety codes, public health standards, occupational health and safety programs, unemployment compensation, and retirement programs.

Perhaps the most systematic way to approach the differences in state and local environments is to examine the following: (1) the level of state wealth, (2) the willingness of state and local governments to tax that wealth, and (3) the proportion of the taxes that state and local governments are willing to direct to higher education.

The level of economic activity in a state and the sum of personal wealth contribute to state wealth. This is measured as tax capacity, which is an index of the potential to obtain revenues for public purposes through various kinds of taxes. McCoy and Halstead (1979, 12) define the tax capacity of a state and its local governments as the amount of revenue they could raise (relative to other state and local governments) if all 50 state-local government systems applied tax rates at the national average to their respective tax bases. The tax base will be shaped by the state's demographic profile and the economic mix of manufacturing, agriculture, and service industries. In fiscal year 1981 the extreme values in relative tax capacity ranged from $3,333 per capita in Alaska (224 percent above the national average) to $737 per capita in Mississippi (28 percent below the national average) (Halstead, 1983a, 21). Thus in fiscal year 1981 Mississippi had only 22 percent of the inherent tax wealth of Alaska from which to support public services.

The willingness of state and local governments to tax their wealth is measured by tax effort, or the revenues collected as a percentage of state and local tax capacity. In fiscal year 1981 Alaska demonstrated the greatest tax effort (with an index 84 percent above the national average), and Nevada the smallest (with an index 38 percent below the national average) (Halstead, 1983a, 22). This means that Alaska demanded more of its tax capacity in that year than did Nevada.

Collected tax revenues represent the funds available to state and local governments and are an end product of tax capacity and tax effort. A state with low tax capacity and high tax effort can collect an average amount of tax revenues. Virginia, for example, collected revenues of $867 per capita in fiscal year 1981 (compared to a national average of $1,029) on the basis of a tax capacity that ranked 30th nationally (6 percent below the national average) and a tax effort that ranked 31st nationally (11 percent above the national average) (Halstead, 1983a, 22).

Several factors determine the proportion of state and local government revenues appropriated for higher education. The commitment to social programs varies widely among the states. Generally, the stronger the competition is for resources in a state, the smaller is the share allocated to any one social service. During the 1970s higher education's priority ranking in the states' list of social services actually declined. There are no indications that higher education's ranking will improve during the 1980s; on the contrary, it seems likely that the demand for support of prisons, health care, and welfare systems will increase significantly, further displacing higher education. Moreover, as state and local governments are asked to carry more of the cost of social services currently funded by the federal government, lower-priority services such as higher education likely will receive smaller shares of state and local resources.

Another determinant of appropriations is the nature of the higher education system in the state. A system composed of many community colleges is probably considerably less expensive to operate than one with a similar number of institutions overall but with more at the four-year level or above. Also, some states, particularly those in the Northeast, traditionally have a very strong independent sector and depend on those institutions to enroll a large number of students who might otherwise attend public institutions. A few states such as New Jersey experience a considerable out-migration of potential students and allocate relatively fewer resources to higher education. Some states, such as Maryland, base their contributions to the independent sector on the level of support for public colleges and universities.

SOURCES OF FUNDS

Colleges and universities in both the public and independent sectors rely on a variety of sources for financial support. Although the sources are similar from one institution to another, the extent to which any one source is tapped depends very much on the institution's character. Thus, independent institutions, for example, usually rely more heavily on student tuition and fees than do public institutions. Large research-oriented universities in both the public and independent sectors receive a greater proportion of their support from government grants and contracts than do four-year public and independent colleges.

Each of the revenue types is discussed below. For each type of revenue the aspects common to public and independent institutions are presented first; features peculiar to the sectors are presented separately. The list below does not identify student aid as a source of institutional revenue because it flows into the institution indirectly through students. However, as noted earlier, federal and state support for higher education via student aid is considerable (the impact of student aid as an indirect source of revenue is discussed as part of tuition and fees). Figures 3a and 3b summarize the proportions of income from the types of revenue above.

Institutional Resources

Source	Type of Revenue	Received Through
Students	Tuition and fees	Charge to customer
Government		
a. Federal	Appropriations	Subsidy
	Grants and contracts	Reimbursement for
	a. Direct costs	services
	b. Indirect costs	
b. State and	Appropriations	Subsidy
local	Grants and contracts	Reimbursement for
	a. Direct costs	services
	b. Indirect costs	
Private	Gifts	Contribution
(individual or	Grants and contracts	Reimbursement for
corporate)	a. Direct costs	services
	b. Indirect costs	
	Contributed services	Subsidy
Institutional	Investment earnings	Investment of
endowment and		working capital
fund balances		and permanent
		funds
Sales and	Educational activities	Charge to customer
services	Auxiliary enterprises	Charge to customer
	Medical services	Charge to customer

Adapted from *Financial Responsibilities of Governing Boards of Colleges and Universities* (Washington, DC: AGB and NACUBO, 1979), p.20.

TUITION AND FEES

Tuition is the price of an instructional service rendered to students, but unlike most prices it represents only a portion of the costs incurred in providing the service. Some of the factors considered in the setting of tuition levels are: (1) tuition at peer institutions, (2) the need to balance the budget, (3) student financial aid needs, (4) tradition or philosophy of the institution or the state system, and (5) general economic conditions. "Price setting" is a very important budget decision that requires an understanding of the institution's market position and the elasticity of student demand. Demand elasticity dictates that when prices are higher fewer students seek admission than when prices are lower. Some institutions, such as the Ivy League universities, need not be so concerned about reduced demand when they raise charges because they now turn away well-qualified students. Colleges and universities with a regional audience, on the other hand, may find that they are much more restricted in setting tuition if they wish to maintain or increase enrollment levels.

To remain competitive, institutions must be sensitive to their peers' net student charges (tuition charges less financial assistance). In comparing peer institutions, the presumed quality of education provided by each and the effect of the net price on enrollment must be considered. Tuition levels are often determined by the amount of income needed to balance the budget within the constraints of institutional philosophy and market position. This factor is closely related to the economic climate at the time the budget is prepared. When costs increase rapidly, tuition will also have to increase markedly. However, the institution must weigh the ability and willingness of prospective students to pay higher tuition. Some institutions have strong traditions that govern the setting of tuition levels. For example, the California system of public higher education has for many years had a no- or low-tuition policy. Other institutions seek to set tuition at a fixed percentage of the estimated annual costs of education.

Fees for special activities or purposes tend to be based as closely as possible on the actual costs of services. Examples of activities or services for which fees are charged include intercollegiate athletics, laboratory usage or breakage, instructional materials, health insurance or health services, student organizations, and debt service.

In the area of student aid the setting of tuition levels has a significant effect on the expenditure side of the revenue equation. Institutions with a strong commitment to student aid, such as those that provide considerable aid from their own funds, must usually plan to increase their aid expenditures to parallel the increase in tuition so as not to price themselves out of their traditional student markets. Also, institutional student aid becomes more important in the face of threatened reductions in federal student aid.

Independent institutions. Tuition and fee income in fiscal year 1981 represented 35.8 percent of all current fund income in four-year independent institutions and 64.0 percent of all income in two-year independent colleges (private correspondence, Stephen D. Campbell).

Because tuition and fee income represents a much greater proportion of institutional income for the independent sector as compared to the public sector, the balancing of the budget through tuition increases generally becomes a primary consideration. Thus, the rate of tuition increases at independent institutions is typically related, under steady-state conditions, to the Consumer Price Index, or the Higher Education Price Index.

Public institutions. Tuition and fee income in fiscal year 1981 represented 12.4 percent of all income in four-year public institutions and 15.2 percent in two-year public colleges (private correspondence, Stephen D. Campbell).

Setting tuition in the public sector is often more complicated and indirect than in the private sector. Rusk and Leslie (1978, 544) argue, for example, that adjusting state appropriations seems to be the major way to influence tuition levels. They also note that tuition increases are higher where state effort is insufficient to satisfy the financial needs of the institutions. Similarly, in states that have a substantial proportion of their enrollments in independent institutions, the public universities have tuition rates much higher than the average. The reverse is also true (Rusk and Leslie, 1978, 534).

By 1980, 20 states had established policies for setting tuition levels (Viehland, Kaufman, and Krauth, 1981, 26). One state based tuition on charges at comparable institutions; one raised tuition according to increases in the Higher Education Price Index; one indexed nonresident tuition to educational costs but had no established policy for setting resident tuition charges; three had formal statements about the factors to be considered in setting tuition levels but had no particular formula; and 14 indexed tuition to increases in educational expenditures. Tuition levels in the latter 14 states were a specific percentage of educational or instructional costs. Generally there is no philosophical basis for the percentage levels chosen; instead, the percentages were selected to yield tuition charges comparable to those in neighboring states, to generate sufficient revenues for current operations, and to be consistent with the proportion of instructional costs traditionally charged to students.

It should be noted that in some states tuition and fee income is part of the legislative appropriation, while in others it is treated independently as an institutional revenue fund and therefore does not appear in the appropriation bill. Generally, institutions have more flexibility in the use of funds if those funds do not appear in the appropriations bill.

FEDERAL STUDENT AID PROGRAMS

The American Council on Education (1982) prepared the following summary of the federal student assistance programs currently in place. The numbers cited are illustrative because federal laws and regulations are often changed.

Pell Grants (formerly BEOG). The Higher Education Act of 1972 established the Basic Education Opportunity Grants program (BEOG) to provide students with a quasi entitlement for a minimum level of assistance that could be used at any postsecondary institution. Although the institution disburses the funds, the individual student's eligibility is determined by a national needs analysis.

The needs analysis system functions as a means test to reduce awards as family income increases. Actual awards are limited by appropriations (a reduction formula applies when funds are insufficient) and by a provision limiting grants to no more than one-half the cost of attendance. In fiscal year 1983 (academic year 1983–84), Congress appropriated $2.857 billion, providing 2.6 million awards with a maximum of $1,800.

Campus-based programs. The Educational Opportunity Grant, now Supplemental Educational Opportunity Grants (SEOG), was established by the Higher Education Act of 1965 to provide federal grants for needy students as selected by the institution. Funds are distributed to institutions according to a state allocation formula based on proportionate undergraduate enrollments. In fiscal year 1983, Congress appropriated $355 million, providing 650,000 grants to needy students in academic year 1983–84.

The College Work-Study (CW-S) program was established by the Economic Opportunity Act of 1964. The federal government provides 80 percent of funds to pay wages of needy students employed by colleges or nonprofit agencies. Funds are distributed to institutions according to a state allocation formula based on that state's proportion of higher education enrollments, high school graduates, and children in poverty-level families. Institutions put up 20 percent, and they select the recipients. In fiscal year 1983, Congress appropriated $590 million, which provided jobs for 925,000 students in academic year 1983–84.

The National Defense Student Loan program, now National Direct Student Loan program (NDSL), established by the National Defense Education Act of 1958, provides low-interest loans for needy students. The federal government provides 90 percent of the capital. Funds are distributed directly to institutions under a state allocation formula based on proportionate enrollments in higher education. Selection of recipients is done by the colleges, which contribute 10 percent and collect the principal and interest paid on previous loans to be recycled for new borrowers. In fiscal year 1983, Congress appropriated $179 million in new federal loan capital, which provided awards to 845,000 students in academic year 1983–84.

State Student Incentive Grants. The 1972 act also established another program, State Student Incentive Grants (SSIG), to encourage the creation of state scholarship programs for needy students. States match federal grants and allocate them to institutions. In fiscal year 1983, Congress appropriated $60 million, providing awards to 240,000 students in academic year 1983–84.

Guaranteed Student Loan program (GSL). The Higher Education Act of 1965 established the Guaranteed Student Loan program, which (1) insures loans made by private lenders to students and reinsures loans guaranteed by state or private nonprofit agencies, (2) subsidizes the in-school interest for students up to a specified income level, and (3) pays a special allowance to the lender to make up the difference between the student interest rate (8 percent in 1983) and market rates. Beginning in 1981, students have had to pay a 5 percent origination fee. The income limitation on eligibility for the in-school interest subsidy was removed in 1978 and reestablished in 1981 at $30,000 of adjusted gross income. Above that limit, the student may borrow only up to the level of "unmet need." The program is an entitlement, with annual costs to be met by the Treasury based on the dollar volume of outstanding loans, money market conditions, and the default rate. In fiscal year 1983, 2.9 million new loans were made to students totaling $6.8 billion, and the cost to the government of the total program was $2.9 billion.

The Education Amendments of 1980 established the parent loan program as part of the Guaranteed Student Loan program. The former was expanded in 1981 to include graduate and professional students and independent students. The new program is called Auxiliary Loans to Assist Students (PLUS). The interest rate was lowered from 14 to 12 percent in 1982. This program does not subsidize in-school interest, but the federal government pays a special allowance to lenders to make up the difference between the borrower's interest rate and market rates. Full-time students may defer principal payments but not interest; other students must pay principal and interest in regular installments beginning 60 days after origination.

Graduate fellowships. The federal government provides Graduate and Professional Opportunities (GPOP) fellowships for minorities ($10 million in fiscal year 1983), public service fellowships ($2 million in fiscal year 1983), and fellowships for minorities to attend law school (CLEO) ($1 million in fiscal year 1983).

STATE STUDENT AID PROGRAMS

Most states have scholarship programs for needy students. State funds for these programs match federal monies provided as State Student Incentive Grants. In several states the support for the scholarship programs far exceeds the federal contribution. Some states also have competitive as well as need-based programs. Because the character of higher education in individual states varies considerably, state aid programs also differ widely. Most state student aid programs have maximum awards, with the limit set at tuition or a dollar ceiling, whichever is less. In some programs awards are also made to students who attend out-of-state institutions.

GOVERNMENT SOURCES OF FUNDING

Public and independent institutions receive funding from the federal government and from state and local governments in the form of direct appropriations and contracts and grants. The awarding of contracts and grants is usually on a competitive basis and does not differentiate between public and independent institutions. There are usually two parts to the grant or contract: the direct costs and the indirect costs. The direct cost portion represents the award to the institution for conducting the actual research or project. The award is restricted in that it can be expended only for the research activity. Included in the direct costs are the salary costs of the investigators, graduate assistants, and support staff and funds for supplies, equipment, and operating costs associated with the research or activity. The indirect cost portion of the award is a reimbursement to the institution for the overhead costs associated with conducting research activities. The indirect costs are generally computed as a percentage of direct costs and include charges for utilities, facilities maintenance, library usage, and the administrative costs of processing research proposals, monitoring the expenditure of contract and grant funds, and complying with reporting requirements (see chapter 13 for a detailed discussion of indirect costs).

The federal government makes appropriations directly to public and independent institutions in the form of categorical support for college libraries, library research and training, veterans' cost of instruction, cooperative education, law school clinical experience, land-grant aid, women's educational equity programs, support of developing institutions, international education, and vocational education. Federal aid is also provided through the College Housing Program.

Independent institutions. Income from federal sources, including appropriations and restricted and unrestricted grants and contracts, in fiscal year 1981 represented 19.2 percent of all current fund income in four-year independent institutions and 4.4 percent in two-year colleges.

Appropriations and grants and contracts income from state and local governments in fiscal year 1981 represented 2.7 percent of all income in both four-year and two-year independent institutions (private correspondence, Stephen D. Campbell).

State and local appropriations to independent institutions take a number of forms. Approximately one-third of the states contract with independent colleges and universities for a wide variety of instructional services. Most of these arrangements involve the "purchase" of student spaces in special programs, such as the health sciences.

About one-fifth of the states support the acquisition of new physical facilities at independent institutions through special state grants or by extending public authority to borrow funds through the sale of public bonds (Benezet, 1976, 27).

Certain states provide direct support to independent institutions in the form of contracts based on the full-time equivalent enrollment of in-state students, and others appropriate funds to independent colleges and universities for capitation grants. Under the Bundy Plan in the state of New York, for example, the state bases aid on the number of degrees conferred at the bachelor's, master's, and doctoral levels.

Public institutions. Income from federal sources, including appropriations and restricted and unrestricted grants and contracts, in fiscal year 1981 represented 14.2 percent of all income in four-year public institutions and 6.8 percent in two-year public colleges.

Appropriations and grants and contract income from state and local sources in fiscal year 1981 represented 45.3 percent of all income in four-year public institutions and 67.3 percent in public two-year colleges (private correspondence, Stephen D. Campbell).

State and local appropriations represent the single largest source of revenue to public institutions. These appropriations cover current operating expenses and capital construction costs.

PRIVATE SOURCES OF FUNDING

Both public and independent institutions receive funds from private sources in the form of gifts, grants and contracts, and contributed services. The sources of these funds are corporations, foundations, churches, alumni, local supporters, members of the institution's board of trustees, and friends.

Independent institutions depend more heavily than public institutions on gifts for a substantial portion of each year's budget. Gifts are credited as current fund income to the extent that they are spent during the budget year. Gifts are designated as unrestricted or restricted. Unrestricted gifts allow an institution greater flexibility because they can be spent for any purpose. Restricted gifts are earmarked by the donor for specified activities. When the activities enhanced by restricted monies are high on an institution's list of priorities, the restricted funds can be used in place of institutional funds, thereby freeing the latter for other uses. Although institutions depend on gift support to varying degrees in their budget planning, this income is not always reliable. In years of economic downturn, for example, corporate giving declines. Also, philanthropic and corporate giving is sensitive to fluctuations in tax laws. And events on campus can have an important bearing on the level of giving by alumni or local supporters. If giving targets are not achieved, the institution must cut expenditures or draw on restricted funds.

Contracts and grants from private sources generally have the direct and indirect cost components noted earlier. The primary difference between contracts and grants from private sources and those from government sources is that the indirect cost recovery rate applied to private contracts and grants is sometimes lower than the rate applied to government contracts and grants.

Some independent church-related colleges are subsidized through the contributed services of members of the religious order. The most significant contributions come in the form of teaching. In some colleges the teaching members of the religious order receive salaries equal to those of lay members, and the order returns the salaries as a gift to the college.

Independent institutions. Revenues from private sources in fiscal year 1981 represented 9.3 percent of all income in four-year independent institutions and 7.7 percent of all income in two-year independent colleges (private correspondence, Stephen D. Campbell).

Public institutions. Revenues from private sources in fiscal year 1981 represented 3.0 percent of all income in four-year public institutions and 0.4 percent in two-year public colleges (private correspondence, Stephen D. Campbell).

INCOME FROM THE INVESTMENT OF ENDOWMENT AND FUND BALANCES

Public and independent institutions often have funds available that can be invested for the purpose of generating income. These include endowment, current, loan, and life income and annuity funds. Endowments are permanent funds established to provide institutions with a regular source of investment income. The portfolio of investments is selected on the basis of both income-generating potential and the potential for long-term growth. A portion of the income earned from endowment fund investments is returned to the endowment so that the endowment can be maintained in real terms to provide a hedge against inflation (see appendix 3). The size of institutional endowment funds varies widely. In 1982 Harvard University and the University of Texas System had endowments in excess of $1 billion; only the 125 largest endowments were more than $2 million. Thus, for the vast majority of institutions in the United States, endowment income is quite small.

The cash flow in most institutions is such that any surplus in the current operating fund is invested on a short-term basis. At the beginning of each semester, for example, when student tuition is usually paid, institutions tend to have more cash on hand than at other time of the year. The excess funds can be invested for the short term. For public institutions, rules governing short-term investment of institutional operating funds vary from state to state. Some states allot funds to institutions on a quarterly basis so that the state itself can invest its monies and collect the income rather than allowing institutions the opportunity to do so. Other states allot their appropriation at the beginning of the year and allow the institutions the flexibility to invest the funds. Use of the earnings from the investment of fund balances may be restricted or unrestricted. Thus, for example, earnings on the investment of restricted student loan fund balances may be used only for student loans.

Independent institutions. Revenues from the investment of endowment and fund balances in fiscal year 1981 represented 5.5 percent of all income in four-year independent institutions and 1.7 percent of all income in two-year independent colleges (private correspondence, Stephen D. Campbell).

Public institutions. Revenues from the investment of endowment and fund balances in fiscal year 1981 represented 0.6 percent of all income in four-year public institutions and 0.1 percent in two-year public colleges (private correspondence, Stephen D. Campbell).

INCOME FROM SALES AND SERVICES

Colleges and universities receive income from the sale of educational and medical services and from auxiliary enterprises. Educational activities might include film rentals, testing services, home economics cafeterias, demonstration schools, dairy creameries, and college theaters (AGB and NACUBO, 1979, 29). Medical services are provided through teaching hospitals, student and staff health centers, and hearing and speech clinics. Auxiliary enterprises, which are generally self-supporting, include activities such as residence and dining halls, student unions, student bookstores, and intercollegiate athletics.

Independent institutions. Income from sales and services in fiscal year 1981 represented 24.8 percent of all income in four-year independent institutions and 15.3 percent of all income in two-year independent colleges (private correspondence, Stephen D. Campbell).

Public institutions. Income from sales and services in fiscal year 1981 represented 22.3 percent of all income in four-year public institutions and 6.9 percent in two-year public colleges (private correspondence, Stephen D. Campbell).

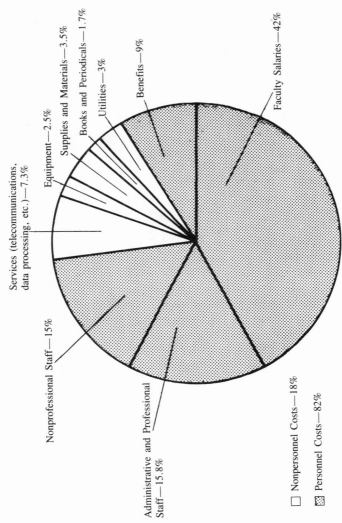

Figure 1: Percentage Allocation of Higher Education Costs, Educational and General, FY 1972

Services (telecommunications, data processing, etc.)—7.3%

Equipment—2.5%

Supplies and Materials—3.5%

Books and Periodicals—1.7%

Utilities—3%

Benefits—9%

Faculty Salaries—42%

Nonprofessional Staff—15%

Administrative and Professional Staff—15.8%

☐ Nonpersonnel Costs—18%

▨ Personnel Costs—82%

Source: D. Kent Halstead, *Inflation Measures for Schools and Colleges* (Washington, DC: National Institute of Education, 1983).

Figure 2: Faculty Pay and the Cost of Living

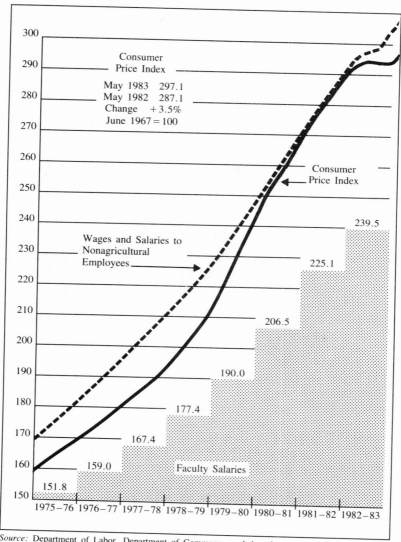

Source: Department of Labor, Department of Commerce, and American Association of University Professors.

Figure 3a: Sources of Current Funds Revenues for Institutions of Higher
Education, by Control and Level of Institution:
Fiscal Year 1981

Fiscal Year and Source	Total, All Institutions	Public Institutions		Independent Institutions	
		Four-Year	Two-Year	Four-Year	Two-Year
1981:	Amount, in Millions				
Total	$65,585	$35,351	$7,845	$21,729	$660
Government[1]	31,645	21,031	5,808	4,758	47
Federal[2]	9,748	5,010	530	4,178	29
State	20,106	15,729	3,947	416	14
Local	1,791	292	1,331	164	4
Private sources	3,177	1,065	35	2,026	51
Students	21,061	8,484	1,701	10,357	518
Tuition and fees	13,773	4,374	1,196	7,781	422
Auxiliary enterprises[3] .	7,287	4,110	505	2,577	96
Institutional[4]	9,703	4,770	301	4,588	43
1981:	Percentage Distribution				
Total	100.0	100.0	100.0	100.0	100.0
Government[1]	48.2	59.5	74.0	21.9	7.2
Federal[2]	14.9	14.2	6.8	19.2	4.4
State	30.7	44.5	50.3	1.9	2.1
Local	2.7	0.8	17.0	0.8	0.6
Private sources	4.8	3.0	0.4	9.3	7.7
Students	32.1	24.0	21.7	47.7	78.5
Tuition and fees	21.0	12.4	15.2	35.8	64.0
Auxiliary enterprises[3] .	11.1	11.6	6.4	11.9	14.6
Institutional[4]	14.8	13.5	3.8	21.1	6.6

[1]Includes appropriations and restricted and unrestricted grants and contracts.

[2]Includes appropriations, restricted and unrestricted grants and contracts, and independent operations (FFRDC).

[3]Includes revenues generated by operations that were essentially self-supporting within the institutions, such as residence halls, food services, student health services, and college unions. Nearly all such revenues are derived from students.

[4]Includes endowment income, sales and services of educational activities, sales and services of hospitals, and other sources.

Note: Details may not add to totals because of rounding.

Source: Unpublished tabulations from the Higher Education General Information Survey (Financial Statistics of Institutions of Higher Education for Fiscal Year 1981).

Figure 3b: Sources of Current Funds Revenues for Institutions of Higher Education

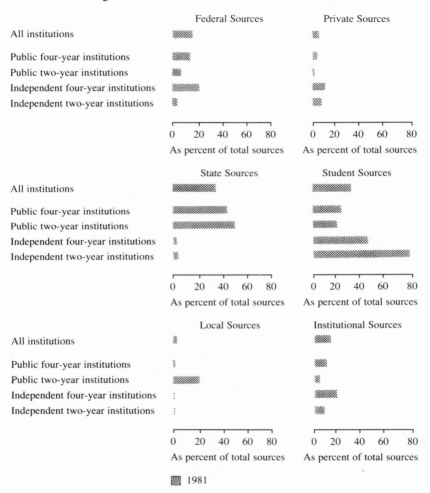

1981

Source: Unpublished tabulations from the Higher Education General Information Survey (Financial Statistics of Institutions of Higher Education for Fiscal Year 1981).

FOR FURTHER READING

A brief profile of higher education in the United States is *The National Investment in Higher Education*, prepared by the Association Council for Policy Analysis and Research (Washington, DC: American Council on Education, 1981). An excellent discussion of the broad economic and political environment within which institutions function is found in Howard R. Bowen's *The Costs of Higher Education: How Much Do Colleges and Universities Spend per Student and How Much Should They Spend?* (San Francisco: Jossey-Bass, Inc., 1980).

Institutional sources of funds are identified in the excellent handbook *Financial Responsibilities of Governing Boards of Colleges and Universities* (Washington, DC: Association of Governing Boards of Universities and Colleges and National Association of College and University Business Officers, 1979). Financing is also discussed by Jacob Stampen, *The Financing of Public Higher Education*, AAHE/ERIC Higher Education Research Report no. 9 (Washington, DC: American Association for Higher Education, 1980), and Louis T. Benezet, *Private Higher Education and Public Funding*, AAHE/ERIC Higher Education Research Report no. 5 (Washington, DC: American Association for Higher Education, 1976).

An analytical examination of the demographic issues of the 1980s is found in Lyman A. Glenny, "Demographic and Related Issues for Higher Education in the 1980s," *Journal of Higher Education*, vol. 51, no. 4 (March/April 1980), pp. 363–380, and in David W. Breneman, *The Coming Enrollment Crisis: What Every Trustee Must Know* (Washington, DC: Association of Governing Boards of Universities and Colleges, 1982).

The financial support of higher education by state and local governments is summarized for the 50 states in Marilyn McCoy and D. Kent Halstead, *Higher Education Financing in the Fifty States: Interstate Comparisons, Fiscal Year 1981*, 3rd ed. (Boulder, CO: National Center for Higher Education Management Systems, 1984). The fiscal capacity of state governments is summarized in *1981 Tax Capacity of the Fifty States* (Washington, DC: Advisory Commission on Intergovernmental Relations, 1983). Institutional costs are profiled in Paul E. Lingenfelter and Freeman H. Beets, *Higher Education Costs: Causes and Containment—A Study of 34 Midwestern Colleges and Universities* (Kansas City, MO: U.S. Department of Education Region VII, 1980). Research Associates of Washington annually publishes an update of the Higher Education Price Index.

The relationship of capital to operating budgets is discussed in Hans H. Jenny (with Geoffrey C. Hughes and Richard D. Devine), *Hang-Gliding, or Looking for an Updraft: A Study of College and University Finance in the 1980s—The Capital Margin* (Wooster, OH, and Boulder, CO: The College of Wooster and John Minter Associates, 1981).

3 / The Budget Process

The actors in the budget process, the timing of their participation, and the sequence of events in the budget cycle are remarkably similar from one institution to another within either the public or independent sector. Thus, in each sector it is possible to describe a generalized budget process. The way this process is tailored to a particular institution depends largely on several major factors: institutional character, participation, trust, openness of the process, centralization of authority, and demand for information.

Furthermore, to fully appreciate the dynamics of the interaction among the participants in the budget process at the various levels, one must also understand the range of roles performed by the actors in the process. The complexity of the process is highlighted by the fact that one actor may, for example, adopt different roles depending on the stage of the process.

Finally, it is important to point out the overlapping nature of budget cycles. In both the independent and public sectors, budgeters are involved in multiple budget cycles that are strongly dependent on their predecessors. In this sense the most important determinant of the current budget is the previous year's budget. To minimize ambiguity and uncertainty, budgeters generally adopt incremental decision-making strategies in which the shape of previous budgets is retained, with changes introduced at the margin.

39

BUDGET FACTORS

INSTITUTIONAL CHARACTER

To understand the budget process, it is crucial first to understand institutional character, an amorphous concept that is difficult to define. Character is made up of factors such as history, mission, array of academic programs, size, geographic location, nature (public or independent), profile of faculty and staff, quality of leadership, financial condition, composition of the student body, degree of faculty participation in governance, alumni support, and reputation of athletic teams. Every institution has its own unique character. Because of the weight of the historical component, character tends to change slowly over time.

The character of the state land-grant university, for example, is different from that of the state college or state regional university or a community college. Each is located in a different part of the state, has a different percentage of commuter students, is more or less attractive to performing artists and groups, has a different array of degree programs and different degree-granting authority, has different political support in the legislature, and has a different history. Similarly, the public urban institution satisfies the needs of a different clientele from that of the rural institution. Institutional character often translates to image. How an institution is perceived by insiders and outsiders influences the behavior of all who have a relationship to the institution.

Each of the dimensions of institutional character contributes to the way in which participants in the budget process will interact and creates part of the framework for interaction. Thus, collegial governance and broader faculty and student participation in the budget process generally are more easily adopted in smaller colleges and universities. In large institutions faculty may be more reluctant to delegate authority to a small group of colleagues. Also, because communication among faculty and administrators is often poorer in large institutions, it may be desirable to devote more attention and resources there to governance processes and communications. Budget participants at public colleges and universities and at the well-endowed and prestigious independent colleges and universities that have relatively steady sources of revenue will establish a different set of parameters for the budget process and ask a different set of questions about the internal allocation of resources from those of participants in institutions that are financially insecure. Institutions in the public sector are accountable to a broader constituency, including legislators and the general public, than are independent colleges and universities. Accordingly, public institutions must respond to more requests for information from external agencies. These demands for information influence the formats for budget requests, the accounting structures, and the methodology for financial audits. Similarly, institutions (both public and independent) whose students are heavily dependent on federal or state aid must use considerable resources in the effort to account for these funds. Considerations such as these can be extended to other dimensions of institutional character. The cumulative result is a unique environment for each institution and a unique framework within which the budget process occurs.

As a management technique, budgeting is approached in many different ways. It is not unusual, therefore, for budgeters to look at how other organizations budget, with an eye to refining their own methodologies. Organizational theorists have noted that more change within organizations occurs through copying from other organizations than from innovation. Higher education, too, tends to adopt from others rather than create instructional programs, instructional methodolgies, administrative structures, computing systems, and research programs. However, grafting the new to the existing is most successful when done with a sensitivity to institutional character. In the Northeast, for example, academic programs designed to attract black students will probably be more successful in urban institutions than in rural ones. Similarly, an institution's character and the nature of its decision-making process will determine how successfully certain budget methodologies can be adopted. It will probably be difficult to introduce a more collegial, participatory form of decision making in a large university that has a history of strong administrative guidance and limited faculty involvement. Clearly, the nature of campus decision making has implications for the budget process. For example, it would be difficult for a large, urban state university to make use of the budget decision-making mechanism (i.e., the Priorities Committee) of Princeton University, with its small, tightly knit intellectual and social community. Other aspects of institutional character also affect the way budget innovations can be transported from one setting to another.

PARTICIPATION

The role of administrators, faculty, and students in the decision-making process in colleges and universities and the quantity and quality of that participation are continuing governance issues, the resolution of which uniquely colors the budget process at individual institutions. (See appendix 1 for the AAUP statements on participation in campus budget processes.) As active participants in the design and implementation of instructional, research, and service programs, faculty demand a role in making the decisions concerning the allocation of resources among programs and activities. As consumers of educational programs, students are concerned about how well their own programs are supported financially. Although students generally are less active in campus governance than faculty or administrators, in an aggregate sense students have a major impact on the flow of resources to instructional programs through enrollment patterns.

The identity of participants in the budget process and the order in which they participate are constantly being reevaluated at each college and university. Administrators, faculty, and students seeking a broader role in the allocation of resources do not always have realistic expectations of what that participation means. Generally, participation in the budget process is not on a democratic basis. Most budget cycles have very tight schedules that prevent wide involvement and leisurely consideration of the issues. Also, making budget decisions concerning educational and support programs requires considerable knowledge of the relationships among campus activities. Because this knowledge and expertise is acquired gradually, a rapid turnover of participants results in discontinuities in the budget process. Also, active participation in the budget process requires a very large commitment of time, even when actors are not involved in day-to-day budgeting.

Different governance structures require different levels of participation. Moreover, participants can enter the budget process at a number of different stages. At Princeton University, for example, the closeness of the campus community is reflected in a governance structure that encourages a high degree of participation by faculty, staff, and students. The budget process at Princeton has been woven tightly into the governance processes through the Priorities Committee, which involves many different members of the university community at all stages in the budget process. A more common model for faculty participation in budgeting is the advisory committee. A committee actively involved in the budget process will have a role in establishing the framework for analysis by addressing questions of budget format, timing, policy issues, and alternative income and expenditure projections. Active involvement is evidenced by substantial consensus-building. Less active faculty advisory committees are usually asked to consider a much narrower range of issues, or issues that are of secondary importance. The extent to which such advisory committee participation is seen as political "window dressing" or as a "rubber stamping" of the decisions of others will determine the level of frustration experienced by committee members.

To insure that the contribution is meaningful, some colleges and universities structure the participation so that it occurs at key points during the budget cycle. Too often, it seems, faculty, student, and administrative budget committees are only peripherally involved in major budget decision making. The most practical role for faculty and students in the process seems to be to help in examining the probable consequences of establishing program and activity priorities and general levels of expenditure. Administrators are normally given the responsibility for implementing the decisions and maneuvering the process on a day-to-day basis. Faculty and student participants are involved in budget planning but not in the day-to-day administration of budgets. One of the disappointing realities of participation is that faculty and students tend to be inadequately rewarded for their contributions. In addition, students are pulled away from their studies and faculty are drawn away from teaching and research.

TRUST

The smoothness with which the budget cycle progresses is determined in large part by the degree of trust among participants at all levels. Trust relationships between public institutions and state agencies are just as important as those within institutions. Trust evolves over time as individuals in the process become more familiar with the expectations, value systems, and behavior of other participants. Trust relationships tend to engender more communication and cooperation, for example, in the exchange of data, information, and analyses. Rather than precluding sharp questioning or lively negotiations among actors in the process, trust provides a framework for the effective and efficient engagement of the actors.

OPENNESS OF THE PROCESS

The degree to which the budget process is open to casual review by those not actively involved in deliberations will define in part the amount of flexibility decision makers have in their negotiations over the allocation of resources. The openness of the process, in turn, is determined in large part by the institution's character and participatory structure for decision making—the more participants there are in the budget process, the more open the process becomes to the institutional community. At some institutions the degree of openness is controlled very carefully to prevent unintended actions that might otherwise flow from budget decisions. For example, when identifying the strong and weak departments in an institution, most budget decision makers tend to be cautious in making their determinations known to the larger academic community so as to avoid creation of a self-fulfilling prophecy, whereby units labeled as weak in fact become weak as faculty morale deteriorates and mobile faculty members depart.

There has been a tendency in recent years to move toward more open or public deliberations in the policy-making and decision-making arenas. This has been most pronounced in the public sector, where "sunshine" legislation mandates that most meetings of public officials be open to the public. While the more open decision-making process may permit more participants to become involved, it has the negative effect of discouraging negotiation. In the budget process, where by definition there are insufficient resources to meet all needs, bargaining is essential and usually involves making trade-offs. Most budget decision makers are reluctant to negotiate in public because they do not want to publicize the issues or items on which they have to compromise. Participants in the budget process thus prefer to negotiate privately in order to maintain "face" with their constituent groups.

In acknowledging that there are needs both for privacy and for increased participation and open communication, some institutions design the budget process to allow the interests of relevant groups to be represented while sensitive discussions about competing programs and activities are carried on. Accordingly, communications to the broader academic community are structured to minimize the negative impact that budget decisions may have on individuals, programs, and activities. The need for openness in the budget process is balanced by the need for privacy during the more delicate deliberations.

CENTRALIZATION OF AUTHORITY

A continual source of tension between decision makers in postsecondary education, especially in the budget process, is the attempt to determine the level of authority at which decisions should be made. There is a natural tendency for decision makers at each level to argue that the range of issues over which they have final responsibility is increasingly limited by higher levels of authority. Senior campus officials at public institutions, for example, may complain that because the state legislature appropriates funds on a line-item basis rather than on a lump-sum basis, the legislature reduces their flexibility to allocate funds as they deem appropriate among the various campus programs. Similarly, department chairpersons sometimes maintain that their decision-making authority is constrained by campus-level officials who establish ceilings for departmental budget requests rather than allowing the chairpersons to specify their actual resource needs. Also, final decisions on tenure that were once decided within the college are now often made at the campus or even system level.

Decisions about the allocation of scarce resources tend to be made at higher levels of authority, as are painful decisions to reduce resources, particularly faculty and staff. Evidence of this tendency is the increasing professionalization of staffs at colleges and universities and the expansion of governors' budget office and legislative fiscal staffs. Thus, the context for decision making about resources has changed significantly in recent years. Decisions that were once made in a very informal way now evolve in a more structured manner. Accompanying the centralization of budget decision authority is an increased concern for accountability and productivity at lower levels. Thus, more documentation is required to justify to higher authorities that resources are allocated effectively and efficiently. A major role of leadership is to provide sufficient decision-making flexibility at all levels of the process.

DEMAND FOR INFORMATION

The budget cycle is structured in large part to transmit information such as that concerning program activities, the utilization of resources, the anticipated resource requirements of programs, or criteria for performance evaluation. When changes in the budget process are introduced (e.g., new formats for the presentation of budget materials or entirely new budget techniques, including program budgeting and zero-base budgeting), the process will be disturbed until the participants become familiar with the changes. Disturbances arise because familiar information is missing and the relevance of new information is not clearly understood. This can be costly in terms of time and emotional involvement because actors in the process must adjust their expectations about the kinds of information transmitted and the kinds of analyses and decisions that they must contribute to the process. A reasonably stable process enables budget actors to anticipate their responsibilities and reduces some of the uncertainty of budgeting. This is not to argue against change in the face of new conditions; it is to suggest that changes should be justified with respect to the costs incurred.

As the number of staff at all levels increases and as decisions about resource allocation move to higher levels of authority, the demand for information increases. In California, for example, during the growth years of the 1960s and 1970s, officials at the University of California used an informal index whereby three additional staff members were needed for each additional staff person hired at the state level just to handle the increased demand for information. Greater involvement by professional staff in academic decision making also often leads to more sophisticated analyses that in turn require more information.

Decision makers are frustrated by the fact that information tends to flow upward in the authority hierarchy. In comparison to the amount of information provided to higher-level decision makers, the amount flowing downward as feedback generally seems to be small. Decision makers sometimes argue that the information imbalance exists because the press of their responsibilities does not allow sufficient time for the formulation of appropriate messages to subordinate levels. There are, however, two additional explanations. First, decision makers tend to collect more information than they can use; and second, they underestimate the information needs of those lower in the authority hierarchy and do not structure effective feedback channels. The two-way flow of information in the budget process is especially important as participants negotiate for resources and adjust their positions to reflect changes in the demands of other participants, the priorities of higher-level decision makers, and the availability of resources.

ROLES

Wildavsky (1979, 160) defines roles as "the expectations of behavior attached to institutional positions." In the budget process actors can assume multiple roles at different stages in the cycle. Here, roles are nothing more than characteristic behaviors in situations that tend to reoccur year in and year out in the budget process. Wildavsky (1979, 161) also observes that "the roles fit in with one another and set up a stable pattern of mutual expectations, which do a great deal to reduce the burden of calculations for the participants." In other words, based on the expected behavior of other actors, participants can begin to estimate the consequences of their actions during the budget process.

Although refined models of role behavior identify a spectrum of distinct roles, the simplest model contains the "spender" or advocate role and the "cutter" or restraining role. As an advocate, for example, the department chairperson's goal is at worst to maintain the department's current resource base, and at best to acquire as many additional resources as possible. An increased budget is symbolic evidence of success to the chairperson's clientele group, the department faculty. Requesting fewer resources than are currently available is usually viewed negatively by clientele groups because such behavior does not satisfy the role of advocate. An increased budget also represents an expansion of services, an added subspecialty in the discipline, additional enrollments, improved personnel benefits, such as satisfactory pay raises for the faculty, or a combination of these.

If the role of the department chairperson is that of advocate for additional resources, what is the role of the college dean responsible for several departments? On the one hand, the dean will be an advocate to the vice president for academic affairs for the departments within the college and will strive to gain as many new resources as possible. The dean's mission is not simply one of resource maximization, however, because there may be programs within the college that the dean believes should be reduced in scope. Overall, however, the dean will not wish to lose resources. On the other hand, the dean probably could not justify a budget request to the vice president for academic affairs that was simply the cumulative total of each department's request. Some discretion must be exercised by the dean in assembling the request, resulting in certain departments being cut back in accordance with priorities. Thus, the dean also assumes the role of cutter in restraining departmental requests. His or her success as a participant in the budget process is measured in terms of the ability to gain additional resources for the college and to restrain departmental desires so as to arrive at a reasonable budget request for the college.

In the public sector this spender-cutter duality appears in higher levels of the budget process also, extending to the governor and the governor's budget office and to the legislature and legislative fiscal staffs. The campus budget office is often viewed internally as a cutter whose role is strictly to insure fiscal responsibility and the prudent management of resources. As seen by state agencies in the public sector, for example, the campus budget office is an advocate for an increased institutional budget. In a similar way one could analyze the multiple roles of each participant in the budget process.

The spender-cutter model summarizes a set of expectations. Generally, advocates will always ask for more resources than they really need because they know that the cutters will reduce budgets somewhat regardless of the amounts requested. The cutters will reduce the budget requests of participants, knowing full well that the requests are padded and that by reducing the budgets there is no danger of injuring the programs. This demonstrates the built-in pressure for expansion that characterizes most budget processes.

OVERLAP IN BUDGET CYCLES

The overlap in budget cycles strongly determines participant behavior in the budget process. In both the independent and public sectors, attention is directed toward more than one budget cycle at the same time. Figure 1 illustrates the annual operating budget cycle for Stanford University; figure 2 illustrates the budget cycle for the University of Maryland, College Park. The fiscal year at Stanford extends from October 1 through September 30. In figure 1, while the budget for fiscal year 1981 was being executed, the 1982 budget was being prepared. Research and analyses and forecasting for the 1982 budget were performed *prior* to the beginning of fiscal year 1981. Budget instructions for fiscal year 1982 were prepared and distributed just as fiscal year 1981 began. Thus, participants in the budget process drew on their experience during fiscal year 1980 in planning for the 1982 budget. In a sense the most important determinant of the 1982 budget was a projection of the 1981 budget that was beginning to be played out as the 1982 budget was being assembled.

The University of Maryland, College Park (see figure 2) has an even longer schedule for budget preparation because of the involvement of state-level agencies. The fiscal year at Maryland extends from July 1 through June 30. During fall 1980, campus officials were required to prepare a preliminary estimate of their budget needs for fiscal year 1983. Thus, the preliminary request for fiscal year 1983 had to be prepared more than six months prior to the end of fiscal year 1981. Based on the campus estimate of needs and state-level projections of revenue availability, the governor set a ceiling during June 1981 for the campus's fiscal year 1983. The guidelines for the campus budget for fiscal year 1983 were established, therefore, just prior to beginning the execution of the budget for fiscal year 1982.

The budget cycle for public institutions is extended even more in states with biennial budgets. Institutional estimates of budget needs for the second year of the biennium have to be based on the budget from three years before. Clearly, much can happen in the intervening two to three years between budget estimation and the beginning of the fiscal year that can make the budget obsolete, particularly in times of rapid economic change. State legislatures are becoming increasingly aware of this problem and are scheduling more interim sessions to discuss and amend the state's budget for the second year of the biennium. In any case, budgeters will not be able to effect change for at least two years because prior budgets are already largely established.

When projecting so far into the future, budgeters reduce their uncertainty by using the most current experience as a base. Adjustments are made at the margin to reflect anticipated changes in revenues and expenditures, which in turn are determined by a host of variables including program mix, enrollments, inflation factors, and investment yields. Scheduled changes such as the introduction of a new degree program or the use of tighter admissions standards can be planned for, but it is difficult to predict more radical disturbances such as oil embargoes, skyrocketing energy costs and interest rates, reductions in federal student assistance, and the impact of national economic trends on the institution's enrollment base. Accordingly, budgeters approach budget development incrementally.

THE BUDGET CYCLE

Except for the timing of events, the budget cycle is similar for both public and independent institutions, although it is longer in the public sector because of the involvement of state-level agencies. Budget cycles described in subsequent sections are generalized for both sectors. It should be noted that the cycles of specific institutions may vary in terms of sequence and actors. The Stanford University and University of Maryland, College Park examples are representative of the more complex budget processes in the independent and public sectors and are useful, though not necessarily ideal, for comparing the budget cycles of specific institutions. In the following discussions, illustrations of the chronology of events assume a fiscal year beginning July 1.

INDEPENDENT COLLEGES AND UNIVERSITIES

ESTABLISHING THE FRAMEWORK FOR BUDGET REQUESTS

Participants in the budget process, including presidents, deans, department chairpersons, faculty, directors of administrative support units, and students, need to be given some framework within which they can present their justifications for resource requests for the coming budget cycle. Unless participants are working under the same assumptions and constraints, budget requests will not be congruent and information from lower levels, such as departments and administrative support units, will have to be ignored or collected anew at higher levels.

This framework for budgeting, often termed budget instructions, budget protocol, or budget guidelines, must in turn be informed by analyses and projections of conditions in budget years to come. These projections and analyses are normally carried out during spring or summer, some 10 to 15 months prior to the beginning of the fiscal year. Analyses include estimates of the impact on enrollment of changes in admissions standards, changes in program offerings, and changes in federal student assistance programs and the availability of aid funds; estimates of income for several years, including investment income, gifts, tuition, and research funding; estimates of expenses for several years, including anticipated increases in faculty and staff salaries, the impact of rapidly changing energy costs, the cost of bringing new or renovated facilities into operation, and the impact of the changing Consumer Price Index on the cost of goods and services; estimates of the impact of affirmative action programs; and a proposed plan of action to reconcile the budget experience of recent years with the anticipated conditions of the next several years. A number of institutions involve faculty in reviewing the overall constraints set and the particular budget instructions used.

The degree of sophistication of the projections and analyses depends largely on the staff resources available, the experience of the analysts, and the accuracy and availability of information (larger institutions tend to have more staff resources and more highly developed information systems than smaller institutions). Participants in the preliminary analytical work often include the vice president for financial affairs, the comptroller, the budget office, the office of institutional studies, and the office of institutional planning. The vice president for academic affairs may be involved in assessing the effects of changes in the instructional programs. In smaller institutions the projections may be done by only a handful of individuals, such as the vice president for financial or business affairs, the director of the budget, and the vice president for academic affairs. In both large and small institutions considerable time and effort is devoted to updating and correcting information bases. At the preliminary analysis stage few formal committees involve faculty, students, or trustees but rather are composed of administrators.

BUDGET INSTRUCTIONS

Budget instructions are usually issued during early fall (about 9 to 10 months before the fiscal year begins) by the institution's central budget officers, including the vice president for finance, the director of the budget, and the vice president for academic affairs or dean of the faculty. Units have approximately one month to prepare their requests. The information contained in the instructions and the manner in which it is presented vary depending on the intended purpose. Some institutions, for example, want the budget instructions or guidelines to be distributed to as much of the campus community as possible. In such instances the instructions are designed to present an overview of the budget process, including a chronology of steps, the institution's longer-range context and outlook, a discussion of particular budget problems for the coming year, a discussion of the working assumptions for preparation of budget requests, and tentative proposed operating budgets for the year ahead. These instructions thus become a kind of status report that communicates proposed changes in the institution's scope of operations and mission.

Often, however, the guidelines are more technical, having been designed for individuals with responsibility for specific parts of the institutional budget. The instructions specify the constraints under which budget requests should be prepared: estimates of inflation factors for operating expenses budgets, estimates of percentage increases in salaries and wages, and conditions under which additional faculty and staff positions can be requested.

Perhaps the most complex aspect of the budget request activity is budgeting and planning for faculty positions. The complexity arises from the special nature of faculty appointments (i.e., 9½, 10, or 12 months), the vastly different market conditions for faculty members in different disciplines, the flexible schedules and assignments of faculty, and the looseness of departmental organization. Budget instructions must address such issues as enrollment trends and their implications for staffing, the distribution of tenured and nontenured permanent faculty, the distribution of part-time faculty, anticipated tenure and promotion decisions, anticipated sponsored research and its effect on faculty salary needs, anticipated faculty leaves of absence without pay and sabbatical leaves, the effect of gifts and endowments restricted to the particular department, the distribution of teaching loads among the faculty, and the instructional schedule of the department as a whole. It is important to remember that faculty salaries and benefits comprise the largest single part of the budget; therefore, plans for faculty staffing greatly influence the budget. Also, because most colleges and universities employ permanent faculty on the basis of contracts of three or more years and tenure commitments, the financial impact of staffing decisions will be felt for many years.

Many institutions with faculties that are stable or declining in size are concerned about the prospect of departments with a very high percentage of tenured faculty and therefore little flexibility to hire young faculty members. To assure the inflow of new faculty, some institutions have developed quota systems that limit the percentage of tenured faculty by department or college or by entire campus. Other institutions, more consistent with AAUP policy, have avoided such quotas (see appendix 1 for the AAUP policy concerning tenure quotas). Where these long-term staffing plans exist, the annual budget instructions usually specify for each department or college the number of tenured positions available, the number of new positions that can be filled, and the number of positions that must be relinquished for purposes of reallocation.

Estimates of operating expenses and support staff costs for academic and nonacademic units are much more straightforward and are usually based on the application of inflation factors for the costs of goods and services to the operating expenses base, to workload data, and to tentative salary step and merit adjustments for administrators and support staff. Requests for additional staff must usually be justified in detail with respect to changes in organization, service loads, and unit mission.

Designers of budget instructions often give too little consideration to the information burdens placed on department chairpersons, deans, and the heads of administrative units. Much of what is demanded is a verification of the existing situation; these data are used by participants at higher levels to correct and update their data bases. In an attempt to reduce some of the paperwork and effort required and to introduce simpler requests for information, some colleges and universities have eliminated the more routine budget forms, requesting information only for exceptions. Thus, departments or administrative units have to respond only when changes in the level of operations or changes in the source of funding are proposed.

PREPARATION OF THE DEPARTMENTAL BUDGET REQUEST

Departmental structure, plan of organization, and bylaws will determine the level of faculty and student participation in assembling the departmental budget request. In any case, the department chairperson assumes a major responsibility for justifying the department's resource needs to higher levels in the budget process.

There is considerable variation from one institution to another and from one department to another in terms of the internal guidelines used to prepare requests. In some cases the department has a formal long-term plan for developing its instructional, research, and service programs. In other cases either the chairperson has a plan of action in mind or there is an implicit understanding among the faculty about how the department is to develop. This plan is usually related to the services to be rendered, including the number of sections to be taught, class size, committee assignments, and release time for research. Generally, departments that have weak leadership do not have a strong basis for preparing and justifying requests and usually seek to maintain the status quo in their budgets.

Larger institutions tend to consolidate departmental budget requests by college or school. Again the college structure, plan of organization, and bylaws will determine the level of participation in preparing the college request. Clearly, department chairpersons are largely responsible for defending their unit's needs during the process. For those cases in which the college budget is not simply the sum of departmental requests, the college dean may be the first level of formal review (see below) in the budget process and may hold budget hearings and perform analyses.

Under the best of conditions departments will prepare a consolidated budget, including salaries and wages and operating expenses. Then departments can present a complete picture of their resource needs to higher levels. However, some colleges and universities have separate budget requests for faculty and administrative support staffing and operating expenses; or allow academic departments to request additional staff throughout the year prior to the beginning of the new fiscal year. The piecemeal nature of these requests gives the departments some flexibility to make last-minute changes because of factors such as faculty resignations or the availability of a leading scholar, though this makes the preparation of budget requests basically a continual process at the departmental level. Requests that change during the budget cycle place additional administrative burdens on the department and, as will be noted below, make it difficult for campus-level officials to review competing program and activity needs simultaneously.

REVIEW OF BUDGET REQUESTS

Budget requests are normally reviewed and analyzed each time they are consolidated for presentation to a higher level of the process, until an institutional budget is ultimately presented to the board of trustees for consideration. Informal reviews occur during preparation of budget requests as department chairpersons discuss the budget situation with their deans, and administrative unit heads with their superiors. The purpose of these discussions is twofold: to encourage the requesting units to be realistic in stating their resource needs, and to begin to provide the first level of reviewers with information about resource needs so that they can begin their analyses.

College-level review. In large institutions with multiple colleges and schools, the first level of review is usually at the college and is held in September or October, approximately eight to nine months before the fiscal year begins. Typically, the dean must consolidate individual departmental requests into a single college request; unless the departments have exercised considerable restraint, the dean will have to pare the requests selectively to generate a college request that will appear reasonable to campus-level reviewers. Many colleges do not have the luxury of a large administrative staff, so the analysis of departmental requests tends to be limited. The dean may assemble a faculty advisory committee to make recommendations or may prepare the college request without formal participation of faculty. In either case departmental chairpersons may be consulted frequently. Where a formal plan for academic programs does not exist, the college request will be shaped on the basis of recommendations from advisory committees or the dean's staff. Questions raised at the dean's level focus largely on academic issues: curriculum design, course scheduling, faculty staffing, program enrollments, and research agendas. There is usually considerable informal interaction between the college and campus levels during college-level reviews, particularly when resources are very limited. College-level officials may request, for example, updates of revenue projections, assistance in performing analyses, or information concerning the use of endowment income and restricted funds.

Campus-level review. The major review of departmental and college budget requests and of requests from administrative units occurs from October through January, about five to nine months before the fiscal year begins. The major participants in the campus-level review include the president, the vice president for business or finance, the vice president for academic affairs, the budget office, and those staff members concerned directly with budgeting. Participation in the process beyond this circle of actors varies from campus to campus. Hearings at which academic and administrative officials defend their budget requests are held as is necessary or customary. Many institutions have advisory committees that make recommendations to the president. Princeton University, for example, has a Priorities Committee, which, while advisory to the president, performs thorough analyses and makes specific, detailed recommendations. This committee is composed of faculty, graduate and undergraduate students, and members of the administration and staff. At Stanford University, the University Advisory Committee on Budget Planning examines issues of long-range importance, reviews the major assumptions for each year's budget planning, and advises the president on planning problems and prospects.

In some cases faculty senates assign to faculty committees the responsibility for an independent review of budget requests. During the campus-level review the board of trustees is often involved, normally through a finance or budget committee. This committee is kept informed about the long-range financial forecast for the institution and about the progress of staff and advisory committee reviews and analyses. The president usually provides the trustees' budget or finance committee with formal budget recommendations in January or February, five to six months before the fiscal year begins.

During the campus-level review in independent colleges and universities, considerable attention is given to sources of funding. Budget staff regularly refine estimates of income from sources over which the institution has limited control, including endowment, gifts, and contracts and grants. Student enrollment projections are updated to reflect the institution's fall semester or quarter experience and are applied against alternative tuition and fee schedules to yield a range of income estimates. Ceilings for departmental and college budget requests in the academic area and for support activity requests are adjusted to fit available resources.

Budget staff and members of advisory committees analyze the various components of budget requests in such categories as faculty staffing, computing, library facilities, special academic programs, physical plant, academic administration, general administration, faculty and staff salary adjustments, tuition, and student aid. The student aid budget is dependent in large part on anticipated tuition levels and current federal student assistance policies. Budget requests for self-support activities, including faculty and staff housing, student housing, food services, intercollegiate athletics, and various services, are analyzed separately in terms of projected revenues.

In conjunction with the revenue estimation and activity analyses, key administrators negotiate among themselves and with the units under their control during the attempt to reshape activity and program plans to fit resource constraints. This process of negotiation is more or less continual, beginning at the earliest stages of the budget process, and is a response to both the changing nature of activities and programs, such as the sudden replacement of building systems, the implementation of new degree programs, the opportunity to hire an outstanding faculty member, and the upgrading of a management information system, and the changing revenue picture, including the nation's slide into a recession, an increase or decrease in the number of student applications, and the receipt of a large gift from a generous alumnus.

Some institutions are more successful than others in using the budget review stage to reduce the uncertainty experienced by participants. Two problems can arise from the structure of this stage. First, the review of budget requests can be stymied if operating units and departments do not provide total requests, or if the requests are not considered simultaneously. In situations where requests for resources cannot be examined together, budgeters must keep a running tally of commitments for periodic comparison with estimates of available resources. Thus, the various kinds of requests cannot be treated as competing claims against a fixed level of funding. Campuses that routinely permit units to request additional staffing or operating funds throughout the year and that approve these requests will be susceptible to this problem. Second, some colleges and universities review the academic programs portion of the budget separately from the administrative support portion. This approach tends to obscure the close relationship between academic and administrative support activities. For example, a significant increase in a department's research activity will result in an increase in the workload of accountants in the comptroller's office or the sponsored programs office. Similarly, the introduction of an on-line computer requisition system can streamline administrative activities in the purchasing department while at the same time reducing the administrative workload in academic departments. Institutions that establish academic and administrative budgets simultaneously seem to be more successful in anticipating the fiscal impact that activities in one area will have on the other.

PREPARATION OF THE DETAILED BUDGET

Formal budget recommendations are presented by the president to the board of trustees between January and March, approximately four to six months before the fiscal year begins. The board's finance or budget committee, which has likely been involved informally in the budget review process, reports to the full board at this time. The board of trustees acts on the general outline of the proposed budget and on specific recommendations for tuition and fees, room and board increases, salary increases, the proportion of endowment income to be applied to the operating budget, and student aid. Assuming that differences of opinion have been reconciled before the formal recommendations are presented to the board of trustees, board approval tends to be routine. The board's interests are usually protected through the work of its budget or finance committee during the budget process. The board evaluates the overall institutional budget from a broad perspective, considering the institution's mission and the implications of environmental conditions, weighing competing program goals, and projecting the effect of current decisions on the future of the institution.

Once the board of trustees approves the budget recommendations, budget staff begin to prepare the detailed budget. This stage of the process generally occurs during the period February through May. Final adjustments are made in the budget to reflect late changes in the revenue picture or in programs and activities.

The approval of budget recommendations and preparation of the detailed budget can be delayed for those institutions that have collective bargaining agreements. The delays might occur every two or three years, the usual frequency of negotiations for collective agreements. In the future, unions may seek to increase the frequency of negotiations as a hedge against the uncertainty of multiyear contracts. Because negotiations most often take place during the spring, the amount of time available to prepare the detailed budget will depend on how quickly an agreement can be reached. If, for example, the cost of wage increases exceeds revenue projections, the scope of operations in the academic and nonacademic areas may have to be reduced. In some situations protracted negotiations delay final settlement until well into the new fiscal year, leaving unit heads to operate for several months without firm knowledge of their new budget.

IMPLEMENTATION OF THE BUDGET

The budget represents an expenditure plan for the institution's programs and activities. Within that plan, however, unit heads must expend their resources in accordance with the institution's accounting structure and cash-flow scheme. Accounting rules restrict the use of certain categories of funds. The cash-flow scheme regulates the expenditure of funds so that it matches as closely as possible the receipt of revenues. Departments may not be able to purchase expensive items of equipment early in the fiscal year, for example, because the institution's primary source of income—tuition and fees—is collected in the fall (for the fall semester) and spring (for the spring semester).

Expenditures are monitored closely throughout the fiscal year by the comptroller's office and the budget office. Staff in these offices project savings in budgeted staff salaries resulting from turnover and project fuel and utilities expenditures as well as other general operating expenditures. These same staff also regularly update income projections, flag problem areas for administrative attention, control the transfer of funds among categories to insure compliance with accounting procedures, and finally, compare actual enrollment patterns to the budgeted patterns to provide key administrators with information for making expenditure readjustments. The comptroller's office usually provides periodic fund balance statements to the operating units, which can then monitor their own expenditures.

CLOSING OUT THE FISCAL YEAR

Most colleges and universities have procedures for the orderly closing of expenditures for the fiscal year. These procedures are intended to allow sufficient time to process paperwork and to discourage last-minute spending. For example, certain types of expenditures can be prohibited within 30 or 60 days of the end of the year, or the routing of purchase requisitions can be changed to allow the budget office or the comptroller's office to monitor more closely the flow of funds.

All institutions perform audits to insure that funds have been accounted for and used properly. Internal auditors work throughout the fiscal year and "perform detailed reviews of activities of the institution to apprise management of the adequacy of controls, policy compliance, procedures for safeguarding assets from fraud, and sometimes performance of employees in carrying out assigned responsibilities" (AGB and NACUBO, 1979, 56). External auditors are usually contracted private accounting firms, although state and federal auditors are considered external for institutions that receive public funds. External auditors test and evaluate the institution's internal financial controls and its compliance with financial policies, normally including in their report a management letter stating that the financial data are accurate and that the accounting systems are trustworthy (see chapter 7). Usually, fiscal audit reports do not evaluate the programs and activities for which funds were expended, but simply account for those funds and evaluate the accounting structure. The work of external auditors complements that of internal auditors; tests performed by the external auditors are similar to those performed by the internal auditors but are not as extensive. Also, state and federal auditors examine only specific programs and activities. Independent colleges and universities usually have up to two months (July and August) to close out the previous fiscal year.

PUBLIC COLLEGES AND UNIVERSITIES

The budget cycle for public institutions is similar to that for independent institutions, with two major exceptions: in the public sector the cycle begins much earlier and it has stages that extend beyond the institution to include actors at the system and state levels.

ESTABLISHING THE FRAMEWORK FOR BUDGET REQUESTS

Most states have some form of statewide master plan for public, and occasionally independent, postsecondary education. Generally, the institutions are heavily involved in the development of such plans, primarily through advisory councils made up of faculty and administrators. The plans can specify the mission of each institution, describe the distribution of academic programs, and even establish enrollment targets. Updated regularly, they become an important component of the framework for budgeting in the public sector.

The structure of public postsecondary education in a state will have considerable bearing on who participates in preliminary planning. In a multicampus university system, officials in the central administrative office may be active in establishing the budget framework for each campus. If the state higher education agency is a consolidated governing board, the central administration tends to have a dominant role in setting the framework for the campuses, whereas if the agency is a coordinating board, the degree to which the coordinating board participates in the establishment of the budget framework depends on the board's statutory authority for budget review.

To reduce the uncertainty of budgeting, some states employ a preliminary asking budget cycle to set institutional ceilings for the "final" asking budget requests. The preliminary asking budget cycle is a means for the state-level agencies to examine institutional "blue-sky" requests, to make an early assessment of institutional needs and compare those needs with projections of the availability of state revenues, and to give the institutions a realistic target for the more detailed budget requests to follow. The stages for the preliminary asking budget cycle closely parallel those of the detailed budget cycle. The difference is largely one of focus. Preparation and review of the preliminary asking budget centers on the broad questions of the merits of entire programs and activities, the interrelationships of these programs and activities, and the establishment of program priorities. The preliminary asking budget cycle tends to consider major issues; the "final" asking budget cycle addresses program details. The major issues often include faculty salaries, program expansion, deferred maintenance, and research programs.

The preliminary asking budget is usually assembled and reviewed during the period October through June, some 12–21 months prior to the beginning of the fiscal year. Guidelines for assembling the preliminary asking budget are provided by the governor's budget office, the consolidated governing board, the multicampus system office, or a combination of these. The guidelines tend to deal with the more mechanical aspects of request submission, containing only minimal information on policies for developing budget requests. The campuses or multicampus system offices may supplement these guidelines with some preliminary information to create a more issue-oriented framework for constructing requests at the department and college levels. Departmental requests are reviewed at the college level, and college-level requests at the campus level. The range of participants, the use of hearings, and the sophistication of analyses vary widely. Because of the preliminary nature of the requests, campus-level analyses tend to be less detailed and thorough than those in settings where there is no preliminary asking budget cycle.

Campus-level recommendations are generally reviewed by the system-level administration in a multicampus structure and by the finance or budget committee of the board of trustees. If modifications in the campus requests are needed, the requests are returned to the campuses for adjustment. The finished preliminary request is then submitted to the board of trustees and, if approved, forwarded to the appropriate state agencies, which might include the higher education coordinating agency, the governor's budget office, and the legislative fiscal staff(s). The state-level review of the preliminary asking budget covers the appropriateness of new activities and programs or major expansions of existing services and the estimates of the amount of resources available for higher education. State agencies may hold hearings to question institutional representatives on the preliminary budget requests. The result of the state-level review of the preliminary requests is establishment of a budget request ceiling for the detailed asking budget. The budget ceiling is usually set by the governor's budget office and indicates the maximum budget request the governor might support in his or her budget message to the legislature in December or January, some six months prior to the beginning of the fiscal year. The budget ceiling then becomes an important part of the framework within which the institutions prepare their detailed asking budgets.

In those states without federal preliminary asking budget cycles, the institutions, multicampus system offices, and state agencies arrive at a framework through informal discussions and negotiations. Normally, the state agencies, especially the governor's budget office and the legislative fiscal staff(s), communicate a budget ceiling or a fiscal range within which institutional requests will be accepted. State agencies will also provide policy guidance on statewide issues such as productivity increases, state-level spending priorities, changes in accounting and purchasing structures, and proposed reallocations among public services.

BUDGET INSTRUCTIONS AND
PREPARATION OF THE BUDGET REQUEST

The preparation of budget instructions and the assembly of departmental budget requests in public institutions are basically similar to those functions in independent colleges and universities.

REVIEW OF BUDGET REQUESTS: THE INSTITUTIONAL LEVEL

The review of budget requests in independent and public institutions is also similar. In the public sector, budget requests are usually prepared and reviewed between July and October, some eight to twelve months before the fiscal year begins.

Budgeters in public institutions are under somewhat less pressure than their counterparts in independent institutions to provide regular projections of the revenue situation for the coming fiscal year. The difference results in large part from the fact that state appropriations at levels reasonably close to the current and previous years are more or less assured, except, of course, when the state experiences serious economic difficulties. A major part of the analytical work of budget review is projecting enrollments and tuition and fee income on the basis of alternative tuition schedules. (Tuition and fee income is significant in that it tends to make up most of the difference between anticipated expenditures and state appropriations or to provide some "flexible" resources for the institution.) As in the independent sector, budgeters project student financial aid needs using alternative tuition and fees plans. Budgeters in public institutions that have large research programs or large endowments and annual gift programs, or both, regularly estimate the expected revenues from these sources, too.

In states that have some form of preliminary asking budget cycle, the review of budgets at the institutional level tends to be perfunctory, focusing on the mechanical aspects of budgeting (the major policy issues are addressed in the preliminary cycle). In these situations budget review is normally performed by budget office staff and does not entail the wide-ranging participation of advisory groups.

REVIEW OF BUDGET REQUESTS: MULTICAMPUS SYSTEM,
CONSOLIDATED GOVERNING BOARD, OR SEGMENTAL BOARD

Institutions that are not part of a multicampus or segmental system typically forward their budget requests to the board of trustees between September and November, some seven to nine months before the fiscal year begins. Review by the board of trustees in this situation is similar to review in the independent sector.

Budget requests from institutions that are part of a multicampus system, consolidated governing board system, or segmental system are reviewed by the central system or board staffs prior to being forwarded to the board of trustees or board of governors. Whether or not the state has a preliminary asking budget cycle, most central system administrations conduct some form of preliminary budget request exercise. Program and activity priorities for the system campuses are established at this time. Accordingly, staff reviews of individual institutional requests are usually routine checks to insure that the requests conform with system priorities and are assembled in the proper format.

An important role of the system-level review is the packaging of the system request for presentation to the state agencies. Depending on statutory requirements or custom, the consolidated budget request may or may not identify individual campuses, though it usually identifies issues of system-wide importance, including faculty salaries, support for libraries, the cost of high-technology programs such as engineering, computer science, and the physical sciences, and problems arising from deferred maintenance. These priority issues are often presented independent of enrollment-related requests for resources. The level of sophistication of budget review and analysis by the system staff is related to staff professionalization, experience, and size.

REVIEW OF BUDGET REQUESTS: STATE AGENCIES

The routing of institutional budget requests at the state level differs from state to state depending on the review role of each agency. Institutional requests are usually forwarded between September and November, seven to nine months before the fiscal year begins. If the state higher education coordinating agency has very strong budget review powers, it may be the sole recipient of the institutional requests. In that case the governor's budget office likely receives information copies and awaits the coordinating agency's recommendations. Legislative fiscal staffs may or may not receive information copies at this time. In states where the coordinating agency has weak budget review authority or is advisory on budget issues, the budget requests are normally forwarded to the governor's budget office with information copies sent to the coordinating agency.

Because several agencies are involved in budget review at the state level, there is often considerable redundancy in the review process. In some states this redundancy leads to increased competition among the staffs. Perhaps the most noteworthy trend at the state level is that legislative fiscal staffs, and some governors' budget staffs, are growing rapidly in size and sophistication. The result is that in certain instances the budget role of state higher education coordinating agencies is being diminished.

Those agencies generally review budget requests in the context of statewide master plans for higher education, enrollment targets for institutions, funding inequities among institutions, state financial conditions, and funding formulas or guidelines. Of all the reviews at the state level, the one performed by the coordinating agency is usually the closest examination of the relationship between major programs and activities and levels of funding. As at the system level, the degree of sophistication of analysis is tied to staff size and experience and the amount of time the agency is given for budget review. In most cases coordinating agencies have at most one month to analyze requests and make recommendations, normally conducting formal or informal budget hearings at which institutional representatives present their budget requests. Staff review may involve advisory councils of campus faculty and administrators.

The role of the coordinating agency, as perceived by other state-level agencies, varies from state to state. In some states it is seen as an advocate of higher education; in others it is viewed as a protector of state interests and hence a "cutter" of institutional budget requests. Most coordinating agencies strive to maintain what is perceived to be a neutral role between the institutions and other state agencies.

The coordinating agency staff makes budget recommendations to its board or council, which in turn makes recommendations to the governor's budget office and the legislative fiscal staff(s). In states where the coordinating agency has strong budget review powers, or where there is considerable trust between the coordinating agency and the governor's budget office, the coordinating agency's recommendations may be adopted without significant change. The governor's budget office staff generally examines the budget requests in relation to state revenue projections, enrollment targets, and funding formulas or guidelines. The more sophisticated budget office staff may examine programs and activities in greater detail by evaluating them on the basis of productivity or outcome measures, while the less sophisticated staff may examine line-item details without giving much attention to the institution's overall program plans. Frequently there is considerable communication between the governor's budget office and the institutions as the analytical work proceeds. However, the flow of information tends to be one-sided as the budget office seeks explanations or additional data to substantiate the institutional requests.

Typically, the executive budget office reviews budgets between October and December, six to nine months before the fiscal year begins. The recommendations are reviewed by the governor and his or her chief aides and become part of the governor's budget message to the legislature and state. In many states the governor presents the proposed budget in January.

Legislative review of the governor's budget usually takes place between January and April, when the legislative is in session, although in some states the legislature does not convene until late spring. The character of the state legislature and its fiscal staff determines the nature of legislative budget review. Some states, such as California, have full-time legislatures meeting throughout the year. These states tend to have large and experienced full-time legislative fiscal staffs. In many states legislators are part-time, meeting for sessions of 30, 60, or 90 days. Most of these legislatures have some permanent staff members to provide continuity and to support legislative committee activities when the legislature is not in session. In highly political states such as Illinois and New York, the minority and majority parties of each house have their own fiscal staffs; other states have a single legislative fiscal staff. The larger legislative fiscal staffs tend to be more sophisticated in terms of program and fiscal review because staff members are allowed to specialize.

Legislative fiscal staffs generally review budget requests while the legislature is in session. In those states where the legislature receives information copies of institutional requests, staffs have the opportunity to conduct preliminary analyses, often working directly or indirectly for the finance and appropriations committees, which hold budget hearings with all state agencies. Higher education's interests may be represented by officials from the state higher education coordinating agency, the consolidated governing board, the central system office, or the institutions. There is also considerable informal lobbying between individual institutions, system officials, and trustees on the one hand and legislators on the other. The legislative budget process is further complicated by committee actions, which often affect the level of appropriations.

Higher education is often one of the last appropriation items dealt with by the legislature and hence is more subject to fluctuations in the availability of state funds and to changes in the levels of other social services. The reason for this situation is that an increasingly large percentage of state activities is supported on an entitlement basis, whereby funding is set by statute and is dictated by the level of demand for services or the volume of activity. Because the higher education appropriation can be adjusted without statutory constraint it can be treated on a discretionary basis. As Caruthers and Orwig (1979, 65–66) note, "Appropriations for higher education are determined in part on the basis of the need described in the budget request and in part on the basis of what resources are available after other state program commitments have been met."

The discretionary nature of the higher education budget makes the setting of tuition and fees all the more important. In some states tuition and fees can be set by the institutions or central system offices, thereby providing some flexibility in filling the gap between expected expenditures and the level of appropriations. In other states, the tuition is formally set by institutional boards but informally controlled by the governor's budget office or the legislature. When tuition and fees are determined in large part by executive budget office or legislative action, institutions lose some flexibility.

APPROPRIATIONS

The appropriations bill passed by the legislature varies considerably from state to state. In some, individual institutions are identified in the appropriations bill and receive direct appropriations; in others, resources are provided to systems or state postsecondary education agencies, which in turn distribute the funds to the institutions; and in others, appropriations are distributed by the governor's budget office.

The content of appropriations bills also varies widely. In some states certain kinds of revenues, such as tuition and fees, athletic fees, sponsored research, and auxiliary enterprises, are not included in the appropriations bill. Thus, the funds may go to the institutions without ever having passed through the state treasury. Direct institutional control of these funds tends to afford the institution more flexibility in the use of its monies.

The degree of detail in the appropriations bill often determines the extent of control exerted by state-level officials and agencies over institutional budgets and the amount of flexibility that institutions have in the use of appropriated resources. Generally, the potential for state-level control is greater as the number of program categories and line items, or objects of expenditure, in the appropriations bill increases.

In most states the appropriations bill also contains legislative directives, which specify legislative intent regarding certain issues. These riders may include cost-of-living and merit adjustments for faculty salaries, enrollment ceilings, expected tuition levels, funding levels for special programs not identified in the appropriations bill, or directions for the distribution of funds among institutions. In some states the governor has line-item veto authority after appropriation.

ALLOCATION OF APPROPRIATED FUNDS

When funds are appropriated on a lump-sum basis to a system of institutions, the central administration must allocate the funds among the institutions. Similarly, when individual campuses receive their allocations, campus officials must distribute the funds among the various programs and activities. The distribution pattern will usually differ from the budget requests. Some resources will be removed to establish contingency funds to provide reserves in case of enrollment shortfalls or other emergencies. Reallocations may be made that alter the historical distribution of resources among institutions or among departments and support activities. Resources must be set aside, for example, for new instructional programs. Budget formulas used in some states to construct budget requests are normally *not* used by system and campus officials in allocating appropriated funds. Instead, allocations tend to be made on the basis of historical expenditures, enrollments, and assessments of programmatic need. Also, because so much of each budget is already committed to continuing activities, the reallocations have to be done at the margin.

IMPLEMENTATION OF THE BUDGET

The expenditure of funds in public institutions is similar to the process in independent institutions.

Some states experience budget pressures during the budget cycle, after appropriations have been made, and must make midcycle adjustments. For example, if one or more state agencies have overspent their resources, deficiency appropriations can be made during the budget cycle if the state has sufficient reserves. A more common situation, however, is a shortfall in state revenues, making midyear cuts in state agency budgets necessary.

CLOSING OUT THE FISCAL YEAR

The difference between closing out the fiscal year in public institutions and doing so in independent institutions is largely one of timing. Whereas the latter often allow two months to complete the closing process, the former must usually accomplish the closing within several weeks of the end of the fiscal year.

As with independent institutions, public institutions are audited internally and externally. The external auditors are either from the legislative audit staff or from private accounting firms with which the state has contracted.

The recent appearance in some states of a new state agency—the program and management audit staff—has implications for higher education. These audit groups are often attached to either the legislative or executive branch and take their cues accordingly. In some states program or management audits are conducted by the executive or legislative branch fiscal audit staff as an adjunct to its more accustomed financial audit responsibilities. Program audit staffs conduct audits of state agency activities, including program management and performance, to determine if those activities are conducted efficiently and effectively. Such audits extend far beyond the traditional questions of financial responsibility. Several state program audit groups have conducted audits of programs and activities in higher education, and the number of such reviews is increasing. As the staffs gain experience, they can be expected to ask more penetrating questions about the conduct of business in higher education.

Figure 1: The Annual Operating Budget Cycle—
Stanford University

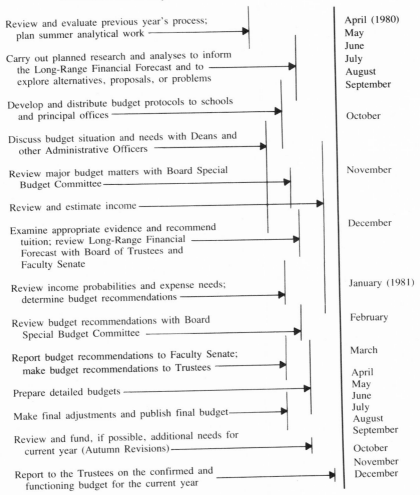

Review and evaluate previous year's process; plan summer analytical work	April (1980) May June
Carry out planned research and analyses to inform the Long-Range Financial Forecast and to explore alternatives, proposals, or problems	July August September
Develop and distribute budget protocols to schools and principal offices	October
Discuss budget situation and needs with Deans and other Administrative Officers	
Review major budget matters with Board Special Budget Committee	November
Review and estimate income	
Examine appropriate evidence and recommend tuition; review Long-Range Financial Forecast with Board of Trustees and Faculty Senate	December
Review income probabilities and expense needs; determine budget recommendations	January (1981)
Review budget recommendations with Board Special Budget Committee	February
Report budget recommendations to Faculty Senate; make budget recommendations to Trustees	March
Prepare detailed budgets	April May June
Make final adjustments and publish final budget	July August September
Review and fund, if possible, additional needs for current year (Autumn Revisions)	October November
Report to the Trustees on the confirmed and functioning budget for the current year	December

Source: Stanford University Operating Budget Guidelines, 1981–82.

Figure 2: Fiscal 1983 Operating Budget Development Process—
University of Maryland, College Park

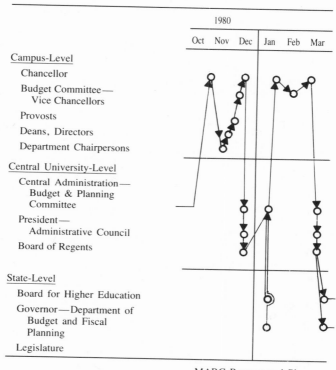

MARC Request and Plan
Update

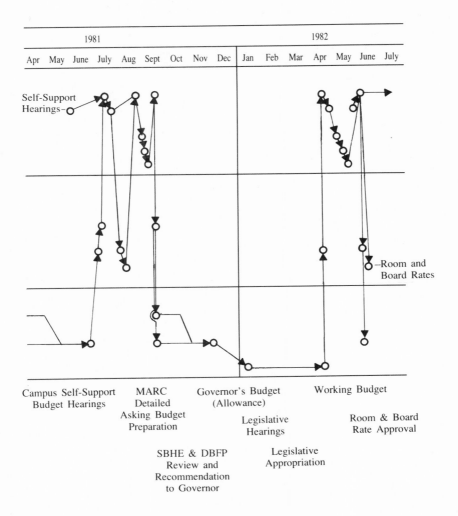

	1981									1982						
Apr	May	June	July	Aug	Sept	Oct	Nov	Dec	Jan	Feb	Mar	Apr	May	June	July

Self-Support
Hearings

Room and
Board Rates

Campus Self-Support
Budget Hearings

MARC
Detailed
Asking Budget
Preparation

Governor's Budget
(Allowance)

Legislative
Hearings

Working Budget

Room & Board
Rate Approval

SBHE & DBFP
Review and
Recommendation
to Governor

Legislative
Appropriation

Note: MARC is the Maximum Agency Request Ceiling set by the governor.

FOR FURTHER READING

A good overview of the higher education budget process is the previously mentioned monograph by J. Kent Caruthers and Melvin Orwig, *Budgeting in Higher Education,* AAHE/ERIC Higher Education Research Report no. 3 (Washington, DC: American Association for Higher Education, 1979).

For technical discussions of institutional budgeting, the reader is referred to sections of *College & University Business Administration,* 4th ed. (Washington, DC: National Association of College and University Business Officers, 1982), and Ray M. Powell, *Budgetary Control Procedures for Institutions* (Notre Dame, IN: University of Notre Dame Press, 1980).

An excellent case examination of institutional budgeting is found in a two-volume report on a Princeton University demonstration project supported by the Ford Foundation: *Budgeting and Resource Allocation at Princeton University* (Princeton, NJ: Princeton University, 1972), and *Budgeting and Resource Allocation at Princeton University,* vol. 2 (Princeton, NJ: Princeton University, 1979).

The budget process at the state level is described in detail in a series of monographs published by the Center for Research and Development in Higher Education at the University of California, Berkeley: Lyman A. Glenny et al., *State Budgeting for Higher Education: Data Digest;* Ralph A. Purves and Lyman A. Glenny, *State Budgeting for Higher Education: Information Systems and Technical Analyses;* Lyman A. Glenny, *State Budgeting for Higher Education: Interagency Conflict and Consensus;* Richard J. Meisinger, Jr., *State Budgeting for Higher Education: The Uses of Formulas;* Frank M. Bowen and Lyman A. Glenny, *State Budgeting for Higher Education: State Fiscal Stringency and Public Higher Education;* and Frank A. Schmidtlein and Lyman A. Glenny, *State Budgeting for Higher Education: The Political Economy of the Process.*

4 / Influencing the Budget Process

The question most frequently asked about the budget process is "How does one effect change through the process?" In other words, "How does one change the pattern of budget allocations?" Knowledge of the economic and political climates and of the actors and the sequence of events is not sufficient to influence the budget process. Successful budgeters must know also what kinds of questions to ask and when to ask them. Such questions can be about the process itself (e.g., Who should participate at each stage of the process? What information should be provided as most useful to participants? How can the timing be adjusted to allow for more complete analyses?), or about the substance of budget decisions (e.g., How much should tuition and fees be increased? How large an increase should the various departments receive next year?). Over time, participants become more adept at phrasing and raising the questions so as to have the most impact. This chapter identifies issues that are common to most colleges and universities and that strongly affect the distribution of resources, and also suggests at which stages in the budget process these issues are typically addressed.

One assumption is that budgeters or participants in the budget process can affect the way in which resources are distributed if they analyze their programs and activities in a logical, orderly manner. The questions raised in this chapter, then, provide a framework for analytical thinking. One must be cautioned, however, that the role of "politics" cannot be overlooked or underestimated in weighing budget outcomes. The political environment or the "spheres of influence" of members of the academic community will vary from institution to institution. Through friendships with trustees or legislators, a dean, for example, may have political connections that provide him with influence far beyond his position. An administrator or faculty member who has participated in the budget process over many years may have gained a knowledge of the institution and a collection of political debts sufficient to make him or her a powerful figure in budget negotiations. Some actors in the process are more articulate spokespersons than others and are more successful in resource acquisition. In general, the more complex the budget process and the interconnections among the actors, the more complex the political environment becomes. The framework adopted in this chapter attempts to show how institutions can strike a balance between rational planning and the inevitable political maneuvering.

The first section addresses institutional character. Although difficult to change, character is a major factor in the allocation of resources, and the assessment of character is a logical first step in determining how budget outcomes are influenced. The next section examines academic, administrative, and revenue factors that can be adjusted at the institutional level to alter the distribution of resources; ways are suggested for faculty and administrators to question the basic assumptions under which budgets have been assembled at their institution. Included is a discussion of the potential hidden costs of administrative and programmatic decisions. The third section examines administrative and revenue factors that come into play at levels beyond the institution. Shaping the budget at these higher levels is very different from doing so within the institution. Institutional actors are often insensitive to this difference, having unrealistic expectations about affecting the process beyond the institution or inappropriate strategies for influencing higher-level decision makers. The fourth section covers some of the analytical tools used by decision makers in determining how to allocate resources (a more detailed discussion is included in part 2). Also discussed are some shortcomings of comparative data. The fifth section touches briefly on methods of financial reporting. Before decision makers can question how resources are allocated, they need information about how resources are actually expended. Without adequate control and reporting mechanisms, decision makers cannot be certain about the consequences of resource allocation decisions.

INSTITUTIONAL CHARACTER:
THE ENVIRONMENTAL FACTORS

As described in chapter 3, institutional character is an amalgam of variables describing an institution's unique qualities. Character is defined in large part through such factors as institutional mission, history, mix of academic programs, size, geographical location, and nature (public or independent). Institutional character carries with it considerable inertia, primarily because of historical tradition and the propensity of most organizations to change slowly. An understanding of an institution's character will provide insight into how decisions are made and resources distributed, but participants cannot expect significant adjustments in the internal and external perceptions of the institution's character each budget cycle. In fact, the causal relationship is probably circular: institutional character changes slowly over time as a result of changes in the distribution pattern of resources, and the allocation of resources may be adjusted to reflect the desire for a different institutional character. It is important to note that the above relationships are loosely articulated. Character does not respond immediately to changes, however major, in funding patterns.

However, there are occasions in an organization's "saga," as Burton Clark (1972) defines the collective understanding of the unique accomplishments in a formal organization, when the character can change more dramatically. Participants in the budget process who recognize these transition periods can strongly influence changes in institutional character and the allocation of resources. Clark (1979, 180) identifies three settings for important changes in the development of organizational sagas or institutional character. The first and most obvious setting is the creation of a new institution. The second setting is what Clark characterizes as a "crisis of decay," during which the institutional community must decide whether to abandon the established behavior or allow the institution to fail. Today this situation is often marked by a change in leadership or a financial crisis brought about by a deteriorating economy, uncontrollable expenses, or plummeting enrollments. In the third setting the institution is ready for evolutionary change, a state difficult to discern because the institution is not in a crisis situation or a steep decline.

One indicator of possible change in institutional character is shifts in the enrollment distribution among the disciplines. During the late 1970s and early 1980s in institutions with a wide array of academic programs, students moved, for example, from the liberal arts and social sciences to the physical sciences in order to pursue degrees having greater marketability. Pronounced changes in student preferences can force budgeters to shift faculty and staff resources to accommodate the new demands. Budgeters must determine whether enrollment shifts indicate short-lived trends or long-term changes in direction and must then decide whether to accommodate the shifts. Actors who participate in the framing of institutional priorities will be every bit as influential as those involved in the budget process. A much different pattern of enrollments evolving over a short period of time may eventually change the character of the institution. If, for example, faculty are to have a major role in shaping their institution's character, they will have to participate in reviewing the implications of enrollment projections.

A second key indicator is the composition of the faculty (in terms, for example, of age, training, disciplines, salaries, and scholarly productivity). During the late 1970s and early 1980s institutions enjoyed a buyer's market for faculty in many disciplines. However, the demands and expectations of new faculty are often different from those of continuing faculty. With the number of faculty vacancies declining, the market in many disciplines has seen an abundance of talented young faculty who, though well trained as researchers, have often been employed by institutions whose primary mission is instruction. This can produce misalignment between mission and faculty expertise and expectations. For example, when a sufficient number of these bright, talented, research-oriented faculty arrive on a campus that does not have a strong research mission, there is strong pressure to strengthen the research component. These young faculty owe their primary allegiance to their disciplines and realize that to maintain their stature in the profession and to ensure their mobility, they must continue active research. Altering the balance between teaching and research can over time affect the character of the institution.

A third indicator is financial condition, particularly in the case of independent institutions. Through careful management of resources and the generosity of alumni and other donors, some colleges and universities have over time accumulated a significant endowment or a working reserve (as opposed to restricted funds) that could serve as the foundation for a new mission.

A fourth indicator of possible change is the perception of the institution held by influential people, including legislators, congressmen and congresswomen, powerful alumni, political figures, and special-interest groups. When influential outsiders believe that the institution has been of some benefit to them, they are more willing to provide financial or political support. Conversely, when these same outsiders perceive that the institution has eroded their position or has not performed satisfactorily, they can lend their weight to an effort to limit resources. Except in crisis situations such as student disturbances or well-publicized confrontations between faculty and administrators, these changes in outside perceptions are slow to accumulate. However, incidents can confirm notions, and notions build on one another.

It is evident that significant changes in the indicators above and in others not listed can lead to broad readjustments in the pattern of resource allocation. Thus, it is always useful for budgeters to analyze their institution's character and estimate its place in the organization's saga. Because noteworthy upheavals in institutional character are generally limited, it seems more practical for budget participants to examine a number of academic, administrative, and revenue factors over which they have much more control on a year-to-year basis. These factors tend to be more tangible and, therefore, more subject to adjustment. The cumulative effect of these adjustments will be an altering of the institution's character.

ADMINISTRATIVE AND REVENUE FACTORS

Questions about the allocation of resources at the institutional level concern four basic areas: the budget process itself, academic and administrative policies and procedures, how revenues are estimated, and the hidden costs of some activities. Though the impact of answers to the questions varies widely from institution to institution, it seems appropriate to raise questions about each area above regardless of the setting.

THE BUDGET PROCESS

Many questions about the institutional budget process are concerned with the degree of involvement of the various actors (see appendix 1 for the AAUP policy statement on faculty participation in the budget process). First is the question of who should be involved in the preparation of budget requests. At the campus level, the issue is whether to give departments a role in assembling the asking budget or to make budget preparation the responsibility of the campus budget staff. The answer will depend on the kind of expectations one wishes to encourage among departments. For example, if it is quite evident that the institution will not have sufficient revenues to satisfy even a fraction of departmental requests for additional resources, it may not be wise to arouse departmental expectations through the preparation of an asking budget. On the other hand, if one views the budget process as a political process in which competing parties present their best arguments for scarce resources and bargain for those resources, it may be appropriate for the departments to be actively involved. In this case requests and justifications are based on information that might not otherwise become available to participants at higher stages in the budget process. The decision to involve departments therefore has the disadvantage of raising expectations that perhaps cannot be met and the advantage of providing additional information about resource needs. As faculty become more aware of the constraints, their expectations become more realistic and the potential for building consensus grows.

Another question is whether the budget format is appropriate. In public institutions budget formats are dictated in large part by the requirements of state-level agencies. To reduce the burden of budget preparation within the institution, budgeters often develop their budgets in accordance with the specifications of those agencies. However, the kinds of information required by state-level officials are often not useful to institutional decision makers. An extreme example of the impact of budget formats was seen in Connecticut during the mid-1970s. State budgeters opted to change to a program budget format, maintaining a parallel flow of budget documentation in the old line-item format (see chapter 8 for a discussion of approaches to budgeting). Because most of the state budgeters were familiar with the line-item approach and did not understand how to frame their analyses around program formats, the program budget documents were collected but not used during the budget review stage. State-level officials usually examine aggregate data that focus more on the institution as a whole than on individual departments or programs. It may be necessary for institutional budgeters to develop parallel budget formats that can be used more effectively for internal decision making.

In both the public and independent sectors it is appropriate to question the structure of the budget and the kinds of information therein. The picture of an institution will vary depending on whether budgets are constructed with object-of-expenditure detail, program categories for program budgeting, or decision packages for zero-base budgeting. Each format requires different information and forces budgeters to ask different kinds of questions about institutional activities.

PARTICIPANTS IN THE BUDGET PROCESS

Budget reviews can involve budget staff and administrators only, or selected faculty and students as well. Constituent groups take part in the review process through a variety of mechanisms, including advisory committees and budget hearings. When faculty or students participate, there is generally a formal procedure on campus for selecting individuals. Also, the nature of the participation (e.g., advisory or decision making), the parts of the budget to be reviewed, and the timing of the review are usually specified. How each of these factors is addressed will influence the outcomes of the budget process. For example, the selection of faculty and student participants by democratic voting may yield individuals who are the most active politically but who are not necessarily the best judges of programs and activities.

Participants not involved in day-to-day budgeting generally need budget staff assistance for background information and analyses. The effectiveness of the participation tends to be a function of the knowledge and experience brought to the review by participants or by budget staff and of the willingness and ability of budget officers to provide data in a form that will facilitate a thorough review.

Another important factor is the nature of the specific budget portions being considered. Reviews that focus on budgets in the academic area may miss the important contributions of administrative and support service budgets. In turn, reviews that focus on individual departments may miss significant relationships among programs. Finally, the timing of participation and the amount of time allotted for review will influence the effectiveness of the participation. Participants need sufficient time to weigh the evidence and examine the consequences of alternative allocation patterns. Resulting recommendations will be more useful to policy makers at higher levels in the budget process if they are available *before* decisions are made and approved by governing boards.

Participants may become frustrated if they believe that the time and effort expended are not adequately recognized by the actors to whom they make recommendations or provide advice, or if the recommendations are ignored. However, not involving members of the academic community guarantees the loss of potentially valuable knowledge and experience. Therefore, the structuring of participation entails a realistic appraisal of the costs and benefits to the institution and to those involved in budget review. At Indiana University, for example, a recent faculty chairperson of the campus budget affairs committee expressed doubt about the value of the committee's role in that it did not deal with the most crucial issues: planning the budget, salary allocation, and plans for increasing revenues (Brown, 1982, 8a). Generally, additional time is required for satisfactory participation, often creating conflicts with budget deadlines.

The degree of openness in the review process will be determined in large part by the character of the institution. Colleges with small faculties and staffs and a strong sense of shared governance will probably have relatively open deliberations. Institutions that are large or that lack a participatory governance structure tend to have a more closed budget review. Usually, an open process is seen as more desirable, particularly by those who do not have an active role in budget review. There are trade-offs, however, in adopting one approach over another. The more open the process is, the more difficult it tends to be for budgeters to ask difficult questions about programs and activities and to negotiate over the allocation of resources. On the other hand, the criteria for distributing resources may be more widely debated and known if the process is open. The opposite tends to be true of more closed deliberations. If budgeters are willing to sacrifice some of the privacy of their deliberations for the sake of broader knowledge of review criteria, they generally have some assurance that the information will be communicated accurately to members of the academic community. Still, budget actors in large institutions, for example, often find that communication channels are unreliable and transmit distorted information. Similarly, the give-and-take of budget review can sometimes yield mixed signals, especially if negotiations occur over a long period of time.

The problem of openness was confronted recently by a large campus that is part of a multicampus state university system. A combined faculty-administration committee was examining the fiscal and academic implications of transferring one or more degree programs to another campus of the system. During the deliberations, the identities of certain programs under examination were released along with statements summarizing the negotiations up to that point. Although the faculty and administrators in each program were cooperating with the review committee, the premature release of information about the review placed these individuals in an awkward position. Several, in fact, drew on the support of strong external constituent groups to block further action. In one program, faculty with the most visibility quickly sought, and were offered, positions in industry or at other universities. The review committee eventually recommended that this much-weakened program be transferred to another campus in the system.

Steps should be taken to provide adequate information about the budget review process to lower levels in the decision hierarchy. Departments or colleges often submit their budget requests (i.e., asking budgets) in the late summer or early fall and receive little information about the requests until the final budget is approved by the legislature (in public institutions) or by the board of trustees (in independent institutions). That is, the departments or colleges do not know how successful their arguments are or how they are perceived by budgeters at higher levels. Departments that begin to make plans for the following year based on their budget request may be shocked in the spring to learn that their expectations had far exceeded the resources eventually allocated. The disparity between asking budgets and appropriated budgets is seemingly magnified in the public setting because legislative action tends to occur long after initial submission. In some institutions the budget office staff or the budget liaison in the office of the vice president for academic affairs provides departments with summaries of budget recommendations at each major step in the review cycle. For special cases the president or the vice president for academic affairs can commit resources to departments even before the final allocation has been determined by the board of trustees or the legislature. If, for example, a department has the opportunity to hire a distinguished scholar or is hosting a major scholarly conference or undertaking a major student recruitment program, it needs some assurance that it will receive the resources necessary to accomplish the task. On a case-by-case basis, the president or the vice president for academic affairs may wish to risk the early commitment of funds to guarantee success. If the burden of these special early commitments is not excessive, the president should be able to adjust the final budget to cover the promises.

ACADEMIC AND ADMINISTRATIVE
POLICIES AND PROCEDURES

Perhaps the single most important way to influence the pattern of budget allocations is to alter the policies and procedures that govern the allocation and expenditure of resources. Because personnel expenditures account for most of the budget, it makes sense to question first the manner in which faculty and staff are utilized.

A useful framework for considering changes in a budget takes into account three factors: (1) increases or decreases resulting from inflation or deflation; (2) increases or decreases in workload; and (3) improvement in or erosion of the quality of a program or activity. Inflation or deflation factors reflect changes in prices of goods and services, including cost-of-living adjustments to salaries and wages. Changes in faculty workload usually reflect changes in enrollment, or demand for course offerings; changes in administrative and staff workload mean changes in the level of service provided. The third factor accounts for qualitative changes in programs and activities. A decision to increase average faculty workload might be made with the expectation that the quality of instruction or advising will decline. Similarly it might be possible to increase faculty workload and yet maintain program quality by introducing into the curriculum new technologies such as computers or television or new instructional modes. Applying the three factors above to budget review enables decision makers to be more discriminating in adopting budget strategies and more accurate in projecting the consequences of those strategies.

Programmatic directions. The first pass at questioning the budget is usually to identify major issues and establish priorities for academic and support programs and activities. Generally, resources are allocated to encourage or promote certain kinds of activities according to the dictates of program priorities. If, for example, research is one such priority, academic departments that are successful in attracting external research funding may be rewarded through the allocation of additional salaries and wages funds to support faculty release time. If higher enrollments are the objective, academic departments that increase their enrollments may be allocated additional faculty positions. If the objective is to increase the use of seminars and the case-study approach, the physical plant operation may need additional funds to renovate classrooms for case-study classes and seminars. Thus, the budget becomes a vehicle for sending messages about how programs and activities are valued.

As budgeters establish program priorities, they also decide the means by which progress is to be measured. Typically, the measures are a balance of quantitative indexes (e.g., student-faculty ratios, student credit hours per FTE faculty member, square footage serviced per member of the janitorial staff) and qualitative indicators (e.g., quality of a department's faculty, national reputation of a department, faculty contact with students, perceived service orientation of support units). Because not all measures can be quantified, budgeters balance quantitative evidence with judgment.

Each of the specific issues discussed below is defined by three broad factors: (1) the extent to which the quality of the activity or program is being improved; (2) the extent to which the activity is responding to an increase in workload; and (3) the extent to which the mission of the activity is being diminished, expanded, or redirected.

Teaching loads. In allocating resources to departments, most institutions use some method of measuring instructional load. Two of the most commonly used indicators are student-faculty ratios and average student credit hours per FTE faculty member. Departments that have heavier credit-hour loads have higher student-faculty ratios and generate on average more student credit hours per faculty member. To determine the policy implications of these ratios, one must also consider the effect of class size on teaching loads. Generally, the indicators are best used only to ask further questions about the instructional process in departments and not as the sole basis for allocating resources.

Departments that depend heavily on laboratory or studio instruction will by the nature of the instructional methodology have lower ratios than departments that have large lectures or sections. Questions can be asked about the extent to which departments depend on labor-intensive instruction: Should they or can they offer more balance between laboratory instruction and large lectures? Does the discipline really need one-on-one instruction, as in the studio training of musicians? Do accreditation standards limit departments to certain instructional methodologies? Could educational technologies such as television or computer-assisted instruction be used to reduce labor-intensiveness in order to allow expanding programs to maintain quality?

In disciplines where student demand is rising, are there ways to serve the students without increasing the number of faculty positions? The apparently obvious answer—to increase faculty teaching loads—is often insufficient. Controlling demand for instructor time calls for a careful examination of instructional methodologies, course and section scheduling, and options such as enrollment rationing. Colorado College, for example, has a point system by which students bid for courses that have enrollment limits. The University of Maryland's College of Business and Management established a minimum grade-point average for a student's first two years as a requirement for admission to the business major, which is in great demand.

Individual faculty teaching loads both within and across departments often differ widely. Within a department the following questions can be raised: Are faculty members with lighter teaching loads given reduced loads as a matter of policy because they are more active and productive as scholars? Are faculty teaching loads skewed by rank, with, for example, full professors teaching two courses per semester and assistant professors three? Do such teaching assignments penalize junior faculty members by making it more difficult for them to find time for research? Do faculty members with equivalent credit-hour production really have the same teaching load? That is, does one individual teach multiple sections of the same course, while the second teaches several different courses? Do some teach chiefly the courses they want to year after year, or is there rotation among some of the courses, especially the basic or service courses? It is also particularly useful to compare the department's current status to its status in various periods in the past. Regarding the interdepartmental situation one can ask the following: Do differences in average faculty teaching loads reflect differences in the reputation, quality, and quantity of scholarly activity in the departments? Is the leadership in some departments more aggressive than in others in terms of the adjustment of instructional workload patterns within the departments? Inevitably, some will argue that any interdepartmental comparison is unfair because the base time period is wrong for their own department.

Course credit weighting factors. As noted above, the allocation of faculty "lines" or positions is frequently done on the basis of a measure of instructional load (e.g., student credit hours taught, headcount enrollment). Typically, the measures of instructional load are composed of elements weighted by level of instruction or level of student. The weights are usually larger for more advanced levels of instruction or levels of student to reflect the belief that instruction at advanced levels is more time-consuming for faculty, and hence more expensive. The relative difference among weights may also reflect institutional priorities in terms of the relative importance of instruction at different levels. For example, lower-level undergraduate courses might be weighted 1.0, upper-level undergraduate 1.5, graduate course work 2.0, and graduate research 3.0. These weights, which are somewhat arbitrary, assume that a faculty member requires twice as much effort to offer one credit hour of graduate course instruction as one credit hour of lower-division undergraduate instruction, or that graduate course work is valued twice as highly as lower-division undergraduate course work, or some combination thereof. Clearly, there are differences between disciplines with respect to the effort required to offer one credit-hour of instruction at a given level. Nonetheless, the weights are usually applied uniformly across an institution.

If the weights used to compute teaching load are indicative of an institution's priorities, a change in weights signifies a change in priorities. If resources are allocated on the basis of weighted student credit hours, for example, a change in weights will lead to a change in the distribution of resources. Figure 1 illustrates that the weighting factors differ greatly across a select group of public institutions. From the range of values, and for a given distribution of "raw," or unweighted, credit hours, it is possible to develop a sense of the size of potential shifts in resources when weights are changed. Figure 2 illustrates the effect on two departments of altering the weighting scheme at a hypothetical institution. The example assumes that the average load of a full-time faculty member is 600 weighted student credit hours. The department that has a relatively larger share of its enrollments at the graduate levels will be authorized a relatively larger number of faculty positions as a result of introducing the richer weighting scheme.

Distribution of faculty ranks. Departments with a higher proportion of junior faculty will tend to be "cheaper" to support because salaries will be lower than in departments with a higher proportion of senior faculty. In addition to the fiscal implications of the distribution of faculty by age and rank, there are several academic concerns: Is the distribution of faculty expertise within a discipline appropriate for both the department's instructional and research missions? Is the proportion of tenured faculty sufficiently low to guarantee a flow of "new blood" into the department? Conversely, should the quality of the experienced teacher be more fully recognized? Do standards for tenure and promotion differ significantly among departments? Should such standards differ when people of higher quality can be hired in some disciplines? Are vacant positions filled at the same rank held by the former incumbent? It should be noted that faculty demographics are often slower to change than institutional policies and procedures.

Distribution of faculty salaries. The distribution of faculty salaries will vary from one department to another for a number of reasons, each of which in turn raises a question about budget policy: Does the distribution of faculty salaries follow closely the pattern of faculty ranks? Does the distribution of faculty salaries reflect more the seniority hierarchy or the contributions and professional accomplishments of the faculty? What are the incentives and disincentives that result? Has the salary difference between entering faculty and faculty with long service to the institution been compressed? If so, is this compression created by market conditions in disciplines such as business, engineering, and computer science? Do some departments achieve economies by filling vacant positions at ranks lower than those of former incumbents? Is this latter strategy necessitated by rapidly rising salaries in the market competition for new faculty? Do the differences in faculty salaries *across* disciplines accurately reflect the differences in the market for faculty?

The salary distribution question frequently arises when a department seeks to fill a vacant faculty position, especially one at the senior ranks. One strategy has been to fill vacant senior professorial posts with junior faculty members. The oft-mentioned advantages of this strategy are: (1) the difference in salaries can be used elsewhere in the department; (2) there is more opportunity to promote junior faculty; and (3) new talent can infuse the department. Before accepting this perspective, however, a department must consider the potential loss of senior faculty leadership. A faculty that is relatively junior usually needs a core of senior faculty positions to provide this leadership.

A question raised frequently by faculty is how to determine the size of faculty and staff salary adjustment pools each year. In the aggregate, salary adjustments depend heavily on the size of the increase in institutional income, which is largely derived from state appropriations, endowment income, and tuition and fees. Generally, the total pool of resources available for salary adjustments is divided into two parts: one for merit adjustments, the other for across-the-board, or cost-of-living, adjustments. At some institutions a portion of the total salary adjustment pool is set aside as a contingency fund for special recruitment and retention needs.

In public institutions the cost-of-living adjustment as a percentage of base salary is frequently mandated for all public employees. There is no national pattern for the relative sizes of cost-of-living and merit adjustments. Ideally, the merit pool is considerably larger than the cost-of-living pool so that an individual's performance can be rewarded.

Typically, the merit adjustment pool allocated to each department or administrative unit is a percentage of total base salaries. If the president, vice president for academic affairs, or deans set aside a portion of the institution's total salary adjustment pool as a contingency fund, the pro rata departmental allocations may be supplemented to reflect differences among departments in terms of market conditions or institutional priorities.

Use of part-time and temporary faculty. As budgets become tighter, more departments and institutions depend on part-time and temporary faculty to make ends meet. Generally, a part-time or temporary faculty member receives less compensation on a course-by-course basis than a permanent faculty member. Also, part-time and temporary faculty can be employed as needed. When student demand shifts, part-time and temporary faculty can be hired or released to accommodate these shifts. One negative feature of part-time and temporary employment is that some individuals become academic gypsies, moving from one temporary position to another. Accordingly, one would expect temporary faculty to be less committed to their institutions. Temporary faculty often receive heavier teaching assignments than permanent faculty, making it more difficult for them to pursue scholarly activities. Also, part-time faculty tend to be less available to students and colleagues because of their other obligations.

To employ part-time and temporary faculty, departments generally must use funds earmarked for adjunct faculty or funds from vacant faculty positions. However, some institutions have policies that prohibit the use of monies from permanent faculty positions for temporary and part-time faculty. Should departments have the latitude to hold faculty positions purposely vacant to provide the resources for temporary hirings? Do large departments have enough faculty turnover or faculty on sabbatical leaves or leaves of absence without pay to generate funds for part-time and temporary faculty without having to hold positions vacant? Do undergraduates experience too large a proportion of their courses with temporary or part-time instructors? Do departments employ budget savings gained in the use of part-time and temporary faculty in the instructional area, or are those savings diverted to other activities such as departmental research and service?

Budgeters in public institutions often must be cautious in attempting to increase flexibility by using part-time and temporary faculty. In some states faculty positions that are vacant for more than one or two years are eliminated from the institution's budget. Other states closely monitor the number of FTE faculty employed, including part-time and temporary faculty, to insure that the number does not exceed the budgeted faculty FTE count.

Sabbatical leaves. Many institutions have a sabbatical leave policy for faculty that provides individuals with one year of leave at half salary or one semester at full salary for every six to ten years of full-time service. For faculty leaves of one year, departments can use the half salary saved to employ part-time instructors to cover the permanent instructor's courses and, if the permanent instructor's salary is sufficiently large, as funding for other activities. Generally, departments lose resources with sabbaticals of one semester at full pay because they must employ substitute instructors and at the same time pay the faculty member's entire compensation. Departments may vary considerably in the handling of sabbatical leaves: Are all faculty granted such leaves when they have met the minimum service requirement? Are faculty required to seek outside funding to cover part of the sabbatical leave? Are only year-long sabbatical leaves at half salary permitted? If one-semester sabbaticals at full pay are permitted, are the absent faculty member's courses canceled or are temporary instructors employed to teach the courses?

Graduate assistants. In institutions that offer graduate-level instruction and have budgeted graduate assistant positions, departments may differ significantly in how the graduate assistants are used. That is, graduate assistants are a source of considerable flexibility. The primary question to be addressed is how departments actually use their graduate assistants (i.e., the extent to which they are used as graders, instructors of independent sections, research assistants, or administrative aides). Another question is the basis on which graduate assistant positions are allocated to faculty— the basis could be seniority, the percentage of teaching load made up of large lecture classes, or scholarly and research productivity. Assistant positions could also be granted across-the-board.

Support staff. The distribution of support staff (e.g., bookkeepers, secretaries, laboratory technicians) may vary a great deal from department to department: Are differences the result of specific instructional methodologies employed, the nature and extent of research activities, instructional loads, service commitments, or simply historical evolution? To what extent should support staffing be adjusted among departments? To what extent can investments in new technologies such as word processing and computerized accounting systems reduce the need for support staff?

Administrative and student support. The academic affairs portion of the institutional budget cannot be understood completely without analyzing its relationship to the administrative and student support budgets. If one assumes that the academic mission (i.e., instruction, research, and service) is primary, academic and student support budgets could be expected to be developed so as to facilitate operations in the academic arena. As happens in most organizations, however, the support operations can sometimes take on a life of their own. Many campuses have policies calling for periodic review of the effectiveness of such operations. Importantly, the reviews are an excellent vehicle for raising and studying budget questions.

The following are some of the many questions that could be asked about support operations: Is this service essential to the campus? Is there a duplication of services on campus? To what extent are new technologies (e.g., computerized accounting, personnel, payroll, and data systems; word processing equipment; energy monitoring systems) being used to reduce the number of staff required and to make operations more efficient?

In examining the physical plant operation, for example, one can ask the following questions: Is the salary structure competitive with market conditions in the area? Has this affected the frequency of vacancies? What steps have been taken to conserve energy in campus facilities? How much would it cost to upgrade campus facilities to achieve significant savings in energy usage? Does the physical plant operation follow a plan of preventive maintenance for campus facilities? What are the long-term costs of deferred maintenance?

In the student affairs operation, for example, one can question the extent to which policies concerning the availability of on-campus student housing influence student enrollment, student retention, and the character of the institution. The fiscal and academic implications of policies in a nonacademic operation on campus are illustrated by the experience of a large university located near a major urban center in the East. This institution has a strong commuter orientation. Students and faculty tend to pursue their cultural and social activities away from campus; accordingly, the campus is not perceived to offer much of a sense of intellectual community. Preference for on-campus student housing is given to upperclassmen; freshmen are not guaranteed housing. This policy may discourage the development of a sense of community among freshmen. If freshmen are not encouraged to view the campus as an intellectual and social community, it becomes more difficult for them to change their impressions when they become sophomores, juniors, and seniors. Thus, a policy controlled by the student affairs office has important implications for the academic environment of the institution. It is interesting to note that one reason the housing policy at this institution has not been altered is concern for a balanced budget. The student housing administrators have fiscal projection models that accurately predict revenues under the existing housing policy. If the policy were to be changed so that freshmen receive preference in on-campus housing, the fiscal models would have to be redesigned, and housing officials there have no historical data base available for inserting new parameters into the models. The officials fear that they might lose money for several years until they are able to predict accurately residential patterns under a new housing policy. This short-run concern for avoiding risks is thus preventing officials from uplifting the intellectual and social environment of the campus. Another way of looking at this situation is to suggest that a willingness to invest resources to cover deficits that might occur during the transition could produce a major benefit in terms of a more positive attitude toward the institution on the part of students. This improved attitude would probably contribute to increased retention and would in the long run help in the effort to attract more students.

Operating expenses. Academic and support departments and activities can be evaluated in terms of how effectively they use their monies for day-to-day operating expenses such as communications, travel, supplies, and equipment. In academic departments, are faculty who are presenting papers or serving on panels the only ones to receive travel funds? Does the department use a priority ranking of the discipline's various professional meetings to ration travel funds? In academic, administrative, and student support areas, are administrators and support staff who are presenting papers or attending workshops the only ones to receive travel funds? Because excessive telephone charges can imperil any unit's budget, budgeters can ask what steps have been taken to subscribe to long-distance telephone services, to design a telephone system that is effective and relatively inexpensive, to monitor long-distance telephone calls and charge faculty for non-business usage, and to disconnect grant-supported telephones when external support ceases. Most institutions have a central purchasing department that orders and stores routine supplies in bulk. To what extent do departments purchase supplies on their own? Do departments take advantage of discounts on purchases of large quantities of supplies? When purchasing equipment, do departments seek educational discounts or prepayment discounts? Do departments take advantage of institutionwide low-cost maintenance agreements for standard pieces of equipment such as typewriters and computer terminals?

REVENUE

Budgets are shaped fundamentally by available revenues, as well as by changes in academic and administrative policies and procedures. Questions of how revenues are projected and of how institutional policies and procedures influence the availability of resources are important considerations to budgeters. In both the public and independent sectors student enrollments are probably the single most influential determinant of institutional income. The independent sector depends more on tuition income than the public sector, though the latter's appropriations from state legislatures are geared primarily to enrollments. Endowment income is a major consideration at only a few institutions in the U.S.; in 1982, fewer than 200 colleges and universities had endowments exceeding $3 million. Many institutions supplement their endowment income with gift revenues. Finally, a small number of institutions have sponsored research programs attracting millions of dollars. Most of these monies are set aside for the research activities themselves, however, and do not constitute a pool of revenues over which an institution has significant control.

Enrollment projections. Projecting student enrollments is an art, not a science (see chapter 12). An institution that projects enrollments accurately over time knows its potential audience and successfully controls a number of key variables, including acceptance rates, student retention rates, tuition levels, and the attractiveness of academic programs.

An institution's character will in large part define the potential population of students. Accordingly, an understanding of an institution's character will shape the kinds of questions raised. What is the target population, and what characteristics of the institution help define that population? Does the target population need to be expanded to obtain a larger pool of potential students? Would this expansion affect the quality of the student body? Are there some components of the institution's character (e.g., array of academic programs, student housing policies, athletic programs) that can be adjusted to make the institution more attractive to prospective applicants? Has the target population changed dramatically in recent years?

As the competition for students increases, some institutions are turning to advertising and recruitment campaigns. Because this can be quite expensive, budgeters usually weigh the costs against the benefits as measured by increased applications or an increase in matriculations. Should the institution employ its own publicity staff, or should it contract for advertising services? What kind of advertising should be undertaken? To what audience should the advertising be directed? Should professional recruiters be hired by the institution? Can recruitment be done to some extent by students, faculty, and alumni?

Every institution has a pool of applicants, and that pool may overlap with pools of other institutions. Applicants are screened by an admissions office and perhaps by a faculty committee, which evaluate each candidate according to institutional entrance criteria. Because many potential students apply to more than one institution and many for various reasons decide not to enter college, a percentage of those admitted will not matriculate. Enrollment projections are usually based on a firm knowledge of the historical acceptance and matriculation rates and on the confidence that the projected rates will not differ from historical patterns. When radical changes are made in institutional character—such as when the institution becomes coeducational, or no longer requires students to live on campus, or changes its admissions criteria—the acceptance and matriculation rates cannot be projected from historical data. Also, enrollment projections must be adjusted to reflect the trend in average student load, which in recent years has been decreasing. Clearly, the number of matriculating students is crucial in that it will determine tuition revenue and, in most public institutions, state appropriations. If the number of candidates offered admission is too small, are admissions standards too strict? If the number of candidates offered admission is too large, are admissions standards too lax? If applicants are required to specify their proposed degree major, does the distribution of candidates offered admission resemble the distribution of faculty resources? To what extent will more attractive student aid packages help to improve acceptance and matriculation rates? If those rates fluctuate widely from year to year, should admissions standards be changed? Are life experiences credited in evaluating candidates for admission? What are the special requirements and obligations associated with equal opportunity in the admissions process? Are transfer students encouraged to apply? Are admittance rates for transfer students adjusted to compensate for changes in the admittance rates of first-time students?

Admissions to graduate programs are usually treated differently from admissions to undergraduate programs. Are admissions handled by an office of graduate studies or by individual departments? Who establishes the criteria for admission to graduate programs? Are the financial aid or graduate assistantship packages attractive to prospective students?

One aspect of enrollment projections is estimating the number of matriculated students who will continue at the institution until graduation. Over time a retention history evolves that is used to guide the projections. Students remain at or depart from institutions for any number of reasons. However, because it makes sense financially (and, one hopes, educationally) to retain as many students as possible, some institutions have introduced retention programs. Budgeters would ask several questions about those programs: Are they necessary? What is their cost and do the costs outweigh the gains? Financial gains can be estimated in terms of net revenue, that is, additional income from tuition and fees and charges for room and board less the incremental costs of financial aid, recruitment, housing, and food services. Are resources, and particularly new staff, needed so that faculty can be released from teaching and other obligations in order to assume more counseling and advising responsibilities? What teaching loads will be imposed on faculty in particular departments and what burdens placed on administrative staff?

Tuition and financial aid. A key variable in the determination of net revenue is tuition less in-house financial aid to students. Tuition levels are typically established in close relationship with enrollment, revenue projections, and expenditures. Roughly, tuition income makes up the gap between total estimated expenditures and the sum of other income. This gap is especially large in most independent institutions. Setting tuition charges, however, is more complex than simply selecting a figure that will yield a balanced budget. If tuition is raised, financial aid must usually be increased as well. Thus, part of the tuition increase must, in essence, be used to fund the increase in financial aid. To what extent will the tuition increase work to reduce enrollment, even with an increase in financial aid? At what point will the tuition increase actually reduce revenue? Should the tuition charged at competitive institutions be used as a benchmark in establishing new tuition levels? Should tuition vary by degree program or student class-level to reflect the different costs of programs? What is the appropriate relationship between undergraduate and graduate tuition charges? Similarly, should financial aid be employed to adjust net charges to particular groups of students? The calculation of net revenue per student is important for small institutions, where incremental increases or decreases in enrollment can determine the fate of faculty and staff positions and basic services.

Generally, student fee structures are considered with tuition charges. The setting of fees is a much murkier area than the setting of tuition levels because most fee income is channeled to auxiliary enterprises, which are self-supporting. Budgeters often use the establishment of fee structures as a means to examine the financial operations of these self-supporting programs. On many campuses, for example, student affairs activities such as intramural athletics, student government, and health clinics are budgeted largely through fees. A number of institutions charge for private music lessons, and others have a laboratory fee to generate income for academic departments that use laboratories in instruction. Some fees are charged to faculty and staff as well as students. Income from parking fees, for example, might be used to maintain parking lots and campus roadways for the benefit of the entire academic community. In some public institutions it may be possible to increase fee levels more than tuition levels because of state oversight in the establishment of the latter. Thus, funding for academic programs might be slighted while self-supporting or nonstate budget activities flourish. Also, institutional advocates of low tuition may be unaware of proposed fee increases because tuition charges and fee charges are sometimes established through separate processes by different participants (see chapter 12).

Endowment. Many actors in the budget process are not familiar with endowments, as these investments are often managed by a committee of the board of trustees, a separate development office, or professional investment counselors. Although budgeters generally need not concern themselves with the day-to-day management of endowments, they can raise questions about the direction of investment policies and the relationship between the policies and the revenue generated for the institution (see chapter 9). How is the investment portfolio balanced to accommodate the need for capital growth on the one hand and operating income on the other? If the portfolio leans too heavily toward capital growth, it may produce insufficient income for the budget. If the portfolio leans too heavily toward income generation, it may not grow enough to keep pace with income needs and inflation. What is the rate of return on the investment portfolio? How does this compare with the returns for other kinds of portfolios? At what rate is income from the endowment drawn down? Should only a portion of the income generated by endowment investments be used as revenue for the budget, with the balance added to the principle so that the endowment will grow? A major policy decision that will influence revenues directly is determining the proportion of investment income allocated to the budget.

Another series of questions can be raised about endowment income. Should it be used primarily to fund continuing activities, or as seed money for new activities? Should part of endowment income be set aside for contingencies? To what extent is endowment earmarked by donors for particular programs and activities? (See chapter 7 for a detailed discussion of fund accounting.)

Gifts. Most institutions receive more income from gifts than from endowment. Gifts are less predictable than endowment income unless an institution has an established record of receiving gifts and employs a staff to pursue them actively. Is it cost-effective to employ a development staff? That is, can the staff recover more in gifts than is spent for salaries and operating expenses? Are there ways in which the institution can pursue gifts more aggressively so that income will be more predictable? Should the institution have an alumni office? For institutions with a religious affiliation, how steady a source of income is the church?

Research funding. In preparing the budget, institutions with substantial sponsored research activity normally project contract and grant revenues. However, historical information concerning the number of contract and grant applications made and the number funded is of questionable value because the priorities for federal research support are changing constantly in today's economic environment. What are the current federal priorities? Does the institution have research activity in those areas? What are the possibilities of joint research enterprises with business and industry? Are there private sources of funding, such as foundations, that might support sponsored programs? Do indirect cost rates differ among sponsored activities such as training programs, laboratory research, or off-campus research? (See chapter 13 for a discussion of indirect cost rates.)

Sponsored research can make a significant contribution to an institution's instructional program by covering part of the costs of graduate education. Research projects often involve graduate students as research assistants. A number of graduate students receive their research training in this way. In addition, research funding complements the institution's allocations to departments by providing additional funds for faculty travel, secretarial support, equipment purchases, and other items.

HIDDEN COSTS

Budgeters do not like to be surprised by unexpected expenditures. So in designing budgets they usually include estimates for equipment and facilities repair and replacement, or they establish a contingency fund to enable the institution to take advantage of opportunities or respond to emergencies. However, many policy decisions, such as those involving the addition of new facilities, the introduction of new degree programs, or the revision of curricula, carry with them hidden costs that become long-term obligations. Opening a new or renovated building, for example, will require funds for building maintenance. Also, a new facility usually needs an initial allocation for equipment and furnishings. If the allocation of equipment to the new facility is significant, funds will have to be provided for equipment maintenance.

The obvious costs of a new degree program are the salaries of additional faculty and staff and the operating expenses associated with day-to-day program administration. New programs also seem to arouse expectations for continued growth. Less obvious are the demands that the new program makes on existing programs. If the new program attracts new students to the institution, the demand for courses in existing programs that are complementary will increase. This may require that additional instructors be hired. If, on the other hand, the new program attracts students from other degree programs, there may be a decline in students taking courses in certain existing departments. Thus, the courses in some departments may become undersubscribed, leaving those departments relatively overstaffed.

Altering the curriculum of one department's program may have fiscal implications for other departments. If, for example, the accounting program changed its requirements to include instruction in computer science, the computer science department may have to employ additional faculty to meet the increased demand. Similarly, if a number of degree programs included a requirement for one or more accounting courses, the accounting department may have to add faculty. Recently the University of Maryland at College Park added a junior-level English composition requirement to all curricula. Now all students must take such a course prior to graduation. The fiscal implications of this curricular modification, which were not evaluated prior to campus senate approval of the measure, include the addition of classroom sections at an approximate cost of $250,000. One question raised by these examples is "Who should provide the resources to meet the increased or shifted demand for instruction?" Clearly, more than one department must bear the burden of curricular changes that affect several programs. The question then is whether the new programs are worthwhile in view of the explicit and hidden costs.

Even the elimination of activities or programs may have hidden costs that erase some or all of the planned savings. For example, programs that depend on one being eliminated will have to find substitutes or provide the services themselves. If personnel are being released, the institution may be obligated to place them in other positions on campus or to provide some severance pay. Facilities that are being "mothballed" may require security and minimal heating during the winter months.

Personnel decisions can have long-term costs if they involve positions protected by tenure or some form of job security. One cost is the loss of budgeting flexibility. Job permanence makes it difficult for budgeters to reallocate positions from one activity to another or to reduce the number of positions in an activity. Moreover, tenured positions require a significant financial investment. If one assumes that an assistant professor is tenured and promoted at age 30 and continues to serve until age 70 at a level salary of $25,000 throughout his or her career, the institution makes a $1 million commitment upon awarding tenure.

Hidden costs may also be a factor when new programs and activities are initiated with seed funding from endowment or grants. Once the program or activity is underway and the seed money has been consumed, it may be necessary to provide continued funding to keep the enterprise alive. There is a natural tendency to want to guarantee the success of initial investments by continuing to invest funds in the new programs and activities. If the long-term financial needs of a new enterprise are anticipated and sources of funding have been identified, there will be fewer hidden costs.

RELATIONSHIP BETWEEN CAPITAL BUDGET AND
ANNUAL OPERATING BUDGET

In the budget processes at many institutions consideration of the relationship of the capital budget to the annual operating budget is often neglected. This lack of coordination is particularly striking in public institutions, where the capital and annual operating budgets are often treated as distinct entities. In those situations the capital budget request is often prepared by the physical facilities planning staff with minimal participation from the academic community.

The capital budget typically addresses new equipment needs, replacement of obsolete or worn-out equipment, renovation of existing facilities, and acquisition of new facilities. In the best of circumstances the capital budget is prepared on the basis of a long-range plan for the capital needs of academic programs and support units.

Across higher education there is no uniformity in the accounting standards for capital depreciation (see chapter 7). In fact, a lively debate continues over whether capital depreciation is a realistic concept for institutions of higher education. Opponents contend that facilities and equipment wear out and should not be depreciated. Capital depreciation, they argue, is valid only in the for-profit sector in relation to taxes. Financial support for the replacement of facilities and equipment should come from gifts and endowment income restricted to that purpose. Capital depreciation is an especially sensitive subject in the public sector, where government agencies seem to want to keep capital expenditures out of the spotlight.

A more practical and realistic approach to capital budgeting, especially in the independent sector, is to build into the annual operating budget a depreciation charge. This charge would be over and above the portion of the annual operating budget devoted to preventive maintenance. The size of the annual capital charge would be set on the basis of a long-range plan for capital development. The monies would be placed in a reserve fund as a means for removing them from the cash flow for use in present and future capital projects. Charging the annual operating budget for depreciation seems to offer more certainty in the capital budgeting process than depending on the timely beneficence of donors.

Participants in the budget process will probably find that capital needs are often seen as less urgent than annual operating needs. Thus, the capital component of the annual operating budget may be seen as a primary candidate for reductions to balance the institution's budget. This tendency to see the capital area as a source of painless cuts should be avoided. Reducing or eliminating a capital depreciation charge from the annual operating budget is trading a short-term financial difficulty for a long-term one that will likely be more debilitating.

STATE FACTORS

In the public sector, institutions have much less control over the budget process once the budget request leaves the institution. The process itself, for example, cannot be modified unless the state-level actors take such action. Institutional actors can raise questions about several significant policy issues, but their success in changing state-level policy direction depends in large part on the persuasiveness of the arguments, the fiscal implications of changes as seen from the state perspective, and the receptivity to such arguments on the part of key state-level decision makers.

POLICY ORIENTATION

At the state level most important decision makers view policy issues through their staffs. Thus, the governor depends heavily on his executive budget office to collect and analyze data and to make recommendations concerning the details of the budget. Similarly, legislators depend on staff members of the legislative fiscal staff(s) for much of their understanding of budgets. On rare occasions, however, these key actors can examine higher education without the filtering effect of the staff. The governor may meet formally with the presidents of institutions or informally with faculty and institutional staff members who are personal friends. Legislators may also have informal relationships with faculty and staff. More commonly, legislators examine higher education directly through budget hearings. Staffs of state higher education coordinating and governing boards generally have the most frequent contact with the institutions, although this contact tends to be through administrators.

Because of the relative infrequency of such contacts, their importance cannot be overemphasized. Institutional representatives, whether acting formally or informally, are under considerable pressure to represent the whole institution when they speak. Sometimes there is the temptation to risk the entire institutional budget for the sake of a special interest in one small part of the budget. Although only a small part is argued or defended in a hearing or meeting, it is the full budget that is under the scrutiny of state-level decision makers. Accordingly, institutional representatives are usually careful to place their commentary in an appropriate context. State-level actors are extremely busy and seek information about state programs from every possible source. If handled sensitively, the face-to-face contact between institutional and state-level actors can be an opportunity for selling budgets and programs.

Contact between state-level staff and institutional actors occurs frequently outside the context of budget hearings. Many of the perceptions of higher education formed by state-level staff members are based on these encounters. The same cautions that apply when institutional actors engage key state-level decision makers also apply to any dealings with the staffs of those state-level persons. In particular, lobbying activities should be coordinated to be effective.

POLICY ISSUES

Issues that might be discussed by institutional and state-level budgeters will vary in nature and importance from one state to another. The following list is illustrative rather than exhaustive.

Budget formulas. Funding levels for many public institutions are determined by budget formulas (see chapter 8). Such formulas in the instructional area are for the most part driven by student enrollments. Many formulas distinguish between graduate and undergraduate instruction; some distinguish among levels of instruction by degree program, academic department, or form of instruction (such as primarily lecture, mixture of lecture and small-group discussion, and laboratory). Many discussions concerning formulas focus on the philosophical underpinnings or on the technical aspects of the formula: Should formulas be enrollment-driven? How should enrollment-driven formulas be modified for situations of enrollment decline? Can funding mechanisms be developed that function on the basis of marginal costs? What should be the relative formula weights among degree programs, among levels of instruction, and among forms of instruction?

State appropriations. How does the state determine what its equitable share of the costs of public instruction should be? How does the state determine an equitable distribution of resources among institutions? What is the relationship between state policy on faculty workload and state appropriations?

Auxiliary enterprises. What are the state's policies concerning support of auxiliary enterprises? Should the state have as much control as it does over auxiliary activities? Can institutional autonomy be increased while state needs for accountability are met?

Continuing education/evening programs/summer programs. To what extent should the state fund continuing education, evening programs, and summer programs? Should these be self-supporting? Can institutions market and advertise for such programs? To what extent will the continuing education program at one institution compete with the instructional programs at other institutions?

Budget reviews. At what level of detail should budgets be reviewed by state officials? How much information about the operation of institutions should be provided? At what level of detail in a budget review does the autonomy of institutions begin to erode?

Tuition levels. How much control should state officials have in establishing tuition levels? What portion of the costs of higher education should be borne by the student through tuition charges? Do state financial aid policies take tuition policies into account? Should there be different tuition charges for different degree programs and different student levels?

Enrollment ceilings. Some states have set enrollment ceilings for each institution as a means of limiting higher education budgets. Should enrollment ceilings be used to redirect students from certain institutions to others?

Financial crisis. How should the higher education community and the state establish processes to develop and review institutional plans for program reductions and mission changes as enrollments decline? What will happen to higher education in the face of falling state revenues or tax and expenditure limitations that force reductions in funding regardless of enrollment trends?

ANALYTICAL TOOLS

Participants new to the budget process may be overwhelmed at first by the profusion of technical jargon, data, analyses, and simulation models. There is a tendency in some settings to allow budget office staff and analysts to establish the framework and set the tone for budget deliberations. Actors with long experience in budgeting generally learn to balance the technical aspects of budgeting with an understanding of how institutions do and should function. Also, experienced actors know that the skills and judgment of the individuals interpreting the analyses will largely determine the actors' own success in the budget arena.

A vast array of analytical tools is available to budgeters: budget formats (e.g., program budgeting, zero-base budgeting), computer simulation models (e.g., EDUCOM-FPM, RRPM, CAMPUS) (see chapter 14), costing studies, enrollment projection models, cross-sectional and time-series analyses, and comparative analyses. (See part 2 for discussions of the technical aspects of many of these tools.) The technical facility to understand or use analytical tools and the gaining of perspective in the application of those tools generally come with experience. Actors who wish to influence the budget process usually understand the assumptions underlying the models and analyses and the limitations of their application to the institution. Analytical tools are, after all, no better than the questions advanced by their designers and users. The most sophisticated users of these tools, whether technicians or policy makers, are the individuals with the most realistic expectations about their application.

The incredibly rapid development and acceptance of microprocessor, or "home computer," technology has made a wide range of management tools readily available to administrators, faculty, and students. Software packages for budget analysis, scheduling, inventory control, and portfolio analysis enable decision makers to simulate a spectrum of alternative environments.

There are now diminished expectations about the feasibility and value of comparative unit-cost data across institutions (see chapter 10). The National Center for Higher Education Management Systems (NCHEMS) pioneered efforts to develop uniform typologies of program classifications and data elements that could serve as the basis for an exchange of data. During the early 1970s the National Commission on the Financing of Postsecondary Education recommended that uniform financial data be collected on a national basis. In recent years some members of the Association of American Universities (AAU) have organized informal data exchanges on an experimental basis in an attempt to refine the comparability and collection of financial data across institutions. Also, the American Association of University Professors (AAUP) conducts an annual faculty salary survey. Although these efforts have made us more sensitive to the complexities of higher education in this country, they have largely been frustrated by the very complexity and diversity of institutions. Every institution is organized differently, has different staffing patterns, has unique policies and procedures that encompass the full spectrum of institutional activities and programs, and has a unique location. In short, each institution has its own personality or character that is reflected in its data. In many ways it is impossible to separate out the variables to yield data that are truly comparable. This difficulty does not mean that such data cannot be used to raise questions about the institutions being compared. In fact, data comparisons should generally be used as the basis for questions about programs and activities, though they should not be definitive justifications for decisions. In weighing the value of comparative data, one must also consider the costs of acquiring the data. Those costs may far outweigh the benefits obtained.

It should be mentioned that the National Center for Educational Statistics (NCES) collects data annually from all colleges and universities through its Higher Education General Information Survey (HEGIS). These HEGIS data concern all aspects of the institutions (including the financial side), but are aggregated in broad categories that allow for only macro-level comparisons among institutions.

Budget formats can become a powerful analytical tool as long as the users understand that formats are simply a device for focusing on questions concerning the allocations of resources and do not provide an accurate picture of organizational reality (see chapter 8). Program budgeting, for example, structures institutional activity around programs. Instead of focusing on discrete pieces of the institution, the program perspective intends to show how the pieces are integrated into coherent wholes labeled programs. A degree program in political science, for example, includes courses offered by departments other than political science: economics, English, foreign languages, sociology, psychology, and others. A budgeter cannot understand or appreciate the complexity of a degree program in political science by examining only the activities of the political science department. The program focus enables us to ask better questions about the distribution of courses a major is required to take, for example, or about the extent to which a department devotes its resources to serving its own majors rather than the majors of other degree programs. The budgeter is reminded, however, of institutional reality—resources are usually allocated to departments and *not* to degree programs.

If used selectively and with sensitivity to organizational dynamics, zero-base budgeting can be another helpful analytical tool. Zero-base budgets portray an institution's activities and programs as if they were being established for the first time. Each activity or program is justified in terms of the resources needed to accomplish certain tasks. In many ways this approach is a luxury because the activities and programs already exist, have a history of resource needs, and typically are not about to be eliminated or drastically diminished. Moreover, in most budget cycles there is insufficient time to ask each program or activity to justify itself *de novo*. Accordingly, the experienced budgeter may earmark only one or a few activities and programs to be subjected to zero-base budgeting to make the review more manageable and to fit time constraints. Unless there are serious questions about all aspects of the program or activity, the budgeter may request that only part of the program or a certain percentage of the program's budget be justified *de novo*.

Cost analysis can also be quite useful when applied judiciously (see chapter 10). As mentioned above, standardized cost information across institutions is available in only a few cases and presents many problems of comparability. Cost analysis, then, is generally best used to study cost behavior over time within an institution. Comparisons among institutions must be made carefully and the results must always be qualified considerably. In a few areas of institutional operation, cost information of high reliability can be obtained (e.g., in lease/purchase decisions, indirect cost recovery formulas, and auxiliary enterprises). For most activities of the institutions, however, cost information is not definitive and is used primarily to raise questions about activities. Comparing the costs of instruction over time, for example, can foster questions about teaching loads (e.g., Has department X reduced its average faculty teaching load from three courses to two?), faculty distribution (e.g., Is degree program X more expensive than degree program Y because program X has more senior, and hence more expensive, faculty, attached to it?), or sponsored research (e.g., Does department A have more faculty engaged in sponsored research than department B, as indicated by the cost of instruction in the two departments?). Cost data in themselves do not tell the budgeter much; plotting trends over time, on the other hand, permits the budgeter to frame interesting questions. Moreover, cost analysis can be incorporated into very sophisticated mathematical models to study a variety of fiscal relationships that are too complex to analyze otherwise.

In general, all other analytical tools should be approached with the same healthy skepticism about underlying assumptions and limitations. To be avoided is the use of analysis simply to provide the appearance of rationality in decision making or to create a sense that definitive answers are available. Moreover, the current issues that can be probed analytically may not be the most significant ones over the long-term. A further caution is that analytical tools that are grounded in historical data may prove deficient in the years ahead if the economy and the social structure of higher education in this country continue to change as rapidly as they have during the past several years. Despite the uncertainties, however, there are risks in *not* performing these analyses.

FINANCIAL REPORTING

All institutions have financial reporting systems. Most of these systems have evolved over time and are still oriented toward the need to *control* the flow of funds. More current systems seek to satisfy not only the need to control expenditures, but also to provide information that can be used to *manage* resources. It is important for budgeters to understand the limitations of their own institution's accounting and budgeting reporting systems if they are to become more sophisticated about the budget process. A knowledge of where data come from is a major first step to understanding how the data can be used and how they are inherently limited. Budgeters' expectations for certain kinds of information may not be met if the financial reporting system has only a control orientation. Even financial reporting systems that are focused more on resource management offer data that suggest questions rather than definitive answers about the institution.

Figure 1: Student Credit Hour Weighting Factors
Reported by AAU Institutions 1982–83

	Lower Div.	Upper Div.	Grad. Instruction	Grad. Research
California	1.0	1.5	2.5	3.5
Colorado[1]	1.0	1.8	3.6	4.7
Minnesota	1.0	1.0	1.5	1.5
Missouri	1.0	2.0	4.0	4.0
Nebraska	1.0	1.6	3.4	6.5
Oregon	1.0	2.0	4.0	4.0
Washington[2]	1.0	1.8	4.3	6.0
	1.67	2.86	4.3	6.0
Wisconsin	1.0	1.7	3.92	6.06

[1]Based on average direct-cost dollars per student credit hour resulting from the Major Research Universities Information Exchange Project.
[2]The higher weights are used for "high-cost" programs such as architecture and engineering.
Source: Private correspondence, Marilyn Brown, University of Maryland, College Park, 1983.

Figure 2: Faculty Staffing as Determined by Weighting Factors

(Assume 1.0 FTE faculty position carries a load of 600 weighted student credit hours.)

Dept. A	Credit Hours by Level of Instruction	Weighting Factor		Weighted Student Credit Hours	
Lower Division	3,000	1.0	1.0	3,000	3,000
Upper Division	4,000	1.5	1.5	6,000	6,000
Graduate Instruction	1,500	2.0	2.5	3,000	3,750
Graduate Research	500	3.0	3.5	1,500	1,750
				13,500	14,500

Number of full-time equivalent faculty positions $= \dfrac{13,500}{600} = 22.5$

$$= \left[\dfrac{14,500}{600} = 24.2 \right]$$

Dept. B

Lower Division	2,000	1.0	1.0	2,000	2,000
Upper Division	3,000	1.5	1.5	4,500	4,500
Graduate Instruction	2,500	2.0	2.5	5,000	6,250
Graduate Research	1,000	3.0	3.5	3,000	3,500
				14,500	16,250

Number of full-time equivalent faculty positions $= \dfrac{14,500}{600} = 24.2$

$$= \left[\dfrac{16,250}{600} = 27.1 \right]$$

FOR FURTHER READING

The readings suggested at the end of chapter 3 also discuss ways in which budget participants can influence the process and the outcomes. Factors in the distribution of resources within an institution are examined in Paul Dressel and Lou Anna Kimsey Simon, *Allocating Resources Among Departments,* New Directions for Institutional Research, no. 11 (San Francisco: Jossey-Bass, Inc., 1976). An excellent discussion of the relationship of capital budgets to annual operating budgets is found in a monograph by Hans H. Jenny (with Geoffrey C. Hughes and Richard D. Devine), *Hang-Gliding, or Looking for an Updraft: A Study of College and University Finance in the 1980s—The Capital Margin* (Wooster, OH, and Boulder, CO: The College of Wooster and John Minter Associates, 1981).

5 / Flexibility

There is a high probability that unforeseen circumstances will shape the outcomes of most planning. It is important to anticipate both disruptions in plans and the possibility of opportunities by incorporating alternative activities or events into the plans. One of the marks of a well-regarded institution is its ability to take advantage of sudden opportunities and to respond to unanticipated problems.

The experienced budgeter at every level of the budget process attempts to build as much flexibility as possible into the budget. Flexibility is defined here as a pool of resources that an individual can use for any purpose or as the ability to manipulate policies and procedures to alter outcomes. In a college or university budget, that pool of resources is usually extremely difficult to obtain or structure because of the heavy demands placed on available resources and the relatively autonomous functioning of departments and activities.

Personnel costs (salaries and wages and associated benefits for all employees) account for approximately 65 to 80 percent of most college or university budgets; fixed expenses such as utilities or maintenance represent approximately 10 to 15 percent. The balance is usually allocated to operating expenses such as service contracts, supplies, communications, noncapital equipment, and travel. Flexibility is usually structured according to the

99

portion of the budget to which it pertains. Typically, restrictions on the uses of funds differ from one expenditure category to another. For example, in many institutions salary and wage monies cannot be expended for operating or fixed expenses, but the latter two funds can be used for salaries and wages. Thus, strategies for obtaining flexibility tend to be tailored to the function, to the expenditure restrictions affecting the institution, and to the level of operation within the institution.

In some circles the notion of flexible resources has the negative connotations of inefficiency and poor administration. Slack in an institutional budget is sometimes erroneously equated to "fat." One extension of this philosophy is that a leaner budget translates into greater accountability. In fact, the most effective organizations tend to be those in which resources can be marshaled as necessary to meet contingencies. Most budgeters guard against intrusions on their slack resources from both above and below in the organization's hierarchy.

In all organizations there is a natural tendency to want to shift uncertainty to other persons. Often department chairpersons, for example, depend over time on deans or campus-level administrators to provide resources over and above their unit budgets for emergencies and opportunities, such as the overexpenditure of operating expense accounts, the costs of replacement faculty hired on short notice to replace ill or incapacitated faculty, and the hiring of an excellent faculty member who recently appeared on the market. Responsibility for uncertainties that arise in departmental operations is thereby shifted to the dean or campus-level administrator. Similarly, deans and college-level administrators may closely monitor departmental spending in order to anticipate problems or establish a reserve of funds to service departmental requests. In public systems of higher education, state-level officials shift uncertainty to system-level or campus-level administrators through statutes mandating that state agencies will not operate at a deficit.

It should be noted that the notion of flexibility changes from one budget cycle to the next as circumstances change. Sources of slack resources must change to adapt to new conditions, as must the strategies employed to obtain the slack. Although budgeters at all levels in the organization seek slack resources, they are naturally reluctant to identify those reserves to other institutional actors for fear of losing them.

Budgeters build flexibility into their plans in anticipation of significant changes in revenue or expenditures. (Although an unanticipated windfall of funds is a relatively infrequent occurrence, a savvy budgeter will know in advance how to spend such resources wisely.) These changes arise from three primary sources: (1) enrollment fluctuations, (2) emergencies, and (3) unforeseen opportunities. The uncertainty surrounding enrollment projections is a major reason for building slack into the budget. If anticipated enrollments fail to materialize, a college or university loses tuition income or state appropriations or both. Unless there are reserve resources to cover the shortfall, the institution will have a deficit budget for that year. Similarly, enrollments above expectations can sometimes tax an institution's budget, even when the extra tuition income is considered, in that extra instructional sections may have to be scheduled with marginal registrations. Enrollments among degree programs may also shift so rapidly that it is not possible to reallocate resources, thereby creating an imbalance of teaching resources and requiring the staffing of additional instructional sections with temporary faculty.

The range of emergencies for which resource reserves are needed is as broad as the imagination. For example, changes in federal student aid policies may place more of the burden of financial assistance on colleges and universities. The federal government may increase the minimum wage base for hourly employees. Soaring prices for gas and oil can send utilities expenditures higher than projected. An especially bitter winter or unseasonably hot summer can also undermine a utilities budget. State revenues might be less than projected, forcing state governments to reduce commitments to public agencies, colleges, and universities. To meet anticipated revenue shortfalls, the state might impose higher salary savings targets. If an institution is self-insured, or has high deductibles, it might have to absorb significant losses arising from fires, severe storms, theft, or vandalism. Major building systems, such as heating and cooling, plumbing, and electrical networks, eventually deteriorate and have to be replaced, sometimes ahead of schedule. A roof or plumbing leak might cause extensive damage to sensitive equipment, personal articles, or building structure. Typically there is no way that any of these events can be anticipated when the budget is planned, some six to eighteen months prior to the beginning of the fiscal year. The best that budgeters can hope for is to set aside sufficient financial reserves or to be relatively free to alter other budget plans to accommodate the contingencies.

Ultimately, flexible funds have their origin in any revenue source: tuition and fee income, unrestricted endowment income, some state appropriations, unrestricted gift income, indirect cost recoveries from sponsored programs, and excess income from auxiliary and self-support activities. What is more important, however, is how reserves can be created and held free of the heavy day-to-day demands of institutional operations. Strategies for the creation of resource reserves are discussed in a subsequent section. The strategies themselves are shaped in large part by a number of environmental factors common to large classes of institutions.

THE REGULATED ENVIRONMENT:
CONSTRAINTS AND OPPORTUNITIES

PUBLIC AND INDEPENDENT INSTITUTIONS

Fiscal transactions in both public and independent institutions are governed by an array of accounting, personnel, and purchasing policies and procedures and federal regulations. Independent institutions have more control over their fiscally related policies and procedures than do public institutions, which usually must conform to guidelines for all state agencies, but there are professional standards in accounting, personnel, and purchasing that tend to be widely adopted and thereby limit any advantage the private sector might enjoy. Also, collective bargaining agreements in both the public and private sectors affect budgeters' flexibility.

Accounting policies and procedures. The complex structure of accounts that many institutions have is intended to guarantee that funds can be monitored and spent only for the intended purposes. For example, many institutions, especially public ones, are restricted in the use of their salaries and wages funds to personnel expenditures only. Operating expenses funds, however, can sometimes be used for salaries and wages as well as for communications, travel, or equipment. Sometimes accounts established to pay for visiting lecturers' honoraria or contractual arrangements with individuals can be replenished by both salaries and wages funds and operating expenses funds. Often accounts are established to track certain kinds of income and to insure that the revenues are spent for specified purposes. Accounts for student activity fees, laboratory fees, or instructional materials fees are examples of this category. For the same reason accounts set up to receive research funds can be used only for project expenditures.

The degree to which faculty and staff adhere to accounting policies and procedures is determined by internal, state, and federal auditors. These auditors examine not only the accuracy of account statements but also the appropriateness of transfers and expenditures and the adequacy of the accounting framework.

The prospective budgeter needs to understand several aspects of his or her accounting structure. First, what is the range of expenditures that can be made from each account? Second, to what extent can funds or charges be transferred across accounts? (Reserves in one part of the account structure may not be useful in other parts; similarly, flexibility in adjusting the accounts may be restricted.)

Personnel policies and procedures. Because salaries and wages account for most of an institutional budget, it seems reasonable to expect that a large part of a budgeter's flexibility will be controlled by institutional personnel policies and procedures. Contract and tenure obligations represent long-term financial commitments on the part of the institution. The manner in which faculty salary structures are set and the ease with which adjustments can be made strongly influence the institution's competitiveness in recruiting new faculty. Likewise, clerical and support staff salary structures, whether based on local market conditions, union pay scales, or statewide public employee scales, affect the ability to hire and retain good staff. If the institution must conform to a state employee salary scale, for example, it may not be able to attract individuals with the special skills required in a college or university setting.

Contractual and tenure policies specify, for example, the lengths of probationary periods, the amount of advance notice to be given for termination of appointment, schedules for performance review, and grievance procedures. In some states these schedules are specified by law, and budget planning is clearly dependent on them. Moreover, the policies governing the appointment of temporary and part-time personnel will determine some of the bounds of budget flexibility. The availability of faculty research appointments that parallel the tenure-track appointments may provide programs with staffing flexibility in that research appointments can be made without the usual tenure commitment. (See appendix 1 for the AAUP policy statement concerning tenure and tenure quotas.)

Princeton University, for example, attempts to build flexibility into its staffing of degree programs by establishing a tenure quota, or a maximum ratio of tenured to total faculty on a department-by-department basis. Departments at the tenure ceiling cannot make tenured appointments until a tenured faculty member departs. Exceptions to the departmental tenure quotas are made when excellent opportunities exist for faculty recruitment. Although the tenure quotas place considerable pressure on junior nontenured faculty, the policy is clearly presented and well publicized so that junior faculty know in advance the probabilities of attaining tenure.

Controlling the number of tenured faculty is only one concern in the application of tenure quotas. Another consideration is the age distribution of tenured faculty. If, for example, the ages are clustered, many faculty will have to be replaced at the same time when the retirement age is reached.

Tenure quotas can be used to control the number of tenure commitments in situations of declining enrollment. The disadvantages of quotas include the limiting of opportunities for junior faculty, the placement of considerable pressure on those faculty, and the potential exclusion of superior faculty from tenure.

Purchasing policies and procedures. Procurement regulations are basically intended to facilitate the orderly and economical purchase of goods and services. As with any bureaucratic procedures, their weight and complexity alone often conspire to undermine convenience and limit flexibility. In many institutions, for example, all purchase requests are funneled through a purchasing department. The volume of activity through this support unit usually dictates how quickly the purchase can be made. Toward the end of the fiscal year, when most campus units are attempting to spend the balances in their operating expenses budgets, the volume of purchase requests is very high and the delays are more frequent. These delays in the purchasing department may in turn cause suspension of some activity in the requesting unit or the loss of early-payment discounts.

In many public institutions the purchasing procedures are governed by state regulations. Often there are ceilings specified above which purchase requests must be placed out on bid. In some cases the bid requests must be advertised (e.g., in the state register) for prescribed lengths of time before purchases can be made. Generally, the purchase must be made through the low bidder; exceptions must be justified to the appropriate authorities. Some states require that proposed purchases over a certain value be reviewed by a state agency before the purchase is actually made. In a growing number of states certain classes of proposed purchases, especially those involving computer-related expenditures, must be reviewed by state agencies. The effect of these purchase regulations is to restrict the maneuverability of budgeters, particularly their flexibility to spend resources as they wish. Flexibility thus becomes a matter of timing as well as the identification of reserve resources.

Federal regulations. In seeking to insure that federal funds are used only for the purpose for which they were granted, the federal government has burdened colleges and universities with a complex set of regulations that absorb considerable institutional manpower, money, and time. Although these regulations are well intentioned, their implementation has severely strained the flexibility of administrators and faculty in day-to-day operations on campus.

The federal government requires, for example, a strict accounting of the use of contract and grant funds and the costs assessed by institutions as indirect cost reimbursement charges. Accounting for indirect costs alone is a time-consuming and inexact science at best. Tracking faculty and staff time is even more difficult. Faculty members involved simultaneously in more than one sponsored research activity must account for their time commitment to each project. This distribution of time must then be translated by the comptroller's office into differential charges against the various research accounts. Most college and university payroll systems cannot respond to the fluctuating commitments to multiple sponsored activities, so typically the charges on a monthly or semester basis are averaged as dictated by the faculty member's cumulative distribution of time to the various projects. Recordkeeping is perhaps even more troublesome for support staff. A secretary, for example, may be responsible to five or six faculty members, each of whom has externally supported research in addition to his or her teaching and service commitments. It is almost impossible to monitor the secretary's effort accurately in terms of commitment to specific research projects, teaching obligations, and professional activities. It is not uncommon for the federal government to charge that certain institutions use research funds to support instructional and other activities. Many of these problems arise from the difficulties in separating and monitoring commitments to multiple activities. In some cases, such as the support of graduate students or postdoctoral fellows, research training is a part of research activity and is acceptable to the federal government. Increased federal oversight in recent years, especially through Office of Management and Budget Circular A-21 regulations, has encouraged colleges and universities to improve and expand their accounting systems while at the same time limiting the free interchange of federal and institutional dollars for a wide range of activities.

Despite restrictions associated with the use of federal funds, some flexibility is nonetheless permitted. Faculty and staff travel that is supported by contracts and grants may release institutional funds that otherwise would have been earmarked for travel. Some contracts and grants support the purchase of expensive equipment that can be used for graduate student training as well as research. Contracts and grants often support graduate students as research assistants, thereby increasing the availability of financial assistance to the institution. Furthermore, some grants and contracts provide salary funds to allow faculty to support staff and purchase release time from the institution for their own activities. The salary monies saved in this manner can be used to hire part-time faculty to meet instructional commitments or to hire additional support staff. Finally, in some institutions the budgeting systems are such that funds equivalent to a portion of the indirect cost reimbursements might be used by the institution to provide seed funding for new or junior faculty or to encourage departments to undertake new research.

Collective bargaining. The existence of a collective bargaining agreement at an institution will restrict the actions that may be taken by the administration during the budget process. Collective bargaining agreements almost always contain stipulated salary increases, rates of pay for summer school and overtime, and mandated employee benefits. These contractual agreements may be modified only with the assent of the collective bargaining representative. Normally, previously negotiated compensation increases are not reduced by a collective bargaining representative, except, on occasion, to prevent layoffs. Because some collective bargaining agreements extend over three or even four years, accurate long-range budget planning is crucial for determining affordable compensation levels.

Although most collective bargaining agreements state specific future salary increases, some agreements have made these increases, or parts thereof, conditional on such factors as inflation, student enrollment, and state appropriations.

In addition, most collective bargaining agreements specify the workload of the faculty. Thus, the institution may not unilaterally increase this workload during the term of the agreement to meet unexpected financial developments. Furthermore, some agreements restrict the use of part-time faculty as replacements for full-time faculty.

Union approval may also need to be sought for early-retirement programs for tenured faculty. These provisions become particularly important because, as of July 1, 1982, the minimum mandatory retirement age for tenured faculty was raised from 65 to 70.

The collective bargaining agreement will almost certainly specify retrenchment procedures, including the order of retrenchment, the required due notice or severance salary, and the required consultation that must precede the retrenchment of faculty. Any plan to resolve a budget crisis through retrenchment must take into account these restrictions and the cost of terminating personnel. For example, some institutions are self-insured for unemployment compensation (i.e., the institution must reimburse the state for payments made to any employee laid off).

Some agreements contain other restrictions with indirect budget implications. The agreement may forbid the use of tenure quotas. In addition, incentives to seek outside funding may be included. For example, the Temple University collective bargaining agreement returns to the dean of each college 10 percent of the increase in overhead recovery on grants. The purpose of this clause is to provide a financial incentive for the dean and faculty of each college to seek additional outside grant support. On the other hand, by contract the central administration has ceded control over 10 percent of the increase in indirect cost recovery that these efforts produce.

Collective agreements allow precise determination of personnel costs well in advance, though they hinder the ability to reduce these costs when unexpected financial problems occur.

PUBLIC INSTITUTIONS

The regulated environment of public institutions extends beyond those areas mentioned above to include formal and informal restrictions concerning state appropriations to institutions. These constraints arise from the quantitative bases used to determine state appropriations and from the control and monitoring of the institutional use of these funds.

Formula allocation procedures. Generally, budget formulas are used as a means for generating institutional requests for funds. By their very nature, formulas are simplified models of the complex expenditure patterns of institutions. A danger in the use of formulas is that decision makers far removed from institutional operations may rely on formulas for an understanding of how the institution actually functions. If, for example, decision makers believe that faculty in some disciplines are not teaching enough students and propose that student-faculty ratios be increased, the net budget effect at the institution might not be at all what was planned. Although adjusting the formula to a higher student-faculty ratio might reduce resources, campus decision makers might decide to absorb the reduction by assigning graduate students heavier teaching loads rather than increasing the burden on faculty. Similarly, decision makers may lighten the impact of a reduction in faculty travel funds by an internal transfer of funds from supplies or equipment to the travel account.

The restrictiveness of formula allocation procedures stems not from their use as a means to generate budget requests, but from the perception of formulas as an implicit or explicit commitment of how funds will be utilized. The more state-level decision makers perceive the formula as an instrument of accountability, the more complex the formula will have to become to mirror the richness of institutional activity and the more restrictive the budget environment becomes.

Enrollment ceilings. To limit institutional demands on the state treasury, some states have placed enrollment ceilings on institutions. In imposing ceilings, states generally agree to support instructional and other costs up to the target enrollments, but require the institution to absorb the costs of educating students in excess of the ceiling. Enrollment ceilings have also been used by state-level policy makers as a mechanism to redistribute enrollments among public institutions within a state. Ceilings are imposed on institutions with the highest student demand, thereby, in theory, discouraging excess enrollments and encouraging students to seek admission to underenrolled institutions. Whatever the policy objective, the net effect on the institution that has enrollment ceilings is a limiting of state appropriations.

Some states apply the concept of enrollment thresholds in making their appropriations to institutions. The state establishes a bandwidth for enrollment projections of, for example, plus or minus 2 percent. If actual enrollments fall within that range, the appropriation is unchanged. If enrollments exceed the projection by more than the bandwidth, the state will provide funds for the additional enrollments (usually those *over* the bandwidth). Similarly, if enrollments are lower than the projection by more than the bandwidth, the institution must return funds. In the example given, the institution is responsible for the enrollments if the latter exceed projections by up to 2 percent and gains excess funds if the actual enrollments are up to 2 percent less than projected.

Appropriations bill language. The contents of the appropriations bill determine much of a public institution's flexibility. Some states do not appropriate funds that are received directly by the institution: tuition income, student and other fees, contract and grant funding. Other states have detailed appropriations that include all of the above items. Frequently in such cases there are intense negotiations between institutions and state officials concerning estimates of these kinds of income. State officials tend to estimate liberally; institutional officials tend to estimate conservatively. In general, the fewer the items included in the appropriations bill, the more control the institution has over that income.

Often the appropriations bill will contain language indicating legislative intent. This portion of the appropriations bill may address such topics as faculty productivity, student-faculty ratios, travel, campus security, and computer facilities and operations. In California, for example, the legislature's joint appropriations committee once inserted language in the appropriations bill calling for the elimination of $75,000 from the budget of the University of California, Berkeley, because the degree program in demography had allegedly been dropped. (The irony of the situation was that the legislator introducing the control language had mistakenly read demography as dermatology, which was not a program on the Berkeley campus.) Although the control language is separate from the actual appropriations, the connection between the two is explicit and generally must be heeded if the institution does not wish to suffer a financial penalty at the hands of an irate legislature during the next session.

State agency staff control. Control over public institutions is exerted not only through state regulations and the language of appropriations bills, but also informally through the actions of the various state agency staffs. Higher education coordinating and governing board staffs are heavily involved in the drafting of statewide plans for higher education, reviewing new and existing degree programs, collecting data, establishing enrollment ceilings, reviewing budget requests, and reviewing plans for capital expenditures. Legislative fiscal staffs and executive budget office staffs shape and interpret policy in the same way as they review higher education budget requests and control higher education expenditures once funds have been appropriated. Often the informal development of policy by these state agency staffs is not subject to tight control by the state's elected officials.

Position control. In some states the appropriations bill specifies not only the dollar amounts available to public institutions, but also the number of faculty and staff positions that can be filled. Clearly, position control limits the way in which salaries and wages funds are expended and limits the flexibility of institutional decision makers to staff their operations as needed. State-level policy makers frequently mention two reasons for the importance of position control. First, it establishes a ceiling on employment in the public sector in the state. This ceiling affords politicians the chance to convince taxpayers that state government is under control. Second, some state governments assume responsibility for benefits packages by way of central accounts (rather than including benefits packages in appropriations to state agencies). Under this arrangement policy makers need to be able to project the size of the benefits package that has to be set aside for the central account. This projection becomes much more difficult if there is no control over the number of staff positions.

How institutions minimize the impact of state position control depends in large part on personnel policies. In some personnel structures temporary appointments of six months or less are not counted against an institution's position total. Moreover, it may be possible to reappoint temporary faculty or staff one or more times without a break in service and still not have the appointment charged against the institution's position total. Also, some campuses establish pools of vacant positions and allocate these to various units. If, for example, a campus had 1,000 faculty and staff positions authorized by the state, of which 50 were vacant at any particular time, campus units might be permitted to fill 50 more positions than currently allocated. Because vacancies might not appear in units where additional staff are most needed, the pool vacancies can be reallocated on a year-to-year basis.

Year-end balances. In most states the balances remaining in state agency accounts at the end of the fiscal year revert back to the state treasury. Unless otherwise controlled, most institutions spend a considerable portion of their budgets in the last several months of the fiscal year in an effort to expend all of their available resources. Given current incentives, this behavior is eminently rational. A common working assumption is that an organization or agency that cannot spend all of its appropriation within the fiscal year should have its budget reduced the following year. Incentives must be altered so that the rational person will do what is desirable, namely, to spend resources only for what is necessary.

Some states employ fiscal controls instead of positive incentives to discourage uneven spending patterns. They control the rate of institutional expenditures through the allotment process whereby funds appropriated to institutions are released by the state treasury on an installment basis (e.g., annually, quarterly, monthly). Generally the more frequent the allotments, the less control the institution has over the timing of its expenditures. (That is, the institution may not be able to commit funds until it has actually received them from the state treasury.)

Some states have adopted a carryover policy for a part or all of state agency year-end balances. As a positive incentive for good fiscal management, state agencies are allowed to retain some or all of their account balances from one fiscal year to another. This policy discourages the hurried and unplanned year-end spending described above. The policy also permits institutions to save enough funds from one fiscal year to another to make expensive purchases that could not otherwise be made within one fiscal year. Implicit in this policy is that the prudent budgeter will always have some positive balance in his or her accounts as a hedge against the uncertainty of price changes and the delays in reporting that occur in most accounting systems. Also, many budgeters purposely wait to make major expenditures until late in the budget cycle to insure that there are resources available for emergencies. This category of year-end spending is carefully planned and not hurried. To require that all year-end balances revert to the state treasury is to penalize the careful money manager.

Even in states in which year-end balances do revert to the treasury, most institutions have some accounts that automatically carry over balances from one fiscal year to another. These accounts, often called carryover or revolving accounts, are typically designated for special purposes, including sponsored research and auxiliary enterprises. Generally transfers between these revolving accounts and the usual state accounts are controlled tightly by transfer regulations to prevent the abuse of revolving accounts as "laundries" for carrying state funds across fiscal years.

Salary savings targets. A number of states have introduced a management device known as salary savings or turnover savings or forced savings. State agencies are targeted to return a percentage of their budgets (usually a percentage of the salaries and wages budget only) to the state treasury at the end of the fiscal year. These targets typically range from 1 to 4 percent of the salaries and wages budget. Thus, for example, if an institution receives an appropriation of $10 million in salaries and wages and is assigned a 4 percent salary savings target, the institution may spend only $9.6 million in salaries and wages and must return $0.4 million to the state treasury.

The practice of salary savings evolved from the historical pattern of year-end savings that accrue to most organizations because of personnel attrition and the usual delays experienced in refilling positions. State-level policy makers observed that these savings in appropriated salaries and wages ranged from 2 to 4 percent. Rather than wait until the end of the fiscal year to collect whatever salary monies went unspent, policy makers decided to set salary savings targets *in advance* to guarantee a known return. In this way the targeted savings could be allocated in advance (i.e., prior to the beginning of the fiscal year), thereby expanding the base of available state resources. Although most targets were based originally on historical patterns of natural salary savings, most states have adjusted the targets to reflect the need for additional resources and the perceived availability of those resources within state agencies. In some states the method for setting salary savings targets is not very sophisticated: if state agencies complain loudly about the targets, state budget officials know that too much has been demanded. Some states also use an increase in the salary savings target to fund a portion of legislatively mandated salary increases. If, for example, a legislature appropriates a 9 percent salary increase, it may provide the public institutions with funds sufficient for only an 8.25 percent increase. The balance of the increase, 0.75 percent, must be provided internally through an increased salary savings target.

The typical pattern of behavior within the institution is for campus-level administrators to distribute the campus target to all units supported by state funds. This distribution is often made on the basis of pro-rata shares of the campus salaries and wages budget, although adjustments might be made to reflect the economies of scale of larger units (i.e., larger units generally have more personnel turnover in absolute terms than smaller units and therefore are in a better position to absorb a larger share of the salary savings target than their proportion of the campus salaries and wages budget would dictate). Any intermediate administrative layers between the campus administration and the department or activity are allocated a target and distribute it in turn to the units under their responsibility. The imposition of salary savings targets requires that the careful department chairperson or administrator identify in advance the source of the savings. This advance planning is all the more important in that position vacancies occur unevenly across campuses. Sometimes staff positions must be held vacant simply to allow sufficient savings to accumulate to meet the target obligation. Sponsored research funding that provides faculty release time, sabbatical leaves, and leaves of absence without pay becomes a source of salary savings for academic departments. Because the first obligation to be met with "flexible" salary monies is salary savings, the savings target ultimately limits the fiscal flexibility of all units across the campus.

SOURCES OF FLEXIBILITY

CHANGING THE FRAMEWORK

Although it would be difficult to quantify, there is probably a considerable amount of flexibility in most institutions that has been eroded or has disappeared over time because the framework for budgeting within the institution has not been reexamined regularly. Given the press of time during the budget cycle, the natural tendency of budgeters is to allocate resources largely on the basis of history (i.e., the previous year's budget). Patterns of allocation are adjusted marginally either across-the-board or in response to special requests made by individual units. The inertia of history is recognizable in the asymmetry of program growth and program decline. When a unit's activities increase, the unit typically requests special increases in personnel and operating expenses to accommodate the increased workload. When the unit's activities decline, however, there usually is not an equally vigorous mechanism to insure that the expenses of running the unit are reviewed and, if possible, reduced.

An institution may be able to recover slack resources by carefully analyzing the distribution of resources across the campus. The best approach seems to be an analysis of only portions of the budget at any one time, or an analysis of how portions of the budget relate to one another (e.g., academic affairs and administrative support and student affairs). Zero-base budgeting or its variants or some form of degree and service program analysis might be applied to closely related academic or support programs. Another analytical strategy might be to investigate activities across some common dimensions, such as secretarial or support staffing, operating expenses budgets, the use of graduate assistants in academic departments, or faculty/staff workloads.

An analytical approach that has gained some currency in both inter- and intrainstitutional studies is the examination of fixed and variable costs. Fixed costs represent the base expenditure for the operation of an institution or activity below which operations could not occur. In essence, fixed costs represent the thresholds for activities. A liberal arts curriculum, for example, requires some core of faculty representing certain disciplines (e.g., philosophy, English, history, art) in order to be considered a curriculum, and an institution requires a certain minimum of facilities or space. This core is supplemented to reflect increases in workload or improvements in the quality of activities. Unless the pattern of resource allocation is periodically studied in detail, the core of fixed costs for most activities or institutions increases with time. If one embraces the principle that fewer fixed costs mean more flexibility, the objective of the budgeter becomes obvious: to "unfix" the fixed costs. In other words, the assumption that some costs are fixed should be challenged regularly during budget reviews. Experienced budgeters have observed that when program and activity planning are linked in advance to the budget process, costs become more variable.

STRATEGIES FOR OBTAINING FLEXIBILITY

A number of specific strategies can be adopted. Because independent institutions have considerably more control over the framework for resource use than do public institutions, most of the strategies detailed below are more commonly observed in the public sector.

Central reserve. Perhaps the most obvious strategy is to create a central reserve of resources (at the institution, college, or department level) by withholding a small percentage of the funds to be distributed to lower levels in the institution. If, for example, an institution projects an increase in revenue of 10 percent for the coming fiscal year, the president may elect to withhold one-tenth of the amount (or 1 percent of the institutional budget) for a discretionary fund. Similarly, deans may elect to withhold a small percentage of any increase in revenues to their colleges or schools and use this pool of resources for discretionary purposes. In turn, the department chairperson may decide to hold back a small part of the faculty and staff salary increment pool as a departmental reserve.

Although some central reserve is essential as a buffer against the uncertainty of a year's budget, the degree to which persons at lower levels in the institutional hierarchy become dependent on this surplus pool determines how much flexibility the reserve truly offers. If departments in a college, for example, regularly petition the dean for supplementary support from the dean's contingency fund, and if the dean regularly provides some or all of the resources requested, the contingency fund becomes de facto a part of the college's regular budget. The contingency fund remains a flexible resource only if it is used for emergencies or unusual opportunities. Central reserves should be viewed as a short-term safety net to keep useful activities going until alternative permanent funding sources are identified. The reserves themselves should not be seen as the permanent source of support for the activities.

Salary or budget savings. In both independent and public institutions reserves can be established through the imposition of a salary or budget savings target on units lower in the institutional hierarchy. Budgeters in public institutions are usually obligated to meet a state-imposed target; accordingly, campus-level officials simply increase the targets of subordinate units to exceed the state obligation and thereby create a small reserve. If, for example, the state targets a small public college for $25,000 in salary savings, the president or chief budget officer may allocate salary savings targets of $35,000 in order to create a central reserve of $10,000 for the president. Budgeters in the campus-level administrations of independent institutions can either set institutionwide salary or budget savings targets based on historical natural savings balances or target programs and activities to conform with institutional objectives.

Within institutions that employ salary or budget savings targets, there is a natural tendency for budgeters at every level of the hierarchy to set higher targets for subordinate units so as to provide a cushion of reserves. This setting of targets for subordinate units is a means of shifting uncertainty to other levels of the authority hierarchy.

Formula adjustments. In some state systems that employ budget formulas, it has been possible for institutions to adjust the formula parameters to their advantage. Although such strategies to gain flexibility generally are not encouraged, they illustrate how budgeters have taken advantage of the underlying incentive structures of the formulas. In situations where the budget formulas are based on the number of student credit hours taught per faculty member, some institutions have increased the credit hour value of certain courses (e.g., physical education, which is taken by many students) to increase artificially the student credit hour productivity of the institution. Formulas that differentiate by level of instruction for credit hour productivity (i.e., whereby credit hours in graduate-level courses are weighted more than credit hours in upper-division courses, which in turn are weighted more than credit hours in lower-division courses) have encouraged some institutions to raise the level of certain courses (e.g., to shift courses from the lower division to the upper division) to gain additional funding. In those states that use enrollment-driven formulas but do not assess penalties for enrolling below projections (the penalty would be the reversion of excess funds to the state), some institutions make optimistic enrollment projections, especially at the higher student levels (e.g., graduate or upper division) that have more weight in the funding formula. State agencies frequently audit the data used in formulas to discourage such improper activities.

Position reversion. Institutions can gain some flexibility through a policy of requiring that all vacant faculty and staff positions in subordinate units revert to the control of a dean or central administrator for possible reallocation. Departments or activities losing positions to the administrator's pool would be given the opportunity to justify having the position returned. In a large university, for example, a college dean might wish to hold several faculty positions vacant in order to be able to take advantage of opportunities to hire excellent faculty who appear on the job market, or to supplement the staffing in selected departments to accommodate enrollment shifts or shifts in program priorities.

Clearly, some positions that revert to the higher-level administrator would have to be returned to the original department or activity because of workload or program priority. However, vacancies will eventually occur in units that are not destined to have the positions returned, resulting in creation of a reserve pool of positions or a source of position reallocations.

Reduction of the grade or rank of vacant positions. Some slack resources can be gained by downgrading the grade or rank of a position when it becomes vacant and shifting the salary savings to other areas. For example, if a full professor earning $45,000 a year departs, the department chairperson might wish to fill the vacancy with an assistant professor earning $23,000. The difference of $22,000 can be diverted to other salaries and wages. As a variant of the position reversion strategy, administrators might automatically downgrade the grade or rank of vacant positions in units under their purview and retain the salary savings. This strategy must be used selectively, however, so as not to undermine the integrity of the program or activity. An academic department, for example, requires a core of senior faculty to provide leadership. Similarly, an academic or administrative support unit may not be able to function well with underexperienced support staff.

Employment of part-time or temporary faculty. A very common source of flexibility is the employment of part-time or temporary faculty in place of permanent faculty. Temporary faculty employed on a course-by-course basis generally are much less expensive. Some department chairpersons purposely hold certain faculty lines vacant so that the funds can be used to employ temporary faculty, thereby increasing the department's teaching capacity. Departments often employ part-time or temporary faculty to replace permanent faculty who have gone on sabbatical leave or leave of absence without pay. The salary savings can be used for student labor, graduate or research assistants, or additional secretarial support, or for salary savings targets imposed by higher levels of authority.

Institutions that depend heavily on temporary faculty must carefully weigh the advantages and drawbacks. Temporary faculty often become academic nomads, moving from one temporary position to another each semester or year because they are unable to find permanent positions in a tight job market. Temporary faculty are frequently not as available to students and colleagues as are permanent faculty. In the public sector, state-level policy makers who note that institutions keep faculty positions vacant in order to employ temporary faculty may decide to reduce the number of permanent faculty positions allocated to those institutions.

Withholding of some salary adjustment funds. In public systems the legislature often appropriates funds for salary adjustments based on the number of authorized faculty and staff lines and the current salaries on those lines. To create a central reserve, campus-level administrators might allocate salary adjustment funds to subordinate units only for those lines currently filled. The salary adjustment funds provided by the state for vacant lines would be retained by campus-level administrators as slack resources. Some of these resources might be used, for example, to increase the salaries of faculty or staff who have been promoted as of the new fiscal year.

Revolving funds. In most state systems, fund balances remaining at the end of the fiscal year revert to the state treasury. Similarly, in many independent institutions year-end balances revert to the president or chief executive officer for use as a reserve or as part of the following year's budget. Most campuses have activities such as sponsored research or auxiliary enterprises with budgets that continue across fiscal years, primarily because the funds involved are not provided by the state. Sometimes these budgets, in the form of revolving or carryover accounts, can be used to carry regular institutional funds across fiscal years. At the end of the fiscal year it may be possible, for example, to transfer charges that have accumulated during the year against the revolving fund to accounts consisting of regular institutional funds. Federal effort reporting and accounting regulations have made it difficult to effect such transfers with federally sponsored program accounts, although these transfers generally are permissible in other revolving accounts.

Balance carryovers. Those state systems or independent institutions that permit the carryover of year-end balances from one fiscal year to another (whereby a part or all of the balances may be retained) have a natural source of budget flexibility. This liberal use of year-end balances reduces the pressures on units to spend all of their resources at year's end and encourages the saving of resources for major purchases or projects.

Sponsored programs. Sponsored research and training activities supported by external funding sources provide institutions with the opportunity for considerable flexibility. Grant and contract proposals include many direct costs (e.g., secretarial support, graduate student support, travel, supplies and materials) that enhance the financial position of the institution. They also provide financial relief for research activities currently supported by the institution, but which legitimately can be supported externally.

Overhead reimbursement. Indirect costs charged to sponsored activities are computed on the basis of the actual expenses incurred by the institution in conducting the activities (see chapter 13). To encourage sponsored research and training, some states allow institutions to use a portion of the indirect cost reimbursement funds for discretionary purposes rather than requiring that the funds be used to offset the operating expenses incurred. In essence, these states are assuming part of the cost of the sponsored activities. Frequently, the overhead reimbursement funds retained by the institution are used as seed funding to encourage additional sponsored activities (such funds can provide, for example, for faculty release time for proposal writing or for equipment purchases or for the establishment of laboratories for new or junior faculty).

Research foundations and research institutes. Many state institutions with significant sponsored program activity establish private research foundations and institutes for receipt of certain grants, contracts, and gifts. Funds processed by these private foundations do not come under the scrutiny of state-level officials, and activities supported through these foundations are not subject to the usual state policies and procedures. If, for example, a state agency must review purchases that are in excess of some fixed amount, scrutiny can be avoided if the purchase is made with foundation funds. The dimensions of the flexibility obtained by creating a private research foundation or institute are defined by the organization's legal structure.

Sabbatical leave policy. Many institutions have a policy of providing faculty members with sabbatical leaves for a full year at half salary or for one-half year at full salary after the individual has served a specified time at the institution. To gain some flexibility when resources are tight, some institutions have altered the standard policy to permit only sabbatical leaves for a full year at half salary. This modification guarantees that the institution will have one-half of the faculty member's salary to use for temporary replacements or for other purposes.

Clearly, this list of strategies to obtain flexibility is not exhaustive. Many other strategies will depend on the policies, procedures, and practices of the particular institution.

FOR FURTHER READING

The literature on flexibility in the budget process is almost nonexistent (perhaps a reflection of the limited flexibility available to most budgeters). An excellent article on budget savings is Anthony W. Morgan's "Flexibility for Whom: The Case of Forced Savings in Budgeting for Higher Education," *Educational Record*, vol. 56, no. 1 (Winter 1975), pp. 42–47.

Four case studies of the effect of state regulation on management flexibility in public institutions are presented in *Management Flexibility and State Regulation in Higher Education*, edited by James R. Mingle (Atlanta: Southern Regional Education Board, 1983).

6 / Retrenchment and Reallocation: Fiscal Issues

This chapter will first examine the continuing debate over the meaning of the term financial exigency. AAUP has defined financial exigency and has specified pertinent policies. Some administrators and faculty have questioned the term's applicability to certain financial crises. A framework reporting both points of view is presented here for considering retrenchment and reallocation strategies. These broad categories of institutional strategies are defined by the time necessary to achieve budget reductions: (1) short-term (1–3 years), focusing on cash-flow management, (2) intermediate-term (2–6 years), focusing on personnel policies, and (3) long-term (3–9 years), focusing on program reduction or elimination and resource reallocation. This framework seeks to be sensitive to the intent of AAUP guidelines concerning faculty welfare and rights while acknowledging the variety of financial crises.

The scope of this chapter is limited somewhat to fiscal issues. A considerable body of literature concerning fiscal stringency and retrenchment has evolved during the past five years. Several of the references herein detail some of the dominant personnel policies and procedures and legal issues attendant to retrenchment. Discussions about retrenchment and reallocation tend to be viewed as negative, no doubt because of the unpleasantness accompanying these processes in many institutions during the past decade. For example, the 1976 retrenchment at the City University of New York (CUNY) is now viewed by faculty and administrators alike as having had disastrous consequences for morale. Also, through the large-scale release of junior faculty, CUNY instantly aged its faculty. For any institution suddenly thrust into a financial crisis, the experience can be damaging. The purpose of this chapter is to encourage administrators and faculty to anticipate financial hard times and to plan ways to avoid or at least minimize the effects.

FINANCIAL EXIGENCY, FINANCIAL STRINGENCY, AND RETRENCHMENT POLICY

In many financial crises, college and university officials consider the prospect of releasing permanent faculty and staff as a way to achieve financial equilibrium. Regardless of the origin of the crises or the numbers and kinds of individuals identified for layoff or termination, the separation of individuals from institutions is a painful process and one to be avoided if at all possible. Ideally, officials can solve an institution's fiscal problems through avenues other than releasing permanent faculty and staff. Sometimes, however, the magnitude of the reductions that must be accomplished within a very short period makes the release of permanent personnel unavoidable.

In 1976 AAUP published a revised and amplified version of its "Recommended Institutional Regulations on Academic Freedom and Tenure," derived from the joint AAUP-Association of American Colleges 1940 Statement of Principles on Academic Freedom and Tenure (see appendix 1 for the 1940 Statement and the 1982 edition of the complete regulations). The document includes the following provisions relating to the termination of faculty appointments for reasons of financial exigency or program discontinuance.

FINANCIAL EXIGENCY

Termination of an appointment with continuous tenure, or of a probationary or special appointment before the end of the specified term, may occur under extraordinary circumstances because of a demonstrably *bona fide* financial exigency, i.e., an imminent financial crisis which threatens the survival of the institution as a whole and which cannot be alleviated by less drastic means. . . .

(Note: . . . there should be a faculty body which participates in the decision that a condition of financial exigency exists or is imminent, and that all feasible alternatives to termination of appointments have been pursued. . . .)

(The responsibility for identifying individuals whose appointments are to be terminated should be committed to a person or group designated or approved by the faculty. . . .)

The faculty member (given notice of a proposed termination) will have the right to a full hearing before a faculty committee. . . . The issues in this hearing may include:

—The existence and extent of the condition of financial exigency. The burden will rest on the administration to prove the existence and the extent of the condition. . . .

—The validity of the educational judgments and the criteria for identification (of faculty members) for termination; but the recommendations of a faculty body on these matters will be considered presumptively valid. . . .

If the institution, because of financial exigency, terminates appointments, it will not at the same time make new appointments except in extraordinary circumstances where a serious distortion in the academic program would otherwise result. . . . The appointment of a faculty member with tenure will not be terminated in favor of retaining a faculty member without tenure, except in extraordinary circumstances where a serious distortion of the academic program would otherwise result.

Before terminating an appointment because of financial exigency, the institution, with faculty participation, will make every effort to place the faculty member concerned in another suitable position within the institution. . . .

The place of the faculty member concerned will not be filled by a replacement within a period of three years, unless the released faculty member has been offered reinstatement and a reasonable time in which to accept or decline it.

DISCONTINUANCE OF PROGRAM OR DEPARTMENT
NOT MANDATED BY FINANCIAL EXIGENCY

Termination of an appointment . . . may occur as a result of *bona fide* formal discontinuance of a program or department of instruction. The following standards and procedures will apply:

—The decision to discontinue . . . will be based essentially upon educational considerations, as determined primarily by the faculty as a whole or an appropriate committee thereof.

(Note: "Educational considerations" do not include cyclical or temporary variations in enrollment. They must reflect long-range judgments that the educational mission of the institution as a whole will be enhanced by the discontinuance.)

—Before the administration issues notice to a faculty member . . . the institution will make every effort to place the faculty member concerned in another suitable position. . . .

(Note: When an institution proposes to discontinue a program or department of instruction, it should plan to bear the costs of relocating, training, or otherwise compensating faculty members adversely affected.)

—A faculty member may appeal a proposed relocation or termination resulting from a discontinuance and has a right to a full hearing before a faculty committee. . . .

The AAUP guidelines, which oppose the dismissal of faculty or the termination of appointments before the end of specified terms, except when stated conditions (i.e., "financial exigency") exist, are designed to prevent administrators from using financial exigency as a justification for capricious actions. Although these guidelines provide a general definition of financial exigency, it is necessary to interpret them and adapt them to specific institutional settings.

Furthermore, the Commission on Academic Affairs of the American Council on Education expressed several concerns with AAUP's "Recommended Institutional Regulations" (Furniss, 1976). First, the commission noted that the regulations state that termination for financial exigency is legitimate only when the whole institution is on the verge of bankruptcy, and that terminations for program discontinuance are legitimate only when the program has been discontinued "based essentially upon educational considerations" that do not include "cyclical or temporary variations in enrollment" or financial stringency. Also, the commission argued that the definition of financial exigency and the conditions under which programs may be discontinued are too general to be practicable. Moreover, the commission was concerned that the vagueness of the definition of financial exigency encourages the courts to provide their own definitions that might differ from the definitions to which the institutions subscribe in good faith.

In the next decade it seems likely that some institutions will face the "edge-of-the-cliff" travails of bankruptcy but that the great majority will face two less severe situations: (1) a debilitating though not immediately life-threatening reduction of revenues such as state appropriations or tuition; and (2) the need to reallocate resources internally. The focus of the debate about resource allocation, especially in hard times, is whether reallocation can in some instances be done on educational grounds to strengthen good programs *and* on the basis of enrollments and finances.

Although the central question concerns guidelines for reallocation, the debate is often about labels. At Michigan State University during fall 1980, for example, administrators chose the term "financial crisis" rather than "financial exigency" to describe the financial situation, arguing that because the institution was public, it was not in danger of collapse but rather of having its academic quality eroded by adverse financial conditions. It is important to understand that the substantive issues are the degree of financial emergency and the procedures to be followed in reallocating and reducing resources.

Brown (1976, 13) notes that cyclical enrollment variations are not grounds for program discontinuance. He argues, in part, against "a pernicious practice, extensively employed in large state systems, of measuring appropriations by formulas that reflect minute fluctuation in enrollments. The intent is doubtless to measure competing claims objectively, but the result must be harmful to stability of employment or of program." Purely enrollment-driven funding formulas are not desirable, particularly in times of declining enrollments. However, they *are* the mechanism some states use to set state appropriations for higher education. Most states consider enrollments in some fashion in establishing levels of state support. Legislatures can and do cut the budgets of public institutions for a variety of reasons; faculty and administrators try to incorporate such possibilities into their fiscal planning.

Donald Cell (1982) argues in favor of accepting enrollments *and* the academic values that originate from disciplinary frameworks as legitimate components of what AAUP terms "educational policy." With respect to enrollments, Cell (1982, 4) states that "consideration of enrollment should . . . not be routinely dismissed by such negative code-words as 'market' or 'financial'; enrollments more fundamentally reflect values held by students which, while we sometimes need to challenge them in the classroom, we should at the same time respect."

Clearly, the quality of academic programs is a significant determinant in resource decisions. A program of mediocre quality and with low enrollments, for example, might be draining resources from better programs. Also, it might be necessary to boost sagging institutional enrollments by reallocating resources to make particular programs more attractive to potential students. Difficulties arising from the internal reallocation of resources probably will touch more campuses than any other fiscal problem. The bitterness surrounding the proposed reallocation at the University of Missouri during the 1981–82 academic year illustrates the magnitude of the potential problems (Desruisseaux, 1982, 1, 12).

The major issue in reallocation is what to do with personnel in all categories: tenured, nontenured, and staff. AAUP guidelines address the elimination of entire academic programs but do not permit, short of financial exigency, the discontinuance of particular tenured faculty because of reduction in scope or reorganization of academic units. In a small institution that holds instruction as its primary mission, for example, there might be insufficient enrollments to justify a five-person, all tenured, art history department. If the institution wishes to reduce its commitment to art history and wishes also to follow AAUP guidelines, its only alternative is to disband the entire program. Moreover, the institution would have to justify the discontinuance of the art history program "essentially upon educational considerations," by which is meant other than enrollment considerations. In dealing with low-demand or low-quality programs, there may be alternatives to the termination of tenured faculty members. If there is sufficient lead time, the size of the program faculty and staff can be allowed to diminish through natural attrition. Also, in some situations faculty members can be redeployed or retrained (see below).

The elusiveness of an agreement among constituencies about the definition of financial exigency is an indication that social, economic, and political forces are pressuring institutions of higher education to such an extent that many of the boundaries between normal operations and the AAUP definition of financial exigency may be blurred. To deal with this problem, governance strategies are being advanced. For example, Donald Cell (1982, 8) makes the following suggestions for providing the maximum protection of tenure while recognizing the financial realities many institutions face: (1) the burden should fall on administrators to show that less harmful economies have been exhausted before the termination of permanent faculty and/or staff is called for; (2) it is the responsibility of an appropriate faculty committee to determine which academic programs should be cut; and (3) within a program, tenured positions should have preferred status over untenured positions except when a serious distortion of the curriculum would result.

PLANNING FOR RETRENCHMENT AND REALLOCATION

Many recent cases of financial stringency have caught institutions unprepared. Generally, the less time faculty and administrators have to react to a fiscal emergency, the narrower the range of options open to them. Moreover, with personnel salaries and benefits comprising the largest part of institutional budgets, substantial reductions will often involve the termination of faculty and staff. For any number of reasons these reductions are the most difficult to make and have potentially the greatest effect on institutional operations. Conversely, the earlier faculty and administrators plan cooperatively for or anticipate financial problems, the more the institution can rely upon normal attrition and provide for informed faculty involvement.

Some of the worst aspects of financial retrenchment can be minimized through what Paul Strohm (1981) terms "pre-exigency planning." Some students of organizational behavior argue that faculty and administrators are so entrenched in their routines and hold so firmly to their expectations that they need the spur of financial stress to motivate them to alter their behavior. Clearly, the impact of planning will vary from one setting to another. Generally, it will be easier to accept strategies that do not involve the termination of personnel than those requiring faculty and/or staff dismissals. It seems reasonable, however, that even on campuses where it is politically difficult in the absence of a fiscal crisis to earmark activities for retrenchment, it will still be possible to establish the guidelines for retrenchment in anticipation of fiscal hard times. There is strong evidence that it is difficult to perform anything more than short-term planning during a fiscal crisis. Donald K. Smith (1976, 33) comments on the experience of the University of Wisconsin System during the 1970s:

> It is all but impossible to do effective midrange or long-range planning for a state system of higher education in the presence of continuing fiscal crises and the kinds of coping actions and improvisations such crises generate.

He also notes that:

> . . . . the disproportions between those actions which might be most wise in the long run, and those actions which may be necessary in order to cope with the crises, become increasingly clear.

Thus, planning to minimize the negative effects of financial stress must be a mid- to long-range activity. In the short term, institutions usually can achieve only modest economies by reducing nonpersonnel expenditures for items such as travel, telephone usage, and the purchase of supplies. Some short-term economies such as reducing library purchases of books and periodicals, deferring maintenance and renovations, and deferring the purchase of replacement equipment may in the long term cause severe financial problems or seriously undermine programs and facilities. This is why large reductions can usually be realized only by reducing personnel costs. The larger the budget reduction sought, the more time will be required to reduce personnel costs through attrition rather than terminating faculty and staff.

In responding to fiscal crises, faculty and administrators must be sensitive to the influence of legal constraints and external factors. Collective bargaining agreements, for example, limit the options available. Also, in public higher education the states have become more involved in personnel matters, thereby introducing another level of actors into the planning process. For example, state-level involvement extends from the negotiation of faculty contracts to control over the number of faculty and staff positions. Also, under some budget formulas institutional income may be affected by adjustments in instructional methodologies or staffing patterns, such as shifts from laboratory-intensive to lecture-intensive instruction or changes in the distribution of faculty ranks. Finally, there is obvious correlation between institutional size and the ability to reallocate resources and to absorb losses.

The responses of specific institutions to financial hard times have been as diverse as the universe of American higher education. Mingle (1982, 9) catalogued a pattern of institutional responses to cutbacks based on the institution's perception of the severity of the fiscal conditions; Sigmund G. Ginsburg (1982, 14–16) prepared a list of suggestions for increasing institutional income and for decreasing institutional expenses. (See appendix 3 for the two lists above. Both contain controversial elements, and neither provides guidance for the whole universe of institutions.) Some cutback strategies are adopted more for their relative ease of implementation than for their appropriateness in addressing a particular situation. The precise order of strategies for implementation will vary from institution to institution and must be debated and evaluated according to basic institutional values and general principles and standards of legal and ethical behavior. No one strategy can be undertaken by itself or necessarily to the exclusion of others. When there is a fiscal crisis, in the short term a number of activities and budget lines might be eliminated completely before personnel retrenchment is begun. For example, one may wish to reduce the travel budget substantially before any personnel reductions, but in the long run one would not wish to eliminate completely a travel budget before personnel reductions because of the importance of communication and interaction among faculty members and their peers in the disciplines.

In considering retrenchment strategies, institutions are cautioned that reducing support staff *too* severely may undermine the integrity of programs and services. As faculty are involved in decisions concerning the allocation of resources, they cannot place an unfair burden of reductions on those individuals who do not participate in the decision making. Equal opportunity programs also must be taken into account.

Institutional strategies typically can be grouped into short term (1–3 years), intermediate-term (2–6 years), and long-term (3–9 years). It is important to note that these strategies can be pursued simultaneously in accordance with a number of general principles suggested by Robert M. O'Neil (1983).

First, planning should involve both administrators and appropriately composed faculty bodies. Experience has shown that durable decisions require active faculty participation.

Second, faculty participants should have access to all available information. At the same time, planners should be sensitive to the implications of this information, especially when it pertains to personnel and programs. Prior understandings should be reached concerning the confidentiality of the information.

Third, planning should not ignore the principles and traditions of the institution; short-term departures from such principles should be avoided. The long-term implications of major changes should be carefully considered, especially if the changes will affect the institution's character.

Fourth, the institution's governing board should be kept well-informed of the progress of fiscal planning. Educating the regents or trustees is a wise investment of time that will be repaid with support of proposed policies and procedures.

Fifth, the impact of the media should be taken into account. Journalists are very concerned about the plight of terminated faculty and are especially receptive to the issue of intellectual freedom.

Sixth, the state legislature should not be ignored. Legislators who are in-

formed about actions that institutions take to remain financially and pro-
grammatically stable will tend to be more sensitive to institutional interests
as state-level policy is being set. Institutional decision makers have to re-
sist the natural inclination to shield the planning process from outside actors.

Seventh, faculty and administrative planners should project the long-
term effect of all retrenchment strategies before implementing them to insure that the changes are desirable. Those planners who wish to perform
sophisticated analyses would be wise to consult the work on planning models at Stanford University (see chapter 14).

SHORT-TERM STRATEGIES

In the short term, institutions can save money simply by reducing their
day-to-day expenditures or can strive to earn a better return on their investments. For example, short-term institutional balances can be invested in in-
terest-bearing accounts. Unless an institution has experienced fiscal
stringency for several consecutive years, savings usually can be achieved
in such areas as supplies, communications, travel, and equipment purchases. Maintenance can be deferred, but with potentially severe long-term
consequences. Faculty positions that become vacant can be held vacant,
filled with lower-salaried faculty, or filled with temporary or part-time faculty. Fewer classes and larger sections can be scheduled. Course duplication can be eliminated to reduce the number of sections offered.

The advantage of short-term strategies is that savings can be realized
quickly. There are several disadvantages, however. First, the savings tend
to be a relatively small fraction of the total institutional budget. Second,
some long-term damage may be done to programs or facilities. If large
numbers of vacant positions are filled by temporary or part-time faculty,
for example, the composition and character of the faculty can be altered
markedly. Faculty contact with students may be reduced. Also, using
career-minded individuals in temporary or part-time slots only adds to the
new breed of "gypsy scholars." Commitment to university research and
service to both the institution and community suffer. Furthermore, position
vacancies do not always occur in programs slated for shrinkage. To meet
student and programmatic demands, it may be necessary to replace some
departing faculty with permanent appointments, thereby diminishing potential savings.

Short-term budget reduction strategies tend to be administered across-
the-board. Imposing an equitable burden on all units on short notice is
more palatable politically than making selective reductions. However,
across-the-board reductions strike strong and weak programs alike; the
long-term effect may be to seriously undermine the institution's strong programs. The administration of selective reductions usually requires strong
leadership from both faculty and administrators.

INTERMEDIATE-TERM STRATEGIES

Most intermediate-range retrenchment strategies alter personnel policies and procedures so as to provide faculty and staff with financial incentives to retire early, resign, or take unpaid leaves of absence. As with most retrenchment strategies, the objective is to provide institutions with budget-reduction alternatives to forced terminations. Ideally, the least productive and least needed faculty and staff would be the ones to depart. In reality, however, it is possible that the best individuals may do so. Moreover, unless used in conjunction with a review, these strategies do not earmark the programs and activities that are lowest in priority and from which it is most desirable to encourage departures. (Program reviews would be conducted regularly, perhaps every five years on a staggered schedule, and might involve separate panels of faculty and external experts in the field.) Of course, vacancies created when productive individuals depart or vacancies in high-priority programs and activities can be filled with less expensive though qualified candidates. Under the best of conditions the strategies listed below would be introduced without the threat of dismissal hanging over the heads of individuals.

These strategies require a period of approximately two to six years to implement successfully. Some of the time will involve formulation and review of the policies and procedures by the appropriate bodies. A schedule of program reviews may require several years to complete. Also, the front-end cost of some strategies is such that a period of several years is required to recoup the initial investment and to begin saving resources. In general, these strategies are not practicable for the institution facing imminent bankruptcy. Used in conjunction with program review, they may provide sufficient budget savings to enable institutions to avoid forced terminations of faculty and staff.

Personnel actions are a delicate subject. Ideally faculty and staff should not be pressured to accept modified terms of employment. A healthy respect for due process on the part of officials should minimize the possibility of coercion and ensure that the individuals who are offered alternate employment programs have a primary role in selecting the programs. It is also important for faculty and staff to realize that not every suggested change in personnel status should be viewed as an adversarial situation. Many changes in personnel programs are entered into by mutual agreement. Implementation of the following strategies is discussed in detail by Kreinin (1982a and 1982b) and Patton (1979, 1981).

Early retirement incentives. Faculty and staff who meet certain age or service criteria can be offered a lump-sum separation allowance for agreeing to retire or resign early. For example, at Temple University, the University of Pittsburgh, and the University of California, the severance packages have contained up to four years of salary. Benefits such as pension contributions, medical and dental insurance, and tuition allowances could be negotiated as part of the package. Another early retirement option is a liberalization of early retirement actuarial differences, whereby the institution buys up part or all of the differences in pension benefits. Institutions can also offer supplemental pensions to be paid from savings accruing to the vacant position. A further inducement to retirement is the promise to hire retiring faculty on a part-time basis for an agreed-upon period.

There are several potential problems with early retirement systems. First, it may be necessary to convince trustees in public and independent institutions and legislators in public systems that early retirement schemes are valid uses of institutional or state funds and will save money. Some states may have legislation that prohibits the use of public monies for such purposes. Also, the rules of some retirement systems may have to be altered to enable individuals to take advantage of early retirement. Second, early retirement incentives may tempt some excellent faculty and staff to depart. To surmount this difficulty, one can design the incentive structure to discourage the best individuals from leaving. For example, severance salaries may be set at the average salary for a particular age cohort on the assumption that the best individuals in the cohort earn more than the average salary. Also, it may be necessary to offer early retirement incentives only to faculty and staff in programs and activities that have been earmarked for shrinkage.

The early retirement program has significant front-end costs such as the package of severance pay plus benefits. However, the direct cost may still be less than that for outright dismissals that often require from one to two years' notice before they become effective.

Early retirement systems have had mixed success. A system developed at Michigan State University largely prevented forced terminations during the 1981–82 academic year. [See Kreinin (1982a and 1982b) and also Moser et al. (1982) for the details of the Michigan State University experience.] However, institutions with a relatively youthful faculty and staff profile have few individuals interested in early retirement. Moreover, the impact of early retirement systems on the retirement rate is likely to be substantial when they are first introduced. Generally, after an initial swell, the overall retirement rate will decline to a level somewhat above the pre-plan rate.

Part-time tenure (partial buy-out). Here, faculty and staff are permitted to choose part-time appointments for any number of years up to a predetermined maximum (e.g., five years at Michigan State University). They would receive a proportionate salary but have some of their benefits package covered in full. To make this option more attractive, the institution can count each year under the arrangement as a full-time employment year for purposes of retirement and sabbatical leave.

130   BUDGET PROCESS

The advantage of this program is that senior faculty and staff find it more appealing than do junior personnel. Senior individuals are more likely to be able to afford a reduced salary because other options are open to them. Accordingly, new junior faculty and staff can enter the ranks. Also, because senior faculty and staff typically have higher salaries than their junior colleagues, the savings from this strategy will be greater if senior personnel comprise a majority of those who take advantage of it.

External placement. To encourage less productive faculty and staff to leave, an institution could pay for the cost of placement in positions outside the institution. This strategy benefits both the institution and the individual. Costs may include the services of testing and counseling agencies and fees charged by position-finders. The costs of relocation could be paid from savings that accrue to the vacant faculty position (such costs probably will be much less than severance payments). Carl Patton (1983, 1a–8a) has suggested that to protect academic due process the option of external placement should be offered to all individuals within programs earmarked for reduction.

The manner in which faculty and staff are identified and approached for this arrangement requires considerable sensitivity, with the assurance of academic due process, and acknowledgment of the faculty's primary role in determining questions of faculty status. Because this strategy focuses attention on individuals, there probably will not be many who take advantage of it.

Mid-career change. A small number of institutions have implemented programs for mid-career change. These programs are designed to either (1) retrain faculty for other positions within the institution, or (2) provide support during the transition from academic to nonacademic employment. Retraining programs designed to keep faculty within the institution are aimed at individuals in academic programs that are shrinking, being eliminated, or changing focus. Selected faculty are given their regular salary plus funds to cover the costs of relocation, tuition, and other expenses associated with a graduate program. A retraining program usually permits one semester or one year of study. Although some individuals do receive advanced degrees, the programs generally are not designed to accomplish this. Those participating in the program have typically negotiated for placement elsewhere in the institution prior to their retraining. Some programs reorient faculty within a discipline (e.g., by providing them with computer skills) in order to accommodate shifts in emphasis, the introduction of new technologies, and changing student demand.

Other programs are geared to retraining faculty for employment elsewhere. Here, institutions may provide individuals with full or partial salaries for a limited period while retraining is taking place. A variation is the guaranteed income option for individuals moving directly to outside positions. With this option the institution can guarantee for a limited period the difference between the individual's current faculty salary and the salary of the new job. The concept can be modified to fit individual cases. For example, the institution can guarantee the full salary difference the first year and some fraction of the difference in later years.

As with the other strategies, trustees and legislators may have to be convinced that the program is an appropriate use of institutional resources.

Leaves. Modest savings can be achieved by altering leave policies. Institutions can encourage or require faculty members to take full-year sabbatical leaves at half pay by withdrawing the option of one semester at full pay available at many institutions. Long Island University offers two-thirds salary for one year as an incentive for year-long sabbaticals and limits the number of one-semester sabbaticals to one-half the total number of all sabbatical leaves. An institution in a weak fiscal position can require faculty to take one half-pay sabbatical at some point in their careers with the institution. Also, institutions can negotiate leaves of absence that provide a certain percentage of a faculty member's salary. In both cases some of the salary monies saved may have to be used to hire temporary replacement instructors; the balance represents the net savings to the institution.

Other. (1) Over a period of several years all 12-month faculty appointments can be reduced to 10-month appointments; or (2) all faculty and staff can be furloughed for several days or annual faculty and staff salaries reduced by a small percentage. Because these arrangements would be mandatory, they would have to be administered across-the-board.

In general, these and other budget-reduction strategies that require alterations in institutional personnel policies and procedures will be most attractive to faculty and staff if the risks associated with career transitions are minimized. Planners will have to project each strategy's break-even point (i.e., where the cost of the program equals the salaries saved) to ensure that savings are achieved.

Any unilateral actions by administrators may place at risk generally accepted principles of tenure and academic due process. Financial savings should not be the only consideration when implementing new personnel policies and procedures; the need to maintain professional relationships is equally important.

LONG-TERM STRATEGIES

Institutions faced with the prospect of reducing budgets significantly, or with the need to reallocate resources internally will have to review carefully their academic programs and nonacademic activities. To achieve economies and maintain or strengthen the quality of the institution, program review must be an active process with a regular schedule of reviews. Generally, passive program shrinkage or elimination through faculty and staff attrition is not sufficient; normal attrition may be politically the least disruptive way to cope with program shrinkage, but it is not at all selective. Faculty and staff do not leave only low-priority or mediocre-quality or low-demand programs and activities. Also, with job mobility declining because of static national economic conditions, normal attrition usually will not free resources quickly enough to satisfy the demands of retrenchment and reallocation.

Program planning is a long-term, continuous activity because of the complexity of the academic enterprise and the need to involve administrators and appropriate faculty bodies. An orderly planning process typically includes at least five elements *before* program reviews are initiated: (1) development of campuswide or systemwide policies and procedures and statements of priorities, (2) development of institutional mission statements, (3) establishment of personnel rules, (4) establishment of planning principles, and (5) establishment of criteria and policies and procedures for the review of new and existing programs and activities.

Although fiscal conditions ultimately are the force behind reallocation and retrenchment processes on most campuses, finances are often overshadowed by well-placed concern for personnel policies and procedures, especially faculty and staff welfare and legal rights and program review criteria.

Program reduction has obvious fiscal and political costs and is a drain on morale. Clearly, these costs will have to be compared with cost savings and other benefits such as the ability to respond to enrollment pressures and hire quality faculty. Institutions sensitive to the professional development of faculty and staff associated with programs about to be reduced or terminated will bear some of the cost of retraining, early retirement, and external placement discussed above. If faculty and staff must be terminated, the institution will take on the costs of severance agreements. Some faculty and staff will contest their dismissals in court; institutions must be prepared to assume the costs associated with these lawsuits. In general, the amount of personnel-related costs will depend on arrangements made for the personnel. When the University of Michigan closed its Department of Population Planning, for example, it honored its contractual obligations and reassigned tenured faculty to other programs. Accordingly, the savings gained from termination of the program and the costs associated with termination were not as great as if tenured faculty had been released. Program reduction or elimination may be a consequence of enrollment decline; the institution must anticipate the loss of revenues from tuition and fees and, in the case of public institutions, the loss of some state appropriations (assuming that they are usually linked to enrollments). Public institutions may not be allowed to reinvest in other programs and activities the savings that accrue through retrenchment. Finally, programs that are heavily supported by external funds may require considerable institutional funds if they are to be continued yet may yield few immediate savings if they are reduced or terminated. The potential future cost of continuing such programs must be carefully considered.

Other costs of reallocation and retrenchment may be more subtle. Faculty may not wish to be associated with a smaller program and may seek employment elsewhere, further eroding the working core of faculty in the program. If, for example, an institution reduced the scope of a program from the Ph.D. to the master's level, as happened in several cases in the state of New York, faculty whose primary interest is in doctoral training and research may not be satisfied with teaching at the undergraduate and master's level. Also, specific programs may have outside benefactors or supporters who may not want to be associated with a losing cause and may sever their ties with the institution if their programs are affected. Thus, one criterion for program evaluation must be external support and visibility. Similarly, certain programs may have special political connections. A political figure may serve on an advisory board or the program may serve a special state or regional political interest such as economic development. In terms of diminished political support the institution as a whole would have to bear the cost of reducing or eliminating such a program. Within the institution, retrenchment and reallocation may cause disruptions in faculty governance unless faculty are closely involved in establishing policies and procedures well in advance of a financial crisis. Even if review criteria and policies and procedures for faculty and staff retrenchment are set, governance groups become reluctant to earmark specific programs or individuals when the time arises. In general, very serious morale problems arise in institutions undergoing faculty and staff retrenchment. Faculty who have provided long and useful service to the institution suddenly find themselves unwanted. If, for example, faculty terminations are decided on the basis of seniority, schisms can develop between junior and senior faculty. Reallocation and retrenchment may also push a campus faculty toward collective bargaining as a way to clarify relevant policies and procedures. Adverse media publicity about program reductions may exacerbate enrollment declines. Finally, situations involving reallocation and retrenchment may uncover deficiencies in administrative leadership, which ultimately may prove advantageous.

The economics of reallocation and retrenchment require that long-term plans be made for programs and activities, which must be held accountable for plan objectives. In the academic area enrollments may have to be restricted so the desired level of service can be provided with the resources available. Enrollments can be controlled by rationing plans that have special admissions criteria for potential students in high-demand programs. Long-range enrollment targets can be established for all academic programs so that planners can better gauge future resource needs (see chapter 12). Programs can be held to the targets, and those that fail to meet them can be subject to a loss of resources.

Long-term enrollment targets can be accompanied by projected staffing patterns. Institutions can project the impact of enrollment levels on decisions about promotion, nonretention, tenure density, and external hiring of junior and senior staff, with the objective of making future staffing decisions more orderly (see chapter 14).

Plans for program reduction and resource reallocation should also anticipate changes in programs and activities. If, for example, an academic program is to be phased out, arrangements must be made to accommodate students in the program pipeline. If tenured faculty in the program being eliminated are to be placed elsewhere in the institution, places must be made for them. The elimination of one degree program will affect other programs that depend on the eliminated one for courses offered or student enrollments. Resources may have to be reallocated to reflect this fallout effect. Also, the impact of reallocation and retrenchment will have to be projected for affirmative action plans in the areas of student enrollments and staffing.

Some institutions have already developed long-term reallocation plans in anticipation of financial hard times and enrollment shifts or declines. The University of Michigan, for example, established a Priority Fund for reallocation purposes. All units in the university have their base budgets reduced one percent each year to provide a pool of resources for the fund. All programs and activities have an opportunity to compete for monies in the fund, although allocations are made only to those with highest priority.

Clearly, if institutions are to adapt, most will have to reallocate resources at some time. Whether the reallocations are done in response to fiscal crises or through the desire to maintain or improve the quality of the institution, they will have to be made selectively. When institutions first encounter financial stringency, they can manage the situations most painlessly through across-the-board reductions. After several years of financial hard times, however, the strongest programs and activities can no longer be penalized at the same rate as the lower-quality or lower-priority ones. Selectivity in accordance with an institution's academic mission and goals should be the guiding factor in retrenchment and reallocation, whether the institution establishes detailed targets centrally or assigns broad targets to large units such as colleges or schools that are then permitted to determine the detailed targets. Above all, the process of reallocation must be sensitive to the character and academic mission of the institution and must involve faculty members.

FOR FURTHER READING

The literature on retrenchment has grown rapidly during the past five years as a number of institutions have experienced financial difficulties. An excellent collection of papers appears in *Challenges of Retrenchment: Strategies for Consolidating Programs, Cutting Costs, and Reallocating Resources,* by James R. Mingle et al. (San Francisco: Jossey-Bass, Inc., 1981). A summary of the major issues addressed by Mingle and his colleagues is found in "Redirecting Higher Education in a Time of Budget Reduction," *Issues in Higher Education,* no. 18 (Atlanta: Southern Regional Education Board, 1982).

Frank M. Bowen and Lyman A. Glenny present several institutional case studies of retrenchment strategies in *State Budgeting for Higher Education: State Fiscal Stringency and Public Higher Education* (Berkeley, CA: Center for Research and Development in Higher Education, University of California, Berkeley, 1976).

A monograph edited by Stephen R. Hample, *Coping with Faculty Reduction,* New Directions for Institutional Research, no. 30 (San Francisco: Jossey-Bass, Inc., 1981), contains several good papers on the programmatic and legal implications of faculty reduction.

A thoughtful paper on retrenchment is Donald K. Smith's "Coping, Improving, and Planning for the Future during Fiscal Decline: A Case Study from the University of Wisconsin Experience," in *The Monday Morning Experience: Report from the Boyer Workshop on State University Systems,* edited by Martin Kaplan (New York: Aspen Institute for Humanistic Studies, 1976).

The American Association for Higher Education (AAHE) has published two monographs on retrenchment: Marjorie C. Mix's *Tenure and Termination in Financial Exigency,* AAHE/ERIC Higher Education Research Report no. 3 (Washington, DC: American Association for Higher Education, 1978) discusses the legal aspects of financial exigency; and Kenneth P. Mortimer and Michael L. Tierney examine the administration of resource reallocation and retrenchment in *The Three "R's" of the Eighties: Reduction, Reallocation and Retrenchment,* AAHE/ERIC Higher Education Research Report no. 4 (Washington, DC: American Association for Higher Education, 1979).

The position of the American Association of University Professors (AAUP) toward tenure, academic freedom, and financial exigency is stated in several documents: William Van Alstyne's "Tenure: A Summary, Explanation, and 'Defense,'" *AAUP Bulletin,* vol. 57, no. 2 (June 1971), pp. 328–333; Ralph S. Brown, Jr.'s "Financial Exigency," *AAUP Bulletin,* vol. 62, no. 1 (April 1976), pp. 5–16; and "1982 Recommended Institutional Regulations on Academic Freedom and Tenure," *Academe,* vol. 69, no. 1 (January-February 1983), pp. 15a–20a. See also Kingman Brewster, Jr.'s "On Tenure," *AAUP Bulletin,* vol. 58, no. 4 (December 1972), pp. 381–383. W. Todd Furniss summarizes the concerns of the Commission on Academic Affairs of the American Council on Education toward the 1976 AAUP retrenchment policy statement in "The 1976 AAUP Retrenchment Policy," *Educational Record,* vol. 57, no. 3 (Summer 1976), pp. 133–139. Furniss also discusses the problems of retrenchment in "Retrenchment, Layoff, and Termination," *Educational Record,* vol. 55, no. 3 (Summer 1974), pp. 159–170. Donald C. Cell, a former secretary/treasurer of AAUP, offers several suggestions for retrenchment policies and procedures in his "Opening Question-Raising Remarks: Tenure and

Exigency Problems," presented at the AAUP Conference on Hard Times, Washington, DC, May 20, 1982 (mimeo).

A detailed case study of an experience with financial exigency is "Academic Freedom and Tenure: City University of New York—Mass Dismissals under Financial Exigency," *AAUP Bulletin*, vol. 63, no. 2 (April 1977), pp. 60–81.

Planning for enrollment shifts and contractions is discussed by William F. Brazziel in "Planning for Enrollment Shifts in Colleges and Universities," *Research in Higher Education*, vol. 9, no. 1 (1978), pp. 1–13; by Robert G. Arns and William Poland in "Changing the University through Program Review," *Journal of Higher Education*, vol. 51, no. 3 (May/June 1980), pp. 268–284; by Kent G. Alm, Elwood B. Ehrle, and Bill R. Webster in "Managing Faculty Reduction," *Journal of Higher Education*, vol. 48, no. 2 (March/April 1977), pp. 153–163; and by Charles L. Cherry in "Scalpels and Swords: The Surgery of Contingency Planning," *Educational Record*, vol. 59, no. 4 (Fall 1978), pp. 367–376.

Mordechai E. Kreinin explains a means of preserving tenure at Michigan State University in the face of financial trouble in "Point of View: For a University in Financial Trouble, a Faculty 'Buy-Out' Plan Can Save Money and Face," *The Chronicle of Higher Education*, vol. 23, no. 20 (January 27, 1982), p. 56, and in "Preserving Tenure Commitments in Hard Times: The Michigan State Experience," *Academe*, vol. 68, no. 2 (March-April 1982), pp. 37–45 (including comments by several respondents). Another response to Kreinin is found in Moser et al., "Buy-outs at MSU," *Academe*, vol. 68, no. 5 (September-October 1982), p. 6. Other alternatives to faculty termination are offered by David D. Palmer and Carl V. Patton in "Mid-Career Change Options in Academe: Experience and Possibilities," *Journal of Higher Education*, vol. 52, no. 4 (July/August 1981), pp. 378–398, and by Patton in "Voluntary Alternatives to Forced Termination," *Academe*, vol. 69, no. 1 (January-February 1983), pp. 1a–8a, and in *Academia in Transition: Mid-Career Change or Early Retirement* (Cambridge, MA: Abt Books, 1979).

The January-February 1983 issue of *Academe* (vol. 69, no. 1) is devoted to the report of a special AAUP Task Force on Faculty and Higher Education in Hard Times.

Part 2

Technical Tools

7 / Fund Accounting

Designing an accounting system is an art form. The system can hide information or it can disclose various aspects of an institution's financial situation. Some accounting systems can do both simultaneously.

Most college and university accounting systems are designed in accordance with generally accepted accounting principles, especially those summarized in *College & University Business Administration,* 4th ed. (Washington, DC: National Association of College and University Business Officers, 1982), and *Audits of Colleges and Universities* (New York: American Institute of Certified Public Accountants, 1975). However, in accounting, as in most disciplines, there is disagreement over how to address certain situations. In those instances the accounting methodologies will differ from one campus to another. The design of the accounting system can also be determined in part by the nature of the institution (e.g., public versus independent, research-oriented versus instruction-oriented) and the institution's history.

An accounting system does not necessarily reflect all financial transactions that may influence the institution's financial status. Frequently these transactions are described in notes to the institution's financial statement. They might include such items as significant additions to plant and pledges of gifts. Items that do not appear in a financial statement might include a planned bequest by an alumnus to be made at an unnamed future date or the donation of rare books or works of art. The latter items increase the value of the institution's assets but would not be included in the financial statement. One must realize, therefore, that the institution's accounting system may not provide a complete financial picture.

What follows is a layman's guide to fund accounting, the basic framework for most college and university accounting systems. This is a brief overview of the most common types of accounts and funds and summarizes selected accounting principles. Attention is given to basic financial statements. The sample institution referred to throughout this chapter is examined in figures 1 through 5.

TYPES OF ACCOUNTS

THE ACCOUNTING EQUATION

The accounting equation involves the balanced relationship among three kinds of economic representations: assets, liabilities, and net worth. Assets are economic values that are owned by or are under the control of the institution. They are of two kinds. The first is cash and that which can be converted into cash, such as investments and accounts receivable. The other type of asset is represented by costs incurred at an earlier date that have not yet been attributed to a given fiscal period. Examples of this second type of asset are capital costs, depreciable equipment, buildings, inventories, prepaid expenses, and deferred charges.

There are also two kinds of liability accounts. The first represents amounts that are owed to organizations or individuals who are outside the institution itself. (An exception to this definition will be discussed later.) In general, liabilities represent amounts owed to others, including creditors, for a variety of reasons. Some liabilities may be amounts that are owed and must be paid in the near term or immediately. Other liabilities may be paid out over a period of many years. The second type of liability account is used to record deferred credits or deferred revenues. These liabilities represent amounts that have been collected in cash or whose collection is anticipated but for which an earnings process has not yet oc-

---

This chapter is a revision of material contained in *Financial Responsibilites of Governing Boards of Colleges and Universities* (Washington, DC: Association of Governing Boards of Universities and Colleges and National Association of College and University Business Officers, 1979), and *Conference for Women Administrators: Financial Management of Colleges and Universities* (Washington, DC: National Association of College and University Business Officers and Committee for the Concerns of Women in New England Colleges and Universities, n.d.). Permission to use this material has been granted.

curred. Until such a process begins, the institution carries these items as a liability.

The relationship between assets and liabilities or the difference between them produces the third kind of account, generally referred to as net worth, equity, or proprietorship. Net worth is also net assets, which represent the net difference between assets and related liabilities. In fund accounting the fund balance equals assets minus liabilities.

The accounting equation is the relationship among these three kinds of accounts and is expressed by the statement that assets minus liabilities equals net worth or by an algebraic transposition of that equation (i.e., assets equal liabilities plus net worth). Another way of interpreting the accounting equation is to state that equities are claims by an owner or creditor against assets.

REAL AND NOMINAL ACCOUNTS

The accounts used in the accounting system to record asset values, liability values, and net worth or fund balance values are referred to as real accounts. These balances carry forward from the beginning of the organization until its end or until the particular type of asset, liability, or net worth no longer exists. Nominal accounts, on the other hand, expire at the end of a given fiscal period (e.g., the fiscal year) and are created anew at the beginning of the next period. Such accounts—called income and expenses—classify the increases and decreases in net worth and provide more detailed information about the sources and uses of net worth throughout the year. For example, increases in net worth may result from sales, gifts, endowment income, or contributions to capital; decreases may reflect expenses or losses in investments, among other possibilities.

In most cases financial statements deal exclusively with either real accounts or nominal accounts (special types of reports may deal with elements of both at the same time). In examining financial statements it is helpful to remember that net worth or fund balances are changed by increases or decreases in assets or liabilities (i.e., by income and expenses).

The concept of double-entry bookkeeping is built on the accounting equation. Thus, for each economic event that is recorded there is a balanced set of entries to record the event (i.e., a debit and a credit). At all times the system must balance so that debits equal credits. The total of assets must likewise equal the total of liabilities and net worth in the system.

The accounting equation and the principles of real and nominal accounts underlie all accounting and apply to fund accounting as well as to other forms of accounting. The next section examines fund accounting and explains why that methodology is used in college and university accounting systems.

TYPES OF FUNDS

RESTRICTED AND UNRESTRICTED FUNDS

Nonprofit organizations as a group often differ from profit-making enterprises in that they are the recipients of gifts, grants, contributions, and appropriations, which are restricted at the direction of the sources for particular purposes, functions, or activities. A donor, for example, may specify that a gift is to be used only for scholarships. This restriction is legally binding on the institution, which has no authority to use that money for any other purpose. That the institution may already have a scholarship program and that the gift would simply help to finance it are irrelevant. Another example of a restriction is a donor's specification that only the income from investing the donation may be used.

Restrictions imposed by a donor differ in two important respects from self-imposed limitations established by the governing board or from other kinds of conditions that characterize the relationship between the donor and the grantee (but which are not restrictions). First, the restriction must be set forth in writing or must be related to a representation made in writing. Second, the language used in the written instrument must be restrictive. Restrictive language is characterized by words that indicate a command or a demand or that establish an absolute limitation. The law distinguishes between restrictive language and precatory language, which represents only a wish, a desire, or an entreaty (but which is not restrictive).

If conditions are documented in writing and if the language is appropriately restrictive, the restrictions cannot be changed by the institution acting alone. In some jurisdictions even the institution and the donor together may not change the restriction once the gift has been accepted with the restrictions imposed. The removal of a restriction or the redirection of the resources into a related activity can be accomplished only through a formal or an informal application of the doctrine of *cy pres*. (This procedure requires formal court proceedings and involves the state attorney general.)

Occasionally, ambiguous language is used in the instruments conveying the donation, and sometimes the original documentation is missing. Legal review is almost always required in such situations. Institutions seeking relief through the courts would, if successful, receive a declaratory judgment.

In summary, it is important to distinguish between those resources that are truly restricted and those that are not. *Cy pres* relates only to externally restricted funds and not to internally designated funds (such as those designated in the budget process). The maintenance of the distinction between these two categories is a paramount responsibility of the fund accounting system.

FUND CLASSIFICATIONS

Resources received by institutions are labeled in several ways to indicate the nature of any pertinent restrictions.

Ownership vs. agency relationship. When an institution receives new monies, the first question is whether the resources actually belong to the institution. Funds that do not belong to the institution are called agency funds and represent assets held by the institution on behalf of others. Alternatively, agency funds represent liabilities for amounts due to outside organizations, students, or faculty that will be paid out on their instructions for purposes other than normal operations. Institutions have on occasion used the agency fund classification inappropriately for funds that officials would like to use outside the constraints of the budget process.

Restricted vs. unrestricted. If the monies received by the institution are indeed owned by the institution, the next question is whether the monies are restricted or unrestricted. As noted earlier, the specific nature of the restrictions must be clearly stated.

Expendable vs. nonexpendable. If the monies received by the institution are restricted, it must be determined whether the monies are expendable or nonexpendable. If the monies are expendable (i.e., can be spent), one must ask for what specific purpose, function, activity, or object. If the purpose or character of the expenditure is such that it is a part of normal operations, it is classified in a category that relates it to current operations. If, on the other hand, the restriction is such that the monies must be spent to acquire land, buildings, equipment, or other types of capital assets, the expenditure is classified as a part of plant funds.

Nonexpendable funds can be distinguished by several types of restrictions. For example, endowment funds cannot be spent. Rather, they must be invested, and only the income can be used. It should be noted that income from the endowment represents a new source of funds, and the nature of this money must be determined by the same series of questions outlined above. It is possible for a donor to restrict both the principal (i.e., the endowment monies) and the investment income.

Certain other funds cannot be spent but must be loaned to students or faculty. Under this arrangement the monies will be loaned, the borrowers will repay the loans, and the same resources will be reloaned to other borrowers.

A third nonexpendable fund is the annuity fund or life income fund. Here, the donor provides money to the institution with instructions to pay to an outside party for a period of time either a certain amount of money (in the case of an annuity fund) or the investment income (in the case of a life income fund).

All funds not restricted by the donor are by definition unrestricted. Generally, all unrestricted funds are to be used first as revenue for current operating purposes. A governing board may also designate unrestricted funds for long-term investments to produce income (in the manner of endowment funds), or for plant acquisition purposes (for which restricted funds are normally used).

Thus, certain unrestricted funds are intended for the same purpose as certain restricted funds. In the reporting of college and university financial matters, as evidenced in financial statements, funds that are either restricted or designated for similar types of activities are classified in a group that has a name indicating the purpose. However, within each one of these groups it is necessary to distinguish between those amounts that are in the group by reason of restrictions imposed by donors and those amounts that are in the group by reason of designation by a governing board.

SELECTED ACCOUNTING PRINCIPLES

Accounting principles are the standards that define how economic transactions are to be classified and reported. Recognition of proper accounting principles is important in establishing a college or university accounting system. Most institutions adhere to the accounting principles set forth by the American Institute of Certified Public Accountants (AICPA). These principles should be reflected in an institution's financial statement. When studying a financial statement that has been audited, one should see in the auditor's report a statement as to whether the financial statement has been prepared in accordance with generally accepted accounting principles. If the auditor notes an exception or denies that proper accounting principles have been followed, it will be difficult to evaluate the financial statement in a meaningful fashion.

FUNDS AND FUND GROUPS

A fund is an accounting entity with a self-balancing set of accounts consisting of assets, liabilities, and a fund balance account, in addition to nominal accounts that measure increases and decreases in the fund balance. Separate funds are established to account for financial activity related to a particular restricted donation, source of restricted funds, or designated amount established by the governing board. These accounting entries are set up to insure the observance of restrictions imposed by donors and of limitations on the use of unrestricted funds that have been established by the governing board. In many cases, however, funds of similar designation and restriction are grouped together for reporting purposes and for purposes of efficient management. Often the assets of like kinds of funds are placed in one set of asset accounts. Similarly, liability accounts related to those assets may be merged. Nevertheless, there would still be a series of individual fund balances for which a separate accounting would have to be performed. The total of all such assets would equal the total of all such liabilities and the total of the fund balances to which they relate. This grouping together for accounting and reporting purposes yields what is termed a fund group. It is important to note that within each fund group it is necessary to continue to distinguish between the balance of funds that are unrestricted and those that are externally restricted. Within the restricted subgroup it is necessary to account for each separate restricted fund balance.

ACCRUAL BASIS OF ACCOUNTING

Accrual-basis accounting is often defined in comparison to cash-basis accounting. In the latter the only transactions recorded are those in which cash comes into the organization or goes out. Thus, an asset or an increase in the fund balance would be recognized only when cash is collected. Similarly, the assets and fund balance would be reduced only when a cash payment is made. Almost nothing else would be accounted for, making the cash basis of accounting rather unsatisfactory for most reporting and management purposes. Accrual-basis accounting was developed in response to this shortcoming in the cash-basis method. The accrual basis recognizes fund balance increments (i.e., revenue) when the amount is earned. Expenses and other types of deductions are recognized when the goods or services have been used up. An asset is recognized as an amount that has been received and has continuing value (i.e., unexpired costs), although a payment may not have been made for this amount. The measurement of revenues and expenses is called the accrual basis of accounting because accruals are used to convert cash receipts into revenue and cash disbursements into expenses.

The objective of accrual-basis accounting is to provide a more satisfactory matching of revenues and other fund balance additions with expenses and other fund balance deductions in the accounting period to which the financial statements relate. In other words, the accrual basis attempts to determine the real economic impact of what has occurred during a given period of time rather than simply determining how much cash was received or disbursed.

INTERFUND ACCOUNTING

The concept of interfund accounting relates to maintaining the integrity and self-balancing characteristics of the individual funds. Problems arise, for example, when cash used for the benefit of one fund actually belongs to another fund. To illustrate, assume that an institution has a scholarship fund of $10,000 and has $10,000 in the bank for that fund. Also assume that in the institution's unrestricted current fund is another $10,000 that is available for any purpose. Assume that the institution makes a payment of

$1,000 to a scholarship recipient out of the unrestricted current fund bank account, whereas the intent was to use the restricted scholarship fund. If the fund balance of the scholarship fund is reduced along with the amount of cash belonging to the unrestricted current fund, both funds would be unbalanced. That is, their assets (when examined separately) would not be equal to their liabilities and fund balances. In the fund that has made the disbursement (i.e., that has given up the cash), an asset account would be established representing the amount due from the fund that is ultimately to finance the activity. This arrangement puts the unrestricted current fund back in balance. In the restricted fund that is to be used for scholarships, a liability account would be established for the $1,000 paid on behalf of the restricted fund, and the fund balance would be charged the same amount. Again, the restricted fund would now be in balance and there would exist an interfund receivable and payable. The asset and liability would at some point be extinguished by a transfer of cash between the funds.

CHART OF ACCOUNTS

The chart of accounts in an accounting system is used to classify each transaction accounted for in the system, facilitating easy and accurate retrieval. It is based on (1) the accounting principles for proper classification of economic phenomena and (2) the reporting needs of management and external parties, calling for segregation of different kinds of transactions so that those transactions may later be aggregated and reported by type. (The chart of accounts of a typical college is provided in appendix 2.)

Accounting systems in higher education usually involve both an alphabetical designation of the account name, which can be read, and a numerical or alpha-numeric designation of the account, which can be used for encoding purposes. This arrangement allows the system to work with a numerical or shortened reference rather than a long rational name.

It is important to remember that the purpose of the chart of accounts is to assist in the locating of discrete kinds of transactions. The only rules are those that make sense in terms of how much information and what kinds of categories should be reported. The information needs of many colleges and universities are the same in certain areas, particularly with regard to the production of basic financial statements.

TYPES OF FINANCIAL STATEMENTS

A college or university's financial statement is generally composed of four segments: (1) balance sheet; (2) statement of changes in fund balances; (3) statement of current fund revenues, expenditures, and other changes; and (4) footnotes to the above segments.

The balance sheet reflects the financial resources of the institution at a given time. The balance sheet contains the assets of the institution, the liabilities, and the fund balances. Thus, the status of the institution is generally expressed in terms of its real accounts. The assets can be viewed as the forms of the institution's financial resources, whereas the liabilities and fund balance are the sources.

The statement of changes in fund balances summarizes the activity within each group of funds during a specific fiscal period. This statement is comparable to the income statement and statement of changes in the stockholders' equity in the for-profit sector. For nonprofit organizations, however, the statement of changes in fund balances covers each set of funds.

The statement of current funds revenues, expenditures, and other changes is a detailed accounting of changes in the current funds column that are included in the statement of changes in fund balances. Sometimes this statement is referred to as the statement of changes in financial position. In fund accounting most useful information is already contained in the balance sheet and the statement of changes in fund balances, often making redundant the information contained in the statement of current funds revenues, expenditures, and other changes. On the other hand, there may be some activity that should be reported and has not been disclosed in any of the statements; this can often be taken care of by enhancing the statements with another presentation summarizing the changes in financial position or by adding footnotes to the financial statements. Footnotes summarize the significant accounting principles used to prepare the statements and provide other information essential to a full understanding of the institution's particular financial environment. No examination of an institution's financial statement is complete without a thorough perusal of the footnotes.

FINANCIAL STATEMENTS: A DETAILED EXAMINATION

INTERRELATIONSHIPS OF THE THREE BASIC STATEMENTS

The balance sheet—a report as of a particular time—states all the financial resources for which the institution's governing board is responsible. In figure 2 the balance sheet has columns for two dates (i.e., current year and prior year). The prior-year column is a point of reference and can be used as a standard to evaluate the current year's financial information. Note that for each category of funds, assets equal liabilities and fund balances for both the current year and the prior year.

The statement of changes in fund balances (figure 2) has a separate column for each fund group. The purpose of this statement is to show the gross additions to and gross deductions from each of the fund groups, to account for any amounts that may have been transferred from one fund group to another, to report the net change in fund balances for the year for each of the fund groups, and to show beginning balances (in order to account for ending balances).

It is worth examining the beginning and ending balances of the statement of changes in fund balances to trace their origins to the balance sheet. For example, at the bottom of the first column of figure 2, the beginning and ending fund balances of unrestricted current funds total $455,000 and $643,000, respectively. In the balance sheet (figure 1) these amounts appear on the liability side opposite the term "fund balance" under the heading "current unrestricted funds." The beginning balance on the statement of changes is the prior year's figure of $455,000. The ending figure is the current year's balance sheet figure of $643,000.

The balance sheet shows amounts for each of the fund balances for each of the fund groups. The statement of changes in fund balances reports all activity that resulted in changes in those fund balances during the year. For each different type of addition or deduction there is a separate line caption. Thus, within the accounting system there are separate classifications so that transactions may be reported separately in the statement. The statement of changes in fund balances addresses only the fund balances, not the assets or liabilities.

The statement of current funds, revenues, expenditures, and other changes covers the activity from the beginning to the end of the fiscal year and essentially expands on the information presented in summary fashion in the statement of changes in fund balances. It relates to current funds only and to transactions that have affected the fund balances of the current funds and has no relationship to assets or liabilities or to changes in funds other than current funds. In figure 3 the final numbers in each of the first two columns are the same as the net changes for the years that appear in the first two columns of the statement of changes, namely, $188,000 and $25,000, respectively.

The accrual basis of accounting can lead to confusion when one examines the statement of current funds, revenues, expenditures, and other changes. As mentioned earlier, certain kinds of funds are provided to the institution with earmarks categorizing them as current operating activity. Accordingly, these funds are classified in the group called current restricted funds. When the amounts are received, they are accounted for as additions to those funds, and such additions are reported in the statement of changes in fund balances. The difference between those two kinds of transactions and any transfers produce the net change in fund balance for the year.

An examination of the statement of current funds, revenues, expenditures, and other changes reveals something a bit unusual in terms of revenues. This statement attempts to match pure revenues with expenditures and other transactions in order to derive a more meaningful report that applies the accrual-basis concept to operations for the year. However, in the accrual basis of accounting one has not "earned" a current restricted fund until that fund has been expended for the purpose for which it was restricted (i.e., a revenue from current restricted funds does not exist until those funds have been expended). This is not unlike the deferred-credit concept in the for-profit sector, whereby a business may receive money from a customer in advance of having rendered the service. The receipt of such monies is treated as a deferred credit. As the services are rendered and the expenses incurred, these amounts are taken into revenue. This reporting convention gives the statement preparer a better basis for matching revenues and expenses, which is one of the objectives of the accrual basis of accounting. The potential confusion here, of course, is that these resources are treated as fund balances rather than as liabilities, as the for-profit sector would treat them. Thus, the two financial statements (figures 2 and 3) seem to conflict.

The differences are reconciled by an adjustment made to the statement of current funds, revenues, expenditures, and other changes. The adjustment represents the difference between the additions to current restricted funds for the current year and the amounts earned and therefore reflected in revenue. In the figures under consideration, the adjustment for the current year is the difference between $1,094,000 of additions (figure 2) and $1,014,000 recognized as revenue (figure 3), or $80,000. However, the adjustment is affected by another transaction (indirect costs recovered), which reduces current restricted fund balances but is not reported as a current restricted fund expenditure because it is an application of such funds to current unrestricted fund revenues. The amount for indirect costs is shown in figure 2 as $35,000. The difference between $80,000 and $35,000 accounts for the $45,000 adjustment, reported in figure 3 as excess of restricted receipts over transfers to revenues. As a result, figure 3 does reconcile with the same changes in fund balance amounts shown in figure 2 for current restricted funds.

The real purpose of the statement of current funds, revenues, expenditures, and other changes, then, is to provide greater detail about the sources of current revenues and the functions for which current funds are expended. One of the basic accounting principles involved in this statement is that at this level of aggregation revenues are to to reported by source and expenditures by function. This statement also enables the reader to identify the total financial activity for current funds during the year. The totaling function is accomplished through the columnar presentation, whereby current unrestricted funds and current restricted funds, revenues, expenditures, and other changes are combined in a column labeled "total." For comparison a total for the preceding year is provided.

It is interesting to note that the statement of current funds, revenues, expenditures, and other changes can be considered in an entirely different manner. If, for example, it is remembered that the purpose of the statement is to disclose certain types of information, the format of the statement is less mysterious than it might be otherwise. Thus, if details as to the sources of revenue are reported on separate lines in the statement of changes in fund balances (instead of being reported as a single amount as in figure 2), it would be possible to eliminate the section on revenues in figure 3, which in turn could be used to provide only the required itemization of expenditures by function for the unrestricted, restricted, and total current funds. Then it would be necessary to tell the reader only how the current restricted fund expenditures were financed. That information could be shown either as a tabulation at the bottom of figure 3 or in the notes to the financial statements. The discussion above is intended to highlight the importance of the information content rather than the specific format.

THE BALANCE SHEET—CURRENT FUNDS

The balance sheet in figure 1 contains all of the assets, liabilities, and fund balances. They are arranged side-by-side in a horizontal fashion for each fund group throughout the statement. This format enables the reader to examine the assets and liabilities and fund balances of each fund group separately, and to see in juxtaposition with the current year's amounts the amounts that pertain to the previous year.

The first major fund group on the balance sheet is current funds. Within the current fund group a distinction is made between unrestricted current funds and restricted current funds. The current funds represent the results of operating inflows and outflows, or the "working capital" position of the institution. Assets and liabilities are the same as for a business if the account "due to other funds" is read as "due to other subsidiaries" and fund balances are understood as the working capital portion of the institution's total net worth, or equity. Assets represent the liquid resources or unexpired costs that pertain to day-to-day operations, and include such items as cash and investments.

The most frequently used basis for carrying assets is historical cost or, in the absence of cost, the fair value of the asset at date of donation. If the institution chooses, it may follow the market value method of accounting, whereby the carrying values for investments are changed from reporting date to reporting date to reflect changes in current market values. If this procedure is followed, all investments of all funds must be accounted for in that fashion.

Another asset listed is accounts receivable. Principles of accounting hold that such assets should be stated at their realizable amounts. Statements often show total accounts receivable less an allowance for doubtful accounts, with the net amount reflecting the difference.

Inventories are unexpired costs representing economic values that will have utility in the succeeding year. Inventories of consumable supplies and supplies for resale are included in this category. Some inventories are carried at the lower of cost or market value. Cost must be determined on some generally acceptable basis (e.g., first-in-first-out, average cost, or last-in-first-out).

Prepaid expenses and deferred charges include items such as prepaid insurance. Here, a policy premium covering more than one year has been paid in advance, with the premium portion that has expired during the year written off as an expense and the unexpired portion carried as the prepaid expense.

The liabilities of current funds are relatively straightforward. The accounts payable and accrued liabilities represent amounts that have to be paid to vendors and others who have provided goods and services to the institution and for which the institution has not yet made a cash disbursement. Student deposits represent amounts that may be applied against tuition at a later date or refunded, depending on the circumstances. Deferred credits represent amounts that have been received in advance by students during registration. After registration and the beginning of classes the credits would be treated as revenue, becoming an addition to the current unrestricted fund balance in that year. (This is another example of the accrual basis of accounting at work.)

The fund balance is shown separately on the statement (in figure 1 it appears as a single amount). If the governing board designates portions of unrestricted current funds for particular current operating purposes, it may be desirable or necessary to subdivide the fund balance between the designated and undesignated portions. It should be kept in mind that a designation is not a restriction.

The assets and liabilities of the current restricted fund group are similar in nature to the assets and liabilities of unrestricted current funds. The same rules and practices apply to the valuation of investments and to accounts receivable. Unbilled charges are usually related to contracts and grants and are amounts that become accounts receivable when billed. A difference between current restricted and current unrestricted funds is that the plural term "fund balances" is used in the restricted current fund, whereas the singular term "fund balance" is used in the unrestricted current fund. Fund balances are grouped in current restricted funds, but because each fund requires separate accountability, the accounts of the institution must maintain a fund balance account for each source and restriction. In the unrestricted current fund there is need for only one fund balance. Any others would simply be disaggregations of the larger fund balance. Such disaggregations reflect designations by the governing board.

The current fund balances, both unrestricted and restricted, are key reflections of the financial viability of the institution. In addition to acting as working capital, the current unrestricted fund balance ($643,000 in figure 1) represents an accumulated reserve from operations, or retained receipts comparable to retained earnings in a business. This most flexible reserve provides both a cushion against future operating deficits and a source of seed money for desirable new programs of instruction, research, and public service.

The current restricted fund balance ($446,000 in figure 1) can be thought of as representing a backlog of future business already committed. The extent of management control over the timing and use of these restricted funds determines the flexibility and importance of the funds in long-range planning. Just as the adequacy of and trends in the amount of working capital and operating reserves in a business must be continually evaluated in terms of sales volume, market risks, inflation, and possible future product needs, so should current fund balances be measured in an educational institution.

The quantity and quality of current fund assets should be routinely reviewed and the offsetting liabilities should be subject to governing board policies and oversight. Excess cash should be temporarily invested in accordance with sound cash management principles. As competition for students intensifies, colleges and universities—particularly the more expensive independent institutions—are under increasing pressure to provide more student assistance. Receivables, which should be compared with operating volumes and with the receivables of peer institutions, are growing. Designing sound collection policies is becoming one of management's more pressing responsibilities.

Inventories ordinarily do not represent very large commitments in service institutions; however, any investment in inventories is not available for other purposes and therefore should be justified by relevant economic considerations. The timing of payments should be in accordance with sound disbursement policies and procedures to avoid either uneconomic prepayments or reputation-damaging late payments. Current fund borrowings should be monitored closely. Techniques for managing and protecting current operating assets and working capital funds include appropriate cash-flow forecasts, reports on the aging of receivables, and reviews of significant changes in inventory levels.

Sometimes an institution's governing board or administration will transfer what might be considered excessive operating reserves, or accumulated current fund balances, to the long-term capital fund groups, with due consideration for any applicable external restrictions. Such transfers would convert the affected operating reserves to invested reserves, possibly increasing investment income but reducing operating flexibility. Likewise, the governing board or administration may "retransfer" any fund balances previously transferred to the long-term capital fund groups back to the current fund balances for needed current expenditures or to make up deficiencies, again with due consideration for any applicable external restrictions. Any retransfer would convert invested reserves to operating reserves, possibly decreasing investment income but increasing operating resources.

Examples of such transfers are shown in the statement of changes in fund balances (figure 2) and are discussed in more detail below. While the mandatory transfers are required by debt instruments or third-party providers, the category "unrestricted gifts allocated" ($650,000) represents management transfers of operating funds to loan, endowment, and plant funds, and the "portion of unrestricted quasi-endowment funds investment gains appropriated" ($40,000) represents a management decision to transfer or retransfer invested funds back to operating funds. Both these transfers should be done in fulfillment of current budgeting and long-range financial plans.

Finally, agency funds represent amounts that are received by the institution but that do not belong to it. Generally, the assets would be cash and investments (see illustration in figure 1). The accountability for these funds is to outside parties; thus the balance sheet shows a liability for the amounts held for others by the institution. This is the only fund group that does not have a fund balance. In this case, assets equal liabilities and there are no net assets that belong to the institution. For this reason the statement of changes in fund balances has no column for the agency fund. Clearly, the institution must account to the various parties for whom it is holding funds by showing receipts and disbursements, but such information is not required in these highly aggregated, general financial statements.

STATEMENT OF CHANGES IN FUND BALANCES

Long-term capital is required to finance assets that will not be recovered or converted to cash within the normal operating cycle. These assets include land, buildings, and equipment; student loans; and investments that provide an earnings base independent of current supporters. Long-term capital is provided directly by gifts and government appropriations, or indirectly through current operating funds.

Current operating funds may be expended for equipment and minor plant renovations directly from current accounts. Or, they may be transferred to the plant funds group, to be expended for debt service, major plant additions, and renewals and replacements, or to loan funds, or to endowment and similar funds, either as required by external agreements or benefactors (mandatory transfers) or as determined by the administration.

The statement of changes in fund balances (figure 2) shows these flows of long-term capital. Under "revenues and other additions," supporters with "private gifts, grants, and contracts—restricted" directly provided $100,000 to loan funds, $1,500,000 to endowment and similar funds, $800,000 to annuity and life income funds, $115,000 to funds for spending on plant, $65,000 for retirement of indebtedness, and $15,000 of "in kind" plant or equipment. An expired term endowment provided $50,000 directly for plant, and state appropriations provided another $50,000 for plant expenditures. Investment income (restricted), realized gains on investments, and accrued interest provided a total of $16,000 to loan funds, $169,000 to endowment and similar funds, and $38,000 to the various plant funds.

Transfers among funds include the long-term capital provided through current operations. Mandatory amounts of $340,000 for debt service (principal and interest) and $170,000 for renewals and replacements were transferred to plant funds as required, while $2,000 was transferred to loan funds for a matching grant. In addition, nonmandatory transfers of unrestricted gifts, which might be considered current operating surpluses, were made by the administration in the amount of $650,000, of which $50,000 was designated for loan funds, $550,000 for quasi-endowment (i.e., amounts set aside by the governing board from expendable funds), and $50,000 for plant. Offsetting this was $40,000 as the "portion of unrestricted quasi-endowment funds investment gains appropriated," or transferred from long-term invested funds to current use.

Loan funds. The loan funds balance sheet reports the assets, liabilities, and fund balances of the institution's lending subsidiary, maintained principally to help students finance their education. This capital in recent years has been provided increasingly by the federal government and accounted for variously as refundable advances (liabilities) or restricted grants (fund balances). Loan funds specifically provided by interested private benefactors become restricted fund balances. The institution must often add matching funds, which then become restricted, or it may transfer unrestricted current funds to increase unrestricted loan resources. These inflows and certain outflows of loan funds, by refunds or write-offs, are illustrated in the statement of changes in fund balances.

Currently, the largest part of the loan fund group is represented by the National Defense Student Loan Program. The amount that has been received since inception, which has not been extinguished through the various kinds of write-off procedures available, must be shown as a separate amount owed to the federal government. This amount is ultimately a liability, but it is accounted for as a fund balance to provide an accounting of the increases and decreases in the amounts owed to the government that otherwise would not appear in the statement of changes in fund balances. It should be noted that when a loan is made, the asset classification changes but the fund balance is not affected.

In figure 1 the cash in the loan fund group is to be loaned to students in the future. The investments represent unloaned resources that will be liquidated when needed for loan purposes. The largest asset category is "loans to students, faculty, and staff, less allowance. . . ." Because these loans are not always repaid, they should be reported at their net realizable value as of the reporting date. The high default rate has led most colleges and universities to make an allowance in their financial statements for doubtful loans receivable.

The fund balance, as illustrated, is divided between refundable federal government grants ($50,000) and university funds (of which $483,000 is restricted and $150,000 is unrestricted).

The statement of changes in fund balances shows the kinds of transactions that affect loan fund balances. Government monies are one source of change, as are private gifts and grants restricted to loan purposes. Investments of these funds yield income and gains that also produce changes in the fund balance. In the illustration (figure 2), there are no entries for the granting of loans or the repayment of loans because these result only in a change from one asset category to another (i.e., from cash to loans receivable). When the loans are collected, the repayments are deducted from loans receivable and are added back to cash.

Deductions from the loan funds on the statement of changes in fund balances include loan cancellations and write-offs, refunds to grantors, and charges for administrative and collection costs. Fund balances are also reduced by losses on investments of unloaned cash.

Endowment and similar funds. The assets of endowment and similar funds are mostly long-term investments. Other assets are uninvested cash, some receivables, and instruments that are convertible to cash. The investments of this fund group are so important that extensive comments concerning them generally appear in the notes to the financial statements.

To understand fully the nature of the investments, two kinds of information must be in either the financial statements or the notes to the financial statements: (1) the basis of accounting (e.g., cost or current market value), and (2) the composition of the investment portfolio (e.g., stocks, bonds, mortgages). If accounting is done on a cost basis, information concerning the current market is required, as is information on the performance of the portfolio (e.g., income, gains, and losses in relation to cost and the market). In the example presented, note 1 to the financial statements illustrates the latter type of disclosure (figure 5).

1. Pooling of investments. The concept of investment pooling poses a special accounting problem with respect to investments of endowments and similar funds (and occasionally other fund groups). Though the ability to identify the assets belonging to each fund balance is important, as a practical matter totals are often recorded only for groups of funds. For example, in the current restricted fund group no attempt is normally made to keep separate cash balances for each current restricted fund. Instead, there is an amount that represents total cash for all current restricted funds. This total together with other assets equals the total amount of all fund balances in that group.

In a similar manner, the assets of the endowment and similar funds may be pooled to purchase investments for the benefit of all participating funds. This calls for a particular kind of accounting that treats the individual funds in the pool equitably in terms of the distribution of the income earned by the investments and the gains and losses from trading in investments.

The pooling concept involves the use of market values as the basis for calculating the distribution of participation units to each fund as it enters the pool. The procedure can be summarized as follows: the market value of all assets at the beginning of the pool is determined; units are given an arbitrary value and are then assigned to each fund depending on how much each has contributed to the pool. From that point on, the number of units held by each participating fund is used as a basis for distributing the income earned by the pooled assets and the gains and losses arising from the sale or exchange of investments held by the pool. When a new fund enters the pool, the current market value of the assets in the pool is recalculated, a new unit value (which may be higher or lower than the original value) is determined, and units are assigned to participants in the pool. This is also done when a fund is to be withdrawn from the pool. Note that the assignment of units to funds does not mean that the assets themselves are carried at market value. In fact, the assets may be carried at either market value or cost, depending on the accounting procedure adopted.

2. Types of funds. The fund balances in the endowment and similar funds group may represent several different conditions—for example, truly restricted funds such as endowment, or monies set aside by the governing board with the direction that they are not to be expended now (but may be in the future) and that only the income is to be used. Truly restricted funds are restricted in perpetuity, requiring the investment of the money contributed, and are referred to simply as endowment funds. The restriction on the second type of funds above has a terminal date or ends when a particular event takes place. This type of fund is known as a term endowment. As of the balance sheet date, by law neither of these types of funds can be expended, and the governing board on its own cannot override that restriction.

By contrast, amounts set aside by the governing board from expendable funds can be expended and are therefore termed "quasi-endowment funds." Sometimes these funds are called "funds functioning as endowments." Both expressions are intended to indicate that the amounts so carried can be withdrawn from this category, restored to the current funds group from which they came, and expended for the purposes for which they were either restricted or designated. The fund group is labeled "endowment and similar funds" in recognition of the nature of quasi-endowment funds. If there are only endowment and term endowment monies, the fund group could be labeled "endowment funds."

3. Principal vs. income. An important consideration in accounting for endowments and similar funds is the need to distinguish between principal and income. Endowment funds are peculiar in that legally they are not trust funds but are viewed as such for certain purposes. However, accounting conventions that have been established for endowment funds are patterned after trust fund concepts, which distinguish between principal and income. These conventions dictate that the principal be preserved for the benefit of the remaindermen of the trust whereas the income is available for the life tenant or the income beneficiary. An institution with an endowment fund, however, is both the remaindermen and the life tenant or income beneficiary. One might ask why this concept is important in this situation. One reason for the need to define income is that the donor has stated that the institution can use only the income. Second, there is another party at issue (i.e., the future generation of students who will benefit from the income). Thus, the governing board has the obligation to balance its investment policies so as not to stress either current income or growth to the advantage of a particular generation of students.

The distinction between principal and income determines what monies are accounted for in the endowment and similar funds group. Principal includes the original contribution (or any additional contributions in the case of endowment or term endowment) or, in the case of quasi-endowment, the original transfers (or any subsequent transfers) made by the governing board. Additions to principal would be realized gains or, in accounting for investments at market, the increases in the carrying value of the investments. Deductions would be losses on investments of the endowment fund.

Income gets its definition from tax law, and includes items such as dividends, interest, rents, and royalties. In the case of real estate, income is the rental income less the expenses of operation and depreciation. The income arising from the investment of endowment and similar funds is accounted for in unrestricted current funds if the income is unrestricted, or in the appropriate restricted fund if the income is restricted. A donor occasionally specifies that the restricted income is to be added to the principal. It is important to note that the addition of income to principal by direction of the governing board does not create a true (new) principal in endowment funds.

Some clarification of terms is in order. Restricted endowment funds are actually endowment funds, the income of which is restricted. Quasi-endowment funds are usually classified as unrestricted and only at times as restricted. Unrestricted quasi-endowment funds are amounts that have been transferred from unrestricted current funds. Restricted quasi-endowment funds are established from restricted current funds set aside for investment (only the income is to be used). The accounting for gains, losses, and income of quasi-endowments follows the same rules as the accounting for true endowments; that is, gains and losses are accounted for as part of the principal of the quasi-endowment fund while the income is accounted for in unrestricted current funds (if the quasi-endowment is restricted).

4. <u>Total-return concept</u>. The total-return concept—a relatively new development—eases restrictions on distinguishing between ordinary income and gains. Its intent is to encourage institutions to invest in growth stocks.

Many states have recently enacted laws patterned after a model law that prescribes how investments of institutions should be managed. Under this law it is legally permissible to use a portion of the gains of true endowment funds for the same purposes as ordinary income is used. (It was always possible for the gains of quasi-endowment funds to be so used.) In most states a portion of the gains may now be transferred from the endowment fund. Normally, there are requirements that such transfers can be made only in the face of gains (i.e., it is not possible to make a transfer that would reduce the fund balance below its historical contributed value).

The total-return concept is the means of determining how much of these gains will be used. First, the total earnings potential of the portfolio is estimated (total return is equal to the ordinary income or yield, plus net gains). A spending rate is then calculated that is sufficiently lower than the total-return earnings rate to ensure that the endowment portfolio is supplemented enough to allow for growth (or, at minimum, to compensate for the ravages of inflation). The spending rate is financed first from ordinary income. If the ordinary income is not sufficient to achieve the spending rate, the difference is financed by means of a transfer from gains. In figure 2 the transfer of $40,000, shown as "portion of unrestricted quasi-endowment funds investment gains appropriated," represents the amount necessary to cover the spending rate.

Annuity and life income funds. Annuity and life income funds, which are trust funds, are a special group of invested funds temporarily committed to supporting donor-designated beneficiaries (i.e., for the lifetime of the beneficiaries, or until specific time periods have expired, after which the remaining funds become institutional capital, operating or long-term, unrestricted or restricted, depending on the agreements with the donors).

This fund group is subdivided into annuity funds and life income funds. If the amounts of such funds are relatively insignificant, they may be reported as a subgroup within the endowment and similar funds group. The assets are cash and investments in other assets convertible to cash. The objective of these assets is to produce income.

The distinction between the two kinds of funds is as follows: in an annuity fund a fixed amount is established by the donor and must be paid out even if the ordinary income from investment of the fund is not adequate for the purpose. For this reason, in the payment of an annuity an institution may incur a liability greater than the amount of the income. In this case some of the original principal may have to be paid back. Thus, annuity funds are accounted for through a liability account that expresses the current value of all future payments that must be made, taking into consideration as well the future earnings. Any excess of the asset value over this liability is the fund balance. Periodically, the liability is reevaluated with regard to the estimated remaining life of the annuitant. The liability is then adjusted, with a corresponding adjustment made in the fund balance.

For a life income fund there is an obligation either to pay only the income earned by the specific investments of the fund or to pay a rate of return earned by a group of funds. Because only the income that has been earned is paid out, the obligation is limited and no liability exists as with the annuity fund.

Of the $2,505,000 shown as annuity and life income fund balances at the beginning of the year in the statement of changes in fund balances, only $10,000 matured and, as a restricted amount, moved to endowment for institutional use. A total of $800,000 was received under new agreements, and an additional obligation of $75,000 in actuarial liability was recorded, resulting in ending fund balances of $3,220,000.

The subject of annuity life income funds involves a number of rather complex tax, accounting, and legal issues. In many states annuity funds are regulated as forms of insurance and are subject to jurisdiction of the state insurance regulatory body (e.g., reserve deposits may be required).

Plant funds. Colleges and universities, as distinct from for-profit enterprises and some nonprofit-oriented ones such as hospitals, have traditionally segregated their plant funds accounting and have generally ignored depreciation. The reason is that most plant funds are originally given or appropriated as restricted or, if not, have been so irrevocably committed to fixed assets that they will never be available for any other purpose. If the resulting plant has been donated, the institution cannot very easily justify charging for depreciation or expecting customers to pay for something that was given in the first place to help those customers.

On the other hand, as shown earlier, some colleges and universities not only make capital expenditures out of current operating accounts but also transfer operating funds to plant for debt repayments and plant renewals and replacements, which could be considered a flow of depreciation-like expenses. The flow of funds into and out of plant accounts and the resulting plant assets and fund balances, or equity, are important in the management and protection of that part of the institution's long-term capital.

Direct external contributions to plant funds and amounts of current operating funds transferred to plant during the fiscal year are shown in the statement of changes in fund balances. At the top section of that statement (figure 2), $230,000 in new funds was added directly to unexpended plant funds from various sources. Under the transfers section at the bottom, $50,000 in unrestricted gifts was allocated by administrative decision from current to plant funds. Out of these receipts and the prior unexpended balance of $2,120,000, a total of $1,200,000 was expended for plant facilities (under "expenditures and other deductions" in the middle section of the statement), leaving an unexpended balance at the end of the year of $1,200,000 for future plant needs.

Similarly, $10,000 in new funds was received directly for renewals and replacements and $170,000 was transferred from current funds under third-party requirements (mandatory). Out of these receipts and the beginning fund balance of $380,000, a total of $300,000 was expended for plant facilities, leaving an ending balance of $260,000 for future renewals and replacements. Retirement of indebtedness received $78,000 in new funds from external sources and $340,000 in mandatory transfers from current operations for principal and interest. Out of those inflows and the $293,000 beginning balance, the institution's debt service obligations on its plant were fulfilled (under "expenditures and other deductions" in the middle of the statement), and $300,000 in debt service funds remained for the future.

The last column shows the changes in the institution's net investment, or equity, in its physical facilities (i.e., in its accumulated historical plant cost less associated liabilities). Of the year's additions to net investment in plant, $15,000 was from gifts in kind, $1,550,000 from expenditures by the other plant fund groups and from current funds, and $220,000 from retirement of indebtedness. During the period, $115,000 of plant facilities was disposed of, for a new addition of $1,670,000 and an ending balance of $38,210,000.

Beginning plant fund balances totaled $39,333,000. With all the above additions and deductions, the ending plant fund balances, or the equity in all plant funds, increased only $637,000, to a new total of $39,970,000. It should be noted that only $1,460,000 of the most flexible unexpended and renewal and replacement funds remained; there had been $2,500,000 at the beginning of the period. The difference was committed irrevocably to "bricks and mortar," or equipment.

Many donors, faculty members, students, and trustees do not realize that depreciation, or the cost of wear and tear on physical facilities, is not usually accounted for in tuition and fee charges or in the expenditures of colleges and universities.

In the statement of changes in fund balances (figure 2), the total of current operating funds made available for plant capital includes, under "revenues and other additions," $100,000 (as stated in the parenthetical note) and $220,000 for "retirement of indebtedness" (not interest), and, under "transfers among funds," $170,000 for renewals and replacements and $50,000 "allocated" to plant. Amounts funded from current operations, but really expended for plant, could be considered capital expenditures in lieu of depreciation. In the year illustrated, this would represent only 1.35 percent of the total investment in buildings and equipment, based on the balance sheet amount of $41,600,000 in figure 1.

The sample institution obviously depends heavily on funds from external sources for plant maintenance as well as plant additions. Unfortunately, externally restricted funds are more likely to be given for additions than for preservation of current physical facilities. Over time, this can result in buildings and equipment deterioration that is not recognized in operating statements or balance sheet valuations.

Several comments can be made about the four subgroups of the plant fund group.

1. Unexpended. Unexpended plant funds arise from restricted grants, gifts, and appropriations that can be used only for the acquisition of plant. In the sample institution's statement of changes in fund balances (figure 2), unrestricted gifts were allocated by the governing board for this purpose. This $50,000 nonmandatory transfer will be accounted for in the unrestricted portion of the balances of unexpended plant funds.

When an expenditure of these funds is made, there is (1) a reduction in the fund balance and in cash, and (2) an equal increase in the plant funds subgroup labeled "investment in plant," where the cost of the asset acquired and the increase in net investment in plant are recorded.

Borrowings are an important source of funding for capital outlay. Monies borrowed for acquisition of new plant and equipment are accounted for in this unexpended plant funds subgroup. When the borrowed money is spent, the charge is against the liability account rather than the fund balance. In the investment in plant subgroup the credit is not to net investment in plant but to the reestablishment of a liability.

Construction in progress may be accounted for in unexpended plant funds until the project is complete. Accountability is then established in the investment in plant subgroup. The procedure most commonly followed is to remove the accountability for construction in progress from the unexpended subgroup as quickly as expenditures are made and to carry the construction in progress in the investment in plant subgroup.

2. Renewals and replacements. This subgroup represents monies set aside to renew or replace plant assets presently in use. Here, too, the fund balances (figure 2) are subdivided between restricted and unrestricted. One of the sources of renewal and replacement funds is a portion of the mandatory transfer ($170,000 in figure 2); when mandatory transfers are received, they are classified as restricted funds. The assets (figure 1) consist of cash, investments, and amounts of money that have been turned over to a trustee in accordance with an indenture. These assets ($100,000) are classified as deposits with trustees. Expenditure of these monies results in the reduction of assets and fund balances in this subgroup. Simultaneously, an equal amount is recorded as an increase in net investment in plant and in the investment in plant subgroup. These expenditures often do not result in the acquisition of a capitalizable asset. The amount of such expenditures not capitalized should be disclosed, as illustrated in the parenthetical note

on the caption "expended for plant facilities" in the statement of changes in fund balances. (The note states "including noncapitalized expenditures of $50,000.")

3. Retirement of indebtedness. Funds for this subgroup may come from contributions or grants that are made for this explicit purpose and are restricted. (This is the case in the sample institution.) Most frequently, the monies for this subgroup come from a mandatory transfer (note the $340,000 shown in the transfer section of the statement of changes in fund balances). Amounts so received are classified as restricted fund balances. If the governing board sets aside excess funds for the retirement of indebtedness, such amounts in excess of what is required would be nonmandatory transfers and would be classified as unrestricted. Funds for retirement of indebtedness are used to meet two kinds of obligations: (1) interest expense, which should be shown separately (see the $190,000 deduction), and (2) amortization of the debt (see the $220,000 deduction). Amortization of the debt results in another set of entries in the investment in plant subgroup. In figure 1 there would be a reduction of the liability for bonds payable equal to the debt amortization payment made in the retirement of the indebtedness funds, and there would be a corresponding credit for increase to the net investment in plant of $220,000. Thus, as debt is reduced the equity in net assets is increased.

4. Investment in plant. The assets of this subgroup consist of the carrying values of land improvements, buildings, equipment, library books, museum collections, and other similar capital holdings with a long-term life. Some of these are depreciable.

These assets are to be carried at their historical cost until disposed of. In earlier years some institutions carried such assets at some other amount (e.g., periodic appraisal value), either out of preference or because the original cost records had been lost or destroyed. When historical cost information is not available, it is permissible for an institution to obtain a professional estimate of the *historical* costs and to use the estimate as the basis for reporting.

Rules must be established by the institution to determine when a particular expenditure results in the acquisition of a capital asset. For example, items of movable equipment should be capitalized, provided they have a significant value and that they have a useful life that extends beyond at least a year. (Otherwise the items do not have capital value.) The value thresholds vary widely from institution to institution. The Cost Accounting Standards Board established costing rules for all contractors employing federal funds and set certain limits beyond which an expenditure is classified as a capital addition. Another rule must be made to determine when a renovation becomes a capital asset. For example, a minor renovation probably has little value associated with it and would not be considered a capitalizable asset. On the other hand, a renovation that extended the life of the asset or permitted an entirely new use of an existing facility will probably be capitalized. Finally, new assets are added to the carrying values of the asset section of this subgroup, and assets that have been sold, destroyed, stolen, lost, or otherwise eliminated from the possession of the institution should be removed from the records (i.e., their carrying values should be removed).

If debt is incurred by the institution to finance working capital, it should not be carried in the plant fund but rather as a liability of current funds. This rule holds even though plant assets may be pledged as collateral against the loan. The reader of financial statements needs to know a great deal about the liabilities of plant funds and other liabilities of a long-term nature that may appear in other fund groups. Some disclosure requirements in this regard are therefore illustrated in the notes to the financial statements (see figure 5).

The fund balance of the investment in plant subgroup is referred to as net investment in plant. It is not classified as restricted or unrestricted because it is simply the accountability for the net asset values carried in this section. No further future use is intended. Thus, any restrictions that may have been imposed on the funds used to finance these assets generally have been met. There are, however, some instances of gifts that carry restrictions of a second-generation nature. For example, the initial restrictions may require that the funds be used for the acquisition of a building. An additional restriction might require that, in the event the building is later sold, the proceeds of the sale be used for a replacement building. This situation is rare, however.

In the statement of changes in fund balances (figure 2), increases in the net investment in plant arise from the expenditure of unexpended plant funds and renewal and replacement funds. Increases also arise from debt reductions (reflected in the decrease in funds for the retirement of indebtedness) and from contributions-in-kind such as a building, land, or equipment.

Decreases in the net investment in plant represent the elimination from the capital assets inventory of those assets that are retired, sold, disposed of, or destroyed. When such assets are eliminated, the total carrying value of the asset is deducted from the asset category and from the net investment in plant. Any cash proceeds received as a result of this retirement are taken in the unexpended plant fund, and, in the absence of any of the secondary types of restrictions mentioned earlier, are classified as an addition to the unrestricted portion of unexpended plant funds. Thus, the net gain or loss from the sale or disposal of the capital asset does not appear separately. Another major deduction would be the depreciation of capital assets (if such a practice is followed).

Net investment in plant can increase for a reason linked to the peculiar operations of colleges and universities. Many institutions include in the operating budgets of the various departments a provision for minor items of equipment. In some cases there is a policy of equipment replacement with respect to certain types of assets. For example, typewriters may be replaced on a scheduled basis. The amount that will be expended annually for this purpose is budgeted in that department. Therefore, the expenditure of current funds for this purpose becomes part of the functional expenditures set forth in the statement of current funds revenues, expenditures, and other changes and in the statement of changes in fund balances for unrestricted or restricted current funds. Another kind of capital outlay that might be financed in a similar manner from current funds expenditures is library books. These expenditures of current funds for the replacement of capital assets are reported first as expenditures of current funds, and are then picked up as assets and as additions to the fund balance of the investment in plant subgroup. In the sample institution $100,000 charged to current fund expenditures is also added to net investment in plant.

STATEMENT OF CURRENT FUNDS REVENUES, EXPENDITURES, AND OTHER CHANGES

Revenues. The sources of revenue include tuition and fee income; appropriations received from federal, state, and local government sources; grants and contracts from these same sources; private gifts, grants, and contracts; endowment income (i.e., income generated by the investments of endowment and similar funds); and sales and services of educational departments as well as sales and services of auxiliary enterprises (see figure 3). The sales and services of a hospital associated with the institution would be shown separately. There may be certain other institutional activities rendering unique services that would be separately accounted for, or accounted for as a separate source.

All unrestricted resources that are earned by the institution or come into the institution for the first time are accounted for initially as unrestricted current fund revenues. By contrast, all restricted amounts are accounted for initially in another fund group depending on the nature of the restriction.

Expenditures. Expenditures are categorized according to the major functions of the institution (e.g., instruction, research, public service). Auxiliary enterprises and hospital expenditures are shown separately.

Mandatory transfers are shown on the statement of current funds, revenues, expenditures, and other changes, together with, but separate from, the current fund expenditures. The transfers are divided according to their relation to the educational and general programs of the institution, to auxiliary enterprises, or to a hospital. On the statement of changes in fund balances, mandatory transfers are shown in the transfers section.

Mandatory transfers. In the example (figure 3) a mandatory transfer represents an amount of cash to be transferred from the unrestricted current fund. It will go to that restricted fund for which the transfer is made. In most cases the transfer is mandated by a debt instrument (e.g., a bond indenture, which requires the periodic setting aside of funds to cover principal repayment), by interest expenses, and by the need to accumulate certain reserves for renewal and replacement. These required amounts are transferred to, accounted for in, and expended from the plant fund group. Through the transfer the amounts are deducted from current funds. In this example the amounts deducted are unrestricted, but when they are accounted for in the plant fund they are classified as restricted amounts because they are placed there by reason of the legally binding instrument.

Another mandatory transfer illustrated in the example is the matching requirement of the National Defense Student Loan program. The loan fund matching requirement in this example is being financed from the unrestricted current fund, and the mandatory transfer is to the loan fund group, where the amount transferred would have to be classified as a restricted balance.

Nonmandatory transfers. These transfers are discretionary in nature and are carried out by the governing board. Generally, they are amounts that are unrestricted and are shifted from one major fund group to another to reflect designations by the board. When unrestricted current funds are transferred on a nonmandatory basis to another fund group, it is imperative that the label "unrestricted" be carried along so that when it appears in the other group the reader knows that the amount transferred can be reversed. (Mandatory transfers, once made in accordance with the bond indenture, can never be reversed because they must be used exclusively to serve the debt.)

Other changes. One such change is the accounting for indirect cost recovery from funding sources. The primary source of this kind of cost recovery is federal funds that are used to finance various sponsored research, training, and other activities. The source of recovery becomes the revenue source used to account for the amount of indirect cost recovery. This accounting is difficult in that indirect costs are part of the total grant received by an institution. This total grant is first accounted for as an addition to a restricted current fund. The indirect cost recovery, however, is not viewed as an expenditure of a restricted fund but rather as an allocation of that amount into unrestricted current fund revenue for the purpose of reimbursing the institution. Two actions must be taken: (1) the amount must be deducted from the fund balance in restricted current funds (this can be seen as a separate line on the statement of changes), and (2) the amount must be recorded as revenue in unrestricted current funds. Although this amount is not separately labeled, it can be traced. In the federal, state, and local grants and contracts amounts in the unrestricted column of the revenue statement (figure 3), these three figures total $35,000, which is equal to the amount of indirect cost recovery deducted from the current restricted fund balances under expenditures and other deductions in figure 2. Another kind of deduction that is shown separately in both statements (in the amount of $20,000) is the refunding to a grantor of an unspent amount of a current restricted fund.

All revenues, additions, expenditures, and mandatory and nonmandatory transfers collectively yield the net change in fund balances for the year. These amounts must be shown at the bottom of the statement of current funds revenues, expenditures, and other changes, and also near the bottom of the statement of changes of fund balances (just before the fund balances themselves).

Encumbrances. An encumbrance is a commitment to pay for goods or services when such are received. The encumbrance is accounted for as a reduction of available funds (i.e., as a commitment), but must at all times be distinguished from true liabilities. True liability exists once goods or services have been received. In many cases that liability may result in the incurrence of an expense (i.e., when a value is carried forward as unexpired costs, it becomes an asset). Therefore, neither encumbrances that are not true liabilities as of the reporting date nor outstanding unliquidated encumbrances are included in the statement. If the latter are reported at all, they are shown either as a segregation of the fund balance to which they relate or as amounts disclosed in the notes to the financial statements.

NOTES TO FINANCIAL STATEMENTS

The purpose of these notes (see figure 5) is to provide further disclosure of key information that is considered necessary according to generally accepted accounting principles for colleges and universities. For example, some notes for the sample institution relate to such matters as the composition, market value, and performance of investments; outstanding commitments in the area of major items of construction; obligations under pension plans; and details concerning liabilities for short- and long-term debt.

The nature and the means of repayment of any significant interfund receivables must be disclosed in the notes to the financial statements. If the interfund receivable cannot be collected from the owing fund, consideration must be given to making a permanent transfer (thereby eliminating the interfund receivable and payable).

In their financial statements many nonprofit organizations, including a number of colleges and universities, record pledges receivable as assets and as accountabilities. However, many institutions document pledges or have relationships with potential donors such that it is not possible to determine the net realizable value of outstanding pledges. In those circumstances uncollected pledges are not included in the basic financial statements, though all significant pledges must be disclosed in the notes, as illustrated in the case of the sample institution.

Figure 1: Sample Educational Institution
Balance Sheet
June 30, 19___
with comparative figures at June 30, 19___

Assets

Current Funds

	Current Year	Prior Year
Unrestricted		
Cash	$ 210,000	$ 110,000
Investments	450,000	360,000
Accounts receivable, less allowance of $18,000 both years	228,000	175,000
Inventories, at lower of cost (first-in, first-out basis) or market	90,000	80,000
Prepaid expenses and deferred charges	28,000	20,000
Total unrestricted	1,006,000	745,000
Restricted		
Cash	145,000	101,000
Investments	175,000	165,000
Accounts receivable, less allowance of $8,000 both years	68,000	160,000
Unbilled charges	72,000	—
Total restricted	460,000	426,000
Total current funds	1,466,000	1,171,000

(cont.)

Liabilities and Fund Balances

Current Funds

	Current Year	Prior Year
Unrestricted		
Accounts payable	$ 125,000	$ 100,000
Accrued liabilities	20,000	15,000
Students' deposits	30,000	35,000
Due to other funds	158,000	120,000
Deferred credits	30,000	20,000
Fund balance	643,000	455,000
Total unrestricted	1,006,000	745,000
Restricted		
Accounts payable	14,000	5,000
Fund balances	446,000	421,000
Total restricted	460,000	426,000
Total current funds	1,466,000	1,171,000

(cont.)

Assets (cont.)

Loan Funds

Cash	30,000	20,000
Investments	100,000	100,000
Loans to students, faculty, and staff, less allowance of $10,000 current year and $9,000 prior year	550,000	382,000
Due from unrestricted funds	3,000	
Total loan funds	683,000	502,000

Endowment and Similar Funds

Cash	100,000	101,000
Investments	13,900,000	11,800,000
Total endowment and similar funds	14,000,000	11,901,000

Liabilities and Fund Balances (cont.)

Loan Funds

Fund balances		
U.S. government grants refundable	50,000	33,000
University funds		
Restricted	483,000	369,000
Unrestricted	150,000	100,000
Total loan funds	683,000	502,000

Endowment and Similar Funds

Fund balances		
Endowment	7,800,000	6,740,000
Term endowment	3,840,000	3,420,000
Quasi-endowment—unrestricted	1,000,000	800,000
Quasi-endowment—restricted	1,360,000	941,000
Total endowment and similar funds	14,000,000	11,901,000

Assets (cont.)

Annuity and Life Income Funds

Annuity funds		
Cash	$ 55,000	$ 45,000
Investments	3,260,000	3,010,000
Total annuity funds	3,315,000	3,055,000
Life income funds		
Cash	15,000	15,000
Investments	2,045,000	1,740,000
Total life income funds	2,060,000	1,755,000
Total annuity and life income funds	5,375,000	4,810,000

Plant Funds

Unexpended		
Cash	275,000	410,000
Investments	1,285,000	1,590,000
Due from unrestricted current funds	150,000	120,000
Total unexpended	1,710,000	2,120,000

(cont.)

Liabilities and Fund Balances (cont.)

Annuity and Life Income Funds

Annuity funds		
Annuities payable	$ 2,150,000	$ 2,300,000
Fund balances	1,165,000	755,000
Total annuity funds	3,315,000	3,055,000
Life income funds		
Income payable	5,000	5,000
Fund balances	2,055,000	1,750,000
Total life income funds	2,060,000	1,755,000
Total annuity and life income funds	5,375,000	4,810,000

Plant Funds

Unexpended		
Accounts payable	10,000	—
Notes payable	100,000	—
Bonds payable	400,000	—
Fund balances		
Restricted	1,000,000	1,860,000
Unrestricted	200,000	260,000
Total unexpended	1,710,000	2,120,000

(cont.)

Assets (cont.)

Renewals and replacements		
Cash	5,000	4,000
Investments	150,000	286,000
Deposits with trustees	100,000	90,000
Due from unrestricted current funds	5,000	—
Total renewals and replacements	260,000	380,000
Retirement of indebtedness		
Cash	50,000	40,000
Deposits with trustees	250,000	253,000
Total retirement of indebtedness	300,000	293,000
Investment in plant		
Land	500,000	500,000
Land improvements	1,000,000	1,110,000
Buildings	25,000,000	24,060,000
Equipment	15,000,000	14,200,000
Library books	100,000	80,000
Total investment in plant	41,600,000	39,950,000
Total plant funds	43,870,000	42,743,000

Liabilities and Fund Balances (cont.)

Renewals and replacements		
Fund balances		
Restricted	25,000	180,000
Unrestricted	235,000	200,000
Total renewals and replacements	260,000	380,000
Retirement of indebtedness		
Fund balances		
Restricted	185,000	125,000
Unrestricted	115,000	168,000
Total retirement of indebtedness	300,000	293,000
Investment in plant		
Notes payable	790,000	810,000
Bonds payable	2,200,000	2,400,000
Mortgages payable	400,000	200,000
Net investment in plant	38,210,000	36,540,000
Total investment in plant	41,600,000	39,950,000
Total plant funds	43,870,000	42,743,000

Assets (cont.)

Agency Funds

Cash	50,000	70,000
Investments	60,000	20,000
Total agency funds	110,000	90,000

Liabilities and Fund Balances (cont.)

Agency Funds

Deposits held in custody		
for others	110,000	90,000
Total agency funds	110,000	90,000

Source: College & University Business Administration, 4th ed. (Washington, DC: National Association of College and University Business Officers, 1982), pp. 456–457.

Figure 2: Sample Educational Institution
Statement of Changes in Fund Balances
Year Ended June 30, 19____

	Current Funds		Loan Funds	Endowment and Similar Funds	Annuity and Life Income Funds	Plant Funds			
	Unrestricted	Restricted				Unexpended	Renewals and Replacements	Retirement of Indebtedness	Investment in Plant
Revenues and other additions									
Unrestricted current fund revenues	$7,540,000								
Expired term endowment—restricted						50,000			
State appropriations—restricted						50,000			
Federal grants and contracts—restricted		500,000							
Private gifts, grants, and contracts—restricted		370,000	100,000	1,500,000	800,000	115,000		65,000	15,000
Investment income—restricted		224,000	12,000	10,000		5,000	5,000	5,000	
Realized gains on investments—unrestricted				109,000					
Realized gains on investments—restricted			4,000	50,000		10,000	5,000	5,000	
Interest on loans receivable			7,000						
U.S. government advances			18,000						
Expended for plant facilities (including $100,000 charged to current funds expenditures)									1,550,000
Retirement of indebtedness									220,000
Accrued interest on sale of bonds								3,000	
Matured annuity and life income restricted to endowment				10,000					
Total revenues and other additions	7,540,000	1,094,000	141,000	1,679,000	800,000	230,000	10,000	78,000	1,785,000

Expenditures and other deductions

Educational and general expenditures	4,400,000	1,014,000							
Auxiliary enterprises expenditures	1,830,000								
Indirect costs recovered		35,000							
Refunded to grantors		20,000	10,000						
Loan cancellations and write-offs			1,000						
Administrative and collection costs			1,000						
Adjustment of actuarial liability for annuities payable					75,000				
Expended for plant facilities (including noncapitalized expenditures of $50,000)						1,200,000	300,000		
Retirement of indebtedness								220,000	
Interest on indebtedness								190,000	
Disposal of plant facilities									115,000
Expired term endowments ($40,000 unrestricted, $50,000 restricted to plant)				90,000					
Matured annuity and life income funds restricted to endowment					10,000				
Total expenditures and other deductions	6,230,000	1,069,000	12,000	90,000	85,000	1,200,000	300,000	411,000	115,000

Transfers among funds—additions/(deductions)

Mandatory:									
Principal and interest	(340,000)							340,000	
Renewals and replacements	(170,000)						170,000		
Loan fund matching grant	(2,000)		2,000						
Unrestricted gifts allocated	(650,000)		50,000	550,000	50,000				
Portion of unrestricted quasi-endowment funds investment gains appropriated	40,000			(40,000)					
Total transfers	(1,122,000)		52,000	510,000	50,000		170,000	340,000	
Net increase/(decrease) for the year	188,000	25,000	181,000	2,099,000	715,000	(920,000)	(120,000)	7,000	1,670,000
Fund balance at beginning of year	455,000	421,000	502,000	11,901,000	2,505,000	2,120,000	380,000	293,000	36,540,000
Fund balance at end of year	643,000	446,000	683,000	14,000,000	3,220,000	1,200,000	260,000	300,000	38,210,000

Source: *College & University Business Administration*, 4th ed. (Washington, DC: National Association of College and University Business Officers, 1982), pp. 458–459.

Figure 3: Sample Educational Institution
Statement of Current Funds Revenues, Expenditures, and Other Changes
Year Ended June 30, 19____

| | Current Year | | | Prior-Year |
	Unrestricted	Restricted	Total	Total
Revenues				
Tuition and fees	$2,600,000		$2,600,000	$2,300,000
Federal appropriations	500,000		500,000	500,000
State appropriations	700,000		700,000	700,000
Local appropriations	100,000		100,000	100,000
Federal grants and contracts	20,000	$ 375,000	395,000	350,000
State grants and contracts	10,000	25,000	35,000	200,000
Local grants and contracts	5,000	25,000	30,000	45,000
Private gifts, grants, and contracts	850,000	380,000	1,230,000	1,190,000
Endowment income	325,000	209,000	534,000	500,000
Sales and services of educational activities	190,000		190,000	195,000
Sales and services of auxiliary enterprises	2,200,000		2,200,000	2,100,000
Expired term endowment	40,000		40,000	
Other sources (if any)				
Total current revenues	7,540,000	1,014,000	8,554,000	8,180,000
Expenditures and mandatory transfers				
Educational and general				
Instruction	2,960,000	489,000	3,449,000	3,300,000
Research	100,000	400,000	500,000	650,000
Public service	130,000	25,000	155,000	175,000
Academic support	250,000		250,000	225,000

Student services	200,000		200,000	195,000
Institutional support	450,000		450,000	445,000
Operation and maintenance of plant	220,000		220,000	200,000
Scholarships and fellowships	90,000	100,000	190,000	180,000
Educational and general expenditures	4,400,000	1,014,000	5,414,000	5,370,000
Mandatory transfers for:				
Principal and interest	90,000		90,000	50,000
Renewals and replacements	100,000		100,000	80,000
Loan fund matching grant	2,000		2,000	
Total educational and general	4,592,000	1,014,000	5,606,000	5,500,000
Auxiliary enterprises				
Expenditures	1,830,000		1,830,000	1,730,000
Mandatory transfers for:				
Principal and interest	250,000		250,000	250,000
Renewals and replacements	70,000		70,000	70,000
Total auxiliary enterprises	2,150,000		2,150,000	2,050,000
Total expenditures and mandatory transfers	6,742,000	1,014,000	7,756,000	7,550,000
Other transfers and additions/(deductions)				
Excess of restricted receipts over transfers to revenues		45,000	45,000	40,000
Refunded to grantors	(650,000)	(20,000)	(20,000)	
Unrestricted gifts allocated to other funds			(650,000)	(510,000)
Portion of quasi-endowment gains appropriated	40,000		40,000	
Net increase in fund balances	188,000	25,000	213,000	160,000

Source: College & University Business Administration, 4th ed. (Washington, DC: National Association of College and University Business Officers, 1982). pp. 460–461.

Figure 4: Sample Educational Institution
Summary of Significant Accounting Policies
June 30, 19_____

The significant accounting policies followed by Sample Educational Institution are described below to enhance the usefulness of the financial statements to the reader.

Accrual Basis

The financial statements of Sample Educational Institution have been prepared on the accrual basis except for depreciation accounting as explained in notes 1 and 2 to the financial statements. The statement of current funds revenues, expenditures, and other changes is a statement of financial activities of current funds related to the current reporting period. It does not purport to present the results of operations or the net income or loss for the period as would a statement of income or a statement of revenues and expenses.

To the extent that current funds are used to finance plant assets, the amounts so provided are accounted for as (1) expenditures, in the case of normal replacement of movable equipment and library books; (2) mandatory transfers, in the case of required provisions for debt amortization and interest and equipment renewal and replacement; and (3) transfers of a nonmandatory nature for all other cases.

Fund Accounting

In order to ensure observance of limitations and restrictions placed on the use of the resources available to the Institution, the accounts of the Institution are maintained in accordance with the principles of "fund accounting." This is the procedure by which resources for various purposes are classified for accounting and reporting purposes into funds that are in accordance with activities or objectives specified. Separate accounts are maintained for each fund; however, in the accompanying financial statements, funds that have similar characteristics have been combined into fund groups. Accordingly, all financial transactions have been recorded and reported by fund group.

Within each fund group, fund balances restricted by outside sources are so indicated and are distinguished from unrestricted funds allocated to specific purposes by action of the governing board. Externally restricted funds may only be utilized in accordance with the purposes established by the source of such funds and are in contrast with unrestricted funds over which the governing board retains full control to use in achieving any of its institutional purposes.

Endowment funds are subject to the restrictions of gift instruments requiring in perpetuity that the principal be invested and the income only be utilized. Term endowment funds are similar to endowment funds except that upon the passage of a stated period of time or the occurrence of a particular event, all or part of the principal may be expended. While quasi-endowment funds have been established by the governing board for the same purposes as endowment funds, any portion of quasi-endowment funds may be expended.

All gains and losses arising from the sale, collection, or other disposition of investments and other noncash assets are accounted for in the fund which owned such assets. Ordinary income derived from investments, receivables, and the like is accounted for in the fund owning such assets, except for income derived from investments of endowment and similar funds, which income is accounted for in the fund to which it is restricted or, if unrestricted, as revenues in unrestricted current funds.

All other unrestricted revenue is accounted for in the unrestricted current fund. Restricted gifts, grants, appropriations, endowment income, and other restricted resources are accounted for in the appropriate restricted funds. Restricted current funds are reported as revenues and expenditures when expended for current operating purposes.

Other Significant Accounting Policies

Other significant accounting policies are set forth in the financial statements and the notes thereto.

Source: College & University Business Administration, 4th ed. (Washington, DC: National Association of College and University Business Officers, 1982), pp. 462–463.

Figure 5: Sample Educational Institution
Notes to Financial Statements
June 30, 19____

1. Investments exclusive of physical plant are recorded at cost; investments received by gift are carried at market value at the date of acquisition. Quoted market values of investments (all marketable securities) of the funds indicated were as follows:

	Current year	Prior year
Unrestricted current funds	$ 510,000	$ 390,000
Restricted current funds	180,000	165,000
Loan funds	105,000	105,000
Unexpended plant funds	1,287,000	1,600,000
Renewal and replacement funds	145,000	285,000
Agency funds	60,000	20,000

Investments of endowment and similar funds and annuity and life income funds are composed of the following:

	Carrying value	
	Current year	Prior year
Endowment and similar funds:		
Corporate stocks and bonds (approximate market, current year $15,000,000, prior year $10,900,000)	$13,000,000	$10,901,000
Rental properties—less accumulated depreciation, current year $500,000, prior year $400,000	900,000	899,000
	13,900,000	11,800,000
Annuity funds:		
U.S. bonds (approximate market, current year $200,000, prior year $100,000)	200,000	110,000
Corporate stocks and bonds (approximate market, current year $3,070,000, prior year $2,905,000)	3,060,000	2,900,000
	3,260,000	3,010,000

(cont.)

Life income funds:

Municipal bonds (approximate market, current year $1,400,000, prior year $1,340,000)	1,500,000	1,300,000
Corporate stocks and bonds (approximate market, current year $650,000, prior year $400,000)	545,000	440,000
	2,045,000	1,740,000

Assets of endowment funds, except nonmarketable investments of term endowment having a book value of $200,000 and quasi-endowment having a book value of $800,000, are pooled on a market value basis, with each individual fund subscribing to or disposing of units on the basis of the value per unit at market value at the beginning of the calendar quarter within which the transaction takes place. Of the total units each having a market value of $15.00, 600,000 units were owned by endowment, 280,000 units by term endowment, and 120,000 units by quasi-endowment at June 30, 19____.

The following tabulation summarizes changes in relationships between cost and market values of the pooled assets:

	Pooled Assets		Net Gains (Losses)	Market Value per Unit
	Market	Cost		
End of year	$15,000,000	$13,000,000	$2,000,000	$15.00
Beginning of year	10,900,000	10,901,000	(1,000)	12.70
Unrealized net gains for year			2,001,000	
Realized net gains for year			159,000	
Total net gains for year			$2,160,000	$ 2.30

The average annual earnings per unit, exclusive of net gains, were $.56 for the year.

2. Physical plant and equipment are stated at cost at date of acquisition or fair value at date of donation in the case of gifts, except land acquired prior to 1940, which is valued at appraisal value in 1940 at $300,000. Depreciation on physical plant and equipment is not recorded.

3. Long-term debt includes: bonds payable due in annual installments varying from $45,000 to $55,000 with interest at 5⅞%, the final installment being due in 19____, collateralized by trust indenture covering land, buildings, and equipment known as Smith dormitory carried in the accounts at $2,500,000, and pledged net revenue from the operations of said dormitory; and mortgages payable due in varying amounts to 19____ with interest at 6%, collateralized by property carried in the accounts at $800,000 and pledged revenue of the Student Union amounting to approximately $65,000 per year.

4. The Institution has certain contributory pension plans for academic and nonacademic personnel. Total pension expense for the year was $350,000, which includes amortization of prior service cost over a period of 20 years. The Institution's policy is to fund pension costs accrued, including periodic funding of prior years' accruals not previously funded. The actuarially computed value of vested benefits as of June 30, 19____ exceeded net assets of the pension fund by approximately $300,000.

5. Contracts have been let for the construction of additional classroom buildings in the amount of $3,000,000. Construction and equipment are estimated to total $5,000,000, which will be financed by available resources and an issue of bonds payable over a period of 40 years amounting to $4,000,000.

6. All interfund borrowings have been made from unrestricted funds. The amounts due to plant funds from current unrestricted funds are payable within one year without interest. The amount due to loan funds from current unrestricted funds is payable currently.
7. Pledges totaling $260,000, restricted to plant fund uses, are due to be collected over the next three fiscal years in the amounts of $120,000, $80,000, and $60,000, respectively. It is not practicable to estimate the net realizable value of such pledges.

Source: College & University Business Administration, 4th ed. (Washington, DC: National Association of College and University Business Officers, 1982), pp. 463–466.

FOR FURTHER READING

Easy-to-understand pamphlets on the interpretation of financial statements are distributed by a number of stockbrokerages. One of the best is offered by Merrill Lynch. Although these documents address the for-profit sector, many of the principles of accounting are relevant to the nonprofit sector as well.

A good introduction to fund accounting is provided by Robert N. Anthony and Regina E. Herzlinger, *Management Control in Nonprofit Organizations,* rev. ed. (Homewood, IL: Richard D. Irwin, Inc., 1980). For those readers willing to tackle a technical discussion of accounting, a thorough text is Ray M. Powell, *Accounting Procedures for Institutions* (Notre Dame, IN: University of Notre Dame Press, 1978). A good overview of the technical aspects of institutional accounting is provided by *College & University Business Administration,* 4th ed. (Washington, DC: National Association of College and University Business Officers, 1982).

8 / Approaches to Budgeting

The purpose of this chapter is to describe briefly several approaches to budgeting: incremental budgeting; planning, programming, and budgeting systems (PPBS); zero-base budgeting; performance budgeting; formula budgeting; and cost-center budgeting. These approaches are not mutually exclusive—aspects of each may overlap. However, each approach is distinctive in its focus of attention and in the emphasis on different kinds of information.

The incremental approach focuses primarily on increases or decreases rather than on the budget base, which presumably was examined in previous years. Planning, programming, and budgeting systems focus on the substance of programs and activities to weigh their costs and benefits (this may have implications for academic freedom and institutional autonomy). Zero-base budgeting attempts to consider *everything* significant. Performance budgeting focuses on measures of program or activity performance. Formula budgeting is concerned mainly with the "fair share" distribution of resources among institutions. Finally, cost-center budgeting calls attention to the relative ability of a unit to be self-supporting.

181

INCREMENTAL BUDGETING

It is difficult to avoid the playful definition that incremental budgeting is how most individuals, departments, and institutions manage their resources most of the time. That is, the financial situations of most individuals, departments, and institutions change only modestly most of the time from one budget cycle to another. This observation allows for the possibility that individual or organizational fortunes may advance or decline. Because the change in financial resources from one fiscal year to another is generally small compared with the financial resource base of the previous year, the way in which individuals and organizations spend their resources typically varies only at the margin from one fiscal year to another. The pattern of expenditures for most individuals, departments, and institutions is largely determined by continuing commitments. (For political and economic reasons it is often extremely difficult to upset these commitments.) The incremental or decremental changes in the base budget from one budget cycle to another tend to be too small to have a major impact on historical spending patterns.

The above observations are not to argue that significant fluctuations in the amounts of resources available or in the demands placed on available resources do not occur from one fiscal year to another. For example, an oil crisis that drives up the cost of energy or a large loss of tuition income resulting from an unanticipated enrollment decline could lead to major reductions in expenditures in other portions of the budget. Such changes would not be considered incremental or decremental.

Incrementalism is as much a framework for analyzing organizational or political behavior as it is an empirical description of that reality. Political scientist Charles E. Lindblom labeled the concept as "the science of muddling through." Within any organization or political arena the key actors usually have different priorities and different value systems that sometimes conflict. The direction of an organization is arrived at through a complex array of negotiations among the key actors. Frequently the only way to accommodate competing plans for the direction of an organization or political coalition is to make changes at the margin only. Also, when the costs of information gathering are high or when there is considerable uncertainty about the future, there is a tendency for organizations to hedge by moving cautiously through modest changes (i.e., to avoid any negative unanticipated consequences of major changes, organizations make adjustments at the margin). Most organizations, like most individuals, seek a stable existence.

In the literature of political science in general and budgeting in particular there has been considerable criticism of the incremental approach to decision making. Some observers, including Lance T. LeLoup (1978, 488–509), have examined the literature of empirical studies in budgeting and argue that though major changes in policy direction *are* made by organizations, those changes are at times masked by historical budget data. Other criticisms such as the following come from the normative level: incrementalism does not encourage rational examination of the full spectrum of policy choices and selection of the best one; the objective of incremental decision making is to minimize conflict rather than to make the best policy choice; incremental budgeting does not examine the budget base or the array of existing fiscal commitments, but focuses on changes to those commitments; incrementalism is driven more by political demands than by analytical assessments of requirements.

The weaknesses of incremental budgeting are also its strengths. It is simpler, easier to apply, more controllable, more adaptable, and more flexible than modern alternatives such as program-planning-budgeting, zero-base budgeting, and indexed entitlements. The fact that traditional incremental budgeting has endured while several budget innovations have had minimal success speaks to the strengths of the incremental approach.

PLANNING, PROGRAMMING, AND BUDGETING SYSTEMS (PPBS)

PPBS evolved in the early 1960s from a number of concepts and techniques that were in large part independent of the budgeting system: operations research, economic analysis, general systems theory, and systems analysis. The PPBS approach is essentially a means to link systematically the planning process to the allocation of resources. Several characteristics of PPBS are its macroeconomic perspective, focus on centralized decision making, long-range orientation, and systematic analysis of alternative choices in terms of relative costs and benefits.

The primary conceptual components of the PPBS approach are the program budget and cost-benefit analysis. A program budget organizes and presents information about the costs and benefits of an organization's activities (i.e., programs). A program plan establishes goals and objectives for the organization and relates them to the organization's activities. The costs and benefits of alternative ways of reaching the goals and objectives are established through an examination of resource requirements and estimated benefits to be gained from alternative programs. An important aspect of the program budget is projection of the costs and outputs of programs over a number of years to provide a long-term view of the fiscal implications of those programs.

The cost-benefit aspect of PPBS involves a rigorous quantitative analysis of policy alternatives. Goals and objectives and the desired degree of achievement of them must be quantified, as must the costs and benefits of policy alternatives.

The PPBS concept has generally been more appealing on paper than in practice. The federal government's experiment with PPBS began in the Defense Department in the early 1960s and was expanded to other federal agencies. However, the federal bureaucracy did not assimilate the PPBS framework and the system died. Several state governments and institutions have also experimented with PPBS or modifications thereof without noteworthy success. The positive features of the PPBS approach continue to encourage other governments and organizations to experiment with it. Those features include grouping activities by function to obtain output-oriented cost information; estimation of future expenditures in cases where multiyear commitments are made; and quantitative evaluation in situations where it is necessary to screen policy alternatives.

The disadvantages of PPBS are numerous. The approach calls for strong central management in that it requires agreement to be reached on goals and objectives. Moreover, in some settings, particularly institutions of higher education, it is difficult to reach an understanding of what constitutes a program. Also, it is difficult to establish specific outcomes for programs that may have joint outcomes. PPBS focuses more on what has to be accomplished than on operational tools for implementation of goals and objectives. Program accounting often yields information of limited value because it reflects arbitrary cost allocations that are frequently not supported by the accounting systems. A particularly troublesome limitation is that, while it makes sense conceptually to aggregate activities in programs, most organizations are not structured by program. That is, a program usually cuts across several organizational units. In most cases resources are allocated by organizational unit rather than program structure because there is greater accountability in the former. With the responsibility for programs spread across several organizational units, it is difficult to control the flow of resources on the basis of program needs. Generally, it is easier to distribute resources to organizational units on the basis of functional needs (e.g., instruction, research, service, physical plant maintenance, and academic support) and to control resources on the same basis.

PPBS also assumes considerable centralized knowledge of the organization and its future direction. The costs associated with collecting this information and performing the detailed analyses of alternative plans can be significant.

ZERO-BASE BUDGETING

Zero-base budgeting is a rationalist decision-making procedure with a microeconomic focus. In contrast to the centralized PPBS approach, zero-base budgeting is initiated at the lowest levels in an organization. It assumes no budgets from prior years; instead, each year's budget is started from a base of zero. Each budget unit in the organization evaluates its goals and objectives and justifies its activities in terms of both the benefits and the consequences of not performing the activities. This evaluation is in the form of a decision package, which includes a description of the activity, a definition of alternative levels of activity (including minimum and maximum levels), measures of performance, and costs and benefits. Decision packages at one level of the organization are ranked in priority order and forwarded to the next level of review. Each package in turn is ranked at successively higher administrative levels and decisions are made regarding the distribution of resources to each unit.

The most obvious disadvantage of zero-base budgeting, and the one most often cited when the method has been put into practice, is that it assumes no budget history. Thus, it does not recognize that some commitments are truly continuing ones (e.g., to tenured faculty and key staff) and cannot be readily reduced or augmented in a short period. Most organizations, especially institutions of postsecondary education, cannot initiate and terminate activities quickly. Accordingly, when zero-base budgeting has been tried, organizations assume a fixed base of support (e.g., 80 percent of the previous year's budget) and apply the zero-base techniques to the balance of the budget. This strategy compromises one of the purported advantages of the method, namely, the elimination of a protected budget base.

Practitioners of zero-base budgeting claim that they gain a much better understanding of their organization through the preparation and review of the decision packages. However, zero-base budgeting requires a great amount of time and paperwork. Also, it is sometimes difficult to reach agreement on priorities. Another complaint is that the centralized pre-audit of lower-level decisions robs those levels of decision-making autonomy and responsibility. Some observers argue that periodic program reviews are a more practical way to carry out the positive aspects of zero-base budgeting.

PERFORMANCE BUDGETING

Performance budgeting emerged in the late 1940s in the second stage of development of public administration budget and planning. During the first stage of development (i.e., the executive budget movement), the budget was viewed as an instrument of expenditure control. Performance budgeting represented a shift to a management orientation by focusing on programs and activities, which became ends in themselves. Performance budgeting addressed activities rather than objectives, and performance budgets consisted of activity classifications, performance measurements, and performance evaluations. Clearly, the intent of performance budgeting was to improve work efficiency.

In recent years there has been a rebirth of interest in this technique, particularly at the state level. In the newer form of performance budgeting, resources (inputs) are related to activities (structure) and results (outcomes).

Sets of specific outcome measures are defined in both qualitative and quantitative terms. Accounting structures relate expenditures of resources to results. Explicit indicators of input/output relationships or indices relating resources to outcomes are defined. Goals are specified in terms of performance measures (i.e., desired input/output ratios).

Difficulties have arisen in applying the newer forms of performance budgeting in the public arena: the development of performance measures has often flowed from the state level down to the institutional level; outcome indicators are sometimes viewed as useless or controversial because they are linked with program budgets at high levels of aggregation; quantitative measures are more widely employed than qualitative measures; and performance measures at high levels of program aggregation are not easily linked with centers of administrative responsibility. Also, performance budgeting often lacks political appeal from the point of view of legislators. They argue that the rational orientation of performance budgeting reduces the amount of influence they can bring to bear for institutions in their area. Also, legislators dislike the complexity and volume of budget documentation.

Tennessee has experimented with performance budgeting as part of its more traditional formula budgeting approach. A small fraction of the state budget for higher education is appropriated to the Tennessee Higher Education Commission for allocation to individual institutions based on proposals for improved instructional performance. It is hoped that this scheme will evolve into a multiyear planning and budgeting cycle, whereby an institution's performance would be evaluated each cycle and its budget share awarded accordingly.

FORMULA BUDGETING

Formula budgeting is a procedure for estimating resource requirements through the application of relationships between program demand and program cost. These relationships are frequently expressed as mathematical formulations that in the instructional portion of an institution's budget can be as simple as a single student-faculty ratio or as complicated as an array of costs per student credit hour by discipline for many levels of instruction (e.g., lower division, upper division, master's, doctoral). The bases of budget formulas can be historical data, projected trends, and parameters negotiated to provide desired levels of funding. Budget formulas are, in summary, a combination of technical judgments and political agreements.

Budget formulas come in all shapes and sizes. Most are based in some way on enrollment or student credit hour productivity data. Within the same overall framework, different formulas usually address the distinct functional areas of an institution's operations. Thus, instructional resources may be requested on the basis of average faculty teaching loads or credit hour costs by student level or course level, applied against historical or projected enrollment levels. Library support may be requested on the basis of enrollments and service relationships. Requests for support of maintenance and physical plant may not be enrollment-based at all, because the operation of the physical plant is a fixed expense relatively immune to shifts in enrollment. Accordingly, the physical plant formulas will probably be based on square footage of facilities and the nature of the facilities.

Some budget formula frameworks do not use distinct formulas for different functional areas. The base method of formula budgeting computes the resource needs for some base function, usually instruction, based on enrollments and instructional costs or workloads, and then computes the needs of the other functional areas (e.g., libraries, academic support, maintenance and physical plant) as a percentage of the base. On the other hand, the staffing pattern method of formula budgeting computes only salary expenditures for the institution. Nonsalary budget requirements can be determined by other methods (e.g., incremental budgeting).

In general, budget formulas are used on a systemwide or statewide basis for state-supported institutions as a basis for generating budget requests. Formulas tend not to be used as a means to distribute resources within an institution, however. By their very nature, budget formulas are simplified models of how institutions operate. This modeling role of budget formulas sometimes puzzles state officials who assume that funds appropriated to institutions should be spent in exactly the same manner as requested through the formulas.

It is not uncommon for a formula-generated budget request to exceed the amount of available state resources. In such cases the formula may be modified to yield a request consistent with available resources, or state officials may simply allocate a percentage of the formula-generated amount.

A number of factors usually are considered by those evaluating alternative formulas: How many portions of institutional budget requests are generated by budget formulas? How closely does the state adhere to the formula-generated request? Do the budget formulas recognize different types of institutions? What is the inherent incentive structure of the budget formulas? (For example: In the instructional area does doctoral-level instruction receive a significantly higher weighting than undergraduate instruction? Does the formula for maintenance and physical plant provide an advantage to a certain type of facility?) Are formula parameters derived from historical data, norms, or projections? How does the formula treat different levels of instruction? Does the formula differentiate among disciplines?

The advantages and disadvantages of formula budgeting have been debated for three decades. Budget formulas were introduced during higher education's growth era of the 1950s and 1960s as means to ensure the equitable and rational distribution of resources. The quantitative nature of most budget formulas gives them the appearance, if not always the reality, of objectivity. Budget formulas tend to reduce conflict in the budget process in that they represent agreed-upon rules for the distribution of available resources. This conflict reduction occurs in part because budget formulas have become a mechanism for relieving legislators of the pressures of institutional lobbying campaigns. By pointing to the formulas, legislators can disclaim control of institutional allocations. At the same time, budget formulas have enhanced institutional autonomy by lowering the level of political influence in budgeting. Budget formulas have also reduced the uncertainty inherent in the budget process by helping institutions and state officials to predict budget needs for future budget cycles. The budget process is simplified in that the same decision rules (i.e., budget formulas) are used from one budget cycle to another.

As with any quantified approach to decision making, there are disadvantages to formula budgeting. Formulas based on historical data, for example, discourage new programs or rearrangements of existing programs. Any new program will be at a disadvantage until it has accumulated its own history. Also, formulas that are applied across a number of institutions are criticized for encouraging homogeneity and mediocrity (critics assume that funding is provided on the basis of some average). Formulas tend to be based on average factors (e.g., costs or enrollments) rather than on marginal ones and thereby favor institutions with increasing enrollments. That is, as enrollments increase, institutions gain more resources than they "deserve" because of the average-factor base. For the same reason, as enrollments decline, institutions lose resources faster than they should. Consequently, some states are seeking formulas that distinguish between fixed and variable costs.

Formulas become restrictive if state officials assume that appropriated resources are to be used within institutions in the same patterns as appeared in the formula-generated budget requests. Formulas are also restrictive in the sense that once they are put in place, it is difficult to modify them significantly because user expectations have solidified.

COST-CENTER BUDGETING

Cost-center budgeting, also known as responsibility-center budgeting or more informally as "every tub on its own bottom" budgeting, is an appealingly simple concept. In an institution every unit that is budgeted in this manner is treated as self-supporting. Thus all expenditures, such as faculty and staff salaries and a share of physical plant costs, must be covered by the unit in question through income generated by tuition and fees, endowment, gifts, and grants. Generally, the concept is applied most successfully to units that are relatively independent in the sense that the instructional and research programs are self-contained (i.e., students in the unit in question take relatively few courses in other units in the institution; students in other units take relatively few courses in the unit in question; and faculty members in the unit in question conduct most of their research in that unit). Graduate schools of business, law schools, and medical schools are examples of such units.

The "every tub on its own bottom" concept is difficult to apply across most institutions because some units have a considerable service or support mission and could not be self-supporting. For example, unless the liberal arts college of a university is so prestigious that it has its own considerable endowment separate from that of the university as a whole, it probably could not generate enough tuition income from its majors to cover its own operating expenses. If the "every tub on its own bottom" concept is to be applied to this liberal arts college, costing procedures must be instituted that "charge" non-liberal-arts programs or units for instructional and other services offered. Those cost allocation schemes can become cumbersome for large institutions and can undermine the utility of the "every tub" concept.

FOR FURTHER READING

Various approaches to budgeting are portrayed briefly in the monograph by J. Kent Caruthers and Melvin Orwig, *Budgeting in Higher Education*, AAHE/ERIC Higher Education Research Report no. 3 (Washington, DC: American Association for Higher Education, 1979). An overview of budget practices is also offered by Aaron Wildavsky, *Budgeting: A Comparative Theory of Budgetary Processes* (Boston: Little, Brown & Co., 1975), and Robert D. Lee, Jr. and Ronald W. Johnson, *Public Budgeting Systems*, 2nd ed. (Baltimore: University Park Press, 1977).

9 / Endowment Management

The endowment of some institutions is large enough to provide a significant portion of the institution's income each budget cycle. The stability of this income becomes an important factor in preparation of the budget. Accordingly, budgeters must have a grasp of the policy issues related to management of the endowment if they are to maintain control over this source of revenue.

Endowment management is the domain of professionals. Generally, the proper role of trustees, administrators, and faculty in endowment management is questioning and setting policies for endowment investment and income spending. Within this framework investment specialists should be given the flexibility to operate on a day-to-day basis because the investment world is complicated and requires considerable knowledge of the burgeoning number of investment options as well as great amounts of time to remain abreast of developments. This chapter focuses on the major policy considerations of endowment management rather than on specific investment strategies.

An excellent summary of approaches to endowment management is contained in a comprehensive study of endowments by The Twentieth Century Fund (1975). This book includes a background paper on endowment management by J. Peter Williamson of Dartmouth College and recommendations regarding endowment policies developed by a blue-ribbon panel of college trustees and investment professionals.

POLICY QUESTIONS

Three major questions confront policy makers who have responsibility for an institution's endowment management. First, what are the institution's goals for endowment growth and endowment income? Second, who should manage the endowment funds? Third, how should the endowment be invested? The second and third questions can be answered only after the first.

INSTITUTIONAL GOALS FOR ENDOWMENT

Perhaps the most basic institutional goal for endowment investment is a maximum total return consistent with acceptable levels of risk. That is, the institution must determine the total return it seeks and match the level of risk with which it is comfortable. Generally, high-return investments are those that involve high risks. An institution that pursues an aggressive investment strategy with the objective of significant endowment growth must tolerate a higher level of risk in its investments than an institution that invests more conservatively in an effort to preserve capital.

E. Eugene Carter (1980, 105–107) suggests six alternative goals to guide endowment management policy.

1. Maximize the value of the portfolio at some future target point (e.g., 20 years).
2. Conserve principal at all costs.
3. Maximize income, while maintaining prudent protection of principal.
4. Maximize marketability.
5. Maximize long-term return.
6. Achieve a variety of objectives.

These alternative goals argue for different investment strategies (to be summarized below). While each goal seems reasonable, the second goal (i.e., conserve principal at all costs) deserves additional comment. John Train (1974, 1) notes:

> Few people succeed in preserving their capital (that is, maintaining their surplus buying power for future use), and even fewer will succeed in the future.
> One of the Rothschilds is said to have observed that if he could be sure of transmitting a quarter of his capital he would settle for that. Alas, he probably didn't make it. . . .

The objective of conserving principal at all costs is an extremely conservative one. In the long term it does not appear to be a particularly wise goal in that it fails to reflect the decline in purchasing power of the endowment over time resulting from inflation.

An institution's goals for endowment investment flow in part from a spending plan for endowment return. Reasonable objectives for a spending plan might include (1) determining an appropriate balance between meeting the institution's current fiscal needs and ensuring that there are sufficient funds available over the long term, and (2) providing for a stable and predictable level of income for current operations. If the institution's endowment goal focuses on total return (here defined as the endowment's interest and dividends earned plus the appreciation or depreciation in the market value of the endowment), the spending plan might be structured so as to minimize pressure on investment counselors to produce interest and dividends at the expense of achieving the highest total return.

In 1969 the Ford Foundation (1972) released the report of a major study of college and university endowment management. The report observed that, in general, institutions had been too conservative in their investments. Endowments had not performed as well as the market, largely because most institutional investment strategies were driven by the desire to preserve capital. Although the thrust of the conclusions was accurate, some critics argue that the Ford Foundation performed a major disservice to institutions by recommending strongly that institutional budgets be based not on cash income but on the endowment's total return. That is, if interest and dividends yielded 4 percent of the endowment annually, and the endowment appreciated 5 percent annually, the institution's spending plan, and hence its budget, should be based on the fact that the institution is "gaining" 9 percent of the value of its endowment annually. In this example, institutions that assume a contribution to the current operating budget of from 4 to 9 percent of the endowment must sell some of the endowment to realize the capital gains. In recommending this, the Ford Foundation considered the fact that the U.S. federal corporate tax structure encourages corporations to retain earnings through capital investment in the corporation rather than distributing those earnings as dividends. Many institutions adopted the total-return concept only to see the value of their endowments plummet during the 1970s as the stock market stagnated. What these institutions failed to take into account in their spending plans was the effect of inflation.

The spending plan must be sensitive to the need for endowment growth, especially in light of current levels of inflation, and to the need for income stability in the face of market fluctuations. If, for example, an institution's total-return goal is 11 percent, a reasonable spending goal might be 5 percent of endowment. This leaves 6 percent of the endowment gain (in both interest and dividends and endowment appreciation) to be reinvested as additional endowment. As long as the level of inflation remains below 6 percent during the year in question, the real value of the endowment will increase. If it appeared that inflation would exceed 6 percent for a long period, it probably would be necessary to lower the spending goal (again assuming the 11 percent annual return on endowment in this example).

Over time, markets tend to fluctuate. The total-return goal is established with an eye to market and endowment performance over a period of several years. (The total-return goal will probably have to be readjusted periodically to reflect changes in the market situation.) The spending goal must reflect not only the need to protect the endowment base against inflation but also the need for a stable level of income for the operating budget. Market fluctuations can be accommodated by having reasonable spending goals (that allow a sufficient buffer against inflation and declines in return) and a pool of reserve resources.

Thus, investment goals and spending plans are driven by two forces: the need to maintain and increase the endowment base and the need for predictable levels of income for the current budget. Decision makers who examine an institution's investment goals and spending plans should not be surprised to find that a portion of the endowment's total return is reinvested.

INVESTMENT COUNSELORS

Once an institution's investment goals and spending plans are established, it is necessary to determine who is going to manage the endowment. In 1977 Princeton University (Herring et al., 1979, 89–97) reexamined its endowment management policies and identified four alternative models for an investment management structure.

1. Retention by the trustees of direct responsibility for specific investment decisions (the earlier Princeton model).

2. Delegation of responsibility for investment decisions to one or more small investment advisory firms whose dominant client would be the institution. The staff of the firm or firms would make actual decisions concerning the purchase and sale of securities, but a trustee committee would maintain a close working relationship with staff members.

3. Delegation of responsibility for investment decisions to one or more banks, insurance companies, or major investment houses.

4. In-house investment management, either by professional investment managers hired as part of the institution's staff or by a captive investment management organization established as a wholly owned but separate legal entity.

In examining the alternative investment models, officials at Princeton University considered a number of factors.

1. The ability to attract and retain experienced investment specialists.

2. The ease with which portfolio managers can be evaluated.

3. The ease with which changes in portfolio management can be effected if necessary.

4. The assurance that the university would receive priority service and that the university's interest would not be subordinated to the interests of other investors.

5. The necessity for an appropriate investment perspective that recognizes the institution as an enduring organization with both current and long-term financial needs.

6. The need to avoid real or perceived conflicts of interest.

7. The cost of investment and advisory services.

An institution's character and the size of its endowment tend to be major determinants in the decision concerning investment counselors. Not to be taken lightly is the thought offered earlier that successful investing requires considerable time, knowledge of investment options, and information.

THE COMMON FUND

One of the practical difficulties faced by many institutions with smaller endowments is the inability to gain access to top-quality endowment management firms. Those firms typically have a minimum account size of $5 million and some require as much as $20 million. The Common Fund, formed with the help of a grant from the Ford Foundation in 1971, is a nonprofit corporation that provides investment management exclusively for educational institutions. More than 200 colleges, universities, and independent schools utilize the services of The Common Fund to manage their endowments, which range in size from $100,000 to $30 million. The Common Fund, governed by a board of trustees elected by its member institutions, employs professional investment firms and has achieved excellent investment results for its member institutions.

INVESTMENT STRATEGIES

Specific investment strategies will be governed in large part by the institution's investment goals and spending plan. Individuals or groups charged with overseeing the management of investments generally should monitor major portfolio selection policies rather than individual investment decisions. The efficacy of selection policies can be measured in part by evaluating over time the performance of the investment managers.

The composition of the investment portfolio can be examined for consistency with investment goals. If, for example, the portfolio is generating an unusually high return, one might ask whether too much risk has been taken on. One should strive to determine the distribution of investments in common stocks, bonds, real estate, and other investments and gauge the reasonableness of the distribution in light of current market conditions and risk-taking policies. In a time of rapidly increasing interest rates, for example, it may be wise to place funds in money market funds and notes that offer relatively high yields. The portfolio should also be evaluated in terms of its diversification. Investments in the portfolio should not be affected in the same way by the same economic, political, and social forces.

Much of the evaluation of an institution's portfolio involves common sense. For example, maintaining a heavy investment in residential real estate restricted by rent control may not be prudent unless there is considerable appreciation in the value of the properties and sufficient cash flow to enable the institution to provide adequate maintenance. Similarly, it does not seem sensible for colleges and universities, as nonprofit organizations, to invest in tax-free municipal bonds. The yields on such bonds are considerably lower than the yields on corporate bonds, reflecting the built-in discount for the tax-free advantage.

Evaluation of the performance of portfolio managers can be done against internal and external standards. Internally, one can ask whether the investment portfolio is providing the level of revenue called for under the institution's spending plan. If the income is less than desired, either the portfolio managers are not performing well or the institution's spending plan is unrealistic. An external measure of the performance of portfolio managers is comparison with the performance of a standard index, such as Standard & Poor's index of 500 stocks or the index of one of several leading mutual funds. Performance over the short term may fluctuate—performance over the long term is the true measure of success.

FOR FURTHER READING

A well-written layman's guide to financial investments is John Train, *The Money Masters* (New York: Harper & Row, 1980). This book profiles the investment strategies of nine great investors and gives a good sense of the complexity and variety of investment approaches. A good textbook is Jack Clark Francis, *Investments: Analysis and Management,* 3rd ed. (New York: McGraw-Hill, 1980). This volume provides a rigorous approach to investment strategies and offers references for readers interested in even more technical detail.

E. Eugene Carter has a good chapter on endowment management in *College Financial Management* (Lexington, MA: Lexington Books, 1980). *Budgeting and Resource Allocation at Princeton University,* vol. 2 (Princeton, NJ: Princeton University, 1979) discusses Princeton's review of its endowment management policies.

10 / Cost Analysis and the Use of Comparative Data

Cost analysis in its different forms is the basis for decisions on the internal allocation of resources at many institutions. At the state level cost analysis is sometimes used to identify problems across institutions or sectors and to allocate resources among institutions. Some users of cost analysis have unrealistic expectations concerning the utility and applicability of this tool, while many potential users are frightened away by its demanding methodology.

The purpose of this chapter is to highlight the strengths and weaknesses of cost analysis and to identify potential problems in the use of broader categories of comparative data. The first section summarizes the framework for cost analysis and provides some simple examples of calculations. Although there are several ways to perform cost analyses, the outline here will loosely follow the procedures recommended by NACUBO in *A Cost Accounting Handbook for Colleges and Universities* (1983). The focus will be on the costing of academic programs and disciplines, including the allocation of those costs and support costs to final cost objectives such as instruction, research, and public service. The second section discusses philosophical and policy issues related to the use of cost analysis. That discussion follows directly from the examination of the technical aspects of the costing methodology.

FRAMEWORK FOR COST ANALYSIS

The form of cost analysis considered here is comprehensive in that it assumes the development of an institutional cost accounting system. It is also assumed that the collection of cost data is an ongoing process from which a longitudinal data base will evolve. Cost analysis can also be a one-time occurrence for a particular decision. For example, a decision on a contract for campus-wide reproduction and printing services would be made on the basis of user demand patterns (including volume and demand schedules) and vendor pricing options and would require data concerning only reproduction and printing services on campus.

Comprehensive cost analysis is a multi-tier process in which costs are pooled in cost centers for attribution to ultimate cost objectives. In the instructional area, cost centers are typically departments, schools, or colleges. Detailed cost analysis can define cost centers as discrete course levels (e.g., lower division, upper division, graduate instruction, graduate thesis research). The most frequently used ultimate cost objectives in higher education are instruction, research, service, and auxiliary enterprises. Thus, the costs of the various activities and operations that define the institution are allocated to appropriate cost objectives by a cost accounting system and the methodology described below.

FIVE-STEP GENERAL COST ACCOUNTING PROCEDURE

A three-tier cost accounting approach works in conjunction with the general five-step procedure. The tiered methodology is used to collect and analyze instructional costs by groupings and levels of cost. Tier one costs are all direct costs that are readily identifiable with a specific cost center or cost objective. Generally, those direct costs consist of the following expenditures associated with the instructional portion of the budget: (1) compensation, including salaries and wages and benefits; (2) supplies and services, including consumable supplies and materials and communications; (3) travel; (4) contractual services; and (5) noncapital equipment, which normally costs less than some predetermined amount (e.g., $1,000) or has an estimated life shorter than some predetermined span (e.g., two years). Tier one costs include those identified through an institutional chargeback system. Thus, in some settings the costs of computing support for instructional programs are factored into tier one costs.

Tier two costs are all tier one costs plus indirect costs that are attributable to a cost center or cost objective. Indirect costs are not readily identifiable with a specific cost center or objective. Indirect costs of instruction are those related to support services that benefit instruction and include the

---

Several examples in this chapter are drawn from an early draft of *Information Exchange Procedures* (State Council of Higher Education for Virginia).

cost of plant maintenance and operation, accounting, purchasing, computing, libraries, and general administration.

Generally, tier one costs are easily determined and not controversial. Accordingly, much institutional cost analysis involves only tier one costs. The attribution of indirect costs to final cost objectives requires allocation or proration methodologies. (See figure 1 for alternative bases for allocating support costs.) Because several alternative allocation schemes are available for each category of support activity, decision makers are likely to be in greater agreement on appropriate methods for attributing direct costs than on methods for attributing indirect costs.

Tier three costs include all tier two costs plus a depreciation or use charge on facilities and capital equipment. Depreciation is defined as "that portion of the cost of limited-life capital assets (buildings and equipment) that expires during a specified period" (Hyatt, 1983). The procedures for allocating tier three costs can vary among institutions. Tier three costs are very useful in the auxiliary enterprise area in determining the extent to which auxiliary enterprises are actually self-supporting.

The following are the five general cost accounting procedures: (1) designate specific cost objectives and cost centers; (2) select consistent categories of cost; (3) assign all tier one costs to designated cost objectives and centers; (4) assign all tiers two and three costs to designated cost objectives and centers as desired; and (5) develop unit cost or output measures.

Typically, the cost objectives or cost centers are derived from the institution's chart of accounts. The most frequently used cost objectives are instruction, research, public service, academic support, student services, institutional support, operation and maintenance of plant, student financial assistance, auxiliary enterprises, hospitals, and independent operations.

Instruction. This includes activities that are part of the institution's instructional program. Departmental research that is not separately budgeted is usually included in instruction. This program generally will exclude academic administrators whose primary assignment is administration (e.g., academic deans). Department and division chairpersons may or may not be included under instruction; if they are not, they are included under academic support. The instruction program can be divided into subprograms such as general academic instruction, off-campus academic instruction, community education, and summer session instruction.

Research. This includes all activities organized specifically to produce research outcomes; such activities are either commissioned by an agency external to the institution or are separately budgeted by an organizational unit within the institution (only specifically budgeted expenditures for departmental research are included). The research program can be divided into subprograms such as bureaus, institutes and research centers, and individual or project research.

Public service. This includes all activities established primarily to provide noninstructional services for individuals and groups external to the institution, such as professional associations. Activities can include seminars, projects, and various organizational entities established to provide services to particular sectors of the public and professional communities. The public service program can be divided into subprograms such as community services, cooperative extension services, public broadcasting services, and professional association affiliations.

Academic support. This generally includes all activities carried out to provide support services that are an integral part of the operations of one of the institution's three primary programs: instruction, research, or public service. It includes the retention, preservation, and display of materials and the provision of services that directly assist the academic functions of the institution. Also included are the media and technology employed by the three primary programs as well as administrative support operations (including development of future instructional activities) within the academic units. Academic support can be divided into subprograms such as libraries, museums and galleries, audiovisual services, academic computer operations, ancillary support, academic administration, personnel development, and course and curriculum development.

Student services. This includes all activities whose primary purpose is to contribute to students' emotional and physical well-being and to their intellectual, cultural, and social development outside the context of the formal program of instruction. Generally excluded from this program are activities operated as essentially self-supporting operations, which are usually reported under auxiliary enterprises. The student services program can be divided into subprograms such as student service administration, social and cultural development, counseling and career guidance, student admissions and records, financial aid administration, and student health services.

Institutional support. This includes all activities whose primary purpose is to provide operational support for the day-to-day functioning of the institution, excluding expenditures for physical plant operations. The institutional support program can be divided into subprograms such as executive management, fiscal operations, general administrative services, logistical services, and public relations and development.

Operation and maintenance of plant. This includes the operation and maintenance of the physical plant, except for auxiliary enterprises and hospitals. (Physical plant operations of and services performed for auxiliary enterprises are allocated to those auxiliary enterprises initially included in this category as joint costs.) Included with all operations established to provide services and maintenance related to campus grounds and facilities are utilities, property insurance, and debt service. The operation and maintenance of plant program can be divided into subprograms such as administration and supervision, custodial service, building repairs and maintenance and care and maintenance of grounds, utilities, property and general liability insurance, property rentals, operation of power plant, and debt service (educational and general plant).

Student financial assistance. This generally includes only monies given in the form of outright grants and trainee stipends to individuals enrolled in formal coursework. The student financial assistance program can be divided into subprograms such as scholarships (for undergraduate students) and fellowships (for graduate students).

Auxiliary enterprises. These are entities that exist to furnish a service to students, faculty, or staff and that charge a fee directly related, though not necessarily equal, to the cost of the service. Auxiliary enterprises are managed as essentially self-supporting operations, and fees are usually established with that objective. However, revenues do not always exceed or equal expenditures in a specific activity. The general public may be served incidentally by some auxiliary enterprises such as residence halls, food services, intercollegiate athletics, and student stores. Covered are all costs, except depreciation, of operating the institution's auxiliary enterprises, including charges for physical plant operations and logistical services relating to auxiliary enterprises. The program can be divided into subprograms such as student auxiliary services, intercollegiate athletics, and faculty/staff auxiliary services.

Hospitals. Encompassed here is the operation of the hospital, including nursing expenses, other professional services, general services, administrative services, fiscal services, and charges for physical plant operations. Activities that take place within the hospital but that are more appropriately categorized as instruction or research are generally excluded.

Independent operations. These include all operations that are independent of or unrelated to the primary programs of the institution (i.e., instruction, research, and public service), although those operations may contribute to the enhancement of the primary programs. This category is often limited to major federally funded research laboratories such as the Lawrence Livermore Laboratory operated by the University of California.

CONSISTENT CATEGORIES OF COST

In cost analysis it is necessary to use a standard set of cost categories. These categories are based on the institution's current classification of objects of expenditure and are uniformly applied across all activities.

INSTRUCTIONAL WORKLOAD MATRIX

For a cost analysis of the instruction portion of institutional activity, the cost centers become the disciplines or the degree programs. Detailed cost analyses of the instructional area are performed at discipline and program levels (i.e., lower division, upper division, graduate instruction, graduate thesis research). (See chapter 11 for a detailed description and examples.) The instructional workload matrix displays the relationship between disciplines and student degree programs by (1) summarizing the credit hour totals that each discipline and each course level within each discipline have contributed to each student degree program, and (2) summarizing the credit hour totals that each student degree and each student level have consumed from each discipline. The elements of the instructional workload matrix are used to distribute the costs of·faculty and staff salaries and departmental operations to the various discipline and degree program cost centers.

CALCULATION OF TIER ONE UNIT COSTS
FOR DISCIPLINES AND PROGRAMS

For costing purposes, it is necessary to associate expenditures with the program classification activities they support. It is common, however, for expenditures represented by a single institutional financial or budget account to support a number of different activities such as research, public service, or instruction across more than one discipline and at multiple course levels. Direct unit costs are developed by first allocating the costs of department salaries and operating expenses to the appropriate levels of instruction. Unit costs are determined by dividing total direct costs at each level by the total credit hours generated at each level. In distributing each account's expenditures and personnel effort to the activities supported by the account, the instructional workload matrix is used. Figure 2 provides an example of the process in schematic form.

Cost analysis requires the establishment of allocation instructions for all salary and compensation accounts used to pay faculty and staff. For each individual one must calculate the percentage of the individual's effort devoted to each task described for the individual (such as teaching a lower division history course, conducting sponsored research in physics, or engaging in academic administration). The allocation of faculty and staff time can be done on the basis of a periodic activity survey, whereby faculty and staff maintain a diary for a typical work period such as a week. An alternative approach is to distribute artificially a faculty or staff member's time. For example, it might be decided that a faculty member should spend two-thirds of his or her time on instruction, one-sixth on research, and one-sixth on public service. Similarly, a department chairperson's administrative responsibilities might be assumed to consume one-third of his or her time. It is also possible to introduce a system of weights for levels of instruction. For example, lower division instruction might have a weight of 1.0, upper division instruction a weight of 1.5, graduate-level instruction a weight of 2.0, and graduate thesis research a weight of 3.0. These weights would be used to distribute faculty time and compensation.

An illustration of a departmental analysis is shown in figure 3. As illustrated, the history department expended a total of $61,400, of which $50,000 was for faculty compensation. Institutional data A identify the faculty members paid from the account, their compensation and activities, and the percentage of time associated with each activity. The proportion of a faculty member's time related to each activity is the basis for distributing compensation to activities. In the example, faculty member I. Doi devoted 50 percent of his time to instruction in history at the lower division level. Proportionally, 50 percent of his compensation is contributed to the column describing that activity, under "derived individual dollar contribution." In similar fashion, the remainder of his compensation is distributed across his activities. The same computation is performed for all other faculty members funded by the history department account.

Each column is then summed, as demonstrated by C in figure 3, to produce the total contribution to each activity by all faculty members. The distribution percentages represent contribution totals as a percentage of the total amount contributed. For example, the distribution percentage of 39.2 percent for lower division history instruction is calculated by dividing the $19,600 contribution total for lower division history by the $50,000 salary total for the history department account.

The procedures described above concern only the faculty compensation objects of instructional accounts. The entire balance in each instructional account can be allocated using the distribution percentages established for the faculty compensation portion of the account if actual usage data are not readily available. To achieve precise results, it is best to use records of the activities that each object within the individual account actually supports. However, obtaining these data is often costly in that it requires establishing new systems of activity analysis. In figure 3 the entire history department expenditure of $61,400—rather than just the $50,000 in compensation—is allocated according to the salary distribution percentages. In most situations the activities illustrated in figure 3 would be more numerous and would include sponsored research and faculty participation in institution-wide governance (categorized under academic support or institutional support).

The calculation of direct unit costs for disciplines is illustrated in figure 4. Once direct expenditures are allocated to the appropriate level of instruction, as shown in figure 3, expenditure totals by level are divided by total credit hours by level to derive the discipline tier one unit costs by level of instruction.

A simplified example of the calculation of tier one unit costs for student programs is illustrated in figure 5. This example uses the discipline unit costs computed in figure 4 for the mathematics and political science disciplines. In practice the matrix shown in figure 5 would be expanded; instead of a row for "average of all other disciplines contributing to math and poli. sci. programs," the discipline contributions would be shown.

TIER TWO COSTING

Tier two costing requires the allocation of activity costs to final cost objectives. Because instruction is a universal final cost objective, the direct costs computed above are simply allocated to the instruction category. Similarly, direct expenditures for research and public service can be allocated to the research and public service cost objectives.

It is more difficult to allocate expenditures for libraries, academic administration, student services, or physical plant operations to the appropriate final cost objectives. Accordingly, a parameter must be selected as the basis for crossing over these expenditures. For example, the costs of general administrative services might be allocated to instruction, research, and public service on the basis of the proportion of direct costs in each of the final cost objectives. Assume, for example, that general administrative services expenditures amount to $3 million. If the direct cost of instruction is $15 million, of research is $10 million, and of public service is $5 million, then 50 percent (i.e., $15 million divided by $30 million) of the general administrative services expenditures should be allocated to instruction. Similarly, 33 percent (i.e., $10 million divided by $30 million) of the general administrative services expenditures should be allocated to research, and 17 percent (i.e., $5 million divided by $30 million) to public service. In this example, instruction would receive $1.5 million of the general administrative services costs, research would receive $1.0 million, and public service would receive $0.5 million.

Other support cost centers that might use direct costs as the basis for allocating expenditures to final cost objectives include academic administration, course and curriculum development, academic personnel development, executive management, fiscal operations, libraries and museums and galleries, logistical services, public relations and development, and capital equipment. Actual usage data might be employed as the basis for allocating expenditures in computing support, audiovisual services, and ancillary support. Semester credit hours might be used to allocate to instruction the following cost centers: student service administration; social and cultural development; counseling and career guidance; financial aid administration; and student recruitment, admissions, and records. Assignable square feet or direct costs might be the basis for allocating the costs of physical plant operations. Figure 1 summarizes alternative bases for allocating support costs.

COST ANALYSIS AND COMPARATIVE DATA

The approach to cost analysis outlined above yields cost information that is frequently compared with similar cost information from other institutions. Caution is urged, however, in the use of such comparative data for decision making.

What these data indicate is sometimes not obvious from examining only the numbers. It should be clear from the above summary of cost analysis procedures that a set of decision rules is used to allocate costs to final cost centers or even to develop direct costs of instruction. These decision rules are often dictated by organizational structure or procedures and will therefore vary from institution to institution. For example, compensation for deans may be classified as executive management rather than academic administration. Also, a department chairperson's administrative responsibilities may account for different percentages of his or her total activity. The cost of physical plant operations may be allocated on the basis of assignable square feet or direct costs. Some institutions include benefits in faculty and staff compensation while others do not. Expenditures for research stations and extension services may or may not be included in an institution's budget. There are clearly enough variations in methodology to limit the comparability of the data.

What does it mean if lower division English costs $15 per credit hour at Institution A and $60 per credit hour at Institution B? One possibility is that Institution A employs more graduate assistants to teach lower division sections. Another explanation is that salaries of the English faculty are higher at Institution B than at Institution A. Or, during the semester in question a distinguished, high-salaried faculty member taught a large lecture class in lower division English at Institution B.

What does it mean if the cost per English degree granted is $1,500 at Institution A and $3,500 at Institution B? As noted above, faculty at Institution B may receive, on average, higher salaries than faculty at Institution A. Another explanation is that an English major requires fewer credit hours to graduate at Institution A than at Institution B. A third explanation is that Institution B has a higher drop-out rate than does Institution A. Institution B generates many credit hours (and related costs) that do not yield degrees because students drop out before completing the degree requirements.

Comparing longitudinal data across institutions also has weaknesses. The numbers alone, for example, will not indicate if changes in unit costs over time result from internal academic and management decisions or from external factors such as shifts in student demand.

One reason comparative data are attractive is that decision makers want to be assured that their institution measures up favorably to peer institutions. Also, considerable pressure has come from state and federal agencies to adopt uniform measures that can be used in funding mechanisms and program reviews. However, there are enough differences in institutional character from one institution to another to make the possibility of producing standardized cost data appear slight. If differences in institutional character are not sufficient reason, the cost of collecting uniform cost information is.

Cost analysis then does have a role in resource allocation decisions as long as costing is limited to internal decision making, particularly regarding specific activities. For example, longitudinal cost information can highlight the impact of changes in the cost of utilities and periodicals or in the cost of maintaining computer equipment. Similarly, cost analysis can be used to weigh the costs and benefits of introducing word processing technology into administrative and academic offices. Cost analysis seems more suitable for gauging the marginal impact of changes in activities when the analysis focuses on the effects of volume factors such as enrollments and square footage, environmental factors such as inflation and shifts in student demand, and policy factors such as revision of operating procedures.

Raymond F. Bacchetti (1977, 5) suggests a spectrum of cost analysis that runs from "hard management" to "soft management":

> By "hard management" is meant the area of plans and operations where cost information can be developed with a high degree of clarity and have considerable influence in the choice of a best course of action. Examples are lease/buy or make/buy analyses, the setting of prices which are closely related to costs (as in overhead reimbursement formulas and auxiliary enterprise charges), and mathematical models which relate rates of change and give valid and reliable information on the effects of certain actions and trade-offs.

> By "soft management" is meant areas where cost information is diagnostic or indicative rather than definitive, where approximations will reveal as much as is necessary to know in order to focus on a course of action. This is the area in which cost information can reveal *that* something is happening but not *what* it is. Examples are charting the relative costs of instruction over time, the setting of prices which are not closely related to costs (such as tuition), and assessing the marginal costs of new students or programs.

Cost analysis that focuses on specific activities rather than on broad disciplines and degree programs is a powerful decision-making tool as long as it is applied with reasonable expectations. The purpose of outlining discipline and degree program cost analysis in this chapter was to underscore some of the inherent weaknesses in using comparative data and to provide a more realistic sense of the limits of cost analysis within the institution.

Figure 1: Alternative Bases for Allocating Support Costs

Support Activities		Actual Usage Data: • job orders processed • purchase orders • requests for service • voucher count	Total Direct Costs	Assign. Square Feet	Total Comp.	Instr./ Res./ Public Service Comp.*	Student Head-counts	Total Hours of Use	Student Credit Hours	Cost Objectives Receiving Support Costs
Academic Support	Libraries	X	X			X		X	X	Instruction, Research, and Public Service
	Museums and Galleries		X					X		Instruction and Public Service
	Audiovisual Services	X				X				Instruction
	Ancillary Support	X	X							Instruction, Research, and Public Service
	Academic Admin. and Personnel Development	X	X							Instruction, Research, and Public Service
	Academic Computing	X	X							Instruction, Research, and Public Service
	Course and Curriculum Development		X			X				Instruction
Student Services	Student Services Administration		X						X	Instruction
	Social and Cultural Activities		X				X		X	Instruction
	Counseling and Career Guidance		X				X	X	X	Instruction
	Financial Aid Administration	X				X			X	Instruction
	Student Admissions and Records	X				X			X	Instruction
	Health and Infirmary Services		X			X		X		Instruction
Institutional Support	Executive Management		X		X					All cost objectives eligible to receive support costs
	Fiscal Operations	X	X		X					
	General Administrative Services	X	X		X					
	Logistical Services	X	X							
	Community Relations		X					X		
Plant Operation and Maintenance	Physical Plant Administration	X	X	X						
	Building and Equipment Maintenance	X	X	X						
	Custodial Services	X	X	X						
	Utilities	X	X	X						
	Landscape and Grounds Maintenance	X	X	X						
	Major Repairs and Renovations	X	X	X						

*Compensation of individuals, such as faculty, involved in the areas of instruction, research, and public service.

Source: James A. Hyatt, *A Cost Accounting Handbook for Colleges and Universities* (Washington, DC: National Association of College and University Business Officers, 1983), p. 19.

Figure 2: Department Analysis

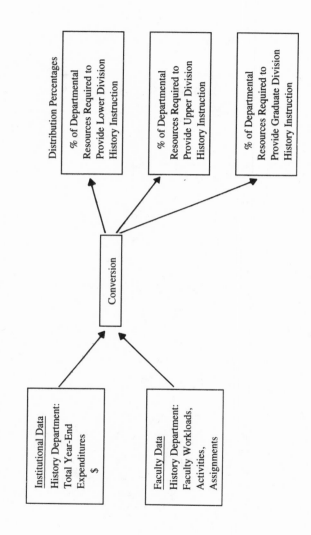

Figure 3: Analysis to Determine Distribution Percentages

Institutional Data [A]

Person Identifier	Payroll Data		Personnel Data	
	Account	Compensation	Activity	Proportion
I. Doi	10-251-01	$20,000	LD History Instruction	50%
			UD History Instruction	30%
			Department Chairperson	20%
				100%
E. Foote	10-251-01	$18,000	UD History Instruction	30%
			GD History Instruction	60%
			Community Education	10%
				100%
P. Bishop	10-251-01	$12,000	LD History Instruction	80%
			LD Sociology Instruction	20%
				100%

[B]

Derived Individual Dollar Contribution

	LD History Instruction	UD History Instruction	GD History Instruction	LD Sociology Instruction	Community Education	History Chairperson	Total
I. Doi	$10,000	$6,000				$4,000	
E. Foote		$5,400	$10,800		$1,000		
P. Bishop	$9,600			$2,400			
Contribution Totals	$19,600	$11,400	$10,800	$2,400	$1,800	$4,000	$50,000
Distribution Percentages	39.2%	22.8%	21.6%	4.8%	3.6%	8%	100%
Crossover Percent	$24,068.80	$13,999.20	$13,262.40	$2,947.20	$2,210.40	$4,912	$61,400

[C]

History Department Expenditures

10-251-01	$50,000	Compensation
10-251-02	2,000	Supplies
10-251-03	8,000	Secretarial Staff
10-251-04	400	Communication
10-251-05	1,000	Travel
10-251	$61,400	

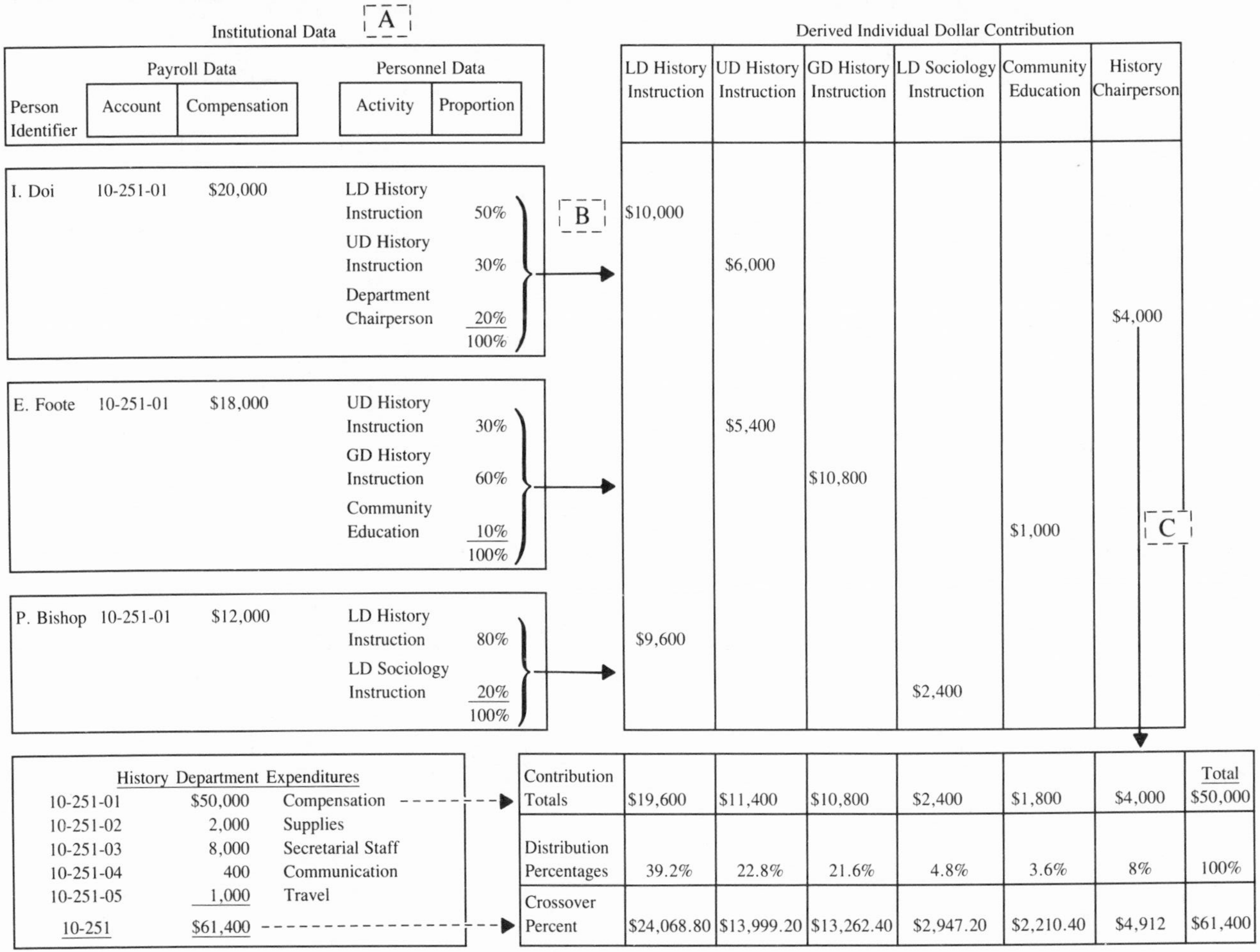

Figure 4: Calculation of Direct Unit Costs for Disciplines

Activity Center	Direct Expenditures	Total Credits Attempted	Discipline Direct Unit Costs
LD Math	$20,000	1,000	$20
UD Math	30,000	1,000	30
LD Poli. Sci.	20,000	2,000	10
UD Poli. Sci.	10,000	500	20

Figure 5: Calculation of Direct Unit Costs for Student Programs

Discipline	Student Program			
	Math Major Lower Level	Math Major Upper Level	Political Science Major Lower Level	Political Science Major Upper Level
LD Math	800 × $20	50 × $20	100 × $20	50 × $20
UD Math	90 × $30	900 × $30	0 × $30	10 × $30
LD Poli. Sci.	200 × $10	10 × $10	90 × $10	1700 × $10
UD Poli. Sci.	50 × $20	0 × $20	50 × $20	400 × $20
Average of All Other Disciplines Contributing to Math and Poli. Sci. Programs	1000 × $40	1500 × $40	2500 × $20	300 × $40
Total Program Costs	$61,700	$88,100	$53,900	$38,300
Total Program Credits	2140	2460	2740	2460
Program Direct Unit Costs	$29	$36	$20	$16

FOR FURTHER READING

A good in-depth introduction to cost analysis is James A. Hyatt, *A Cost Accounting Handbook for Colleges and Universities* (Washington, DC: National Association of College and University Business Officers, 1983). For additional information on reporting and accounting structures for use in cost analyses, see K. Scott Hughes, Jerry H. Leonard, and M. J. Williams, Jr., *A Management Reporting Manual for Colleges* (Washington, DC: National Association of College and University Business Officers, 1980). Cost analysis methodologies are also discussed by Daniel D. Robinson, Howard W. Ray, and Frederick J. Turk in "Cost Behavior Analysis For Planning in Higher Education," *NACUBO Professional File*, vol. 9, no. 5 (May 1977).

James A. Hyatt offers some cautions on the use of national data for comparative analysis in "Using National Financial Data for Comparative Analysis," in *Successful Responses to Financial Difficulty,* edited by Carol Frances, New Directions for Higher Education, no. 38 (San Francisco: Jossey-Bass, Inc., 1982). The same volume contains an excellent paper by Martin Kramer, "What the New Indicators Cannot Tell Us," which discusses the limitations of comparative data.

Three good commentaries on cost analysis are Raymond F. Bacchetti, "Using Cost Analysis in Internal Management in Higher Education," *NACUBO Professional File*, vol. 9, no. 1 (January 1977); Robin Jenkins and James Topping, "Costing for Policy Analysis," *Business Officer*, vol. 13, no. 12 (June 1980); and Stephen R. Hample, "Cost Studies in Higher Education," *AIR Professional File*, no. 7 (Fall 1980).

11 / Instructional Workload Matrix

The instructional workload matrix displays in matrix format the relationship between disciplines and student degree programs (in some institutions disciplines are equivalent to departments). Degree programs are composed of course offerings from a number of different disciplines (or departments if appropriate). The distribution of credit hours taken by a particular major will be determined by the institution's degree requirements, including distribution requirements and mandatory courses such as English composition, and the student's own interests as reflected in his or her elective courses. The instructional workload matrix for an institution represents the cumulative impact of individual student major profiles on the student credit hour distribution for the institution.

CONTRIBUTION AND CONSUMPTION REPORTS

The relationship between disciplines and student degree programs can be shown in two ways. First, the instructional workload matrix displays credit hour totals that each discipline and course level within each discipline have contributed to each student degree program. Second, the matrix displays the credit hour totals that each student degree and student level have consumed from each discipline. Figure 1 illustrates this relationship. For example, the lower division biology discipline, generally the freshman-

213

and sophomore-level courses in biology, contributes a total of 595 credit hours to lower division biochemistry majors, 732 credit hours to lower division English majors, and so forth, summing to a total contribution of 3,050 credit hours. On the other hand, lower division biochemistry majors, generally those students classified as freshman or sophomore biochemistry majors, consume 595 lower division credit hours from the biology discipline, 708 lower division credit hours from the English discipline, and so forth, summing to a total consumption of 2,837 credit hours.

The development of an instructional workload matrix is computationally straightforward. The process sums the credit hours produced by each student major at each course level. Figure 2 illustrates the data requirements and computations necessary to build the matrix. Following this same process of aggregation for each student registration record will yield a matrix similar to that shown in figure 1.

In the instructional workload matrix, disciplines are rows and programs are columns. Thus, the disciplines in figure 2 represent translations of course prefixes and numbers into a description of appropriate rows of the matrix. For example, Sue Kay's enrollment in BIO 104 is translated into lower division biology (because the course number—104—is in the 0-299 course range that is designated as lower division). In figure 2 this enrollment is identified as discipline A. Similarly, the programs in figure 2 represent translations of majors and student levels into a description of appropriate columns of the matrix. Sue Kay's data are translated from BIOC major and LD (lower division) student level into the "biochemistry-lower div." instructional workload matrix program. In figure 2 this enrollment is identified as degree program (or major) B.

Figure 3 is the contribution and consumption report for the fall 1982 semester at the University of Maryland, College Park. This particular report aggregates disciplines and degree programs by colleges and the five academic divisions (Agriculture and Life Sciences; Arts and Humanities; Behavioral and Social Sciences; Human and Community Resources; and Mathematics, Physical Sciences, and Engineering). Also, note that here degree programs are treated as rows and disciplines as columns. Majors in the College of Business and Management in the Division of Behavioral and Social Sciences, for example, consume 30,229 credit hours in various disciplines. Of this total 19,470 are consumed in the College of Business and Management. This means that business and management majors take approximately 64.4 percent (i.e., 19,470 divided by 30,229) of their coursework in the College of Business and Management. Similarly, majors in the College of Agriculture in the Division of Agriculture and Life Sciences consume 16,377 credit hours in various disciplines. Of this total 7,493 are consumed in the College of Agriculture. This means that agriculture majors take approximately 45.8 percent (i.e., 7,493 divided by 16,377) of their coursework in the College of Agriculture.

If, on the other hand, one examines the College of Business and Management as a contributor of credit hours (i.e., as a discipline), the college is seen to contribute 30,762 credit hours to various majors or degree programs across the campus. Of this total, 19,470 credit hours are contributed to business and management majors. This means that 63.3 percent (i.e., 19,470 divided by 30,762) of the teaching load of the College of Business and Management is directed to business and management majors and 36.7 percent to non-business-and-management majors. Similarly, the College of Agriculture is seen to contribute 12,149 credit hours to various majors or degree programs across the campus. Of this total, 7,493 credit hours are contributed to agriculture majors. This means that 61.7 percent (i.e., 7,493 divided by 12,149) of the College of Agriculture teaching load is directed to agriculture majors and 38.3 percent to non-agriculture majors. Thus, the College of Agriculture performs a slightly larger service role (i.e., 38.3 percent vs. 36.7 percent) for other majors than the College of Business and Management. If the Department of English discipline and the English major were disaggregated from this table, one would find that the Department of English performs a significant service mission in that it contributes a large majority of its credit hours to non-English degree programs. That is, most of the credit hours consumed in the Department of English are taken by non-English majors.

The distribution of student credit hours produced by degree programs and disciplines will form the basis for discipline costs and degree program costs. Discipline costs are those costs incurred in teaching specific academic disciplines; discipline unit cost is the cost of a single semester or quarter credit hour of instruction and is usually given by level of instruction. Program costs normally refer to the costs of a student major and program unit cost to the cost of a full-time equivalent student in a specific student major. As noted above, degree programs usually require the contribution of several disciplines. Program costs reflect the resources coming from those disciplines. The instructional workload matrix ultimately becomes the means by which discipline costs are attributed to a degree program or degree program unit. The matrix is an excellent means of tracing over time the changes in student demand and teaching loads. Accordingly, it becomes a powerful tool for examining how instructional resources should be allocated across the institution.

Several examples in this chapter are drawn from an early draft of *Information Exchange Procedures* (State Council of Higher Education for Virginia).

Figure 1: Instructional Workload Matrix

Degree Programs

Disciplines	Biochemistry Lower Div.	Biochemistry Upper Div.	English Lower Div.	English Upper Div.	Psychology Lower Div.	Psychology Upper Div.	Total
LD Biology	595		732		1,283	440	3,050
UD Biology		980		840		440	2,260
LD English	708		2,430	315	1,792	220	5,455
UD English		294		2,100		1,430	3,824
LD Math	1,003		1,579		1,024	220	3,626
UD Math		588	729	630		440	1,658
LD Chemistry	531			1,024		110	2,394
UD Chemistry		784		630		660	2,074
Totals	2,837	2,646	5,470	5,539	4,099	3,960	24,551

Figure 2: Development of an Instructional Workload Matrix

Selected Student Registration Records

Activity Term	Student Name	Course	Prefix No.	Major	Student Level	Semester Credits	IWLM Discipline	IWLM Program
FA	Sue Kay	BIO	104	BIOCHEM	LD	3	LD BIO	BIOCHEM-LD
SP	Robert Allen	BIO	112	PSYCH	LD	3	LD BIO	PSYCH-LD
SP	Mary Smith	ENGL	210	ENGL	UD	3	LD ENGL	ENGL-UD
FA	Arnold Black	MATH	256	ENGL	UD	3	LD MATH	ENGL-UD
FA	Michael Lee	CHEM	100	BIOCHEM	LD	5	LD CHEM	BIOCHEM-LD
SP	Robert Trent	BIO	104	PSYCH	LD	3	LD BIO	PSYCH-LD

Note: Lower division courses carry numbers from 0 through 299.
Upper division courses carry numbers from 300 through 499.

Instructional Workload Matrix

Degree Programs / Disciplines	Biochemistry Lower Div.	Biochemistry Upper Div.	English Lower Div.	English Upper Div.	Psychology Lower Div.	Psychology Upper Div.
LD Biology	③	Sue Kay's Course			6	
UD Biology						
LD English				3		
UD English						
LD Math				3	4	
UD Math						
LD Chemistry	5					
UD Chemistry						

Figure 3: Course Credit Hour Contribution/Consumption by College/Division, University of Maryland, College Park, Fall 1982

Student Col/Div	Total	ALSC			A & H				BSOS			HUCR					MPSE			Other		
		Total	Col. of Agri.	Other	Total	Sch. of Arch.	Col. of Jour.	Other	Total	Col. of BuM.	Other	Total	Col. of Educ.	Col. of HE	Col. of PERH	Other	Total	Col. of Engr.	Other	Ungr. Stud.	Alld. Hlth.	Other Courses
Grand Total	445968	51388	12149	39239	114346	4434	4675	105237	110586	30762	79824	62995	24143	15743	21550	1559	105045	32584	72461	957	—	651
ALSC—Total	45121	25532	8356	17176	6571	69	15	6487	3947	264	3683	2373	430	368	1572	3	6520	332	6188	105	—	73
Col. of Agri.	16377	10872	7493	3379	1728	27	—	1701	1329	144	1185	880	224	169	484	3	1534	216	1318	9	—	25
Other	28744	14660	863	13797	4843	42	15	4786	2618	120	2498	1493	206	199	1088	—	4986	116	4870	96	—	48
A & H—Total	62684	2017	554	1463	42680	3435	3859	35386	9124	818	8306	3759	1011	838	1892	18	4884	55	4829	139	—	81
Sch. of Arch.	3907	57	21	36	3211	2836	9	375	198	9	189	209	25	51	133	—	223	8	215	9	—	—
Col. of Jour.	12547	401	110	291	7006	9	3247	3750	3418	377	3041	818	186	195	437	—	847	21	826	30	—	27
Other	46230	1559	423	1136	32463	590	612	31261	5508	432	5076	2732	800	592	1322	18	3814	26	3788	100	—	54
BSOS—Total	118729	4347	1032	3315	24301	303	270	23728	68715	25942	42773	9323	2024	1998	5292	9	11648	125	11523	209	—	186
Col. of BuM.	30229	457	217	240	2994	24	45	2925	23804	19470	4334	1846	347	336	1163	—	1029	38	991	24	—	75
Other	88500	3890	815	3075	21307	279	225	20803	44911	6472	38439	7477	1677	1662	4129	9	10619	87	10532	185	—	111
HUCR—Total	59134	3088	582	2506	9973	113	117	9743	6717	1121	5596	35356	17289	10202	6576	1289	3894	62	3832	40	—	66
Col. of Educ.	26843	979	186	793	4636	21	15	4600	2538	530	2008	16487	15630	375	455	27	2142	56	2086	22	—	39
Col. of HE	20611	1426	305	1121	3739	77	87	3575	2925	483	2442	11413	951	9672	790	—	1078	3	1078	15	—	15
Col. of PERH	7930	548	71	477	720	3	9	708	644	57	587	5748	597	85	5066	—	258	3	255	—	—	12
Int. Ed. Dev.	1635	108	14	94	633	12	6	615	388	18	370	259	31	45	185	—	247	3	244	—	—	—
Other	2115	27	6	21	245	—	—	245	222	33	189	1449	80	25	82	1262	169	—	169	3	—	—
MPSE—Total	107978	9212	825	8387	15292	375	99	14818	8727	968	7759	4587	826	604	3157	—	69884	31691	38193	261	—	15
Col. of Engr.	60636	4993	577	4416	5957	189	42	5726	2892	215	2677	2009	332	195	1482	—	44617	30847	13770	153	—	15
Other	47342	4219	248	3971	9335	186	57	9092	5835	753	5082	2578	494	409	1675	—	25267	844	24423	108	—	—
UNGR STUD—Total	39057	3671	487	3184	12456	133	243	12080	11281	1424	9857	5268	1360	1385	2508	15	6197	69	6128	169	—	15
Gen. Studies	8653	461	157	304	2217	18	72	2127	2914	383	2531	2556	782	569	1190	15	502	6	496	3	—	—
Indiv. Studies	592	51	9	42	201	2	15	184	111	15	81	119	35	30	54	—	26	—	26	84	—	—
Other	29812	3159	321	2838	10038	113	156	9769	8256	1011	7245	2593	543	786	1264	—	5669	63	5606	82	—	15
ALLD HLTH—Total	8018	2720	23	2697	1977	6	3	1968	1371	36	1335	861	298	197	366	—	1073	—	1073	4	—	12
Allied Health	2896	925	6	919	635	3	—	632	595	21	574	277	49	43	185	—	451	—	451	1	—	12
Nursing	4342	1560	14	1546	1128	3	3	1122	691	15	676	528	242	145	141	—	432	—	432	3	—	—
Pharmacy	780	235	3	232	214	—	—	214	85	—	85	56	7	9	40	—	190	—	190	—	—	—
OTH MAJ—Total	5247	801	290	511	1096	—	69	1027	704	189	515	1468	905	151	187	225	945	250	695	30	—	203
Net Contribution (+) Consumption (−)		+6267	−4228	+10495	+51662	+527	−7872	+59007	−8143	+533	−8676	+3861	−2700	−4868	+13620	−2191[1]	−2933	−28052	+25119	−38100	−8018	−4596

[1]Includes 1,635 I.E.D. credit hours.

Note: Air Science course credits (548) have been included in BSOS.

Source: Office of Institutional Studies, University of Maryland, College Park.

FOR FURTHER READING

A very good introduction to the instructional workload matrix is provided by its creator, Sidney Suslow, in "Induced Course Load Matrix: Conception and Use," in *Assessing Computer-based Systems Models,* edited by Thomas R. Mason, New Directions for Institutional Research, no. 9 (San Francisco: Jossey-Bass, Inc., 1976), pp. 35–52.

12 / Enrollment Forecasting

The forecasting of institutional enrollments has recently been linked more closely than ever with the budget process. There is no reason to expect this close relationship to change over the next decade.

The reasons for elevation of the importance of enrollment forecasting are clear. During the three decades of growth in higher education following World War II, enrollment demand grew, in general, more rapidly than institutional capacity. Institutions were able to accommodate this demand by adjusting admissions standards and by increasing in size. Although for most institutions the resource base lagged behind rising enrollments by one or more years, the certainty of future enrollment growth and increased resources continued to fuel the expansion. As Hoenack and Weiler (1979, 89) note, "To the extent that capacity grew smoothly, the simple extrapolation of trends produced accurate forecasts and economic analysis had relatively little to contribute to enrollment forecasting."

During the 1980s, however, the size of the traditional college-going age group will diminish, and enrollment demand will not exceed capacity except in a relatively small number of selective institutions or in those whose local demographic profiles are at odds with the national trend. Accordingly, competition among institutions for students will intensify. Institutions will seek to maintain or expand their share of enrollments by recruiting more actively, advertising more extensively, making programs more attractive, and enlarging the population of potential students to include older and part-time students. More and more planners are accepting the fact that future enrollments are no longer simple projections of the past, and institutional budgets, which are determined in large part by student enrollments, are more susceptible to fluctuations in enrollment demand. Under these conditions accurate enrollment forecasts become essential in planning resource commitments.

From the layman's perspective projecting enrollments is a mysterious art, whereby past enrollment data are stirred in a computer with an assortment of variables and parameters to arrive at a projection. The mathematical models used to forecast enrollments are often quite complex and can be understood only by experts. Behind the equations, however, lie sets of assumptions that are more significant determinants of the projections than the methodologies themselves. The purpose of this chapter is to identify the kinds of issues that forecasters must address before projection models can be applied. Those issues can be clustered loosely into three categories: (1) demographic and other factors outside the control of the institution, (2) policy variables over which the institution has some control; and (3) modeling methodologies. The reader will be referred to other sources for technical aspects of enrollment projection model development.

FACTORS OUTSIDE THE CONTROL
OF THE INSTITUTION

Enrollment forecasts have to recognize national demographic trends, local demographic patterns, and the environment created by federal, state, and local policies toward higher education.

National demographic data are readily available. One of the most frequently quoted statistics is the number of live births, which decreased nationwide by 27 percent between 1960 and 1974 (U.S. Bureau of the Census, 1979, table 1). Accordingly, the number of 18-year-olds in the population will decline from a peak of 4.3 million in 1979 to 3.2 million in 1994 (Breneman, 1982, 9). The population of 18-year-olds will begin to grow again in the late 1990s.

The national trend in live births will be moderated on a state and local level by several additional factors, including high school graduation rates, college entry rates, college retention rates, enrollment rates for older age groups, enrollments of foreign students, enrollments of graduate and professional students, and the distribution of full-time and part-time attendance. Also, state and local demographics for women, minorities, religious denominations, income levels, and older students will strongly influence enrollment projections.

Blacks and Hispanics will make up an increasing percentage of the 18-year-old population during the 1980s and 1990s. In 1977, for example, the average age of all whites was 30.2, of blacks 24.1, and of Hispanics 22 (U.S. Bureau of the Census, 1978a and 1978b). However, the high school graduation rates of minority students are considerably below those of the majority population (Glenny, 1980, 365–366). In 1977 the high school graduation rate for whites age 18 to 24 was 83.9 percent, for blacks 69.8 percent, and for Hispanics 55.5 percent (Breneman, 1982, 17). The impact of these statistics is more severe for institutions that draw large numbers of students from minority populations.

Projections of the number of high school graduates also show considerable variation from state to state. These projections are important in enrollment forecasting in that the majority of full-time enrollees are recent high school graduates. During the next decade several states, including New York, Massachusetts, Connecticut, Rhode Island, and Delaware, are projected to have declines of greater than 40 percent. Illinois, Iowa, Maryland, Michigan, Minnesota, New Jersey, Pennsylvania, and Ohio are projected to experience declines of between 34 and 40 percent. On the other hand, states such as Arizona, Idaho, Louisiana, Nevada, Oregon, Texas, Utah, and Wyoming project increases in the number of high school graduates by 1995 (Breneman, 1982, 11–12).

College attendance rates are as important as high school graduation rates. In February 1978 the Bureau of the Census reported that the college attendance rate of those age 18 to 24 had dropped from 41.3 percent in the peak year of 1969 to 38.8 percent. During the same period the attendance rate for males in that age group dropped from 44.3 to 35.3 percent, while the rate for females increased from 37.8 to 43.2 percent (Glenny, 1980, 366).

It has been difficult to project enrollments for individuals over age 25 largely because opportunities open to the adult learner have multiplied. Also, many of these persons are not enrolled for college credit or in degree programs. It is important to note that the number of adult men over age 25 entering some area of education has not increased significantly since 1975 (Glenny, 1980, 368). It may be that enrollments of adult men over age 25 have reached a plateau (expiring G.I. Bill benefits for Vietnam-era veterans may be a contributing factor). The marked increase in enrollments of adult women may represent a one-time "catching up" phenomenon (Breneman, 1982, 10).

Federal student loan policies have an important effect on the number of potential students. It appears that the dramatic increase in federal student aid through such vehicles as Basic Educational Opportunity Grants (now Pell Grants), Department of Education loan and grant programs, the G.I. Bill, and specific agency grants will not be sustained in the coming decade.

Also, labor market conditions may influence enrollments to the extent that potential students regard enrollment as an investment. Factors considered by many students are costs incurred while attending college, such as foregone earnings, and benefits received as a result of the college experience, such as improved employment prospects. It is clearly difficult to gauge the impact of labor market conditions on enrollment projections.

FACTORS OVER WHICH THE INSTITUTION
HAS SOME CONTROL

An institution can control to some extent the population from which it draws its enrollments by altering the institution's unique character. Certain aspects of character are susceptible to changes in policy and must be considered by persons involved in enrollment projection at the institutional level. Factors that affect enrollment patterns but are not immediately responsive to policy actions are the diversity and quality of programs, the location of the institution, and the prestige of the institution. The nature of programs changes over time, and enrollment projections can be adjusted to recognize any qualitative changes.

Enrollment projections are also sensitive to the average course load taken by students. Normally, enrollments are measured in terms of head-counts (i.e., the number of students) or full-time equivalent (FTE) students (i.e., the total number of credit hours taken divided by the defined load for an FTE student). Typical defined loads are 15 credit hours per semester for undergraduates and 12 credit hours per semester for graduate students. If the number of part-time students increases, for example, or if full-time students take lighter course loads than before on average, more headcount students are needed to yield the same FTE enrollment.

Institutions exercise considerable control over enrollments through their admissions policies. Generally, enrollment patterns allow enrollment planners to determine the impact of changes in admissions standards. Institutions with a declining pool of applicants might lower entrance requirements to enlarge the pool of potential students or might increase the requirements significantly to attract a very different population of potential applicants. In public institutions the mix of in-state and out-of-state students can be modified, sometimes on a day-by-day basis toward the end of the admissions cycle. Both public and independent institutions can alter the geographical mix of the student body (including the proportion of foreign students), the policies for admission of transfer students, the mix of undergraduate and graduate students, and the mix of part-time and full-time students.

Enrollment projections should incorporate information about the student attrition rate for the range of degree programs. Institutions that have sought to reduce attrition by introducing retention programs should consider the impact of such programs in their enrollment projections.

Tuition and fee levels directly influence enrollments. In the enrollment projections of the University of Minnesota, for example, each $100 of increased charges is assumed to yield a 0.85 percent decrease in enrollments. The assumed enrollment decrease per $100 increase in charges varies across states and institutional types. Enrollment planners usually compare their institution's tuition and fee structure to that of competitors, and the rate of price increases to the general rate of inflation and the growth of family incomes.

The effect of financial aid policies on enrollment levels also must be anticipated. Data on the extent to which increases in tuition and fees are offset by institutional financial aid and state and federal student aid must be built into enrollment projections.

In general, the present financial value of any projected changes in enrollment must be estimated as follows: (1) first, estimate net revenue by subtracting the incremental costs of financial aid, recruitment, housing, and food services for the students gained or lost from the additional income from tuition and fees and room and board charges; (2) second, estimate net revenue from this group of students during subsequent years until their graduation. This calculation requires two steps: (a) reduce the estimated number of students in the group each year until the point of graduation, according to the projected attrition rate; and (b) state the resulting net revenue charges that will be derived from the remaining group in future years in terms of present value—this process is called discounting. The discount rate might, for example, be the rate of return on the institution's investment portfolio.

MODELING TECHNOLOGIES

The objective of enrollment forecasting techniques is to provide statistically accurate projections of future enrollments using parameters that are readily defined from available data. Enrollments are normally projected by using flow models, which compute the number of students passing through the institution under various conditions. There are three general types of flow models: (1) the grade progression ratio method, (2) Markov chain models, and (3) cohort flow models (Hopkins and Massy, 1981, 352–363).

The grade progression ratio method is the least sophisticated mathematically and hence requires the smallest amount of data. It is the ratio of students in one class level at time t to students in the next lower class level at time t-1. Only three such ratios are required to project undergraduate enrollments. The limitation of this modeling procedure is that it assumes that all students in one level advance between one time period and the next. Thus, it can be applied only for making year-to-year (rather than semester-to-semester or quarter-to-quarter) projections. Also, it does not recognize the realities of student flow: some students remain at a given level for more than one year, and other students drop out temporarily to return in subsequent years. The grade progression ratio method is usually viewed as too unsophisticated to provide accurate enrollment projections for institutions and tends to be employed more at the state level.

The Markov chain model, like the grade progression ratio method, uses transition fractions (i.e., the fraction of students in a class in one period that can be found in the next higher class in a subsequent period), but also incorporates the flow of students who remain in the same class level in consecutive time periods. Furthermore, the model can account for flows of transfer students at each class level.

The Markov chain model requires considerably more data than the grade progression ratio method. For four student levels the Markov chain model requires seven transition ratios per term. Thus, the total number of transition ratios required is 14 for a two-semester academic year or 21 for a three-quarter academic year. The use of transition ratios between semesters or quarters enables the model to produce estimates of attrition between terms. Moreover, the model should provide more accurate fall term enrollment estimates than the grade progression ratio method because the estimates are based on enrollments in the preceding spring term. The computation of transition ratios is often difficult in that institutional information systems usually do not distinguish among continuing students according to their previous student level.

A four-state Markov model (for the four student levels) does not account for the two-way flow of undergraduate temporary dropouts, who return to campus after one or more terms away. With four states the model assumes instead that students returning after having dropped out are continuing directly from the preceding term. The Markov model can be modified to accommodate temporary dropouts through the addition of one or more "vacation states." These vacation states require transition ratios for flows between active and temporary dropout levels. For most institutions the information demands here are considerable.

Although the Markov chain model is more satisfying structurally than the grade progression ratio method, its projections are subject to errors that can arise if transition ratios are undifferentiated as to the origins of the students being tracked. Also, built into the model is an unrealistic assumption: a student's remaining at his or her current level in the subsequent term does not depend on the length of time the student has already spent in the current level.

The cohort flow model groups students into cohorts and tracks the longitudinal progression of those cohorts through the institution, as opposed to the cross-sectional models that project enrollments on the basis of an enrollment profile for the term immediately preceding. Cohorts are identified by the period of entry, student level at entry, and other descriptors such as sex or race. The parameters are "survivor fractions" in that the enrollment in a given class level is the total of the survivors from all previous cohorts.

The cohort flow model requires more data than do the previous two models. Distinct survivor fractions must be computed for type of cohort, class level, academic term, and maximum elapsed time for enrollment. (In the cohort flow model the elapsed time for undergraduate enrollment will typically extend beyond four years to account for students who drop out temporarily.) Most data required for the cohort flow model must come from individual student files and are quite expensive to obtain. However, the model offers much greater precision in its projections than do the other two models. Also, in some institutions the enrollment patterns of certain cohort types are remarkably stable over a period of several years. Accordingly, survivor fractions do not need to be updated frequently.

The above three modeling techniques assume as input the number of new students entering the institution in a given term. The computation of the number of new students involves a separate structural model for which several methodologies are available, including (1) linear models using generalized least squares and (2) models that are nonlinear in the estimated coefficients and residuals of separate structural equations and that require Monte Carlo techniques for development of estimates of forecast errors. These models have parameters such as academic ratings, sex, race, residence, income level (own or parents'), and other financial aid available. Public institutions also consider the grade-to-grade advancement ratios of elementary and secondary school students, the mortality of these students, and their migration patterns. The University of Minnesota, for example, includes labor-force variables and a factor to account for changes in Gross National Product (Hoenack and Weiler, 1979).

In projecting enrollments one should be sensitive to the limits of error in the modeling process. The size of the confidence interval for projections can be computed statistically and can in turn provide an estimate of the range of income anticipated for an enrollment-based budget. Interval forecasts are especially important in public sector budget negotiations concerning whether the state or the institution is fiscally responsible for under- or overenrollments.

FOR FURTHER READING

Discussions of policy issues related to enrollment projections are found in David W. Breneman, *The Coming Enrollment Crisis: What Every Trustee Must Know* (Washington, DC: Association of Governing Boards of Universities and Colleges, 1982), and Lyman A. Glenny, "Demographic and Related Issues for Higher Education in the 1980s," *Journal of Higher Education,* vol. 51, no. 4 (May/June 1980), pp. 363–380.

The technical aspects of enrollment forecasting are discussed in David S. P. Hopkins and William F. Massy, *Planning Models for Colleges and Universities* (Stanford, CA: Stanford University Press, 1981). See also Sidney Suslow's article, "Benefits of a Cohort Survival Projection Model," in *Applying Analytic Methods to Planning and Management,* edited by David S. P. Hopkins and Roger G. Schroeder, New Directions for Institutional Research, no. 13 (San Francisco: Jossey-Bass, Inc., 1977), pp. 19–42. Enrollment forecasting at the University of Minnesota is described in Stephen A. Hoenack and William C. Weiler, "The Demand for Higher Education and Institutional Enrollment Forecasting," *Economic Inquiry,* vol. 17, no. 1 (January 1979), pp. 89–113.

13 / Indirect Costs of Sponsored Programs

Institutions with a sizable commitment to research and other sponsored activities generally receive a significant portion of their income from funding agencies and other external sources. Funds received for sponsored programs are intended to cover the direct and indirect costs of these activities. Direct costs are those that can be readily identified and charged to a specific sponsored activity with reasonable accuracy; they include salaries and benefits of individuals engaged in the activity and the materials and equipment employed in conducting the activity. Indirect costs are those incurred for the general support and management of sponsored activities but that cannot be easily or directly attributed to a particular activity. Indirect costs are real and represent an overhead charge for undertaking sponsored activities at an institution. In essence, a funding agency pays for the use of an institution's facilities. These overhead charges include the costs of general administration, physical plant and maintenance, and the library.

DIRECT AND INDIRECT COSTS

The classification of particular expenditures as direct or indirect costs depends on an institution's structure and the way it is organized to conduct research and other sponsored activities. For example, institutions that assign secretaries to pools rather than to specific projects generally charge secretarial support as an indirect cost. Similarly, some institutional computer centers maintain individual accounts for each user, while other centers are budgeted centrally and do not monitor or charge individual users directly. Computer-related charges that can be tied to specific projects are direct costs; expenditures for a centrally budgeted computer center without chargebacks are indirect costs. The following are examples of expenditures that can be accounted for as direct or indirect costs, depending on institutional organization: secretarial support; computer support; administrative and clerical support; purchasing; social security, retirement contributions, and group insurance; vacations, holidays, and sick leave; hospitalization and medical services; liability insurance and workers' compensation; postage and communications; office supplies; books and periodicals; maintenance and janitorial services; security expenses; utility costs; mortgage payments; and depreciation of buildings and equipment.

At times faculty and staff contend that in seeking external funding their institution is not competitive because of its high indirect cost rate. The difference in rates is attributable to differences in institutional organization and hence in what is accounted for as a direct cost and an indirect cost. It is reasonable to expect that for a given sponsored program the combined total of direct costs and indirect costs would not vary from one institution to another by much more than differences in cost of living or in salary profiles for the program participants. Thus, an inordinate amount of attention given to indirect cost rates can present a misleading picture of the costing of sponsored programs.

Colleges and universities determine the rate for reimbursement of indirect costs using guidelines prepared by the federal government: Office of Management and Budget Circular A-21. These guidelines reflect the outcome of negotiations between government officials and institutional officials over the share of indirect costs of sponsored programs that government agencies should bear. OMB Circular A-21 has been revised and reissued several times since its earliest embodiment appeared following World War II.

OMB Circular A-21 deals exclusively with the costs of conducting sponsored programs. It excludes for-profit operations and certain types of expenditures that OMB classifies as unallowable. Allowable costs under federally sponsored research agreements are (1) all expenses that have been incurred solely for the work on the activity (direct costs) and (2) a share of other costs that are incurred primarily for administrative and service support functions related to the sponsored program (indirect costs) (American Council on Education and Council on Governmental Relations of the National Association of College and University Business Officers, 1981, 3). Unallowable costs include research conducted by an institution using its own funds; interest; fund raising and investment management costs; patent costs; entertainment; commencement and convocation costs; student activities costs; cost overruns; and the costs of general public relations activities. The sum of direct and indirect costs represents the total cost of the sponsored activity.

OMB Circular A-21 suggests that the following expenditures are direct costs: salaries and wages of persons employed on the sponsored activity; employee benefits, including social security and retirement plan contributions (these costs may be categorized as indirect costs in certain situations); supplies consumed by the sponsored activity; travel related to the sponsored activity; communication charges attributable to the sponsored activity only; costs of equipment acquired for specific use in a sponsored program; computer time and services, including programming, related to a sponsored program; and renovations to accommodate a sponsored program.

Similarly, the following expenditures are generally considered indirect costs: general administration, including accounting, payroll, purchasing, and administrative offices; expenditures for staff and operations of offices with responsibility for the administration of sponsored programs; plant operation and maintenance, including utilities, janitorial service, maintenance and repairs, and mortgage payments; library expenditures for staff, books, and periodicals; expenditures for administration at the department and college levels; depreciation and use allowance (pro rata share of replacement costs attributable to a sponsored program); and administration of student affairs, admissions, and registrar's offices.

COMPUTATION OF INDIRECT COST RATES

The OMB Circular A-21 guidelines specify, for costing purposes, the major functions of institutions of higher education: instruction, including departmental research; organized research; other sponsored activities; and other institutional activities. It is necessary to determine the proportion of the costs of the indirect cost categories that are directly attributable to the sponsored programs. The total indirect costs are apportioned among the major functions using formulas with various allocation bases.

For example, the cost of operations and maintenance might be allocated to each function based on the net assignable square feet allotted to a particular function (subject to further refinements for shared space or unusual situations). Plant expenses also might be allocated on the basis of salaries. Accordingly, the fraction of total plant costs attributed to sponsored programs will be based on the proportion of total institutional salaries actually charged to sponsored programs. The costs of departmental administration also might be allocated on the basis of total direct salaries. Thus, if sponsored programs pay $20 million in salaries, and if the other functions combined account for $60 million in salaries, 25 percent of departmental administration costs are allocated to sponsored programs. The costs of general administration can be allocated in a similar manner. An alternative method is to use faculty activity reports to determine the proportion of faculty and staff effort devoted to sponsored programs. The allocation of library costs might be based on a study of library usage. The proportion of usage attributed to students could be attributed to instruction. Faculty and staff usage could be allocated among the various functions in proportion to direct salaries, as in departmental administration.

The total of indirect costs attributable to sponsored programs is expressed as a percentage of modified total direct costs. This base consists of salaries and wages, employee benefits, material, supplies, services, travel, and subgrant and subcontract expenditures up to $25,000 each.

Institutions may use more than one indirect cost rate to reflect different kinds of sponsored activities. Sponsored programs conducted exclusively off campus may have a lower rate than on-campus activities to reflect the fact that campus facilities are not used. A program that involves only fellowships or scholarships may have a minimal indirect cost rate to reflect the low costs (generally administrative) of operating the program.

Indirect cost rates are computed by the institution each year based on a cost study as described above. The institution's worksheets are subject to audit by a federal agency. It is not unusual for several years to elapse after submission of the indirect cost rate calculations before an audit is conducted. The audit report often leads to negotiations over indirect cost rates between the federal government and the institution.

COST SHARING

Some sponsoring federal agencies require that in the case of research grants the institution share the costs of the research activity. The cost sharing is accomplished by the institution's absorbing of a portion of the cost of faculty time associated with the activity or by its absorbing of other direct costs such as computer usage, communications, and supplies. The cost of sharing is a very real one in that the institution assumes responsibility for partial support of the research activity and loses the flexibility to use those monies elsewhere. The effect would be the same if the institution "underbid" a research grant to make a proposal more attractive to a funding agency. Although the institution would receive external funding, that funding would be at some cost to available resources. This has to be anticipated in constructing the institution's annual budget.

NONFEDERAL FUNDING AGENCIES

Institutions generally apply the same indirect cost rates to grants and contracts from nonfederal and federal sponsors. In some instances, however, the charter or the funding policies of a private foundation or a voluntary health agency do not permit the payment of indirect costs to the same extent as do federal sponsors. In receiving only partial payment of overhead costs, the institution is sharing the cost of the grant or contract activity. As with explicit cost sharing, this cost has to be anticipated by budget planners.

INSTITUTIONAL AND STATE POLICIES— INDIRECT COST REIMBURSEMENTS

Overhead reimbursement funds are incorporated into the institutional budget somewhat differently in the public and independent sectors. In both cases, however, it is not uncommon for faculty members to argue that, because the institution must maintain its buildings and pay for utilities and have an office of sponsored programs anyway (regardless of whether the institution receives a particular grant and reimbursement for indirect costs), the overhead reimbursement funds should be treated as "free" monies to be used without restriction. This perspective tends to downplay the fact that there are real indirect costs associated with the conduct of sponsored activity.

Independent institutions generally treat indirect cost reimbursements as unrestricted revenue. In constructing a budget, therefore, planners in independent institutions use overhead reimbursements as one of several sources of income. In institutions where units operate as independent cost centers and are essentially self-supporting on the basis of their own revenues (e.g., tuition, endowment, and sponsored programs), a portion of the indirect cost reimbursements is usually returned to the unit generating the sponsored activity.

State practices differ widely concerning the use of indirect cost reimbursements as a source of revenue for public institutions. Some states retain all overhead reimbursements or use them as an offset against state appropriations to the institution. In the latter case the total anticipated revenue from indirect cost reimbursements is included in the total budget of the institution. Other states allow institutions to retain a portion of indirect cost reimbursements as unrestricted income. Under these conditions institutions often distribute overhead reimbursements as a form of seed money to the units generating the sponsored activity. The units are encouraged to use this funding to further their research or other sponsored activities through, for example, the purchase of equipment or the support of junior faculty projects. States that return to the institution a portion of indirect cost reimbursements look on these unrestricted funds as investments in the institution's sponsored programs.

FOR FURTHER READING

A brief discussion of the nature of indirect cost reimbursements is found in *Direct and Indirect Costs of Research at Colleges and Universities* (Washington, DC: American Council on Education and the Council on Governmental Relations of the National Association of College and University Business Officers, 1981). Chapter 4:7, "Indirect Costs of Sponsored Programs," of *College & University Business Administration*, 4th ed. (Washington, DC: National Association of College and University Business Officers, 1982) contains a somewhat more detailed but nontechnical discussion of the subject. Detailed, step-by-step procedures for the computation of indirect cost rates are presented in *Indirect Cost Rates (Long Form): A Manual for Preparation of Indirect Cost Studies,* which is revised and updated annually for NACUBO's workshop on indirect cost rates—long form.

During the late 1970s Princeton University reexamined its policies and procedures governing indirect cost reimbursement rate calculations. The issues are discussed in chapter 5, "Changing the Indirect Cost Rate," of *Budgeting and Resource Allocation at Princeton University: Report of a Demonstration Project Supported by the Ford Foundation,* vol. 2, by Carol P. Herring et al. (Princeton, NJ: Princeton University, 1979).

14 / Budgeting and Mathematical Modeling

Quantitative tools for budget planning in higher education have appeared in great number in the last decade. Many of these tools are termed mathematical models. In modeling, basic assumptions about a category of behavior are made explicit and the relationships among key factors that characterize the behavior are systematically described. A mathematical model takes shape if the relationships can be described algebraically.

Modeling is intended to be a means for addressing problems in a more orderly fashion and with greater rigor than might otherwise be brought to bear. It can also be a cost-effective way to simulate behavior under different conditions. If it is assumed that there is no one "correct" solution to a problem, modeling can be used to sample a range of alternative responses. By comparing the model's forecasts with reality, the model can be refined and understanding of the process being modeled can be increased. Modeling is useful for identifying variables that are important in describing a situation. In modeling certain behavior, factors assumed to be important may be found in fact to have little impact on the process. The converse is also true. Thus, modeling concentrates attention on the factors that have the greatest influence.

Mathematical models have not been universally adopted by institutions

235

of higher education. There is some concern that the use of models will give the misleading impression that administrators have a firm understanding of educational processes. Also, much in the educational process cannot be quantified. The use of quantitative tools conjures up the "business model" in the minds of many who view that approach as inappropriate for institutions of higher education.

However, quantitative examination of certain categories of activities within institutions can be accomplished without complete knowledge of the educational process: faculty flow (recruitment, promotion and tenuring, and departure), enrollment projection, course and facilities scheduling, utilities usage, inventory management, and endowment management. These activities are self-contained enough to allow simulation without the use of a complex model. (Complex models *can* be developed for these activities, however.) Furthermore, recent developments in computer technology have made it easier for individuals lacking a quantitative orientation to experiment with models. Inexpensive microprocessors with nontechnical software packages are sufficiently powerful for all but the most complex modeling exercises.

The purpose of this chapter is to outline the recent directions of mathematical modeling in higher education. The technical aspects of mathematical models are well documented in the references cited at the end of the chapter.

TYPES OF MODELS

Mathematical models can be grouped into two broad categories: sensitivity testing and Monte Carlo or stochastic modeling. Sensitivity testing involves solving mathematical relationships under different assumptions. Modeling of this type asks the question "What if . . .?" under changing circumstances and is probably the most frequently used tool for persons with nonmathematical backgrounds. Stochastic modeling involves solving mathematical relationships by assigning probabilities to the variables. In the latter a computer is normally used to select values randomly from the probability distribution. (Another kind of model is the optimization model. It is not a "what if" model; rather, it asks how best to accomplish something. Large-scale optimization models are used infrequently in academic management mainly because they require an explicit statement of the benefit function. That is, there must be a metric to determine how close one comes to attaining the objective. More frequently, suboptimization models are employed to search alternative means of satisfying an objective at the lowest cost, the objective being a narrowly defined activity. For example, suboptimization modeling might demonstrate that accounting and recordkeeping costs in the bursar's area can be minimized using a certain kind of computer.)

Within these broad categories two approaches to modeling have appeared in higher education: the package model and the locally designed model. Package models employ generalized relationships that are applicable to behavior in many different settings. Most of these models are used to predict resource needs. The unique elements of an environment are introduced into the model when assigning values for the variables. Models purchased as packages tend to be inflexible and complex. Examples of model packages include CAMPUS (Comprehensive Analytical Methods for Planning in University/College Systems), HELP/PLANTRAN (Higher Education Long-Range Planning/Planning Translator), RRPM (Resource Requirements Prediction Model), SEARCH (System for Evaluating Alternative Resource Commitments in Higher Education), and SPEPM (Statewide Post-Secondary Education Planning Model).

Locally designed models usually simulate behavior or a process in a specific setting. The relationships and assumptions specified in such models are often localized to the extent that the model is not readily transferable to other settings. Closely related to the locally designed model is a package labeled as a generalized system. This package is not a true model in that the institution specifies its own definitions of variables, assumptions, equations, and report formats. In essence the system is a software matrix within which a model can be designed locally. An example of the generalized system is EFPM (EDUCOM Financial Planning Model), marketed by the nonprofit consortium EDUCOM. EFPM is an outgrowth of model development at Stanford University.

The large-scale package models seem to be the least utilized of the quantitative tools. A number of factors work against their adoption. First, the problem is often poorly matched to the models because of the models' generalized nature. In many cases it is more appropriate to identify the problem and then design a model to provide solutions. Second, the large-scale packages are frequently too broad in scope. By encompassing too many variables, the models simulate behavior in too much detail to be practical for frequent use. Models that are too detailed are expensive to maintain because of the high cost of collecting the data necessary to fuel them. Third, the equations developed may not reflect a changing environment. Models are refined through testing with historical data. Those that can simulate the past with reasonable accuracy may not be appropriate for a future context. Fourth, the large-scale package models are often too complicated. The frustrations of attempting to master such models may outweigh the perceived benefits to daily decision making and planning.

COMPREHENSIVE MODELS

The logic of comprehensive package models is illustrated by figure 1, and the planning factors employed in two of the better known models,

CAMPUS and RRPM, are summarized in figure 3. RRPM uses the instructional workload matrix (see chapter 11) as the basis for inserting information concerning student programs. CAMPUS, on the other hand, uses less aggregated data on specific courses or activities. The CAMPUS model can generate projections at the lowest organizational levels but requires much more data and many more planning constraints than RRPM. As an indication of the amount of data needed to operate these models, Hussain and Mason (1973, 75) note that at the University of Colorado in the early 1970s there were over 2,000 activities and that for each activity up to 16 data elements on resource loading had to be specified.

Both CAMPUS and RRPM have student flow modules that track the flow of students through the institution by using pass-fail rates at each level, repeat rates at the same level, drop-out rates at each level, and transfer rates between programs. Both models can also calculate costs for academic and support programs and unit costs for student programs by contact hour, credit hour, and FTE for different levels of aggregation. CAMPUS has a revenue module with student revenue components (tuition) and public funding components (formula computation that is varied to fit local conditions). CAMPUS does not have revenue components for student aid or portfolio management, although endowment income, grants, contracts, and gifts are included. RRPM does not have a revenue module.

LOCALLY DESIGNED MODELS

Mathematical models have evolved from comprehensive systems to small models with a more limited scope. The latter are attractive because they are generally less complex than comprehensive models, can be designed for more effective accommodation of local conditions, employ fewer variables and hence require fewer data, and can be easily adapted to many microprocessors and minicomputers.

Perhaps the most frequently encountered mathematical model is for faculty flow. It is quite easy to model the impact on faculty size and composition of promotion rates, hiring rates at the different ranks, and rates of resignations and other departures. Figure 2 presents a simplified model of faculty flow that can be computed on a hand-held calculator. This model assumes that there are only three faculty ranks: assistant, associate, and full professor. In a given year each rank pool can be increased by additions and decreased by departures. The assistant professor pool, for example, can be augmented by hiring new assistant professors. The pool is depleted to the extent that assistant professors are promoted or are denied tenure and required to leave the institution, resign their appointments to accept employment elsewhere, retire, are medically disabled, or die. The associate professor pool can be augmented by hiring new associate professors or by promotion of assistant professors. Departures from the associate professor pool are similar to those from the assistant professor pool. The augmentation and depletion of the full professor pool proceeds in the same manner.

Each of the flows into and out of a pool can be expressed as a proportion of the number of faculty in that pool or in the pool of next lower rank. Furthermore, it is assumed that the proportion of faculty moving from one classification to another during a given cycle (normally one year) is predictable. For the simplified model presented in figure 2, the simulation can be performed using historical data to determine the proportions or by testing different proportions to reflect proposed policy changes such as the application of tenure quotas or the extension of the probationary period of assistant professors from five to six years. Beginning with the number of faculty in each pool at the present time (the initial state), one computes the changes in each pool that result from the various flows. The calculations are repeated for successive years, with the previous years' projections for each pool as the base.

Computer modeling of faculty flow allows for the use of more detailed descriptions of the faculty ranks. Colgate University, for example, projected the effect of policy changes with a flow model in which the faculty was described by six characteristics: age; rank; date of next tenure decision, of promotion, or of retirement; number of years of service (for junior faculty only); sex; and minority status (Nevison, 1980, 154). The Colgate University simulation employed seven faculty ranks: instructor, assistant professor (nontenured and tenured), associate professor (nontenured and tenured), and full professor (nontenured and tenured). Because of the relatively small size of the Colgate faculty, the simulation model (1) could be based on the characteristics of individual faculty, such as age, sex and minority status, and (2) was more sensitive to changes in faculty composition or simulated changes in policies than models of large faculties requiring the clustering of faculty in groups.

In the Colgate University model, the proportions of faculty moving from one classification to another become the probabilities that an individual faculty member will change his or her characteristics. Within the instructor rank, for example, an individual may resign, with the probability based on his or her number of years of service; or the individual may be promoted to assistant professor, with the probability based on years of service. Whether promoted or not, the individual ages one year. If the individual is not promoted, he or she gains another year of service. Similar probabilities of promotion and departure for nontenured and tenured faculty are incorporated into the model.

The Colgate University simulation model was used to gauge the impact of two sets of policy alternatives: the mandatory retirement age of 68 versus the federally mandated age of 70, and a tenure ratio guideline of 55 percent versus a guideline of 65 percent. It was determined that the change in mandatory retirement age would not impair Colgate University's ability to tenure deserving junior faculty (Nevison, 1980, 160–61). Also, an increase in tenure ratio from 55 to 65 percent would increase faculty salary costs only 3 percent over 20 years (Nevison, 1980, 163). Clearly, the advantage of this simulation was that the impact of alternative policies could be projected, with the results helping to inform the decision-making process.

The simulation of faculty flow at large institutions often involves the use of a Markov chain model, which describes the faculty in terms of the number of individuals in each of several classifications, or "states." The number of states in a Markov chain model depends on the number of faculty characteristics used, and the number of states is doubled for each additional characteristic in the model. The transition from one state to another is characterized by a probability distribution that is in turn determined by factors such as age or years of service in rank. Sometimes it is assumed that the proportion of faculty moving from one classification to another remains constant each year of the projection, although the transition probabilities can be adjusted from one year to another to reflect changing conditions. Algebraic equations based on the proportions summarize the distribution of faculty in the next year. The equations are grouped and solved using matrix algebra.

Stanford University uses a flow model with a 17-state Markov transition matrix (Bloomfield, 1977, 5–6). The states, which are specifically selected to describe the tenure and promotion system at Stanford, are summarized in figure 4. Oregon State University, on the other hand, employs a faculty flow model using 161 states (Bloomfield, 1977, 7). The state definitions for the Oregon State University model are summarized in figure 5. The huge data base needed to operate that model (a year-by-year historical profile of the entire faculty) is made possible by a computerized personnel data base.

The use of financial planning models extends beyond analyses of faculty flow. During the late 1970s Wesleyan University, for example, used the EFPM system to study possible changes in its student aid policies (Hopkins et al., 1982, 11–12). The Wesleyan model included all the variables that influenced the student aid budget: enrollment projections and profiles of the financial aid population; schedules of student charges (tuition and fees, room and board, books and personal expenses); projections of parental contributions and self-help (summer earnings, academic-year jobs, academic-year loans); loan programs; and forecasts of various sources of funds to underwrite the student aid budget. The model projections demonstrated that the institution would have to alter its financial aid policies to reduce financial aid commitments in order for the institution to avoid serious deficits.

The Maryland State Board for Community Colleges used the EFPM system to project the effect of annual growth in full-time faculty on annual growth in total faculty salaries and the relationship between the annual growth in county funding and the annual growth in tuition income (Hopkins et al., 1982, 14–15). Using the model the board was able to determine how to balance the system budget, in light of anticipated enrollment changes, through modifications in state aid, tuition, county support, student-faculty ratios, faculty salaries and benefits, faculty FTEs, and administrator and staff FTEs.

A number of other institutions have employed interactive planning models to simulate the fiscal implications of changes in faculty and staff size and enrollments and in energy costs, cost-of-living factors, salaries, tuition, income, and numerous other variables. Stanford University used TRADES, the forerunner of the EFPM system, to model its financial situation. The TRADES planning variables included FTE regular faculty, undergraduate student headcount, graduate student headcount, annual real growth in tuition price, annual real growth in faculty salaries, annual real growth in staff salaries, annual real growth in per unit utilities costs, annual real growth in staff benefits, ratio of FTE tenured faculty to total FTE regular faculty, ratio of FTE academic support staff to regular faculty, stipulated endowment payout ratio as a percentage of market value at beginning of the year, and a budget enrichment factor as a fraction of the preceding year's total budget (Dickmeyer et al., 1979, 63–76). Harvard University, operating under the "every tub on its own bottom" fiscal philosophy, used the basic forecasting models developed at Stanford University to project financial requirements for the Faculty of Arts and Sciences, the Graduate School of Education, buildings and grounds, and the Harvard College library. For each of these units, budgets were divided into a small number of income and expenditure categories and projections were made on the basis of alternative conditions (Zeckhauser, 1979, 93–114).

Figure 1: Basic Logic for CAMPUS and RRPM

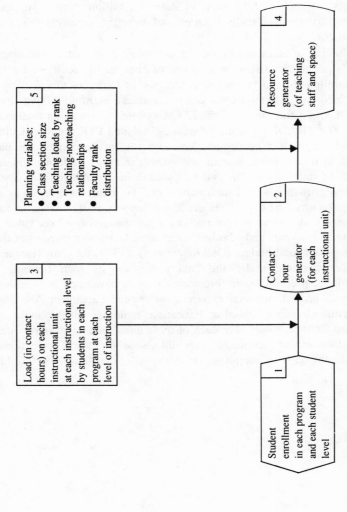

Source: K. M. Hussain, "Comprehensive Planning Models in North America and Europe," in *Assessing Computer-based Systems Models*, edited by Thomas R. Mason. New Directions for Institutional Research, no. 9 (San Francisco: Jossey-Bass, Inc., 1976), p. 89.

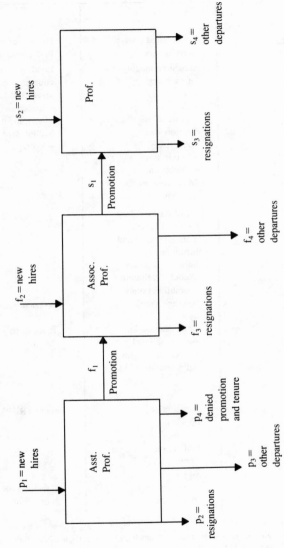

Figure 2: Faculty Flow Model

Figure 3: Some Planning Factors in RRPM and CAMPUS

	CAMPUS VIII	RRPM 1.3
INSTRUCTIONAL		
Student programs	By detailed course activity mix	By mix of credit hours in department/discipline
	Resource loading of each activity	Loading of groups of courses at different
	−Space	levels and fields
	−Personnel type	−Space
	−Time of offering	−Equipment
	Section size	Section size
	−Average	−Average
	−Maximum	
	−Minimum	
	Maximum number of sections	
Faculty	Substitution policy	
	Contract length	
	Turnover rates and hiring policy	
	Sabbatical policy	
	Weekly availability	
	Promotion policy	
	Average salaries by rank	Average salaries by rank
	Rank distribution	Rank distribution
	Academic level	Academic level
	Workload weights	
	Administrative load	
SPACE		
	Substitution policies	(not in RRPM 1.6)
	Availability	Availability
	Utilization	
	Type	Type
	Size	Size
	Construction coefficients	Construction coefficients

Source: K. M. Hussain and Thomas R. Mason, "Planning Models in Higher Education: A Comparison of CAMPUS and RRPM," in *Tomorrow's Imperatives Today: Proceedings of the 13th Annual Forum,* edited by Robert G. Cope (Association for Institutional Research, 1973), p. 76. Copies are available from the Association for Institutional Research, Tallahassee, FL.

Figure 4: State Definitions for the Stanford Faculty Flow Model

State	Description
1	Nontenure—first year
2	Nontenure—second year
3	Nontenure—third year
4	Nontenure—fourth year
5	Nontenure—fifth year
6	Nontenure—sixth year
7	Nontenure—seventh year
8	Tenure—age 30 to 34
9	Tenure—age 35 to 39
10	Tenure—age 40 to 44
11	Tenure—age 45 to 49
12	Tenure—age 50 to 54
13	Tenure—age 55 to 59
14	Tenure—age 60 to 64
15	Retirement
16	Resignation
17	Death

Source: Stefan D. Bloomfield, "Comprehensive Faculty Flow Analysis," in *Applying Analytic Methods to Planning and Management,* edited by David S. P. Hopkins and Roger G. Schroeder. New Directions for Institutional Research, no. 13 (San Francisco: Jossey-Bass, Inc., 1977), p. 6.

Figure 5: State Definitions for the Oregon State University Comprehensive Faculty Flow Model

Variables	Categories	Number
Tenure status	Nontenured, tenured	2
Rank	Instructor, assistant professor, associate professor, professor	4*
Years in rank	0–3, 4–6, 7–9, 10+	4
Age	0–39, 40–49, 50–59, 60+	4
Years of service	0–3, 4+	2*

*The combination of all possible values of the above variables yields 256 possible states. This total was reduced by deleting states corresponding to nontenured full professors (32 states) and by deleting reference to years of service for tenured faculty (64 states). With the addition of a final absorbing state for separation from the university, this model contains 161 states.

Source: Stefan D. Bloomfield, "Comprehensive Faculty Flow Analysis," in *Applying Analytic Methods to Planning and Management,* edited by David S. P. Hopkins and Roger G. Schroeder. New Directions for Institutional Research, no. 13 (San Francisco: Jossey-Bass, Inc., 1977), p. 7.

FOR FURTHER READING

Several works describe planning models in layman's terms. *Assessing Computer-based Systems Models,* edited by Thomas R. Mason, New Directions for Institutional Research, no. 9 (San Francisco: Jossey-Bass, Inc., 1976) focuses on comprehensive planning models to the exclusion of locally designed models. A detailed comparison of the CAMPUS and RRPM models is offered by K. M. Hussain and Thomas R. Mason, "Planning Models in Higher Education: A Comparison of CAMPUS and RRPM," in *Tomorrow's Imperatives Today: Proceedings of the 13th Annual Forum,* edited by Robert G. Cope (Association for Institutional Research, 1973), pp. 102–107. Copies are available from the Association for Institutional Research, Tallahassee, FL. This paper complements one by K. M. Hussain in *Assessing Computer-based Systems Models.*

An overview of locally designed mathematical planning models is presented in *Applying Analytic Methods to Planning and Management,* edited by David S. P. Hopkins and Roger G. Schroeder, New Directions for Institutional Research, no. 13 (San Francisco: Jossey-Bass, Inc., 1977). The authoritative guide to mathematical modeling is *Planning Models for Colleges and Universities,* by David S. P. Hopkins and William F. Massy (Stanford, CA: Stanford University Press, 1981). This book is difficult reading for those untrained in mathematics and operations research, but a perusal of selected chapters is rewarding to anyone interested in planning models. The volume consolidates much of the authors' technical work that has appeared in numerous scholarly journals over the past decade.

A useful summary of case-study experiences with planning models is *Financial Planning Models: Concepts and Case Studies in Colleges and Universities,* edited by Joe B. Wyatt, James C. Emery, and Carolyn P. Landis (Princeton, NJ: EDUCOM, 1979). Many of the cases in this volume refer to the Stanford University experience with TRADES or to the EFPM system, a generalized model adapted from TRADES. Recent experience with the EFPM system is found in *EDUCOM Bulletin,* vol. 17, no. 3 (Fall 1982). This special issue focuses on financial planning models.

The literature on faculty flow models is extensive. A sampling is offered by Barbara Lee Bleau, "Faculty Planning Models: A Review of the Literature," *Journal of Higher Education,* vol. 53, no. 2 (March/April 1982), pp. 195–206. Christopher H. Nevison, "Effects of Tenure and Retirement Policies on the College Faculty: A Case Study Using Computer Simulation," *Journal of Higher Education,* vol. 51, no. 2 (March/April 1980), pp. 150–166, discusses the use of faculty flow models at Colgate University. Another good summary of faculty flow models is found in a paper by Stefan D. Bloomfield, "Comprehensive Faculty Flow Analysis," in *Applying Analytic Methods to Planning and Management* (see above).

Appendix 1

AAUP Documents

A. ACADEMIC FREEDOM AND TENURE: 1940 STATEMENT OF PRINCIPLES AND INTERPRETIVE COMMENTS

In 1940, following a series of joint conferences begun in 1934, representatives of the American Association of University Professors and of the Association of American Colleges agreed on a restatement of principles set forth in the 1925 Conference Statement on Academic Freedom and Tenure. This restatement is known to the profession as the 1940 Statement of Principles on Academic Freedom and Tenure.

The 1940 Statement *is printed below, followed by interpretive comments as developed during 1969 by representatives of the American Association of University Professors and the Association of American Colleges.*

The purpose of this statement is to promote public understanding and support of academic freedom and tenure and agreement upon procedures to assure them in colleges and universities. Institutions of higher education are conducted for the common good and not to further the interest of either the individual teacher[1] or the institution as a whole. The common good depends upon the free search for truth and its free exposition.

---

[1]The word "teacher" as used in this document is understood to include the investigator who is attached to an academic institution without teaching duties.

Academic freedom is essential to these purposes and applies to both teaching and research. Freedom in research is fundamental to the advancement of truth. Academic freedom in its teaching aspect is fundamental for the protection of the rights of the teacher in teaching and of the student to freedom in learning. It carries with it duties correlative with rights. [1][2]

Tenure is a means to certain ends; specifically: (1) Freedom of teaching and research and of extramural activities and (2) a sufficient degree of economic security to make the profession attractive to men and women of ability. Freedom and economic security, hence, tenure, are indispensable to the success of an institution in fulfilling its obligations to its students and to society.

ACADEMIC FREEDOM

(a) The teacher is entitled to full freedom in research and in the publication of the results, subject to the adequate performance of his other academic duties; but research for pecuniary return should be based upon an understanding with the authorities of the institution.

(b) The teacher is entitled to freedom in the classroom in discussing his subject, but he should be careful not to introduce into his teaching controversial matter which has no relation to his subject. [2] Limitations of academic freedom because of religious or other aims of the institution should be clearly stated in writing at the time of the appointment. [3]

(c) The college or university teacher is a citizen, a member of a learned profession, and an officer of an educational institution. When he speaks or writes as a citizen, he should be free from institutional censorship or discipline, but his special position in the community imposes special obligations. As a man of learning and an educational officer, he should remember that the public may judge his profession and his institution by his utterances. Hence he should at all times be accurate, should exercise appropriate restraint, should show respect for the opinions of others, and should make every effort to indicate that he is not an institutional spokesman. [4]

ACADEMIC TENURE

(a) After the expiration of a probationary period, teachers or investigators should have permanent or continuous tenure, and their service should be terminated only for adequate cause, except in the case of retirement for age, or under extraordinary circumstances because of financial exigencies.

---

[2]Bold-face numbers in brackets refer to Interpretive Comments which follow.

In the interpretation of this principle it is understood that the following represents acceptable academic practice:

(1) The precise terms and conditions of every appointment should be stated in writing and be in the possession of both institution and teacher before the appointment is consummated.

(2) Beginning with appointment to the rank of full-time instructor or a higher rank, [5] the probationary period should not exceed seven years, including within this period full-time service in all institutions of higher education; but subject to the proviso that when, after a term of probationary service of more than three years in one or more institutions, a teacher is called to another institution it may be agreed in writing that his new appointment is for a probationary period of not more than four years, even though thereby the person's total probationary period in the academic profession is extended beyond the normal maximum of seven years. [6] Notice should be given at least one year prior to the expiration of the probationary period if the teacher is not to be continued in service after the expiration of that period. [7]

(3) During the probationary period a teacher should have the academic freedom that all other members of the faculty have. [8]

(4) Termination for cause of a continuous appointment, or the dismissal for cause of a teacher previous to the expiration of a term appointment, should, if possible, be considered by both a faculty committee and the governing board of the institution. In all cases where the facts are in dispute, the accused teacher should be informed before the hearing in writing of the charges against him and should have the opportunity to be heard in his own defense by all bodies that pass judgment upon his case. He should be permitted to have with him an adviser of his own choosing who may act as counsel. There should be a full stenographic record of the hearing available to the parties concerned. In the hearing of charges of incompetence the testimony should include that of teachers and other scholars, either from his own or from other institutions. Teachers on continuous appointment who are dismissed for reasons not involving moral turpitude should receive their salaries for at least a year from the date of notification of dismissal whether or not they are continued in their duties at the institution. [9]

(5) Termination of a continuous appointment because of financial exigency should be demonstrably bona fide.

1940 INTERPRETATIONS

At the conference of representatives of the American Association of University Professors and of the Association of American Colleges on November 7–8, 1940, the following interpretations of the 1940 *Statement of Principles on Academic Freedom and Tenure* were agreed upon:

1. That its operation should not be retroactive.

2. That all tenure claims of teachers appointed prior to the endorsement should be determined in accordance with the principles set forth in the 1925 Conference Statement on Academic Freedom and Tenure.

3. If the administration of a college or university feels that a teacher has not observed the admonitions of Paragraph (c) of the section on *Academic Freedom* and believes that the extramural utterances of the teacher have been such as to raise grave doubts concerning his fitness for his position, it may proceed to file charges under Paragraph (a) (4) of the section on *Academic Tenure*. In pressing such charges the administration should remember that teachers are citizens and should be accorded the freedom of citizens. In such cases the administration must assume full responsibility and the American Association of University Professors and the Association of American Colleges are free to make an investigation.

1970 INTERPRETIVE COMMENTS

Following extensive discussions on the 1940 Statement of Principles on Academic Freedom and Tenure *with leading educational associations and with individual faculty members and administrators, a Joint Committee of the AAUP and the Association of American Colleges met during 1969 to reevaluate this key policy statement. On the basis of the comments received, and the discussions that ensued, the Joint Committee felt the preferable approach was to formulate interpretations of the* Statement *in terms of the experience gained in implementing and applying the* Statement *for over thirty years and of adapting it to current needs.*

The Committee submitted to the two Associations for their consideration the following "Interpretive Comments." These interpretations were approved by the Council of the American Association of University Professors in April, 1970, and endorsed by the Fifty-sixth Annual Meeting as Association policy.

In the thirty years since their promulgation, the principles of the 1940 *Statement of Principles on Academic Freedom and Tenure* have undergone a substantial amount of refinement. This has evolved through a variety of processes, including customary acceptance, understandings mutually arrived at between institutions and professors or their representatives, investigations and reports by the American Association of University Professors, and formulations of statements by that Association either alone or in conjunction with the Association of American Colleges. These comments represent the attempt of the two associations, as the original sponsors of the 1940 *Statement,* to formulate the most important of these refinements. Their incorporation here as Interpretive Comments is based upon the premise that the 1940 *Statement* is not a static code but a fundamental document designed to set a framework of norms to guide adaptations to changing times and circumstances.

Also, there have been relevant developments in the law itself reflecting a growing insistence by the courts on due process within the academic community which parallels the essential concepts of the 1940 *Statement;* particularly relevant is the identification by the Supreme Court of academic freedom as a right protected by the First Amendment. As the Supreme Court said in *Keyishian v. Board of Regents* 385 U.S. 589 (1967), "Our Nation is deeply committed to safeguarding academic freedom, which is of transcendent value to all of us and not merely to the teachers concerned. That freedom is therefore a special concern of the First Amendment, which does not tolerate laws that cast a pall of orthodoxy over the classroom."

The numbers refer to the designated portion of the 1940 *Statement* on which interpretive comment is made.

1. The Association of American Colleges and the American Association of University Professors have long recognized that membership in the academic profession carries with it special responsibilities. Both Associations either separately or jointly have consistently affirmed these responsibilities in major policy statements, providing guidance to the professor in his utterances as a citizen, in the exercise of his responsibilities to the institution and students, and in his conduct when resigning from his institution or when undertaking government-sponsored research. Of particular relevance is the *Statement on Professional Ethics,* adopted by the Fifty-second Annual Meeting of the AAUP as Association policy and published in the *AAUP Bulletin* (Autumn, 1966, pp. 290–291).

2. The intent of this statement is not to discourage what is "controversial." Controversy is at the heart of the free academic inquiry which the entire statement is designed to foster. The passage serves to underscore the need for the teacher to avoid persistently intruding material which has no relation to his subject.

3. Most church-related institutions no longer need or desire the departure from the principle of academic freedom implied in the 1940 *Statement,* and we do not now endorse such a departure.

4. This paragraph is the subject of an Interpretation adopted by the sponsors of the 1940 *Statement* immediately following its endorsement which reads as follows:

> If the administration of a college or university feels that a teacher has not observed the admonitions of Paragraph (c) of the section on Academic Freedom and believes that the extramural utterances of the teacher have been such as to raise grave doubts concerning his fitness for his position, it may proceed to file charges under Paragraph (a) (4) of the section on Academic Tenure. In pressing such charges the administration should remember that teachers are citizens and should be accorded the freedom of citizens. In such cases the administration must assume full re-

sponsibility and the American Association of University Professors and
the Association of American Colleges are free to make an investigation.

Paragraph (c) of the 1940 *Statement* should also be interpreted in keep-
ing with the 1964 "Committee A Statement on Extramural Utterances"
(*AAUP Bulletin,* Spring, 1965, p. 29) which states inter alia: "The controlling principle is that a faculty member's expression of opinion as a citizen
cannot constitute grounds for dismissal unless it clearly demonstrates the
faculty member's unfitness for his position. Extramural utterances rarely
bear upon the faculty member's fitness for his position. Moreover, a final
decision should take into account the faculty member's entire record as a
teacher and scholar."

Paragraph V of the *Statement on Professional Ethics* also deals with the
nature of the "special obligations" of the teacher. The paragraph reads as
follows:

> As a member of his community, the professor has the rights and ob-
> ligations of any citizen. He measures the urgency of these obligations in
> the light of his responsibilities to his subject, to his students, to his pro-
> fession, and to his institution. When he speaks or acts as a private person
> he avoids creating the impression that he speaks or acts for his college or
> university. As a citizen engaged in a profession that depends upon free-
> dom for its health and integrity, the professor has a particular obligation
> to promote conditions of free inquiry and to further public understanding
> of academic freedom.

Both the protection of academic freedom and the requirements of
academic responsibility apply not only to the full-time probationary as well
as to the tenured teacher, but also to all others, such as part-time and teaching assistants, who exercise teaching responsibilities.

5. The concept of "rank of full-time instructor or a higher rank" is intended to include any person who teaches a full-time load regardless of his
specific title.*

6. In calling for an agreement "in writing" on the amount of credit for
a faculty member's prior service at other institutions, the *Statement* furthers
the general policy of full understanding by the professor of the terms and
conditions of his appointment. It does not necessarily follow that a professor's tenure rights have been violated because of the absence of a written
agreement on this matter. Nonetheless, especially because of the variation
in permissible institutional practices, a written understanding concerning
these matters at the time of appointment is particularly appropriate and advantageous to both the individual and the institution.

---

*For a discussion of this question, see the "Report of the Special Committee on Academic
Personnel Ineligible for Tenure," *AAUP Bulletin,* Autumn, 1966, pp. 280–282.

7. The effect of this subparagraph is that a decision on tenure, favorable or unfavorable, must be made at least twelve months prior to the completion of the probationary period. If the decision is negative, the appointment for the following year becomes a terminal one. If the decision is affirmative, the provisions in the 1940 *Statement* with respect to the termination of services of teachers or investigators after the expiration of a probationary period should apply from the date when the favorable decision is made.

The general principle of notice contained in this paragraph is developed with greater specificity in the *Standards for Notice of Nonreappointment*, endorsed by the Fiftieth Annual Meeting of the American Association of University Professors (1964). These standards are:

Notice of nonreappointment, or of intention not to recommend reappointment to the governing board, should be given in writing in accordance with the following standards:

(1) *Not later than March 1 of the first academic year of service,* if the appointment expires at the end of that year; or, if a one-year appointment terminates during an academic year, at least three months in advance of its termination.

(2) *Not later than December 15 of the second academic year of service,* if the appointment expires at the end of that year; or, if an initial two-year appointment terminates during an academic year, at least six months in advance of its termination.

(3) At least twelve months before the expiration of an appointment after two or more years in the institution.

Other obligations, both of institutions and individuals, are described in the *Statement on Recruitment and Resignation of Faculty Members,* as endorsed by the Association of American Colleges and the American Association of University Professors in 1961.

8. The freedom of probationary teachers is enhanced by the establishment of a regular procedure for the periodic evaluation and assessment of the teacher's academic performance during his probationary status. Provision should be made for regularized procedures for the consideration of complaints by probationary teachers that their academic freedom has been violated. One suggested procedure to serve these purposes is contained in the *Recommended Institutional Regulations on Academic Freedom and Tenure,* prepared by the American Association of University Professors.

9. A further specification of the academic due process to which the teacher is entitled under this paragraph is contained in the *Statement on Procedural Standards in Faculty Dismissal Proceedings,* jointly approved by the American Association of University Professors and the Association of American Colleges in 1958. This interpretive document deals with the issue of suspension, about which the 1940 Statement is silent.

The 1958 Statement provides: "Suspension of the faculty member during the proceedings involving him is justified only if immediate harm to himself or others is threatened by his continuance. Unless legal considerations forbid, any such suspension should be with pay." A suspension which is not followed by either reinstatement or the opportunity for a hearing is in effect a summary dismissal in violation of academic due process.

The concept of "moral turpitude" identifies the exceptional case in which the professor may be denied a year's teaching or pay in whole or in part. The statement applies to that kind of behavior which goes beyond simply warranting discharge and is so utterly blameworthy as to make it inappropriate to require the offering of a year's teaching or pay. The standard is not that the moral sensibilities of persons in the particular community have been affronted. The standard is behavior that would evoke condemnation by the academic community generally.

B. 1982 RECOMMENDED INSTITUTIONAL REGULATIONS ON ACADEMIC FREEDOM AND TENURE

Recommended Institutional Regulations on Academic Freedom and Tenure *set forth, in language suitable for use by an institution of higher education, rules which derive from the chief provisions and interpretations of the 1940* Statement of Principles on Academic Freedom and Tenure *and of the 1958* Statement on Procedural Standards in Faculty Dismissal Proceedings. *The* Recommended Institutional Regulations *were first formulated by Committee A on Academic Freedom and Tenure in 1957. A revised and expanded text, approved by Committee A in 1968, reflected the development of Association standards and procedures as set forth in the 1961* Statement on Recruitment and Resignation of Faculty Members, *the 1964* Statement on the Standards for Notice of Nonreappointment, *and the 1966* Statement on Government of Colleges and Universities.

Reprinted from Academe, *vol. 69, no. 1 (January–February 1983), pp. 15a–20a.*

The current revision, approved by Committee A in 1982, is based upon the Association's continuing experience in evaluating regulations actually in force at particular institutions. The 1982 revision is also based upon further definition of the standards and procedures of the Association as set forth in the 1970 Interpretive Comments *of the 1940* Statement of Principles, *the 1971 Council* Statement on Freedom and Responsibility, *the 1971* Statement on Procedural Standards in the Renewal or Nonrenewal of Faculty Appointments, *the 1972* Statement of Principles on Leaves of Absence, *recommended procedure adopted by the Council in 1976 on* Termination of Faculty Appointments because of Financial Exigency, Discontinuance of a Program or Department, or Medical Reasons, *the 1976 policy* On Discrimination, *and the 1977 statement* On Processing Complaints of Discrimination on the Basis of Sex. *The Association will be glad to assist in interpretation of the regulations or to consult about their incorporation in, or adaptation to, the rules of a particular college or university.*

FOREWORD

These regulations are designed to enable the [named institution] to protect academic freedom and tenure and the requirements of academic due process. The principles implicit in these regulations are for the benefit of all who are involved with or are affected by the policies and programs of the institution. A college or university is a marketplace of ideas, and it cannot fulfill its purposes of transmitting, evaluating, and extending knowledge if it requires conformity with any orthodoxy of content and method. In the words of the United States Supreme Court, "Teachers and students must always remain free to inquire, to study and to evaluate, to gain new maturity and understanding; otherwise our civilization will stagnate and die."

1. STATEMENT OF TERMS OF APPOINTMENT

(a) The terms and conditions of every appointment to the faculty will be stated or confirmed in writing, and a copy of the appointment document will be supplied to the faculty member. Any subsequent extensions or modifications of an appointment, and any special understandings, or any notices incumbent upon either party to provide, will be stated or confirmed in writing and a copy will be given to the faculty member.

(b) With the exception of special appointments clearly limited to a brief association with the institution, and reappointments of retired faculty members on special conditions, all full-time faculty appointments are of two kinds: (1) probationary appointments; (2) appointments with continuous tenure.

(c) Except for faculty members who have tenure status, every person with a teaching or research appointment of any kind will be informed each year in writing of the appointment and of all matters relative to eligibility for the acquisition of tenure.

2. PROBATIONARY APPOINTMENTS

(a) Probationary appointments may be for one year, or for other stated periods, subject to renewal. The total period of full-time service prior to the acquisition of continuous tenure will not exceed _____ years,[3] including all previous full-time service with the rank of instructor or higher in other institutions of higher learning [*except* that the probationary period may extend to as much as four years, even if the total full-time service in the profession thereby exceeds seven years; the terms of such extension will be stated in writing at the time of initial appointment].[4] Scholarly leave of absence for one year or less will count as part of the probationary period as if it were prior service at another institution, unless the individual and the institution agree in writing to an exception to this provision at the time the leave is granted.

(b) The faculty member will be advised, at the time of initial appointment, of the substantive standards and procedures generally employed in decisions affecting renewal and tenure. Any special standards adopted by the faculty member's department or school will also be transmitted. The faculty member will be advised of the time when decisions affecting renewal or tenure are ordinarily made, and will be given the opportunity to submit material believed to be helpful to an adequate consideration of the faculty member's circumstances.

(c) Regardless of the stated term or other provisions of any appointments, written notice that a probationary appointment is not to be renewed will be given to the faculty member in advance of the expiration of the appointment, as follows: (1) Not later than March 1 of the first academic year of service if the appointment expires at the end of that year; or, if a one-year appointment terminates during an academic year, at least three months in advance of its termination; (2) not later than December 15 of the second academic year of service if the appointment expires at the end of that year; or, if an initial two-year appointment terminates during an academic year, at least six months in advance of its termination; (3) at least twelve months before the expiration of an appointment after two or more years of service at the institution. The institution will normally notify faculty members of the terms and conditions of their renewals by March 15, but in no case will such information be given later than _____.[5]

---

[3][Under the 1940 *Statement of Principles on Academic Freedom and Tenure*, this period may not exceed seven years.]

[4][The exception here noted applies only to an institution whose maximum probationary period exceeds four years.]

[5][April 15 is the recommended date.]

(d) When a faculty recommendation or a decision not to renew an appointment has first been reached, the faculty member involved will be informed of that recommendation or decision in writing by the body or individual making the initial recommendation or decision; the faculty member will be advised upon request of the reasons which contributed to that decision. The faculty member may request a reconsideration by the recommending or deciding body.

(e) If the faculty member so requests, the reasons given in explanation of the nonrenewal will be confirmed in writing.

(f) Insofar as the faculty member alleges that the decision against renewal by the appropriate faculty body was based on inadequate consideration, the committee which reviews the faculty member's allegation will determine whether the decision was the result of adequate consideration in terms of the relevant standards of the institution. The review committee will not substitute its judgment on the merits for that of the faculty body. If the review committee believes that adequate consideration was not given to the faculty member's qualifications, it will request reconsideration by the faculty body, indicating the respects in which it believes the consideration may have been inadequate. It will provide copies of its findings to the faculty member, the faculty body, and the president or other appropriate administrative officer.

3. TERMINATION OF APPOINTMENT BY FACULTY MEMBERS

Faculty members may terminate their appointments effective at the end of an academic year, provided that they give notice in writing at the earliest possible opportunity, but not later than May 15, or 30 days after receiving notification of the terms of appointment for the coming year, whichever date occurs later. Faculty members may properly request a waiver of this requirement of notice in case of hardship or in a situation where they would otherwise be denied substantial professional advancement or other opportunity.

4. TERMINATION OF APPOINTMENTS BY THE INSTITUTION

(a) Termination of an appointment with continuous tenure, or of a probationary or special appointment before the end of the specified term, may be effected by the institution only for adequate cause.

(b) If termination takes the form of a dismissal for cause, it will be pursuant to the procedure specified in Regulation 5.

Financial Exigency

(c.1) Termination of an appointment with continuous tenure, or of a probationary or special appointment before the end of the specified term, may occur under extraordinary circumstances because of a demonstrably *bona fide* financial exigency, i.e., an imminent financial crisis which threatens the survival of the institution as a whole and which cannot be alleviated by less drastic means.

[Note: Each institution in adopting regulations on financial exigency will need to decide how to share and allocate the hard judgments and decisions that are necessary in such a crisis.

As a first step, there should be a faculty body which participates in the decision that a condition of financial exigency exists or is imminent,[6] and that all feasible alternatives to termination of appointments have been pursued.

Judgments determining where within the overall academic program termination of appointments may occur involve considerations of educational policy, including affirmative action, as well as of faculty status, and should therefore be the primary responsibility of the faculty or of an appropriate faculty body.[7] The faculty or an appropriate faculty body should also exercise primary responsibility in determining the criteria for identifying the individuals whose appointments are to be terminated. These criteria may appropriately include considerations of age and length of service.

---

[6]See "The Role of the Faculty in Budgetary and Salary Matters," (*AAUP Bulletin,* 62 [Winter, 1976], pp. 379–81), and especially the following passages:

The faculty should participate both in the preparation of the total institutional budget, and (within the framework of the total budget) in decisions relevant to the further apportioning of its specific fiscal divisions (salaries, academic programs, tuition, physical plants and grounds, etc.). The soundness of resulting decisions should be enhanced if an elected representative committee of the faculty participates in deciding on the overall allocation of institutional resources and the proportion to be devoted directly to the academic program. This committee should be given access to all information that it requires to perform its task effectively, and it should have the opportunity to confer periodically with representatives of the administration and governing board. . . .

Circumstances of financial exigency obviously pose special problems. At institutions experiencing major threats to their continued financial support, the faculty should be informed as early and specifically as possible of significant impending financial difficulties. The faculty—with substantial representation from its nontenured as well as its tenured members, since it is the former who are likely to bear the brunt of the reduction—should participate at the department, college or professional school, and institutionwide levels, in key decisions as to the future of the institution and of specific academic programs within the institution. The faculty, employing accepted standards of due process, should assume primary responsibility for determining the status of individual faculty members.

[7]See "Statement on Government of Colleges and Universities" (*AAUP Bulletin,* 52 [Winter, 1966], pp. 375–79), and especially the following passage:

Faculty status and related matters are primarily a faculty responsibility; this area includes appointments, reappointments, decisions not to reappoint, promotions, the granting of tenure, and dismissal. The primary responsibility of the faculty for such matters is based upon the fact that its judgment is central to general educational policy.

The responsibility for identifying individuals whose appointments are to be terminated should be committed to a person or group designated or approved by the faculty. The allocation of this responsibility may vary according to the size and character of the institution, the extent of the terminations to be made, or other considerations of fairness in judgment. The case of a faculty member given notice of proposed termination of appointment will be governed by the following procedure.]

(c.2) If the administration issues notice to a particular faculty member of an intention to terminate the appointment because of financial exigency, the faculty member will have the right to a full hearing before a faculty committee. The hearing need not conform in all respects with a proceeding conducted pursuant to Regulation 5, but the essentials of an on-the-record adjudicative hearing will be observed. The issues in this hearing may include:

(i) The existence and extent of the condition of financial exigency. The burden will rest on the administration to prove the existence and extent of the condition. The findings of a faculty committee in a previous proceeding involving the same issue may be introduced.

(ii) The validity of the educational judgments and the criteria for identification for termination; but the recommendations of a faculty body on these matters will be considered presumptively valid.

(iii) Whether the criteria are being properly applied in the individual case.

(c.3) If the institution, because of financial exigency, terminates appointments, it will not at the same time make new appointments except in extraordinary circumstances where a serious distortion in the academic program would otherwise result. The appointment of a faculty member with tenure will not be terminated in favor of retaining a faculty member without tenure, except in extraordinary circumstances where a serious distortion of the academic program would otherwise result.

(c.4) Before terminating an appointment because of financial exigency, the institution, with faculty participation, will make every effort to place the faculty member concerned in another suitable position within the institution.

(c.5) In all cases of termination of appointment because of financial exigency, the faculty member concerned will be given notice or severance salary not less than as prescribed in Regulation 8.

(c.6) In all cases of termination of appointment because of financial exigency, the place of the faculty member concerned will not be filled by a replacement within a period of three years, unless the released faculty member has been offered reinstatement and a reasonable time in which to accept or decline it.

Discontinuance of Program or Department Not Mandated by Financial Exigency[8]

(d) Termination of an appointment with continuous tenure, or of a probationary or special appointment before the end of the specified term, may occur as a result of *bona fide* formal discontinuance of a program or department of instruction. The following standards and procedures will apply.

(d.1) The decision to discontinue formally a program or department of instruction will be based essentially upon educational considerations, as determined primarily by the faculty as a whole or an appropriate committee thereof.

[Note: "Educational considerations" do not include cyclical or temporary variations in enrollment. They must reflect long-range judgments that the educational mission of the institution as a whole will be enhanced by the discontinuance.]

(d.2) Before the administration issues notice to a faculty member of its intention to terminate an appointment because of formal discontinuance of a program or department of instruction, the institution will make every effort to place the faculty member concerned in another suitable position. If placement in another position would be facilitated by a reasonable period of training, financial and other support for such training will be proffered. If no position is available within the institution, with or without retraining, the faculty member's appointment then may be terminated, but only with provision for severance salary equitably adjusted to the faculty member's length of past and potential service.

[Note: When an institution proposes to discontinue a program or department of instruction, it should plan to bear the costs of relocating, training, or otherwise compensating faculty members adversely affected.]

(d.3) A faculty member may appeal a proposed relocation or termination resulting from a discontinuance and has a right to a full hearing before a faculty committee. The hearing need not conform in all respects with a proceeding conducted pursuant to Regulation 5 but the essentials of an on-the-record adjudicative hearing will be observed. The issues in such a hearing may include the institution's failure to satisfy any of the conditions specified in this section. In such a hearing a faculty determination that a program or department is to be discontinued will be considered presumptively valid, but the burden of proof on other issues will rest on the administration.

---

[8]When discontinuance of a program or department is mandated by financial exigency of the institution, the standards of section 4(c) above will apply.

Termination for Medical Reasons

(e) Termination of an appointment with tenure, or of a probationary or special appointment before the end of the period of appointment, for medical reasons, will be based upon clear and convincing medical evidence that the faculty member cannot continue to fulfill the terms and conditions of the appointment. The decision to terminate will be reached only after there has been appropriate consultation and after the faculty member concerned, or someone representing the faculty member, has been informed of the basis of the proposed action and has been afforded an opportunity to present the faculty member's position and to respond to the evidence. If the faculty member so requests, the evidence will be reviewed by the Faculty Committee on Academic Freedom and Tenure [or whatever title it may have] before a final decision is made by the governing board on the recommendation of the administration. The faculty member will be given severance salary not less than as prescribed in Regulation 8.

Review

(f) In cases of termination of appointment, the governing board will be available for ultimate review.

5. DISMISSAL PROCEDURES

(a) Adequate cause for a dismissal will be related, directly and substantially, to the fitness of faculty members in their professional capacities as teachers or researchers. Dismissal will not be used to restrain faculty members in their exercise of academic freedom or other rights of American citizens.

(b) Dismissal of a faculty member with continuous tenure, or with a special or probationary appointment before the end of the specified term, will be preceded by: (1) discussions between the faculty member and appropriate administrative officers looking toward a mutual settlement; (2) informal inquiry by the duly elected faculty committee [insert name of committee] which may, failing to effect an adjustment, determine whether in its opinion dismissal proceedings should be undertaken, without its opinion being binding upon the president; (3) a statement of charges, framed with reasonable particularity by the president or the president's delegate.

(c) A dismissal, as defined in Regulation 5(a), will be preceded by a statement of reasons, and the individual concerned will have the right to be heard initially by the elected faculty hearing committee [insert name of committee].[9] Members deeming themselves disqualified for bias or interest will remove themselves from the case, either at the request of a party or

---

[9][This committee should not be the same as the committee referred to in Regulation 5(b)(2).]

on their own initiative. Each party will have a maximum of two challenges without stated cause.[10]

(c.1) Pending a final decision by the hearing committee, the faculty member will be suspended, or assigned to other duties in lieu of suspension, only if immediate harm to the faculty member or others is threatened by continuance. Before suspending a faculty member, pending an ultimate determination of the faculty member's status through the institution's hearing procedures, the administration will consult with the Faculty Committee on Academic Freedom and Tenure [or whatever other title it may have] concerning the propriety, the length, and the other conditions of the suspension. A suspension which is intended to be final is a dismissal, and will be treated as such. Salary will continue during the period of the suspension.

(c.2) The hearing committee may, with the consent of the parties concerned, hold joint prehearing meetings with the parties in order to (i) simplify the issues, (ii) effect stipulations of facts, (iii) provide for the exchange of documentary or other information, and (iv) achieve such other appropriate pre-hearing objectives as will make the hearing fair, effective, and expeditious.

(c.3) Service of notice of hearing with specific charges in writing will be made at least twenty days prior to the hearing. The faculty member may waive a hearing or may respond to the charges in writing at any time before the hearing. If the faculty member waives a hearing, but denies the charges or asserts that the charges do not support a finding of adequate cause, the hearing tribunal will evaluate all available evidence and rest its recommendation upon the evidence in the record.

(c.4) The committee, in consultation with the president and the faculty member, will exercise its judgment as to whether the hearing should be public or private.

(c.5) During the proceedings the faculty member will be permitted to have an academic advisor and counsel of the faculty member's choice.

(c.6) At the request of either party or the hearing committee, a representative of a responsible educational association will be permitted to attend the proceedings as an observer.

(c.7) A verbatim record of the hearing or hearings will be taken and a typewritten copy will be made available to the faculty member without cost, at the faculty member's request.

(c.8) The burden of proof that adequate cause exists rests with the institution and will be satisfied only by clear and convincing evidence in the record considered as a whole.

---

[10][Regulations of the institution should provide for alternates, or for some other method of filling vacancies on the hearing committee resulting from disqualification, challenge without stated cause, illness, resignation, or any other reason.]

(c.9) The hearing committee will grant adjournments to enable either party to investigate evidence as to which a valid claim of surprise is made.

(c.10) The faculty member will be afforded an opportunity to obtain necessary witnesses and documentary or other evidence. The administration will cooperate with the hearing committee in securing witnesses and making available documentary and other evidence.

(c.11) The faculty member and the administration will have the right to confront and cross-examine all witnesses. Where the witnesses cannot or will not appear, but the committee determines that the interests of justice require admission of their statements, the committee will identify the witnesses, disclose their statements, and if possible provide for interrogatories.

(c.12) In the hearing of charges of incompetence, the testimony will include that of qualified faculty members from this or other institutions of higher education.

(c.13) The hearing committee will not be bound by strict rules of legal evidence, and may admit any evidence which is of probative value in determining the issues involved. Every possible effort will be made to obtain the most reliable evidence available.

(c.14) The findings of fact and the decision will be based solely on the hearing record.

(c.15) Except for such simple announcements as may be required, covering the time of the hearing and similar matters, public statements and publicity about the case by either the faculty member or administrative officers will be avoided so far as possible until the proceedings have been completed, including consideration by the governing board of the institution. The president and the faculty member will be notified of the decision in writing and will be given a copy of the record of the hearing.

(c.16) If the hearing committee concludes that adequate cause for dismissal has not been established by the evidence in the record, it will so report to the president. If the president rejects the report, the president will state the reasons for doing so, in writing, to the hearing committee and to the faculty member, and provide an opportunity for response before transmitting the case to the governing board. If the hearing committee concludes that adequate cause for a dismissal has been established, but that an academic penalty less than dismissal would be more appropriate, it will so recommend, with supporting reasons.

6. ACTION BY THE GOVERNING BOARD

If dismissal or other severe sanction is recommended, the president will, on request of the faculty member, transmit to the governing board the record of the case. The governing board's review will be based on the record of the committee hearing, and it will provide opportunity for argument, oral or written or both, by the principals at the hearings or by their representatives. The decision of the hearing committee will either be sustained, or the proceeding returned to the committee with specific objections. The committee will then reconsider, taking into account the stated objections and receiving new evidence if necessary. The governing board will make a final decision only after study of the committee's reconsideration.

7. PROCEDURES FOR IMPOSITION OF SANCTIONS OTHER THAN DISMISSAL

(a) If the administration believes that the conduct of a faculty member, although not constituting adequate cause for dismissal, is sufficiently grave to justify imposition of a severe sanction, such as suspension from service for a stated period, the administration may institute a proceeding to impose such a severe sanction; the procedures outlined in Regulation 5 will govern such a proceeding.

(b) If the administration believes that the conduct of a faculty member justifies imposition of a minor sanction such as a reprimand, it will notify the faculty member of the basis of the proposed sanction and provide the faculty member with an opportunity to persuade the administration that the proposed sanction should not be imposed. A faculty member who believes that a major sanction has been incorrectly imposed under this paragraph, or that a minor sanction has been unjustly imposed, may, pursuant to Regulation 15, petition the faculty grievance committee for such action as may be appropriate.

8. TERMINAL SALARY OR NOTICE

If the appointment is terminated, the faculty member will receive salary or notice in accordance with the following schedule: at least three months, if the final decision is reached by March 1 (or three months prior to the expiration) of the first year of probationary service; at least six months, if the decision is reached by December 15 of the second year (or after nine months but prior to eighteen months) of probationary service; at least one year, if the decision is reached after eighteen months of probationary service or if the faculty member has tenure. This provision for terminal notice or salary need not apply in the event that there has been a finding that the conduct which justified dismissal involved moral turpitude. On the recommendation of the faculty hearing committee or the president, the governing board, in determining what, if any, payments will be made beyond the effective date of dismissal, may take into account the length and quality of service of the faculty member.

9. ACADEMIC FREEDOM AND PROTECTION AGAINST DISCRIMINATION

(a) All members of the faculty, whether tenured or not, are entitled to academic freedom as set forth in the 1940 *Statement of Principles on Academic Freedom and Tenure,* formulated by the Association of American Colleges and the American Association of University Professors.

(b) All members of the faculty, whether tenured or not, are entitled to protection against illegal or unconstitutional discrimination by the institution, or discrimination on a basis not demonstrably related to the faculty member's professional performance, including but not limited to race, sex, religion, national origin, age, physical handicap, marital status, or sexual or affectional preference.

10. COMPLAINTS OF VIOLATION OF ACADEMIC FREEDOM OR OF
DISCRIMINATION IN NONREAPPOINTMENT

If a faculty member on probationary or other nontenured appointment alleges that a decision against reappointment was based significantly on considerations violative of (1) academic freedom or (2) governing policies on making appointments without prejudice with respect to race, sex, religion, national origin, age, physical handicap, marital status, or sexual or affectional preference, the allegation will be given preliminary consideration by the [insert name of committee], which will seek to settle the matter by informal methods. The allegation will be accompanied by a statement that the faculty member agrees to the presentation, for the consideration of the faculty committees, of such reasons and evidence as the institution may allege in support of its decision. If the difficulty is unresolved at this stage, and if the committee so recommends, the matter will be heard in the manner set forth in Regulations 5 and 6, except that the faculty member making the complaint is responsible for stating the grounds upon which the allegations are based, and the burden of proof will rest upon the faculty member. If the faculty member succeeds in establishing a *prima facie* case, it is incumbent upon those who made the decision against reappointment to come forward with evidence in support of their decision. Statistical evidence of improper discrimination may be used in establishing a *prima facie* case.

11. ADMINISTRATIVE PERSONNEL

The foregoing regulations apply to administrative personnel who hold academic rank, but only in their capacity as faculty members. Administrators who allege that a consideration violative of academic freedom, or of governing policies against improper discrimination as stated in Regulation 10, significantly contributed to a decision to terminate their appointment to an administrative post, or not to reappoint them, are entitled to the procedures set forth in Regulation 10.

12. POLITICAL ACTIVITIES OF FACULTY MEMBERS

Faculty members, as citizens, are free to engage in political activities. Where necessary, leaves of absence may be given for the duration of an election campaign or a term of office, on timely application, and for a reasonable period of time. The terms of such leave of absence will be set forth in writing, and the leave will not affect unfavorably the tenure status of a faculty member, except that time spent on such leave will not count as probationary service unless otherwise agreed to.[11]

[Note: Regulations 13, 14, and 15 are suggested in tentative form, and will require adaptation to the specific structure and operations of the institution; the provisions as recommended here are intended only to indicate the nature of the provisions to be included, and not to offer specific detail.]

13. GRADUATE STUDENT ACADEMIC STAFF

(a) The terms and conditions of every appointment to a graduate or teaching assistantship will be stated in writing, and a copy of the appointment document will be supplied to the graduate or teaching assistant.

(b) In no case will a graduate or teaching assistant be dismissed without having been provided with a statement of reasons and an opportunity to be heard before a duly constituted committee. (A dismissal is a termination before the end of the period of appointment.)

(c) A graduate or teaching assistant who establishes a *prima facie* case to the satisfaction of a duly constituted committee that a decision against reappointment was based significantly on considerations violative of academic freedom, or of governing policies against improper discrimination as stated in Regulation 10, will be given a statement of reasons by those responsible for the nonreappointment and an opportunity to be heard by the committee.

(d) Graduate or teaching assistants will have access to the faculty grievance committee, as provided in Regulation 15.

14. OTHER ACADEMIC STAFF

(a) In no case will a member of the academic staff[12] who is not otherwise protected by the preceding regulations which relate to dismissal proceedings be dismissed without having been provided with a statement of

---

[11][See "Statement on Professors and Political Activity," *AAUP Bulletin*, 55 (Autumn, 1969), pp. 388–389.]

[12][Each institution should define with particularity who are members of the academic staff.]

reasons and an opportunity to be heard before a duly constituted committee. (A dismissal is a termination before the end of the period of appointment.)

(b) With respect to the nonreappointment of a member of such academic staff who establishes a *prima facie* case to the satisfaction of a duly constituted committee that a consideration violative of academic freedom, or of governing policies against improper discrimination as stated in Regulation 10, significantly contributed to the nonreappointment, the academic staff member will be given a statement of reasons by those responsible for the nonreappointment and an opportunity to be heard by the committee.

15. GRIEVANCE PROCEDURE

(a) If any faculty member alleges cause for grievance in any matter not covered by the procedures described in the foregoing Regulations, the faculty member may petition the elected faculty grievance committee [here name the committee] for redress. The petition will set forth in detail the nature of the grievance and will state against whom the grievance is directed. It will contain any factual or other data which the petitioner deems pertinent to the case. Statistical evidence of improper discrimination, including discrimination in salary,[13] may be used in establishing a *prima facie* case. The committee will decide whether or not the facts merit a detailed investigation; if the faculty member succeeds in establishing a *prima facie* case, it is incumbent upon those who made the decision to come forward with evidence in support of their decision. Submission of a petition will not automatically entail investigation or detailed consideration thereof. The committee may seek to bring about a settlement of the issue satisfactory to the parties. If in the opinion of the committee such a settlement is not possible or is not appropriate, the committee will report its findings and recommendations to the petitioner and to the appropriate administrative officer and faculty body, and the petitioner will, upon request, be provided an opportunity to present the grievance to them. The grievance committee will consist of three [or some other number] elected members of the faculty. No officer of administration will serve on the committee.

NOTE ON IMPLEMENTATION

The Recommended Institutional Regulations here presented will require for their implementation a number of structural arrangements and agencies. For example, the Regulations will need support by:

(a) channels of communication among all the involved components of the institution, and between them and a concerned faculty member,

---

[13][See Scott, *Higher Education Salary Evaluation Kit*, American Association of University Professors, 1977.]

(b) definitions of corporate and individual faculty status within the college or university government, and of the role of the faculty in decisions relating to academic freedom and tenure,

(c) appropriate procedures for the creation and operation of faculty committees, with particular regard to the principles of faculty authority and responsibility.

The forms which these supporting elements assume will of course vary from one institution to another. Consequently, no detailed description of the elements is attempted in these Recommended Institutional Regulations. With respect to the principles involved, guidance will be found in the 1966 *Statement on Government of Colleges and Universities,* jointly formulated by the American Council on Education, the Association of Governing Boards of Universities and Colleges, and the American Association of University Professors.

C. STATEMENT ON GOVERNMENT OF COLLEGES AND UNIVERSITIES

AMERICAN ASSOCIATION OF UNIVERSITY PROFESSORS
AMERICAN COUNCIL ON EDUCATION
ASSOCIATION OF GOVERNING BOARDS OF UNIVERSITIES AND COLLEGES

Editorial Note. The Statement which follows is directed to governing board members, administrators, faculty members, students, and other persons in the belief that the colleges and universities of the United States have reached a stage calling for appropriately shared responsibility and cooperative action among the components of the academic institution. The Statement is intended to foster constructive joint thought and action, both within the institutional structure and in protection of its integrity against improper intrusions.

It is not intended that the Statement serve as a blueprint for government on a specific campus or as a manual for the regulation of controversy among the components of an academic institution, although it is to be hoped that the principles asserted will lead to the correction of existing weaknesses and assist in the establishment of sound structure and procedures. The Statement does not attempt to cover relations with those outside agencies which increasingly are controlling the resources and influencing the patterns of education in our institutions of higher learning; e.g., the United States Government, the state legislatures, state commissions, interstate associations or compacts and other interinstitutional arrangements. However it is hoped that the Statement will be helpful to these agencies in their consideration of educational matters.

Students are referred to in this Statement as an institutional component coordinate in importance with trustees, administrators, and faculty. There is, however, no main section on students. The omission has two causes: (1) the changes now occurring in the status of American students have plainly outdistanced the analysis by the educational community, and an attempt to define the situation without thorough study might prove unfair to student interests, and (2) students do not in fact presently have a significant voice in the government of colleges and universities; it would be unseemly to obscure, by superficial equality of length of statement, what may be a serious lag entitled to separate and full confrontation. The concern for student status felt by the organizations issuing this Statement is embodied in a note "On Student Status" intended to stimulate the educational community to turn its attention to an important need.

This Statement, in preparation since 1964, is jointly formulated by the American Association of University Professors, the American Council on Education, and the Association of Governing Boards of Universities and Colleges. On October 12, 1966, the Board of Directors of the ACE took action by which the Council "recognizes the Statement as a significant step forward in the clarification of the respective roles of governing boards, faculties, and administrations," and "commends it to the institutions which are members of the Council." On October 29, 1966, the Council of the AAUP approved the Statement, recommended approval by the Fifty-third Annual Meeting in April, 1967,[14] and recognized that "continuing joint effort is desirable, in view of the areas left open in the jointly formulated Statement, and the dynamic changes occurring in higher education." On November 18, 1966, the Executive Committee of the AGB took action by which that organization also "recognizes the Statement as a significant step forward in the clarification of the respective roles of governing boards, faculties and administrations," and "commends it to the governing boards which are members of the Association."

---

[14]The Annual Meeting approved the Statement.

I. INTRODUCTION

This Statement is a call to mutual understanding regarding the government of colleges and universities. Understanding, based on community of interest, and producing joint effort, is essential for at least three reasons. First, the academic institution, public or private, often has become less autonomous; buildings, research, and student tuition are supported by funds over which the college or university exercises a diminishing control. Legislative and executive governmental authority, at all levels, plays a part in the making of important decisions in academic policy. If these voices and forces are to be successfully heard and integrated, the academic institution must be in a position to meet them with its own generally unified view. Second, regard for the welfare of the institution remains important despite the mobility and interchange of scholars. Third, a college or university in which all the components are aware of the interdependence, of the usefulness of communication among themselves, and of the force of joint action will enjoy increased capacity to solve educational problems.

II. THE ACADEMIC INSTITUTION: JOINT EFFORT

A. Preliminary Considerations

The variety and complexity of the tasks performed by institutions of higher education produce an inescapable interdependence among governing board, administration, faculty, students, and others. The relationship calls for adequate communication among these components, and full opportunity for appropriate joint planning and effort.

Joint effort in an academic institution will take a variety of forms appropriate to the kinds of situations encountered. In some instances, an initial exploration or recommendation will be made by the president with consideration by the faculty at a later stage; in other instances, a first and essentially definitive recommendation will be made by the faculty, subject to the endorsement of the president and the governing board. In still others, a substantive contribution can be made when student leaders are responsibly involved in the process. Although the variety of such approaches may be wide, at least two general conclusions regarding joint effort seem clearly warranted: (1) important areas of action involve at one time or another the initiating capacity and decision-making participation of all the institutional components, and (2) differences in the weight of each voice, from one point to the next, should be determined by reference to the responsibility of each component for the particular matter at hand, as developed hereinafter.

B. Determination of General Educational Policy

The general educational policy, i.e., the objectives of an institution and the nature, range, and pace of its efforts, is shaped by the institutional charter or by law, by tradition and historical development, by the present needs of the community of the institution, and by the professional aspirations and standards of those directly involved in its work. Every board will wish to go beyond its formal trustee obligation to conserve the accomplishment of the past and to engage seriously with the future; every faculty will seek to conduct an operation worthy of scholarly standards of learning; every administrative officer will strive to meet his charge and to attain the goals of the institution. The interests of all are coordinate and related, and unilateral effort can lead to confusion on conflict. Essential to a solution is a reasonably explicit statement on general educational policy. Operating responsibility and authority, and procedures for continuing review, should be clearly defined in official regulations.

When an educational goal has been established, it becomes the responsibility primarily of the faculty to determine appropriate curriculum and procedures of student instruction.

Special considerations may require particular accommodations: (1) a publicly supported institution may be regulated by statutory provisions, and (2) a church-controlled institution may be limited by its charter or bylaws. When such external requirements influence course content and manner of instruction or research, they impair the educational effectiveness of the institution.

Such matters as major changes in the size or composition of the student body and the relative emphasis to be given to the various elements of the educational and research program should involve participation of governing board, administration, and faculty prior to final decision.

C. *Internal Operations of the Institution*

The framing and execution of long-range plans, one of the most important aspects of institutional responsibility, should be a central and continuing concern in the academic community.

Effective planning demands that the broadest possible exchange of information and opinion should be the rule for communication among the components of a college or university. The channels of communication should be established and maintained by joint endeavor. Distinction should be observed between the institutional system of communication and the system of responsibility for the making of decisions.

A second area calling for joint effort in internal operations is that of decisions regarding existing or prospective physical resources. The board, president, and faculty should all seek agreement on basic decisions regarding buildings and other facilities to be used in the educational work of the institution.

A third area is budgeting. The allocation of resources among competing demands is central in the formal responsibility of the governing board, in the administrative authority of the president, and in the educational function of the faculty. Each component should therefore have a voice in the determination of short- and long-range priorities, and each should receive appropriate analyses of past budgetary experience, reports on current budgets and expenditures, and short- and long-range budgetary projections. The function of each component in budgetary matters should be understood by all; the allocation of authority will determine the flow of information and the scope of participation in decisions.

Joint effort of a most critical kind must be taken when an institution chooses a new president. The selection of a chief administrative officer should follow upon cooperative search by the governing board and the faculty, taking into consideration the opinions of others who are appropriately interested. The president should be equally qualified to serve both as the executive officer of the governing board and as the chief academic officer of the institution and the faculty. His dual role requires that he be able to interpret to board and faculty the educational views and concepts of institutional government of the other. He should have the confidence of the board and the faculty.

The selection of academic deans and other chief academic officers should be the responsibility of the president with the advice of and in consultation with the appropriate faculty.

Determinations of faculty status, normally based on the recommendations of the faculty groups involved, are discussed in Part V of this Statement; but it should here be noted that the building of a strong faculty requires careful joint effort in such actions as staff selection and promotion and the granting of tenure. Joint action should also govern dismissals; the applicable principles and procedures in these matters are well established.[15]

D. External Relations of the Institution

Anyone—a member of the governing board, the president or other member of the administration, a member of the faculty, or a member of the student body or the alumni—affects the institution when he speaks of it in public. An individual who speaks unofficially should so indicate. An official spokesman for the institution, the board, the administration, the faculty, or the student body should be guided by established policy.

It should be noted that only the board speaks legally for the whole institution, although it may delegate responsibility to an agent.

---

[15]See the 1940 *Statement of Principles on Academic Freedom and Tenure* and the 1958 *Statement on Procedural Standards in Faculty Dismissal Proceedings*. These statements have been jointly approved or adopted by the Association of American Colleges and the American Association of University Professors; the 1940 Statement has been endorsed by numerous learned and scientific societies and educational associations.

The right of a board member, an administrative officer, a faculty member, or a student to speak on general educational questions or about the administration and operations of his own institution is a part of his right as a citizen and should not be abridged by the institution.[16] There exist, of course, legal bounds relating to defamation of character, and there are questions of propriety.

III. THE ACADEMIC INSTITUTION: THE GOVERNING BOARD

The governing board has a special obligation to assure that the history of the college or university shall serve as a prelude and inspiration to the future. The board helps relate the institution to its chief community: e.g., the community college to serve the educational needs of a defined population area or group, the church-controlled college to be cognizant of the announced position of its denomination, and the comprehensive university to discharge the many duties and to accept the appropriate new challenges which are its concern at the several levels of higher education.

The governing board of an institution of higher education in the United States operates, with few exceptions, as the final institutional authority. Private institutions are established by charters; public institutions are established by constitutional or statutory provisions. In private institutions the board is frequently self-perpetuating; in public colleges and universities the present membership of a board may be asked to suggest candidates for appointment. As a whole and individually when the governing board confronts the problem of succession, serious attention should be given to obtaining properly qualified persons. Where public law calls for election of governing board members, means should be found to insure the nomination of fully suited persons, and the electorate should be informed of the relevant criteria for board membership.

Since the membership of the board may embrace both individual and collective competence of recognized weight, its advice or help may be sought through established channels by other components of the academic community. The governing board of an institution of higher education, while maintaining a general overview, entrusts the conduct of administration to the administrative officers, the president and the deans, and the con-

---

[16]With respect to faculty members, the 1940 *Statement of Principles on Academic Freedom and Tenure* reads: "The college or university teacher is a citizen, a member of a learned profession, and an officer of an educational institution. When he speaks or writes as a citizen, he should be free from institutional censorship or discipline, but his special position in the community imposes special obligations. As a man of learning and an educational officer, he should remember that the public may judge his profession and his institution by his utterances. Hence he should at all times be accurate, should exercise appropriate restraint, should show respect for the opinions of others, and should make every effort to indicate that he is not an institutional spokesman."

duct of teaching and research to the faculty. The board should undertake appropriate self-limitation.

One of the governing board's important tasks is to insure the publication of codified statements that define the over-all policies and procedures of the institution under its jurisdiction.

The board plays a central role in relating the likely needs of the future to predictable resources; it has the responsibility for husbanding the endowment; it is responsible for obtaining needed capital and operating funds; and in the broadest sense of the term it should pay attention to personnel policy. In order to fulfill these duties, the board should be aided by, and may insist upon, the development of long-range planning by the administration and faculty.

When ignorance or ill-will threatens the institution or any part of it, the governing board must be available for support. In grave crises it will be expected to serve as a champion. Although the action to be taken by it will usually be on behalf of the president, the faculty, or the student body, the board should make clear that the protection it offers to an individual or a group is, in fact, a fundamental defense of the vested interests of society in the educational institution.[17]

IV. THE ACADEMIC INSTITUTION: THE PRESIDENT

The president, as the chief executive officer of an institution of higher education, is measured largely by his capacity for institutional leadership. He shares responsibility for the definition and attainment of goals, for administrative action, and for operating the communications system which links the components of the academic community. He represents his institution to its many publics. His leadership role is supported by delegated authority from the board and faculty.

As the chief planning officer of an institution, the president has a special obligation to innovate and initiate. The degree to which a president can envision new horizons for his institution, and can persuade others to see them and to work toward them, will often constitute the chief measure of his administration.

---

[17]Traditionally, governing boards developed within the context of single-campus institutions. In more recent times, governing and coordinating boards have increasingly tended to develop at the multi-campus, regional, systemwide, or statewide levels. As influential components of the academic community, these supra-campus bodies bear particular responsibility for protecting the autonomy of individual campuses or institutions under their jurisdiction and for implementing policies of shared responsibility. The American Association of University Professors regards the objectives and practices recommended in the 1966 Statement as constituting equally appropriate guidelines for such supra-campus bodies, and looks toward continued development of practices that will facilitate application of such guidelines in this new context. (Adopted by the AAUP Council in June 1978.)

The president must at times, with or without support, infuse new life into a department; relatedly, he may at times be required, working within the concept of tenure, to solve problems of obsolescence. The president will necessarily utilize the judgments of the faculty, but in the interest of academic standards he may also seek outside evaluations by scholars of acknowledged competence.

It is the duty of the president to see to it that the standards and procedures in operational use within the college or university conform to the policy established by the governing board and to the standards of sound academic practice. It is also incumbent on the president to insure that faculty views, including dissenting views, are presented to the board in those areas and on those issues where responsibilities are shared. Similarly the faculty should be informed of the views of the board and the administration on like issues.

The president is largely responsible for the maintenance of existing institutional resources and the creation of new resources; he has ultimate managerial responsibility for a large area of nonacademic activities, he is responsible for public understanding, and by the nature of his office is the chief spokesman of his institution. In these and other areas his work is to plan, to organize, to direct, and to represent. The presidential function should receive the general support of board and faculty.

V. THE ACADEMIC INSTITUTION: THE FACULTY

The faculty has primary responsibility for such fundamental areas as curriculum, subject matter and methods of instruction, research, faculty status, and those aspects of student life which relate to the educational process. On these matters the power of review or final decision lodged in the governing board or delegated by it to the president should be exercised adversely only in exceptional circumstances, and for reasons communicated to the faculty. It is desirable that the faculty should, following such communication, have opportunity for further consideration and further transmittal of its views to the president or board. Budgets, manpower limitations, the time element, and the policies of other groups, bodies and agencies having jurisdiction over the institution may set limits to realization of faculty advice.

The faculty sets the requirements for the degrees offered in course, determines when the requirements have been met, and authorizes the president and board to grant the degrees thus achieved.

Faculty status and related matters are primarily a faculty responsibility; this area includes appointments, reappointments, decisions not to reappoint, promotions, the granting of tenure, and dismissal. The primary responsibility of the faculty for such matters is based upon the fact that its judgment is central to general educational policy. Furthermore, scholars in a particular field or activity have the chief competence for judging the work of their colleagues; in such competence it is implicit that responsibility exists for both adverse and favorable judgments. Likewise there is the more general competence of experienced faculty personnel committees having a broader charge. Determinations in these matters should first be by faculty action through established procedures, reviewed by the chief academic officers with the concurrence of the board. The governing board and president should, on questions of faculty status, as in other matters where the faculty has primary responsibility, concur with the faculty judgment except in rare instances and for compelling reasons which should be stated in detail.

The faculty should actively participate in the determination of policies and procedures governing salary increases.

The chairman or head of a department, who serves as the chief representative of his department within an institution, should be selected either by departmental election or by appointment following consultation with members of the department and of related departments; appointments should normally be in conformity with department members' judgment. The chairman or department head should not have tenure in his office; his tenure as a faculty member is a matter of separate right. He should serve for a stated term but without prejudice to re-election or to reappointment by procedures which involve appropriate faculty consultation. Board, administration, and faculty should all bear in mind that the department chairman has a special obligation to build a department strong in scholarship and teaching capacity.

Agencies for faculty participation in the government of the college or university should be established at each level where faculty responsibility is present. An agency should exist for the presentation of the views of the whole faculty. The structure and procedures for faculty participation should be designed, approved, and established by joint action of the components of the institution. Faculty representatives should be selected by the faculty according to procedures determined by the faculty.[18]

The agencies may consist of meetings of all faculty members of a department, school, college, division, or university system, or may take the form of faculty-elected executive committees in departments and schools and a faculty-elected senate or council for larger divisions or the institution as a whole.

---

[18]AAUP regards collective bargaining, properly used, as another means of achieving sound academic government. Where there is faculty collective bargaining, the parties should seek to assure appropriate institutional governance structures which will protect the right of all faculty to participate in institutional governance in accordance with the 1966 Statement. (Adopted by the AAUP Council in June 1978.)

Among the means of communication among the faculty, administration, and governing board now in use are: (1) circulation of memoranda and reports by board committees, the administration, and faculty committees, (2) joint *ad hoc* committees, (3) standing liaison committees, (4) membership of faculty members on administrative bodies, and (5) membership of faculty members on governing boards. Whatever the channels of communication, they should be clearly understood and observed.

ON STUDENT STATUS

When students in American colleges and universities desire to participate responsibly in the government of the institution they attend, their wish should be recognized as a claim to opportunity both for educational experience and for involvement in the affairs of their college or university. Ways should be found to permit significant student participation within the limits of attainable effectiveness. The obstacles to such participation are large and should not be minimized: inexperience, untested capacity, a transitory status which means that present action does not carry with it subsequent responsibility, and the inescapable fact that the other components of the institution are in a position of judgment over the students. It is important to recognize that student needs are strongly related to educational experience, both formal and informal. Students expect, and have a right to expect, that the educational process will be structured, that they will be stimulated by it to become independent adults, and that they will have effectively transmitted to them the cultural heritage of the larger society. If institutional support is to have its fullest possible meaning it should incorporate the strength, freshness of view, and idealism of the student body.

The respect of students for their college or university can be enhanced if they are given at least these opportunities: (1) to be listened to in the classroom without fear of institutional reprisal for the substance of their views, (2) freedom to discuss questions of institutional policy and operation, (3) the right to academic due process when charged with serious violations of institutional regulations, and (4) the same right to hear speakers of their own choice as is enjoyed by other components of the institution.

D. THE ROLE OF THE FACULTY IN
BUDGETARY AND SALARY MATTERS

The Statement that follows was prepared by the Association's Committee T on College and University Government. It was approved by the Council of the American Association of University Professors in May 1972 and endorsed by the Fifty-eighth Annual Meeting as Association policy.

I. GENERAL PRINCIPLES

The purpose of this Statement is to define the role of the faculty in decisions as to the allocation of financial resources according to the principle of shared authority as set forth in the 1966 *Statement on Government of Colleges and Universities,*[19] and to offer some principles and derivative guidelines for faculty participation in this area. On the subject of budgeting in general, it is asserted in the 1966 *Statement on Government:*

> The allocation of resources among competing demands is central in the formal responsibility of the governing board, in the administrative authority of the president, and in the educational function of the faculty. Each component should therefore have a voice in the determination of short- and long-range priorities, and each should receive appropriate analyses of past budgetary experience, reports on current budgets and expenditures, and short- and long-range budgetary projections. The function of each component in budgetary matters should be understood by all; the allocation of authority will determine the flow of information and the scope of participation in decisions.

Essentially two requirements are set forth in this passage:

A. *Clearly understood channels of communication and the accessibility of important information to those groups which have a legitimate interest in it.*

B. *Participation by each group (governing board, president, and faculty)*[20] *appropriate to the particular expertise of each.* Thus the governing board is expected to husband the endowment and obtain capital and operat-, ing funds; the president is expected to maintain existing institutional re-

---

[19]Jointly formulated by the American Council on Education, the Association of Governing Boards of Universities and Colleges, and the American Association of University Professors.

[20]The participation of students in budgetary decisions affecting student programs and student life is taken for granted in this document, but no attempt is made to define the nature of that participation here.

Part D of this appendix is reprinted from *AAUP Bulletin,* vol. 58, no. 2 (June 1972), pp. 170–172.

sources and create new ones; the faculty is expected to establish faculty salary policies and, in its primary responsibility for the educational function of the institution, to participate also in broader budgetary matters primarily as these impinge on that function. All three groups, the *Statement on Government* makes clear, should participate in long-range planning.

II. FACULTY PARTICIPATION IN BUDGETING

The faculty should participate both in the preparation of the total institutional budget, and (within the framework of the total budget) in decisions relevant to the further apportioning of its specific fiscal divisions (salaries, academic programs, tuition, physical plants and grounds, etc.). The soundness of resulting decisions should be enhanced if an elected representative committee of the faculty participates in deciding on the overall allocation of institutional resources and the proportion to be devoted directly to the academic program. This committee should be given access to all information that it requires to perform its task effectively, and it should have the opportunity to confer periodically with representatives of the administration and governing board. Such an institution-level body, representative of the entire faculty, can play an important part in mediating the financial needs and the demands of different groups within the faculty and can be of significant assistance to the administration in resolving impasses which may arise when a large variety of demands are made on necessarily limited resources. Such a body will also be of critical importance in representing faculty interests and interpreting the needs of the faculty to the governing board and president. The presence of faculty members on the governing board itself may, particularly in smaller institutions, constitute an approach that would serve somewhat the same purpose, but does not obviate the need for an all-faculty body which may wish to formulate its recommendations independent of other groups. In addition, at public institutions there are legitimate ways and means for the faculty to play a role in the submission and support of budgetary requests to the appropriate agency of government.

Budgetary decisions directly affecting those areas for which, according to the *Statement on Government*, the faculty has primary responsibility—curriculum, subject matter and methods of instruction, research, faculty status, and those aspects of student life which relate to the educational process—should be made in concert with the faculty. Certain kinds of expenditures related to the academic program, such as the allocation of funds for a particular aspect of library development, student projects under faculty sponsorship, or departmental equipment, will require that the decision-making process be sufficiently decentralized to permit autonomy to the various units of the faculty (departments, divisions, schools, colleges, special programs) in deciding upon the use of their allocations within the broader limits set by the governing board, president, and agencies representative of the entire faculty. In other areas, such as faculty research programs, or the total library and laboratory budget, recommendations as to the desirable funding levels for the ensuing fiscal period and decisions on the allocation of university funds within the current budget levels should be made by the university-level, all-faculty committee as well as by the faculty agencies directly concerned.[21] The question of faculty salaries, as an aspect of faculty status, is treated separately below.

Circumstances of financial exigency obviously pose special problems. At institutions experiencing major threats to their continued financial support, the faculty should be informed as early and specifically as possible of significant impending financial difficulties. The faculty—with substantial representation from its nontentured as well as its tenured members, since it is the former who are likely to bear the brunt of any reduction— should participate at the department, college or professional school, and institution-wide levels, in key decisions as to the future of the institution and of specific academic programs within the institution. The faculty, employing accepted standards of due process, should assume primary responsibility for determining the status of individual faculty members.[22] The question of possible reductions in salaries and fringe benefits is discussed in Section III below. The faculty should play a fundamental role in any decision which would change the basic character and purpose of the institution, including transformation of the institution, affiliation of part of the existing operation with another institution, or merger, with the resulting abandonment or curtailment of duplicate programs.

Before any decisions on curtailment become final, those whose work stands to be adversely affected should have full opportunity to be heard. In the event of a merger, the faculties from the two institutions should participate jointly in negotiations affecting faculty status and the academic programs at both institutions. To the extent that major budgetary considerations are involved in these decisions, the faculty should be given full and timely access to the financial information necessary to the making of an informed choice. In making decisions on whether teaching and research programs are to be curtailed, financial considerations should not be al-

---

[21]For obvious reasons, the focus here is on fundings from the resources of the institution, and not from external agencies such as private contractors or the federal government. Even in these cases, however, it may be possible in certain circumstances for the faculty to play a part in deciding further on the allocation of a particular grant to various purposes related to the project within the institution. There should be careful faculty and administrative scrutiny as to the methods by which these funds are to be employed under the particular contract.

[22]On the question of due process and appropriate terminal settlements for individual faculty members (on tenure or prior to the expiration of a term appointment) whose positions are being abolished, see the 1982 *Recommended Institutional Regulations on Academic Freedom and Tenure*, Regulation 4(c).

lowed to obscure the fact that instruction and research constitute the essential reason for the existence of the university. Among the various considerations, difficult and often competing, that have to be taken into account in deciding upon particular reductions, the retention of a viable academic program necessarily should come first. Particular reductions should follow considered advice from the concerned departments, or other units of academic concentration, on the short-term and long-term viability of reduced programs.

III. FACULTY PARTICIPATION IN DECISIONS RELATING
TO SALARY POLICIES AND PROCEDURES

The *Statement on Government* asserts that "the faculty should actively participate in the determination of policies and procedures governing salary increases." Salaries, of course, are part of the total budgetary picture; and, as indicated above, the faculty should participate in the decision as to the proportion of the budget to be devoted to that purpose. However, there is also the question of the role of the faculty as a body in the determination of individual faculty salaries.

A. *The Need for Clear and Open Policy.* Many imagined grievances as to salary could be alleviated, and the development of a system of accountability to reduce the number of real grievances could be facilitated, if both the criteria for salary raises and the recommendatory procedure itself were (1) designed by a representative group of the faculty in concert with the administration, and (2) open and clearly understood.[23] Such accountability is not participation *per se,* but it provides the basis for a situation in which such participation can be more fruitful.

Once the procedures are established, the person or group who submits the initial salary recommendation (usually the department chairman, singly or in conjunction with an elected executive committee of the department) should be informed of its status at each further stage of the salary-determination process. As the 1966 Statement points out, the chief competence for the judgment of a colleague rests in the department, school, or program (whichever is the smallest applicable unit of faculty government within the institution), and in most cases the salary recommendation presumably derives from that judgment. The recommending officer should have the opportunity to defend that recommendation at a later stage in the event of a serious challenge to it.

B. *Levels of Decision-Making.* Not all institutions provide for an initial salary recommendation by the departmental chairman or his equivalent; the Association regards it as desirable, for the reasons already mentioned, that

---

[23]This section does not take into account those situations in which salaries are determined upon according to a step system and/or a standard salary is negotiated for each rank. The salary policy and, in effect, individual salaries are public information under such systems.

the recommendation normally originate at the departmental level. Further review is normally conducted by the appropriate administrative officers; they should, when they have occasion to question or inquire further regarding the departmental recommendation, solicit informed faculty advice by meeting with the departmental head or chairman and, if feasible, the elected body of the faculty. It is also desirable that a mechanism exist for review of a salary recommendation, or of a final salary decision, by a representative elected committee of the faculty above the departmental level in cases involving a complaint.[24] Such a committee should have access to information on faculty salary levels. Another faculty committee, likewise at a broader level than that of the department, may be charged with the review of routine recommendations.

Of the role of the governing board in college and university government, the *Statement on Government* says: "The governing board of an institution of higher education, while maintaining a general overview, entrusts the conduct of administration to the administrative officers, the president and the deans, and the conduct of teaching and research to the faculty. The board should undertake appropriate self-limitation." The Statement adds that "in the broadest sense of the term" the board "should pay attention to personnel policy." The thrust of these remarks is that it is inadvisable for a governing board to make decisions on individual salaries, except those of the chief administrative officers of the institution. Not only do such decisions take time which should be devoted to the board's functions of overview and long-range planning, but such decisions also are in most cases beyond the competence of the board.

When financial exigency leads to a reduction in the overall salary budget for teaching and research, the governing board, while assuming final responsibility for setting the limits imposed by the resources available to the institution, should delegate to the faculty and administration concurrently any further review of the implication of the situation for individual salaries, and the faculty should be given the opportunity to minimize the hardship to its individual members by careful examination of whatever alternatives to termination of services are feasible.

C. *Fringe Benefits.* The faculty should participate in the selection of fringe benefit programs and in the periodic review of those programs. It should be recognized that of these so-called fringe benefits, at least those included in Committee Z's definition of total compensation have the same standing as direct faculty salaries and are separated for tax purposes. They should be considered and dealt with in the same manner as direct payment of faculty salary.

---

[24]See the *Recommended Institutional Regulations on Academic Freedom and Tenure*, Regulation 15, "Grievance Procedures."

Appendix 2

NACUBO Documents

A. INSTITUTIONAL BUDGETING

Institutional budgeting is the process whereby the plans of an institution are translated into an itemized, authorized, and systematic plan of operation, expressed in dollars, for a given period. Budgets are the blueprints for the orderly execution of program plans; they serve as control mechanisms to match anticipated and actual revenues and expenditures.

A primary purpose of budgeting is to provide an opportunity to examine the composition and viability of an institution's resource base for each program and activity. The resource base includes a variety of sources and is typically composed of both restricted and unrestricted funds. Development of a budget should also insure that all institutional activities and programs are simultaneously examined to determine, in light of available resources, which should be supported. The process should communicate institutional priorities to various constituencies, identify specific commitments, and es-

Part A of this appendix is reprinted from *College & University Business Administration*, 4th ed. (Washington, DC: National Association of College and University Business Officers, 1982), pp. 314-331.

tablish preliminary control over institutional resources. The result of this process is a document that is used to monitor and control the ongoing operations of an institution.

The budget process is influenced by the unique characteristics of an institution, such as mission, size, affiliation, organization, and financial structure. Other influences on the process include operating contraints imposed on the institution by government regulations and by social and economic factors.

There are two types of budgets: (1) the operating budget, which is a financial plan of current operations that encompasses both estimated revenues and estimated expenditures for a specified period, normally one fiscal year, and (2) the capital budget, which outlines expenditures for new construction, major repairs or renovations, and major items of equipment. The capital budget is typically for a specified period, which can vary from one to five years, depending on budget requirements.

While this chapter deals primarily with developments and implementation of the operating budget, it is important to note that capital and operating budgets should be integrated. For example, a change in the operating budget, such as the addition of new academic programs and library holdings, can have implications for the capital budget in the form of new space requirements. Similarly, construction of a new facility can result in the need for additional maintenance personnel and funds for utilities that must be reflected in the operating budget.

Development of operating and capital budgets should be preceded by development of an institutional plan. Through the planning process, participants establish program goals and objectives, examine alternative program choices, and develop a controlled budget strategy. The period covered by institutional plans can vary, but the first year of the plan should serve as the basis for developing the institution's budgets.

FACTORS AFFECTING THE BUDGET PROCESS

A number of factors, both internal and external to the institution, have a significant influence on development and implementation of the budget. These are described below.

INTERNAL FACTORS

Mission. A review of the institution's mission statement should be an integral part of the planning and budgeting process. This review should include the constituencies served by the institution; institutional priorities; programs and services provided by the institution; and roles played by instruction, research, and public service. Such a review should aid in determining sources of revenues and ways in which resources are allocated.

Management style. The management style of an institution influences the way in which budgets are developed and implemented. The focus of management decisions, whether centralized or decentralized, can affect not only development of the budget but also the degree and type of budget control. For example, if the management style is participatory, more time may be required for budget preparation and implementation. In addition, a management style that encourages consultation and participation can lead to a greater interest in budget control.

Fiscal policies. The extent to which academic units, service operations, and auxiliary enterprises are required to be fiscally self-sufficient can have a marked effect on the budget. The institution's position on this issue not only affects availability of unrestricted funds for core academic programs, but also determines whether the primary emphasis in the budgeting of these operations will entail simply a review of earnings activities or will also involve allocation decisions.

Type and degree of accountability. Individual budget units may be held accountable for generating a specific number of contact hours per faculty or student credit hours per academic term. Budget units, such as departments or support programs, may also be designated as responsibility centers and held accountable for expenditures for such items as faculty and staff salaries, supplies, and equipment. An institution may implement a system of incentives for sound planning and budgeting by encouraging units to reduce costs and by permitting them to use the savings for other purposes, such as for equipment or faculty and staff travel, although care should be taken to avoid using nonrecurring savings for recurring budget increases. An institution's policy with regard to taking risks or its willingness to explore new ways of serving its constituents, such as offering off-campus or continuing education programs, also influences the development, implementation, and control of the budget and the level of autonomy it allows departments.

Debt policies. An institution's policy on the use of borrowed funds to meet operating expenses or to fund capital projects can significantly affect development of both capital and operating budgets. An institution's debt policy should establish (1) circumstances under which the institution will assume additional debt and (2) criteria for determining the appropriate level of debt. Public institutions are normally prohibited by law from running deficits and are subject to strict regulations concerning external borrowing and the issuance of bonds to fund capital projects. Restrictions on the use of external borrowing are less severe for independent colleges and universities, but an institution's use of borrowed funds for current operations or capital projects should be examined critically during the planning and budgeting process.

Compensation goals and policies. In developing the budget, managers should examine the advantages and disadvantages of providing various levels of compensation. The institution must assess its ability to provide levels of compensation that are competitive with those of other local employers and with peer institutions. The college or university also needs to assess the importance it places on merit, promotion, and longevity among its personnel and to balance this factor against the institution's ability to provide adequate compensation to retain its employees. The advantages of improving employee benefits should also be considered. At unionized institutions, collective bargaining contracts are a principal determinant in the formulation of compensation goals and policies. Further, this area may be controlled in public institutions by the state appropriation process and by state civil service systems that dictate support staff compensation.

Pricing policies. An institution's policy on setting tuition, fees, and rates for auxiliary and support services, such as housing, food services, computing services, and plant operation and maintenance, must be examined. For example, it must be determined whether rates for room and board should cover full costs or whether the institution should subsidize these operations. Also, the extent to which the funding of the budget depends on governmental student aid programs should be considered in developing tuition rates.

EXTERNAL FACTORS

Sources of support. Changes that would significantly affect an institution's traditional sources of support should be considered in developing the budget. For example, changes in the practices of the federal, state, or local government relative to funding higher education can significantly affect public institutions. Changes in the levels of gifts received or in endowment income, and changes in the amount of revenue generated by tuition and fees, can also have major implications for both independent and public institutions.

Inflation. Managers should examine the effect of inflation on faculty and staff purchasing power and the ways in which changes in prices of goods and services affect the institution's total budget. To study the effects of inflation, some institutions use the Higher Education Price Index (HEPI), which measures changes in the costs of goods and services purchased by colleges and universities. Methods by which the inflationary effect may be offset should also be considered; these could include energy conservation programs, quantity purchasing, and consolidation of service functions among institutional units and even with other institutions.

Government regulations. Examples of government requirements that affect the budget include health and safety regulations (Occupational Safety and Health Act and similar state laws), access for the handicapped (the Rehabilitation Act of 1973, especially Sections 503 and 504), federal, state, and local reporting requirements, and state control over program changes.

Competition for students. The degree of competition among institutions, both public and independent, to attract and retain students can significantly affect an institution's ability to obtain adequate revenues for operating its academic and support programs.

Demographic trends. Changes in the pool of students of traditional college age (18–22 years of age) can affect an institution's ability to attract students and can have a major effect on colleges and universities that have provided services primarily to students of traditional college age. As a result of the projected decline in that age group, many institutions have examined alternative methods of providing services, including off-campus programs or programs for nontraditional students. Some have also increased course offerings in program areas that are gaining in student demand. The ratio of resident to nonresident students may be an important revenue factor if there is a nonresident tuition differential at an institution.

Government financial control. In developing their budgets, public institutions must be aware of state and local restrictions on the expenditure of funds, such as purchasing regulations, travel restrictions, limitations on out-of-state enrollment, and restrictions on budgetary transfers imposed by state and local appropriating bodies. Public *and* independent institutions must also be aware of governmental restrictions on student aid and sponsored programs.

Reversion of unexpended revenues to the state can also be of major concern to public institutions. In addition, shortfalls in state revenues can result in mid-period reductions in previously approved institutional budget levels. Other external factors, such as condition of the national, state, and local economy, also must be considered in developing the budget.

BUDGET DEVELOPMENT

In order to understand the budget development process, there must be understanding of the context in which budgets are developed. Aspects of budget development are discussed below.

PARTICIPANTS IN THE BUDGETING PROCESS

This chapter deals with major institutional participants in the budgeting process. However, the budget is often influenced by expressed needs of other constituents that are both internal and external to the institution. These include special-interest groups composed of students, faculty, and staff; alumni; legislators; private industry; and federal, state, and local agencies. While some of these groups may not be directly involved in preparation of the budget, their concerns must be addressed in both the planning and budgeting processes.

Major institutional participants in the budget development process usually include the governing board, chief executive officer, senior administrators, budget officer (who is often the chief business officer), and planning and budgeting staff. In addition, some colleges and universities seek participation from faculty and students.

Roles of participants vary among colleges and universities. In some cases, the chief business officer may also be the budget officer, while at other institutions the positions may be separate, with the budget officer reporting to the chief business officer or to the chief executive officer. In any case, the success of the budgeting process depends on the leadership and support of the chief executive officer and the commitment of the institution's faculty and staff.

Since planning and budgeting are integrated, participants in the planning process often are involved in budgeting. Below are brief descriptions of the roles of participants in the budgeting process.

Governing board. The board organizes itself to oversee the process, reviews the institution's mission, evaluates the effect of conditions such as demographic trends, evaluates competing program goals, reviews proposals for new programs, and reviews and approves institutional budgets.

Chief executive officer. This officer initiates planning and budgeting efforts, communicates with the planning and budgeting staff, approves policies to be used in developing the budget, reviews program plans and budgets, approves budget recommendations, and presents the budget to the governing board.

Planning and budgeting group. Typically, this group is composed of senior administrators, with possible representation from constituent groups. The chief executive officer should serve as chairperson of this group, which is the determining body in development of the institution's short- and long-range plans and budget.

Budget officer (or chief business officer). This officer coordinates budget activities among operating units, works with the planning and budgeting staff and constituent groups, develops the schedule for preparation and implementation of the budget, coordinates the data base for budgeting, prepares the budget for presentation to the governing board, and may be responsible for developing and implementing a system of budget control.

BUDGET TECHNIQUES

Many techniques have been proposed to help facilitate and improve the budgeting process, but there is danger in viewing any of these as effective in all institutional settings and in dealing with all program areas. Instead, such techniques should be viewed as management tools that can be effective in addressing specific problem areas of an institution at particular times.

Below are descriptions of various budget techniques and a brief critique of advantages and disadvantages associated with each.

Incremental budgeting. Under this approach, which is the most common form of budgeting, each line item, such as faculty salaries, is considered for an increment. Incremental increases are often tied to increases in inflation or changes in institutional rates or prices. During periods of fiscal stringency, however, items can be held at current levels or considered for a decrement. Assumptions underlying incremental budgeting are that the current basis for allocating resources is appropriate and that present programs are to be continued. Incremental budgeting is easy to understand and is widely accepted by governing boards and legislators. But only in a limited way, through internal reallocations, does it encourage an institution either to justify existing programs or to eliminate programs that are not productive.

Open-ended budgeting. This technique calls for institutional cost centers, such as academic and support units, to submit budget requests at the level considered appropriate by the unit head. The central budget officer or a group of senior administrative officers then adjusts the budget to meet resources. This adjustment usually takes place in negotiation sessions. Advantages of this process are increased constituent involvement and the linking of planning and budgeting activities of the units. Disadvantages are frequent incompatibility of budget requests with resources and the need for several rounds of negotiations before the request matches available resources.

Quota budgeting. In this technique, institutional cost centers are given a control figure and then requested to build a budget based on this allotment. Control figures may be predicted on a percentage increase or decrease in current levels or on specific dollar amounts based on an analysis of current revenues. Advantages of quota budgeting are that cost centers can ascertain the total budget at an early date and that constituent groups are made aware of the overall budget picture as reflected in quota figures. Disadvantages are that there is a tendency to base the new budget almost entirely on the old one and that program review is not encouraged, since quotas are often placed on line items rather than on programs.

Alternative-level budgeting. This requires that several alternative budget levels (generally two or three) be prepared. For example, levels of 10 percent below present budget level, 5 percent below present budget level, and 5 percent above present budget level may be designated by administrators. Alternative-level budgeting provides a good method of obtaining details of program evaluation and classification of program priorities. It also involves the judgment of persons at operating levels and forces administrators to be cognizant of program priorities. Disadvantages of alternative-level budgeting include the amount of work involved in preparation at various levels and the degree of uncertainty created as to which level will be funded. Alternative-level budgeting also suffers from the same disadvantages as incremental and quota budgeting in that it nurtures a tendency to base the new budget almost entirely on budgets of prior years.[1]

Formula-base budgeting. This is a technique by which financial needs or operating requirements of an institution may be determined through application of a formula. Most formulas are based on enrollment data and/or credit-hour production. Formula budgeting is normally applied on a statewide basis for state-supported institutions rather than as an internal budgeting procedure for individual institutions. An understanding of formula budgeting, however, is essential for those public institutions that receive their funds on the basis of an instructional, library, physical plant, or other type of budget formula. State legislatures and their staffs often use formula results in determining institutional appropriations but they do not necessarily fund programs at 100 percent of formula.

An advantage associated with formula budgeting is that it appears to provide equitable treatment among institutions. Further, formulas are quantitatively based and thus may provide a rational and objective approach to resource allocation. However, formula budgeting is not a simple method of determining funding levels; formulas must often be refined or new ones developed. In addition, actual appropriations can be considerably lower than the funding level determined by a formula. Still another disadvantage of formulas is that in periods of fluctuating enrollments only marginal reductions in expenditures can be achieved; thus, formula budgeting may become inappropriate. It may not recognize the different missions of the several institutions affected by the formula.

Program budgeting. Program budgeting attempts to combine the planning and budgeting process by making planning objectives (outcomes) an integral part of an institution's operating budget. Institutional programs, such as instruction or research, are the central factor in program budgeting. The program budget attempts to establish and clarify resource requirements of these programs and determine the cost of achieving given objectives. It further contributes to decision making by providing an analysis of the anticipated costs and benefits associated with alternative program decisions. Some criticisms of program budgeting are that institutions have different interpretations of what constitutes a program and that it is difficult to establish specific outcomes for many programs that may have joint outcomes.

Zero-base budgeting. Zero-base budgeting assumes nothing about prior budgets, but starts from zero each year to build a new budget. Under zero-

[1]Adapted from *Program Budgeting/Universities*, Ohio Board of Regents, Columbus, 1974.

base budgeting, each budget unit, or "decision unit," is requested to evaluate its goals and objectives and to justify its activities both in terms of the benefits provided by the unit and the consequences of not providing services. This is accomplished by having each budget unit develop a series of decision packages. Each decision package describes an activity, function, or goal of the unit and defines alternative service levels. These should include a minimum level of service, below which the unit would be unable to provide necessary services, and a maximum level, in which all the unit's current and future activities are funded. Once decision packages have been developed, the unit manager ranks them in priority order. Decision packages are then ranked centrally and decisions are made relative to the allocation of resources to each unit. It is evident that some reductions or additions called for in zero-base budgeting cannot be achieved easily, and sometimes not at all. This is because an institution cannot quickly or easily adjust its costs. It may be difficult, for example, to relocate or terminate personnel in a short time. Fixed costs that have been financed over several years also make budget changes difficult in the short run. This kind of inflexibility impedes adoption and strict implementation of zero-base budgeting, even though it has much to offer from a management point of view. Other disadvantages of this technique are the time and paperwork required for its completion.

The budget techniques described above, or a combination of these in a single budget cycle, are those most frequently used in developing institutional budgets. However, other techniques, such as performance budgeting and incentive budgeting, have been used in recent years. Regardless of the technique selected, its most important characteristic should be that it meets the management needs of the institution.

DEVELOPING THE OPERATING BUDGET

The operating budget is specific and detailed and presents the plan to finance approved academic and support services for a set fiscal period, usually one or two years. This budget is determined largely by needs of academic programs and support services within limits of available resources. Individual unit budgets are developed by department heads, using institutional budget guidelines approved by the governing board, with appropriate contributions by faculty and staff. The traditional operating budget is then developed by integrating all unit budgets. The chief executive officer, chief academic officer, and chief business officer all have responsibilities for developing the operating budget. The governing board is responsible for reviewing and approving major policies and for final approval of the comprehensive budget. Specific steps in developing the budget are:

1. Determination and communication of budget guidelines.
2. Estimations of current fund revenues and expenditures.
3. Internal budget hearings with academic and support units.
4. Preparation of institutional budget requests.
5. Presentation of the budget to the governing board and adoption of the institutional budget.

The sequence of these steps may vary, depending on management style and other factors affecting the institution. The sequence also points up the issue of whether the budget is developed from the bottom up or from the top down. In this chapter, it is assumed that development of the budget, through issuance of budget guidelines, comes from the top down. Preparation of budget requests for each budgetary unit, however, comes from the bottom up.

Determination and communication of budget guidelines. These guidelines influence preparation of the budget and indicate the institution's position on such items as salary and wage increases, tuition rates, levels of support for various types of student aid, improvements in certain programs, implementation of new programs, and reduction or elimination of existing programs.

The chief executive officer, other senior administrators, and the budget officer are typically involved in development of budget guidelines. Constituent groups may also be involved. Once guidelines are formulated, the budget officer is responsible for communicating them to the heads of budget units, such as deans, directors, and department heads, by means of a budget memorandum.

Estimating current fund revenues and expenditures. Compilation of revenue estimates is usually the responsibility of the budget officer, although at some institutions the chief business officer may assume this function. For many revenue items, estimates should be based on information supplied by other administrative officers. For example, anticipated revenues from tuition and fees generally are based on estimated enrollment data prepared by the registrar or director of admissions. These estimates should also take into account such factors as general economic conditions, trends of enrollment both within the institution and in similar institutions, and attrition rates.

In estimating investment earnings, the income from each item in the portfolio should be projected, with due consideration to economic trends, dividend records of stocks held, and the effect of any unanticipated changes in the portfolio. The investment officer or investment counselor should assist in preparing such estimates. Estimates of revenues from gifts and unrestricted grants should consider past experience, plans for appeals for funds, and alumni activities.

Because of the significance of sponsored programs, separate estimates should be made of revenues and expenditures related to them. The magnitude of these programs affects all other operating areas, such as space and personnel. Budgets for sponsored programs should be separately identified within the regular budget and adjusted during the year as new projects are undertaken and others are terminated.

Estimates of revenues from auxiliary enterprises should be based on enrollments and on past experience in the operations of these units. Revenues should be estimated on a gross basis, including value of allowances for such items as room and board furnished to counselors and for other perquisites for staff members employed in the various enterprises; these also must be shown as expenses. The director of auxiliary enterprises or manager of each enterprise should prepare a budget for review by the budget officer and acceptance by the chief business officer.

Estimates of revenues from other sources should be based on past experience and adjusted for probable conditions. There are many specific techniques for constructing estimates. For example, gift forecasts can be based on current pledges on hand and miscellaneous income can be extrapolated based on current trends. Estimates of the prior year's balances that may be available for rebudgeting and estimates of balances of quasi-endowment, expired-term endowment, and other funds that might be transferred to current funds for operating purposes should also be considered in preparing estimates of availability of total unrestricted current funds.

Federal, state, and local appropriations must be estimated with the realization that such support ultimately depends on actions of legislative bodies. If such appropriations are included in the federal, state, or local budgets—and thus have approval of the legislative body—the figures can then be accepted as final and the estimates can be used for institutional budget making. In those cases where the budget of the federal, state, or local government does not have approval of the appropriate legislative body, the chief business officer or other administrator must communicate with someone in the legislative body who is knowledgeable of the particular programs to be funded. It must be remembered that funds from these sources are not available for use until they are appropriated.

In estimating expenditures, general goals established in the long-range plan and specific instructions of the chief executive officer for developing the annual budget should guide department heads and others in preparing budget requests. Among such goals are plans for expansion of physical plant, improvement of existing programs, and development of new programs. Consideration must be given to the effect of fluctuations in pricing and of policies for salaries, promotions, and employee benefits. Guidelines such as student-faculty ratios, class size, teaching loads, and staff patterns may also aid in estimating departmental expenditures.

The annual operating budget should provide for contingencies. The amount in contingency accounts depends on available resources, past experience, and extent of economic and other uncertainties at the time the budget is prepared. If resources are insufficient to accomplish objectives of the long-range plan, the base of support must be increased or the plan must be cut back. Authority for assigning contingency funds generally is vested in the chief executive officer.

Internal budget hearings with academic and support units. When revenue has been estimated and expenditure guidelines have been determined, it is possible to provide deans and other administrative officers with a predetermined amount that their budget requests should not exceed. Prior to formal preparation of the budget, a set of budget guidelines is distributed to operating units of the institution. As noted above, these guidelines incorporate data on economic and enrollment trends, preliminary forecasts of workload change (such as student-faculty ratios), and overall budget assumptions. Based on these guidelines, each unit prepares an expenditure request and justification for the request.

After the budget requests have been prepared, a round of discussions or internal budget hearings is initiated between the central administration and key personnel in each of the operating units. During these discussions, questions concerning program efficiency and the need for adequate program resources are reviewed by the budget officer, the senior administrators on the budgeting and planning staff, and unit heads. If budget cuts are envisioned, these discussions may require a more detailed review of the performance of each unit.

Preparation and development of preliminary institutional budget. After the budget has been discussed with personnel from operating units, a preliminary institutional budget, based on requests by each budget unit, is prepared by the budget office.

Preparation of unit budget requests normally involves the use of standardized forms. The content and arrangement of items in budget-request forms are most useful if they follow the pattern of the budget itself and if the account classifications correspond to those in the accounting records and in internal and annual financial reports.

Budget-request forms and final budgets usually reflect the three major object classifications—personnel compensation, supplies and expenses, and capital expenditures. Supporting schedules prepared in development of the budget may assign amounts within major classifications to subordinate object categories. For example, personnel compensation might be subdivided in supporting schedules into separate amounts for faculty and professional salaries, support staff salaries, technicians' wages, and student wages. Minor object classifications such as travel, telephone and communications, and printing might be detailed in supporting schedules under the major classification of supplies and expenses. Such subordinate categories are used for management information, with budget controls normally applying to major object classifications and selected minor classifications.

Budget forms should include columns for comparative figures for at least the preceding fiscal period, the current-year budget projected to the end of the year, and the budget year. Before forms are distributed to department heads and others, historical data, supplied by the business office, should be reviewed. Forms also should provide space for amounts recommended at each level of review.

Departmental budget requests should be tabulated in summary form to show both changes in amounts from the budget of the current year and comparisons with actual expenditures of previous years. These summary reports permit the review of deparmental budget requests with minimal effort.

Presentation and adoption of the budget. Institutional managers need to be particularly sensitive to the manner in which budgets are presented to their governing boards and external agencies. These groups must be made aware of costs and benefits of offering programs, consequences of reducing support services such as plant operation and maintenance, effects of demographic trends on institutional enrollment, and effects of other factors described earlier in this chapter. Data on enrollments and program service requirements, for example, are useful in demonstrating the need for additional resources.

Use of internal budget studies can aid in collecting and using data on economic and enrollment trends and in evaluating efficiency of operating units. For budget presentation, the use of graphs is valuable to highlight trends in such areas as utility costs and inflation or to point up the effect of various factors on the financial condition of the institution. Presentation of the budget to the governing board should also include a comparison of the proposed budget with budgets of previous years, explanations of major changes, descriptions of programs added or eliminated, and wage and salary policies.

Once the governing board has approved the budget, a copy of each unit's approved budget should be sent to the unit head. Copies of the approved budget should also be sent to appropriate administrative officers and divisions of the business office.

SPECIAL CONDITIONS AFFECTING THE BUDGET PROCESS

Various special conditions must be considered in development and implementation of the budget. Unanticipated shortfalls in state revenue, for example, can force public institutions or other institutions receiving appropriations to make mid-period reductions in previously approved budget levels. Similarly, independent institutions can experience revenue shortfalls because of declines in tuition and fee revenues, endowment income, or gift income.

If an institution is forced to reduce its budget, it must deal with the issue of whether to make proportionate reductions in all units or to make selected reductions in certain areas. Institutions that make across-the-board or proportional adjustments to all units feel that this has the appearance of treating all units equally. However, proportional adjustments may impair the future vitality of an institution by reducing support to strong as well as to weak units. To avoid this situation, other institutions have implemented budget adjustments based on program priorities. In this strategy, programs are evaluated on their operational costs relative to their contribution to objectives of the institution. Though this approach tries to make maximum use of resources, it can result in considerable turmoil in the institution.

External reporting requirements also affect the budget process. Budget procedures for public institutions differ from those of independent institutions because of requirements of external funding agencies. Timing and flexibility of budget procedures, for example, can be affected by the need to supply workload and enrollment data in support of budget requests. These data may also be requested on a regular basis throughout the budget cycle. As a result, the timing involved in the budget process for public institutions can become critical, with the budget officer involved not only with budgets for the current fiscal period but also with budgets for the most recent and upcoming fiscal periods.

BUDGET CONTROL

An essential element of budgeting is the establishment of effective budget control. Without adequate controls, the utility of a budget is substantially reduced. A principal purpose of budget control is to insure that expenditures do not exceed allocations. The degree and types of control exercised at an institution depend on external factors, such as inflation, as well as the organizational structure of the institution (centralized or decentralized) and the extent to which control mechanisms are integrated into the budget process.

There are two stages of budget control: (1) preliminary control established by the budget and (2) control that is concurrent with expenditures. Preliminary control can take the form of budget standards that are used in constructing the budget. A budget standard can be defined as the ratio of the amount of input or service provided, such as faculty effort, to the amount of output, such as student credit hours. This ratio is often used to calculate the number of faculty positions that should be added to the budget to meet projected student demand. Other types of preliminary control can relate to use of facilities and their operation and maintenance, such as expenditure per square foot. Preliminary control can also involve the establishment of policies governing the activities of institutional units, for example, purchasing control. In addition, the budget may reflect certain institutional policies, such as access for handicapped students or energy-reduction programs, which relate to specific areas of the budget.

The second stage of budget control runs concurrently with operation of the budget. The institutional budget officer or controller has responsibility for overall budget control within the institution, including responsibility to call attention to major departures from budget allocations and to take appropriate follow-up action. The unit head, however, has primary responsibility for control of expenditures within the budget unit and must insure that appointment of staff members and salaries involved do not exceed budget allocations. In addition, expenditures for supplies and equipment should not exceed amounts allocated for these purposes. Unit heads must also plan expenditures for their units so that allocations will last through the entire fiscal year. In this regard, allocating budgets into quarterly or monthly amounts may be helpful.

In exercising budget control, some type of position control is often helpful. In most cases this involves an administrative officer who reviews all requests to fill vacant positions to determine whether adequate funds are available. In some institutions, budgets for vacant positions are withdrawn from the budget-unit allocation and pooled centrally in the contingency fund or they are reallocated on an institutionwide basis. At other institutions, the department involved is able to retain these savings and use them for other purposes. At state-supported institutions, these savings may revert to the state. Some institutions use such savings as a budget resource and accordingly require a certain amount of savings from unit managers.

BUDGET REPORTS

Budget control is normally implemented at the institutional level through the use of budget reports. There are two levels of budget reporting. One is at the budget-unit level and the other is at the institutional-management level. Reports comparing actual results with budget projections should be prepared at least monthly and sent to individual budget units on a timely basis. At the institutional-management level, a report of operations and variance analysis should be prepared at least quarterly. For the purpose of this report, variance is defined as the difference between planned and actual performance.

BUDGET ACCOUNTING

For institutions of any size, the utility of the budget as a management and control device is lost if budget controls do not appear as an integral part of accounting reports. Integration of budget-control accounts with the accounting system brings under accounting control those records relating to revenues not yet realized and unexpended balances of budget allocations.

As a part of the budget system, provisions must be made for outstanding obligations. There are various methods for handling these, any one of which is acceptable as long as it is part of a total budget system and provides for proper control points. The methods vary from a detailed, central encumbrance system that is kept as part of formal accounting records to a decentralized, informal memorandum record of commitments kept by each budget unit. The method selected should provide effective control and useful information, but should not be inflexible or unreasonably expensive.

In the accounting and budget-control system, there may be records that should be kept locally, that is, at the point of use. In these cases, local records should correlate with, but not duplicate, centrally kept summary records.

BUDGET REVISIONS

The budget consists of a series of estimates, many of which are prepared months in advance of the fiscal period to which they relate. Since conditions change with the passage of time, there should be continuous review of data on which budget estimates are based. The budget should be revised periodically so that it always represents an up-to-date estimate of revenues and a realistic plan for expenditures.

Assignment of responsibility, designation of authority, and procedures for budget revisions should be documented, then approved by the governing board of the institution. The adopted policy should allow the greatest degree of flexibility at each level of authority consistent with maintenance of appropriate administrative responsibility and adherence to approved policies and goals.

Revised estimates of revenues should be initiated by the same officers responsible for the original estimates, and should be subjected to the same general procedure of review before they are approved and recorded in the books of account.

Requests for increased expenditure allocations usually are initiated at the unit level and reviewed by respective deans and the budget officer before being submitted to the chief executive officer. If amounts are within the total of the contingent account or accounts, in the approved budget, or are covered by increases in estimated revenues or decreases in expenditures, the chief executive officer usually has authority to approve such requests. However, if amounts involved are large enough to change the anticipated net results of the original budget, the governing board should give formal approval before increased expenditures are authorized. Budget supplements and transfers should be in writing, with appropriate administrative approvals.

The integrity of the budget process requires that all foreseeable expenditure needs compete in the same process at the same time. To avoid circumventing the central budget process, it is desirable that those budget requests that could have been anticipated in the original budget be deferred, if possible, to the next budget cycle where they can compete with alternative resource needs.

POSTPERFORMANCE REVIEW

Postperformance review involves critical analysis of a completed budget period and focuses on the following elements:

1. Budget versus actual expenditures and revenues during the period.
2. Budget revisions during the period.
3. Achievement of goals during the period.

The results of the postperformance review should be summarized and presented to the chief executive officer and, ultimately, to the governing board. These results are often useful in development of the institution's subsequent year's budget and other plans.

BUDGET VERSUS ACTUAL EXPENDITURES AND REVENUES

The purpose of reviewing budgeted versus actual expenditures and revenues is to examine the areas in which variations from the budget occurred and to determine the reasons for these variances. This information can be useful in assessing financial estimates contained in the institution's planning documents and in making more realistic budget estimates for the next budget period. An analysis of variations between budgeted and actual revenues also encourages institutional managers to assess the consequences of either underestimating or overestimating revenues. For example, if tuition revenue is underestimated, based on conservative enrollment estimates, and if enrollments actually exceed the projected level, the result can be overcrowded classes and a strain on support services, such as housing and food services. Conversely, if tuition revenues are overestimated and enrollments are below projected levels, this can result in the hiring of unnecessary faculty and in excessive operating costs.

Variations in institutional expenditures also result from unrealistic budget estimates. Favorable expenditure variances occur when actual expenditures are less than the amount budgeted. Favorable variations can mean that a budget unit was able to reduce its costs by operating more efficiently or they can indicate that the unit was unable to achieve some of the goals set for it at the start of the budget period.

Unfavorable variances occur when expenditures exceed budgeted amounts. If the budget is not brought into balance by addition of new revenue, the institution may run a deficit for the year. Good planning and budgeting, therefore, require that all budget variations be analyzed and that this analysis be used in developing subsequent budgets and plans.

EVALUATION OF BUDGET REVISIONS

During the budget period a number of revisions may be necessary. These result from a need to adjust the budget for changes in actual budget and expenditure patterns. As part of the budget review it is useful to examine the rationale underlying these revisions and to assess their effect on subsequent institutional plans and budgets. A revision, for example, may result from a high turnover rate in a budget unit and the shift of resulting salary savings to meet other operating expenses. This type of revision, however, may also result from a budget unit's leaving a number of positions vacant in order to use the savings for other purposes. There may be good reasons underlying each of these practices but it is important that they be substantiated, since they can affect the way in which future budgets are constructed. In a similar manner, a revision occurring during one budget period, such as the establishment of a new faculty position, can result in a recurring commitment of funds in future budgets. A budget review of revisions can therefore yield valuable information for developing future budgets and plans.

ACHIEVEMENT OF GOALS

Another aspect of budget review attempts to ascertain whether goals set for an institution and for each of its budget units were achieved during the budget period. Estimates of institutional revenues should be compared to actual revenues and an analysis should be made of reasons for significant variation in anticipated revenues. An examination should be conducted to determine whether goals, such as provisions of certain types and levels of services, were achieved. If a unit, for example, had anticipated generating a certain number of student credit hours and fell short of this goal, an analysis of factors underlying this discrepancy could be useful in developing future plans and budgets.

If an institution has developed a contingency fund for dealing with emergencies, it is useful to examine the extent to which this fund was used. If the fund was inadequate to meet contingencies, additional funds may need to be budgeted for future periods. If the contingency fund is relatively untouched, it may be more productive to use a portion of the fund for other purposes.

Though most institutions have methods for developing the budget and nearly all have a procedure for implementing the budget, few have a formal procedure for reviewing or auditing performance of the budget. However, such review is essential, since it provides important information for the planning and budgeting process.

B. CHART OF ACCOUNTS

1. General Ledger Accounts

CURRENT FUNDS—UNRESTRICTED

Asset Accounts

Cash
Petty Cash
Investments
Accounts Receivable—*detailed as needed, for example:*
 Students
 Hospital Patients
 Governmental
 Unbilled Charges
Notes Receivable—*detailed as needed*
 Allowance for Doubtful Accounts and Notes—*credit balance account associated with each type of receivable*
Inventories—*detailed as needed, for example:*
 College Store
 Dining Halls
 Central Stores
 Plant Operation and Maintenance Supply Store
Prepaid Items and Deferred Charges—*detailed as needed*
Due from Other Fund Groups

Part B of this appendix is reprinted from *College & University Business Administration.* 4th ed. (Washington, DC: National Association of College and University Business Officers, 1982), pp. 440-454.

Liability and Fund Balance Accounts

Notes Payable
Accounts Payable and Accrued Expenses—*detailed as needed*
Deferred Credits
Deposits
Due to Other Fund Groups
Fund Balances—Allocated—*detailed as needed, for example:*
  Auxiliary Enterprises
  Reserve for Encumbrances
  Reserve for Computer Use Survey
  Reserve for Faculty Self-Improvement Program
Fund Balance—Unallocated

Operating Accounts. The following control accounts in the general ledger for actual revenues, expenditures, and other changes are supported in detail by Current Funds Revenues and Current Funds Expenditures and Other Changes accounts in subsidiary ledgers. If desired, several control accounts may be provided in lieu of single control accounts:
  Revenues Control—*credit account*
  Expenditures and Other Changes Control—*debit account*
When budgetary accounts are carried in the general ledger, the following control accounts would appear in the chart of accounts. They are supported in detail by Current Funds Revenues and Current Funds Expenditures and Other Changes accounts in subsidiary ledgers:
  Estimated Revenues *or* Unrealized Revenues
  Expenditures and Other Changes Allocations *or* Budget Allocations for Expenditures and Other Changes
  Unallocated Budget Balance *or* Unassigned Budget Balance

CURRENT FUNDS—RESTRICTED

These accounts are to be used if the assets and liabilities of such funds are separated from those of Unrestricted Current Funds.

Asset Accounts

Cash
Investments
Accounts Receivable—*detailed as needed, for example:*
  Governmental
  Other
  Unbilled Charges
  Allowance for Doubtful Accounts—*credit balance account*
Due from Other Fund Groups

Liability and Fund Balance Accounts

Accounts Payable
Due to Other Fund Groups
Fund Balances—Allocated—*detailed as needed, for example:*
Reserve for Encumbrances
Auxiliary Enterprises
Fund Balances—Unallocated
Both of the fund balance accounts may be control accounts supported by separate subsidiary ledger accounts for each restricted current fund and for each type of fund balance. Additional control accounts may be provided as required or desired.
Operating Accounts. Expenditures of restricted current funds may be recorded in the operating accounts of unrestricted current funds, in which case transfers of restricted current funds to current funds revenues accounts would be made to finance such expenditures. When this is not done, operating accounts for each current restricted fund must provide for proper classification of expenditures by object, as well as providing for appropriate categorization of sources of additions, deductions other than expenditures, and transfers to and from other funds.

LOAN FUNDS

Asset Accounts

Cash
Investments
Notes Receivable from Students, Faculty, and Staff Allowance for Doubtful Loans—*credit balance account*

Liability and Fund Balance Accounts

Accounts Payable to Collection Agencies
Due to Other Fund Groups
Refunds Payable on Refundable Government Grants
Fund Balances—*This may be a control account supported by separate subsidiary ledger accounts for each fund. Separate accounts should be carried to identify the sources of funds available for loans, such as donor- and government-restricted loan funds, including funds provided by mandatory transfers required for matching purposes, unrestricted funds designated as loan funds, and funds returnable to the donor under certain conditions. Accounts to identify allocations of fund balances should be provided. Accounts may be maintained to identify resources available for loans to students separately from those for faculty and staff.*

ENDOWMENT AND SIMILAR FUNDS

Asset Accounts

Cash
Accounts Receivable
Notes Receivable
    Allowance for Doubtful Accounts and Notes—*credit balance account*
Prepaid Items
Investments—*detailed as needed, for example:*
    Bonds
        Allowance for Unamortized Bond Premiums
        Allowance for Unamortized Bond Discounts
    Preferred Stocks
    Common Stocks
    Mortgage Notes
    Real Estate
        Allowance for Depreciation—*credit balance account*
Due from Other Fund Groups

Liability and Fund Balance Accounts

The fund balance accounts should be classified as to Endowment, Term Endowment, and Quasi-Endowment Funds, even though the investments of the funds may be merged in one or more investment pools.
Payables—*detailed as needed, for example:*
    Mortgages Payable
    Notes Payable
    Accounts Payable
Collateral Due on Securities Loaned
Due to Other Fund Groups
Balances of Endowment Funds
Balances of Term Endowment Funds
Balances of Quasi-Endowment Funds—Unrestricted
Balances of Quasi-Endowment Funds—Restricted
In order to differentiate between the balances of funds for which the income is unrestricted and those for which the income is restricted, the following accounts may be employed:
Balances of Endowment Funds—Unrestricted
Balances of Endowment Funds—Restricted—*detailed as needed, for example:*
    Professorships
    Instructional Departments
    Scholarships
    Library
    Loan Funds
Note. The balances of term endowment funds also may be identified in this manner.

Undistributed Gains and Losses on Investment Transactions—*Separate accounts should be established for each investment pool.*

Undistributed Share Adjustments—*Separate accounts should be established for each investment pool.*

ANNUITY AND LIFE INCOME FUNDS

If the funds in this section are pooled for investment purposes, accounts for the assets may be classified as shown below for each investment pool. If any funds are separately invested, accounts should be set up for the investment of such funds.

Asset Accounts

Cash
Accounts Receivable
Notes Receivable
   Allowance for Doubtful Accounts and Notes—*credit balance account*
Investments—*detailed as needed, for example:*
   Bonds
      Allowance for Unamortized Bond Premiums
      Allowance for Unamortized Bond Discounts
   Preferred Stocks
   Common Stocks
   Mortgage Notes
   Real Estate
      Allowance for Depreciation—*credit balance account*
   Due from Other Fund Groups

Liability and Fund Balance Accounts

Accounts Payable
Annuity Payments Currently Due
Annuities Payable
Life Income Payments Currently Due
Due to Other Funds for Advances on Annuity Payments
Due to Other Funds for Advances to Income Beneficiaries
Undistributed Income—Annuity Funds
Undistributed Income—Life Income Funds
Balances of Annuity Funds
Balances of Life Income Funds
   These may be control accounts supported by subsidiary ledger accounts for each fund. Within the two categories the accounts may be listed alphabetically by name, or they may be classified in any other manner at the discretion of the institution.
Undistributed Gains and Losses on Investment Transactions—*Separate accounts should be established for each investment pool.*

Undistributed Share Adjustments—*Separate accounts should be established for each investment pool.*

Income, Expenditure, and Transfer Accounts

Income from Investments—*credit account, detailed by each agreement*

Expenditures and Transfers—*debit account, detailed by each agreement*

PLANT FUNDS—UNEXPENDED

Asset Accounts

Cash

Investments

Receivables—*detailed as needed*

   Allowance for Doubtful Accounts—*credit balance account*

Due from Other Fund Groups

Construction in Progress—*alternatively can be shown in Investment in Plant subgroup of Plant Funds*

Liability and Fund Balance Accounts

Accounts Payable

Notes Payable

Bonds Payable

Mortgages Payable

Due to Other Fund Groups

Fund Balances—*This may be a control account supported by subsidiary ledger accounts which should differentiate between unrestricted and restricted funds.*

PLANT FUNDS—FUNDS FOR RENEWALS AND REPLACEMENTS

These accounts should be used if the assets of such funds are separated from the assets of other subgroups of Plant Funds.

Asset Accounts

Cash

Accounts Receivable

   Allowance for Doubtful Accounts—*credit balance account*

Investments

Deposits with Trustees

Due from Other Fund Groups

Liability and Fund Balance Accounts

Accounts Payable

Due to Other Fund Groups

Fund Balances—*This may be a control account supported by subsidiary ledger accounts which should differentiate between unrestricted and restricted funds.*

PLANT FUNDS—FUNDS FOR RETIREMENT OF INDEBTEDNESS

These accounts should be used if the assets of such funds are separated from the assets of other subgroups of Plant Funds.

<u>Asset Accounts</u>

Cash
Accounts and Notes Receivable
  Allowance for Doubtful Accounts—*credit balance account*
Investments
Deposits with Trustees
Due from Other Fund Groups

<u>Liability and Fund Balance Accounts</u>

Accounts Payable
Due to Other Fund Groups
Fund Balances—*This may be a control account supported by subsidiary ledger accounts which should differentiate between unrestricted and restricted funds.*

PLANT FUNDS—INVESTMENT IN PLANT

<u>Asset Accounts</u>

Land
Buildings
  Allowance for Depreciation—*credit balance account*
Improvements Other than Buildings
  Allowance for Depreciation—*credit balance account*
Equipment
  Allowance for Depreciation—*credit balance account*
Library Books
Art Museums and Collections
Construction in Progress—*alternatively can be shown in the Unexpended Plant Funds subgroup of Plant Funds*

<u>Liability and Fund Balance Accounts</u>

Accounts Payable
Notes Payable
Bonds Payable

Mortgages Payable
Leaseholds Payable
Due to Other Fund Groups
Net Investment in Plant—*detailed as needed*

AGENCY FUNDS

Asset Accounts

Cash
Accounts Receivable
Notes Receivable
   Allowance for Doubtful Accounts and Notes—*credit balance account*
Investments
Due from Other Fund Groups

Liability Accounts

Accounts Payable
Due to Other Fund Groups
Deposit Liabilities—*Accounts for each agency fund should be carried either in the general ledger or in subsidiary ledgers.*

2. Current Fund Revenues Accounts
(Separate Restricted and Unrestricted Accounts)

TUITION AND FEES—*detailed as needed, for example:*

Regular Session
Summer Session
Extension
Continuing Education

FEDERAL APPROPRIATIONS

STATE APPROPRIATIONS

LOCAL APPROPRIATIONS

FEDERAL GRANTS AND CONTRACTS

STATE GRANTS AND CONTRACTS

LOCAL GRANTS AND CONTRACTS

PRIVATE GIFTS, GRANTS, AND CONTRACTS—*detailed as needed*

ENDOWMENT INCOME—*detailed as needed, for example:*
Income from Funds Held by Others Under Irrevocable Trusts

SALES AND SERVICES OF EDUCATIONAL ACTIVITIES—*detailed as needed, for example:*

Film Rentals
Testing Services
Home Economics Cafeteria
Demonstration Schools
Dairy Creameries
Food Technology Divisions

SALES AND SERVICES OF AUXILIARY ENTERPRISES—*detailed as needed, for example:*

Residence Halls
Faculty Housing
Food Services
College Union
Intercollegiate Athletics
Additional revenue accounts may be established for sources of sales, types of products and services, and cash and interdepartmental sales.

SALES AND SERVICES OF HOSPITALS—*detailed as needed, for example:*

Daily Patient Services
Nursing Services
Other Professional Services
Health Clinics *if an integral part of the hospital*

OTHER SOURCES—*detailed as needed, for example:*

Investment Income
Sales of Scrap

INDEPENDENT OPERATIONS—*detailed as needed by organizational units*

3. Current Funds Expenditures and Transfers Accounts

Current funds expenditures accounts should bear identifying codes and symbols that will identify functions, such as Instruction, Institutional Support, and Scholarships and Fellowships; identify organizational units, such as Department of Physics, Controller's Office, and Registrar's Office; and identify the object of expenditures, such as Personnel Compensation, Supplies and Expenses, and Capital Expenditures. If desired, interdepartmental purchases, as contrasted with purchases from external sources, also may be identified by code or symbol. The object coding and symbols should be designed to provide for common usage of the objects throughout the entire chart of accounts, although, of course, there will be individual object codings that will be used only for particular functional categories.

EDUCATIONAL AND GENERAL

Instruction

Accounts by divisions, schools, colleges, and departments of instruction following the administrative organization of the institution. The five functional subcategories are:

General Academic Instruction
Occupational and Vocational Instruction
Special Session Instruction
Community Education
Preparatory and Adult Basic Education
  Adult Basic Education
  Compensatory Education
  Doctoral Language Requirements Courses
  English for Foreign Students
  General Educational Development (GED)
  High School Completion
  Manpower Development Training (MDTA)
  Reading—Study Skills
  Remedial Instruction
  Speed Reading

Research

Accounts by individual projects, classified by organizational units. The two functional subcategories are:

Institutes and Research Centers
Individual or Project Research

Public Service

Accounts by activities, classified by type of activity, such as:

Community Service
Conferences and Institutes
Cooperative Extension Service
Public Lectures
Radio
Regional Medical Program

Television
Testing Services

Academic Support

Accounts by activities, classified by type of activity, such as:

Libraries
Museums and Galleries
Audiovisual Services
Ancillary Support
  Demonstration School
  Departmental Stores
  Dramatic Art Productions
  Educational Television
  Elementary School
  Herbarium
  Optometry Clinic
  Photographic Laboratory
  Psychology Clinic
  Shop Services
  Veterinary Medical Teaching Hospital
  Vivarium
Academic Administration and Personnel Development
  Dean's Office
Computing Support *excluding administrative data processing*
Course and Curriculum Development *if separately budgeted*

Student Services

Accounts by activities, classified by type of activity, such as:

Student Services Administration
Social and Cultural Activities
  Cultural Programs
  Intramural Athletics
  Housing Services
  Intercollegiate Athletics *if operated as an integral part of Department of Physical Education and not essentially self-supporting*
  Public Ceremonies
  Recreational Programs
  Student Organizations
Counseling and Career Guidance
  Counseling
  Placement
  Foreign Students' Program

Financial Aid Administration
  Financial Aid Office
  Loan Records and Collection
Student Admissions and Records
  Admissions Office
  Registrar's Office
Health and Infirmary Services *if not an integral part of a hospital nor operated as an essentially self-supporting operation*

Institutional Support—*detailed as needed, for example:*

Executive Management
  Governing Board
  Chief Executive Office
  Chief Academic Office
  Chief Business Office
  Academic Senate
  Planning and Budgeting
  Investment Office
  Legal Counsel
Fiscal Operations
  Accounting
  Cashiers
  Contract and Grant Administration
General Administrative Services
  Administrative Data Processing *(computer center for administrative services)*
  Administrative Information Systems
  Auditing, Internal and External
  Commencements
  Convocations
  Employee Personnel and Records
  Environmental Health and Safety
Logistical Services
  Business Management
  Material Management
    Inventory
    Receiving
    Storehouse
  Purchasing
  Service Departments
    Duplicating
    Motor Pool
    Mail and Messenger
  Security *(police, etc.)*
  Telephone and Telegraph *unless charged to departmental budgets*
  Transportation *including motor pool, unless operated as a service department*

Printing
Space Management
Community Relations
Development Office
Public Information
Publications
Catalogues and Bulletins
Relations with Schools
Alumni Office
Fund Raising
General
General Insurance Other than Property Insurance
Interest on Current Funds Loans
Memberships
Provision for Doubtful Accounts and Notes

Operation and Maintenance of Plant

Accounts for all organizational units and functions, such as:

Physical Plant Administration
Building and Equipment Maintenance
Custodial Services
Utilities
Landscape and Grounds Maintenance
Major Repairs and Renovations
Other Services
For subaccounts under each of the major accounts listed above, see Administrative Service supplement 3:3:2.

Scholarships and Fellowships

Accounts as needed and desired for scholarships, fellowships, grants-in-aid, trainee stipends, prizes, and awards.
Tuition and Fee Remissions *other than those properly classified as staff benefits*

Accounts may be set up for instructional divisions and departments, such as:

School of Medicine
Department of Physics

Mandatory Transfers, Educational and General—*detailed to show subcategories, such as:*

Provision for Debt Service on Educational Plant
Loan Fund Matching Grants

Nonmandatory Transfers, Educational and General *(to and from)—detailed to show significant subcategories, such as:*

Loan Funds
Quasi-Endowment Funds
Appreciation on Securities of Endowment and Similar Funds
Plant Funds
    Renewals and Replacements of Plant Assets
    Additions to Plant Assets
    Voluntary Payments on Debt Principal

AUXILIARY ENTERPRISES, HOSPITALS, AND INDEPENDENT OPERATIONS

Auxiliary Enterprises

Accounts as needed and desired for such enterprises as included in the Current Funds Revenues accounts.
Provision should be made for identification of mandatory and nonmandatory transfers—to and from—by significant subcategories.

Hospitals

Accounts as needed and desired. Provision should be made for identification of mandatory and nonmandatory transfers—to and from—by significant subcategories.

Independent Operations

Accounts as needed and desired for organizational units.
Provision should be made for identification of mandatory and nonmandatory transfers—to and from—by significant subcategories.

4. Classification of Expenditures by Object

The object classification of expenditures identifies that which is received in return for the expenditures. Object classification has importance as a tool for internal management, but should be considered complementary to the classification of expenditures by function and organizational units and should not replace these classifications in the various schedules of current funds expenditures. The value of object classification will depend on the usefulness of the information it provides to management. The classifications may be omitted from published financial reports or they may be used to any degree considered desirable by the institution. The use of object classifications and the related identifying codes and symbols should not be carried to an extreme; the number of categories should be limited to those that will be of significant value to management.

Three major object classifications are found in most colleges and universities: Personnel Compensation, Supplies and Expenses, and Capital Expenditures. Breakdowns of objects within these major categories may be necessary or desirable in some situations.

PERSONNEL COMPENSATION

This classification includes salaries, wages, and staff benefits. In the various salary and wage expense accounts, it may be desirable to distinguish between groups of faculty and other staff members, such as full-time and part-time personnel; student and nonstudent workers; and professional, secretarial, clerical, skilled, and nonskilled employees. Appropriate code numbers and symbols within this category will aid in identifying, collecting, and summarizing information.

SUPPLIES AND EXPENSES

Because of their general significance to nearly all organizational units within an institution, it may be beneficial to identify significant categories of these expenditures, such as supplies, telephone, travel, and contractual services.

CAPITAL EXPENDITURES

The following object categories within this classification (which includes both additions to and renewals and replacements of capital assets) may prove helpful in the accounting and reporting systems of educational institutions: scientific equipment, laboratory apparatus, office machines and equipment, library books, furniture and furnishings, motor vehicles, machinery and tools, building remodeling, minor construction, and livestock.

Appendix 3
Strategies for Increasing Revenue And Decreasing Expenditures

Mingle (1982, 9) surveyed a number of institutions that had recently experienced financial hard times. He catalogued institutional responses to cutbacks in ascending order of the perceived severity of the financial conditions on campus. (The following list is not prescriptive but is based on observation.)

RESPONSES TO CUTBACKS

Restrict travel, telephone, supply purchases.

Postpone equipment purchases.

Cut library budget.

Tighten tenure requirements.

Reduce energy costs through conservation and/or technological improvements.

Employ part-time in place of full-time faculty.

Reduce secretarial staff.

Defer maintenance and renovation projects.

Adjust investment policy to maximize short-term gains.

Reduce course offerings; increase class size.

Increase tuition, room and board fees.

Initiate a student health fee or increase other special fees.

Require larger/earlier deposits.

Reduce number of resident advisors, counselors, other student services personnel.

Eliminate general fund support of intercollegiate athletics.

Initiate special one-time surcharges to students.

Lease, convert, or close excess dormitory space.

Impose a hiring freeze—reduce cost through attrition.

Cut staffs of public information, alumni offices.

Reduce or eliminate summer school offerings.

Terminate professional administrative staff (associate deans, assistant vice presidents, etc.).

Close the university press.

Close the natural history/art museum.

Eliminate the intramural sports program.

Reorganize governance structure—eliminate "colleges," "departments"; replace with "divisions."

Eliminate low producing/low priority elective courses; terminate non-tenured faculty who teach them.

Discontinue low priority academic programs; transfer tenured faculty to related departments.

Declare a state of financial exigency; close major academic units, departments, colleges, schools.

Terminate tenured faculty.

Merge institution with stronger institution.

Close the institution; transfer endowment and other assets to related purpose.

Mingle observed that, in general, temporary faculty and staff were terminated before any others. Next tended to be support staff such as secretaries, clerks, and maintenance workers, then nonteaching professional and administrative staff. Typically, the last individuals to be terminated were nontenured faculty and finally tenured faculty.

The following list of ways to increase income and decrease expenses was assembled by Sigmund G. Ginsburg (1982, 14–16). The list is *not* in suggested order of implementation; moreover, many of these ideas will be inappropriate for a given institution.

IDEAS FOR INCREASING UNIVERSITY INCOME

1. Increase unrestricted gifts by emphasizing such gifts in fund-raising drives.
2. Sell university land and/or assets.

3. Sell fine arts properties owned by the university.

4. Increase the number of programs/courses geared to needs of business, industry, government, and other groups to increase enrollment and income.

5. Increase research geared to needs of business, industry, government, and other institutions, thus increasing direct income and overhead.

6. Increase enrollment in continuing education courses and programs geared to the adult, nontraditional market. Focus on time, place, type, and method of instruction and delivery of programs, courses, and services in order to attract new students.

7. Increase fees and charges to auxiliaries, thereby increasing income for general funds.

8. Emphasize cable television instruction.

9. Shift investment portfolio, sacrificing growth to some extent but gaining greater income. This might necessitate reducing general funds support to areas that get increased income from the investment policy change affecting their endowment or restricted fund holdings.

10. Use a total funds approach to budgeting, thereby reducing general funds expenditures by using other funds available to units.

11. Institute differential tuition pricing to cover additional costs in certain colleges.

12. Institute new fees, such as laboratory fees in particular areas, to cover additional costs or costs of services provided.

13. Review present fees to determine if they should be increased to cover costs.

14. Increase tuition.

15. Review possibilities for increasing revenue-generating activities. Institutions should be concerned about impact on other suppliers of services and thus about public outcry. There should also be concern about taxes on unrelated business income.

16. Reduce the number of credits covered by the flat tuition rate.

17. Change investment policies with regard to options and other investment opportunities.

18. With outside assistance, carefully review overhead charges to the university hospital, if there is one. Such a review may result in more accurate overhead charges.

19. Increase overhead charges to auxiliaries, if possible.

20. Reduce the grant overhead sharing formulas currently applied.

21. Institute some type of surcharge on collateral employment of faculty and staff.

22. Form private practice corporations similar to those in a medical center to generate additional income for faculty and the university. This may apply to areas such as engineering, law, architecture, chemistry, or physics.

23. Attempt to get state subsidy dollars for academic credit for cooperative programs.

24. In a total funds approach or in "off-loading" of general funds, consider the expendable portions of endowment funds and the existing quasi-endowment and gift funds and the interest they may earn each year.

25. Continue (and if necessary, increase) emphasis on charging academic year salaries to grants and contracts.

26. Consider establishing joint research ventures with business and industry.

27. Consider establishing specific training courses attuned to a particular company's needs.

28. Carefully review overhead percentage charges to grants and contracts to determine if rates can be revised and successfully negotiated with the government.

29. Increase fund-raising results through creative approaches and emphasis on effectiveness and efficiency.

30. Review scholarship and loan opportunities, policies, and programs to encourage increased enrollment or to maintain enrollment and retention.

31. Improve recruitment of students, admissions procedures, and marketing of the university.

32. Emphasize retention of students.

33. Improve public relations, academic quality, public service, human relations, and a "good-place-to-enroll" image of the university to improve enrollment and fund raising.

34. Include depreciation changes in charges to auxiliaries and in the auxiliaries' fees.

35. Continue efforts in the area of money management in order to increase funds available.

IDEAS FOR DECREASING UNIVERSITY EXPENSES

1. Reduce the number of positions at the university.

2. Freeze or reduce salaries.

3. Change benefit coverage or plans.

4. Reduce tuition remissions generally, or in particular areas where "paying" students could take a limited number of spaces (e.g., in law, medicine, or selected graduate programs).

5. Carefully analyze enrollment in certain courses to determine if most students are on tuition remission. This might lead to a reduction in the number of courses offered.

6. Reduce the number of courses and the number of course sections.

7. Reduce duplication of courses (i.e., similar courses given in two or more colleges or departments).

8. Assign a percentage cut to each vice-presidential area.

9. Postpone major building projects.

10. Reduce support to auxiliaries.

11. Phase out, eliminate, or reduce expenditures for public service functions of the university.

12. Phase out, eliminate, or reduce expenditures for nonacademic functions, services, and activities that are not essential to support the academic mission of the university.

13. Reduce expenditures and phase out or eliminate academic majors, programs, units, services, and activities that are not:

    a. Central to the mission of the institution;

    b. Of major importance to the university; and

    c. Of high quality and/or low cost (and where there is little likelihood that the institution could afford to raise or generate income to offset costs).

In essence, spend resources only on those areas that are of great importance; do not spread resources too far. Bolster and support the good, potentially good, and required rather than bringing everything to a level of mediocrity. Prune, and use a scalpel now rather than having to swing a hatchet later.

14. Contract out certain support services.

15. Emphasize energy cost savings throughout the university, including not only major items such as heating or cooling buildings or converting boilers, but also smaller items such as shutting off lights, reducing use of elevators, and reducing the number of fans or heaters.

16. Emphasize economy, planning, efficiency, and care in use of supplies, paper, telephone, duplicating, mail, and printing, and reduce expenditures in these areas.

17. Reduce travel, entertainment, and conference expenditures, and reduce the number of off-campus workshops.

18. Increase productivity by reducing paperwork and red tape and encouraging delegation and job enrichment and enlargement, thus reducing the need for part-time staff and perhaps allowing the elimination of several positions.

19. Increase number of courses and/or credit hours taught per faculty member.

20. Fill some portion of vacant faculty positions with qualified adjunct faculty and graduate assistants.

21. Reduce service hours in various areas.

22. Reduce overtime.

23. Increase student employment as substitute for other employees.

24. Restructure summer school compensation.

25. Review evening session compensation.

26. Change the calendar if this would help enrollment or energy costs.

27. Emphasize flex-year approaches and job sharing in order to reduce personnel costs.

28. Where possible, employ part-time employees or 9- or 10-month employees rather than full-time employees.

29. Reduce or eliminate external temporary services.

30. Reduce telephone costs by purchasing a new system.

31. Reduce number of hours offices are open during registration.

32. Reduce maintenance and custodial expenses (e.g., provide cleaning services or painting less often, or ask staff members to place wastebaskets in the hall at night).

33. Reduce computer services and costs; make departments pay for what they use.

34. Update mailing lists, thereby reaching the right people and eliminating wasted postage.

35. Computerize more systems, thereby reducing the number of staff necessary.

36. Increase job satisfaction and decrease turnover through training, job enhancement and enlargement, and concern for staff. This could increase productivity and reduce the number of staff necessary.

37. Recover for general funds use the savings on salaries of persons on full-time academic leave.

38. Reduce or eliminate sabbaticals if these cost additional sums.

39. Encourage early retirements if these are, in the long run, cost effective. (There may be important programmatic reasons for encouraging early retirements.)

40. Cross-train faculty so that those who have fewer students or courses because of enrollment trends can teach in other areas where there is ample enrollment. This would reduce the need for new full-time faculty or for adjunct faculty.

41. Reduce the number of visiting scholars and lecturers.

42. Reduce the number of graduate assistantships and stipends paid.

43. Reduce or cancel university-paid memberships and entertainment.

44. Encourage leave without pay for staff.

45. Close campus at certain times or individual buildings in order to save utility and maintenance costs.

46. Reduce library expenditures.

47. Reduce university subscriptions to newspapers, magazines, and journals.

48. Disassemble peripheral research units.

49. Eliminate rentals; transfer items to campus.

50. Increase workloads, thereby eliminating the need for some positions.

51. Review university organizations and hierarchy to determine if some units or positions can be eliminated or consolidated, thereby reducing the number of positions at all levels, including middle, upper, and top administration.

52. Consider evening college and summer school as part of the general workload.

53. Shift general fund positions and expenditures to nongeneral positions and expenditures.

54. Reduce the number of support staff, secretarial staff, and assistant and associate directors and deans.

55. Negotiate with the city for more free services (or charge for services provided to the city).

56. Reduce costs in auxiliary services.

57. Reduce or eliminate external consultants; use faculty.

58. Reduce or eliminate academic no-need scholarships.

59. Consider fiscal separation of the medical center, if there is one.

60. Off-load general fund scholarships onto restricted fund scholarships.

61. Insure that individuals on tuition remission and scholarships apply for all the aid to which they are legally entitled. This may save some general funds.

62. Coordinate and reduce advertising and publication and printing expense; convince advertisers to pay for certain publications; introduce advertising in alumni publications.

63. Reduce expenses for recruitment of staff.

64. Reduce expenditures for equipment, furnishings, typewriters, calculators, and computer terminals.

65. Reduce insurance coverage.

66. Reduce support to the university foundation, if there is one.

67. Eliminate Mastercard and Visa charges.

68. Eliminate university payment to the bookstore for staff discounts.

69. Encourage greater use of word processing and typing pools in order to reduce the number of staff.

70. In lieu of salary increases, consider paying the employees' share of retirement costs. This would result in more take-home pay for employees.

71. Furlough all or some staff for a number of days each year; this would be unpaid vacation.

72. Review time spent on various functions to determine if these functions can be eliminated or reduced, thereby eliminating staff, reducing the number of full-time staff, or freeing staff to take on other duties.

73. Reduce the number and level of services and activities provided.

74. Consider combining academic programs, units, or services, thereby reducing some support costs or adding teaching time.

75. Consider combining nonacademic programs, units, or services, thereby reducing some support costs.

76. Change notification procedures for faculty and nonfaculty regarding nonrenewal of contracts or layoffs, thereby realizing savings more quickly if nonrenewals or layoffs are necessary.

77. Improve productivity and quality of service by improving recruitment of staff, setting high standards of performance, and emphasizing evaluation.

78. Increase the number of students required for a course to be run; enforce the minimum. This would reduce the number of low-enrollment courses offered (some exceptions will always be necessary).

79. Reduce number of independent study courses.

80. Defer major and minor repairs and maintenance as much as possible.

81. Temporarily extend 10-year write-off program so that less money has to be set aside each year.

82. Emphasize use of new video and instructional technology to reduce academic operational costs.

83. Emphasize interlibrary loans, use of technology, and other means of cost savings in order to reduce library expenditures.

84. Allow typing and clerical support staff in one area to work temporarily in other areas or to be given work from other areas when time is available in one unit and there are needs in other units. This may reduce part-time, or even full-time employee costs or the cost of overtime.

85. Encourage implementation of an effective suggestion system to focus on decreasing expenses, increasing income, and increasing productivity.

FOR FURTHER READING

The Mingle observations are reported in *Challenges of Retrenchment: Strategies for Consolidating Programs, Cutting Costs, and Reallocating Resources,* by James R. Mingle et al. (San Francisco: Jossey-Bass, Inc., 1981). Sigmund G. Ginsburg's list of strategies was published as "120 Ways to Increase Income and Decrease Expenses" in *Business Officer,* vol. 16, no. 6 (December 1982), pp. 14–16. Minor editorial changes have been made in Ginsburg's original list.

Bibliography

Advisory Commission on Intergovernmental Relations. *1981 Tax Capacity of the Fifty States*. Washington, DC: The Commission, 1983.

Advisory Committee on Endowment Management. *Managing Educational Endowments: A Report to the Ford Foundation*. New York: Ford Foundation, 1969.

Alm, Kent G., Elwood B. Ehrle, and Bill R. Webster. "Managing Faculty Reductions." *Journal of Higher Education*, vol. 48, no. 2 (March/April 1977), pp. 153–163.

American Association of University Professors. "Academic Freedom and Tenure: City University of New York—Mass Dismissals under Financial Exigency." *AAUP Bulletin*, vol. 63, no. 2 (April 1977), pp. 60–81.

———. "1982 Recommended Institutional Regulations on Academic Freedom and Tenure." *Academe*, vol. 69, no. 1 (January-February 1983), pp. 15a–20a.

———. Report of the AAUP Task Force on Faculty and Higher Education in Hard Times. *Academe*, vol. 69, no. 1 (January-February 1983).

American Council on Education and the Council on Governmental Relations of the National Association of College and University Business Officers. *Direct and Indirect Costs of Research at Colleges and Universities*. Washington, DC: ACE, 1981.

Anthony, Robert N., and Regina E. Herzlinger. *Management Control in Nonprofit Organizations*. Rev. ed. Homewood, IL: Richard D. Irwin, Inc., 1980.

325

Arns, Robert G., and William Poland. "Changing the University through Program Review." *Journal of Higher Education,* vol. 51, no. 3 (May/June 1980), pp. 268–284.

Association Council for Policy Analysis and Research. *The National Investment in Higher Education.* Washington, DC: American Council on Education, 1981.

Association of Governing Boards of Universities and Colleges and the National Association of College and University Business Officers. *Financial Responsibilities of Governing Boards of Colleges and Universities.* Washington, DC: AGB and NACUBO, 1979.

Bacchetti, Raymond F. "Using Cost Analysis in Internal Management in Higher Education." *NACUBO Professional File,* vol. 9, no. 1 (January 1977).

Benacerraf, Paul, et al. *Budgeting and Resource Allocation at Princeton University: Report of a Demonstration Project Supported by the Ford Foundation.* Vol. 1. Princeton, NJ: Princeton University, 1972.

Benezet, Louis T. *Private Higher Education and Public Funding.* AAHE/ERIC Higher Education Research Report no. 5. Washington, DC: American Association for Higher Education, 1976.

Bleau, Barbara Lee. "Faculty Planning Models: A Review of the Literature." *Journal of Higher Education,* vol. 53, no. 2 (March/April 1982), pp. 195–206.

Bloomfield, Stefan D. "Comprehensive Faculty Flow Analysis." In *Applying Analytic Methods to Planning and Management,* edited by David S. P. Hopkins and Roger G. Schroeder, pp. 1–18. New Directions for Institutional Research, no. 13. San Francisco: Jossey-Bass, Inc., 1977.

Bowen, Frank M., and Lyman A. Glenny. *State Budgeting for Higher Education: State Fiscal Stringency and Public Higher Education.* Berkeley, CA: Center for Research and Development in Higher Education, University of California, Berkeley, 1976.

Bowen, Howard R. "The Art of Retrenchment." *Academe,* vol. 69, no. 1 (January-February 1983), pp. 21–24.

———. *The Costs of Higher Education: How Much Do Colleges and Universities Spend per Student and How Much Should They Spend?* San Francisco: Jossey-Bass, Inc., 1980.

Brazziel, William F. "Planning for Enrollment Shifts in Colleges and Universities." *Research in Higher Education,* vol. 9, no. 1 (1978), pp. 1–13.

Breneman, David W. *The Coming Enrollment Crisis: What Every Trustee Must Know.* Washington, DC: Association of Governing Boards of Universities and Colleges, 1982.

Brewster, Kingman, Jr. "On Tenure." *AAUP Bulletin,* vol. 58, no. 4 (December 1972), pp. 381–383.

Brown, Mary Ellen. "The Experience of One Committee (or, What is the Sound of One Hand Clapping?)." *Academe,* vol. 68, no. 1 (January-February 1982), pp. 7a–8a.

Brown, Ralph S., Jr. "Financial Exigency." *AAUP Bulletin,* vol. 62, no. 1 (April 1976), pp. 5–16.

Brown, Ralph S., Jr., and Matthew W. Finkin. "The Usefulness of AAUP Policy Statements." *Educational Record,* vol. 59, no. 1 (Winter 1978), pp. 30–44.

Carter, E. Eugene. *College Financial Management.* Lexington, MA: Lexington Books, 1980.

Caruthers, J. Kent, and Melvin Orwig. *Budgeting in Higher Education.* AAHE/ ERIC Higher Education Research Report no. 3. Washington, DC: American Association for Higher Education, 1979.

Cell, Donald C. "Opening Question-Raising Remarks: Tenure and Exigency Problems." Paper presented at AAUP Conference on Hard Times, Washington, DC, May 20, 1982. Mimeo.

Change Panel on Academic Economics. *Colleges and Money: A Faculty Guide to Academic Economics.* New York: Change Magazine and Educational Change, 1976.

Cherry, Charles L. "Scalpels and Swords: The Surgery of Contingency Planning." *Educational Record,* vol. 59, no. 4 (Fall 1978), pp. 367–376.

Committee on College and University Accounting and Auditing. *Industry Audit Guide: Audits of Colleges and Universities.* New York: American Institute of Certified Public Accountants, 1973.

Cope, Robert G., ed. *Tomorrow's Imperatives Today: Proceedings of the 13th Annual Forum.* Association for Institutional Research, 1973.

Desruisseaux, Paul. "Missouri Campus Bitterly Divided over How to 'Reallocate' Funds." *The Chronicle of Higher Education,* vol. 24, no. 12 (May 19, 1982), pp. 1, 12.

Dickmeyer, Nathan, David S. P. Hopkins, and William F. Massy. "TRADES: A Model for Interactive Financial Planning." In *Financial Planning Models: Concepts and Case Studies in Colleges and Universities,* edited by Joe B. Wyatt, James C. Emery, and Carolyn P. Landis, pp. 63–76. Princeton, NJ: EDUCOM, 1979.

Dressel, Paul, and Lou Anna Kimsey Simon. *Allocating Resources Among Departments.* New Directions for Institutional Research, no. 11. San Francisco: Jossey-Bass, Inc., 1976.

Ennis, Richard, and J. Peter Williamson. *Spending Policy for Educational Endowments.* New York: The Common Fund, 1976.

Ford Foundation. *Managing Educational Endowments: A Report to the Ford Foundation.* 2nd ed. New York: The Foundation, 1972.

Frances, Carol, ed. *Successful Responses to Financial Difficulty.* New Directions for Higher Education, no. 38. San Francisco: Jossey-Bass, Inc., 1982.

Francis, Jack Clark. *Investments: Analysis and Management.* 3rd ed. New York: McGraw-Hill, 1980.

Furniss, W. Todd. "The 1976 AAUP Retrenchment Policy." *Educational Record,* vol. 57, no. 3 (Summer 1976), pp. 133–139.

———. "Retrenchment, Layoff, and Termination." *Educational Record,* vol. 55, no. 3 (Summer 1974), pp. 159–170.

Ginsburg, Sigmund G. "120 Ways to Increase Income and Decrease Expenses." *Business Officer*, vol. 16, no. 6 (December 1982), pp. 14–16.

Glenny, Lyman A. "Demographic and Related Issues for Higher Education in the 1980s." *Journal of Higher Education*, vol. 51, no. 4 (March/April 1980), pp. 363–380.

―――. *State Budgeting for Higher Education: Interagency Conflict and Consensus*. Berkeley, CA: Center for Research and Development in Higher Education, University of California, Berkeley, 1976.

Glenny, Lyman A., et al. *State Budgeting for Higher Education: Data Digest*. Berkeley, CA: Center for Research and Development in Higher Education, University of California, Berkeley, 1975.

Halstead, D. Kent. *Higher Education Prices and Price Indexes: 1975 Supplement*. Washington, DC: National Institute of Education, 1976.

―――. *How States Compare in Financial Support of Higher Education, 1982–83*. Washington, DC: National Institute of Education, 1983a.

―――. *Inflation Measures for Schools and Colleges*. Washington, DC: National Institute of Education, 1983b.

―――. *Tax Wealth in Fifty States*. Washington, DC: National Institute of Education, 1978.

Hample, Stephen R. *Coping with Faculty Reduction*. New Directions for Institutional Research, no. 30. San Francisco: Jossey-Bass, Inc., 1981.

―――. "Cost Studies in Higher Education." *AIR Professional File*, no. 7 (Fall 1980).

Herring, Carol P., et al. *Budgeting and Resource Allocation at Princeton University: Report of a Demonstration Project Supported by the Ford Foundation*. Vol. 2. Princeton, NJ: Princeton University, 1979.

Hoenack, Stephen A., and William C. Weiler. "The Demand for Higher Education and Institutional Enrollment Forecasting." *Economic Inquiry*, vol. 17, no. 1 (January 1979), pp. 89–113.

Hopkins, David S. P., and Roger G. Schroeder, eds. *Applying Analytic Methods to Planning and Management*. New Directions for Institutional Research, no. 13. San Francisco: Jossey-Bass, Inc., 1977.

Hopkins, David S. P., and William F. Massy. *Planning Models for Colleges and Universities*. Stanford, CA: Stanford University Press, 1981.

Hopkins, David S. P., Lawrence L. Landry, Burton Sonenstein, and James D. Tschectelin. "Financial Modeling: Four Success Stories." *EDUCOM Bulletin*, vol. 17, no. 3 (Fall 1982), pp. 11–15.

Hughes, K. Scott, Jerry H. Leonard, and M. J. Williams, Jr. *A Management Reporting Manual for Colleges*. Washington, DC: National Association of College and University Business Officers, 1980.

Hussain, K. M. "Comprehensive Planning Models in North America and Europe." In *Assessing Computer-based Systems Models*, edited by Thomas R. Mason. New Directions for Institutional Research, no. 9. San Francisco: Jossey-Bass, Inc., 1976.

Hussain, K. M., and Thomas R. Mason. "Planning Models in Higher Education: A Comparison of CAMPUS and RRPM." In *Tomorrow's Perspectives Today: Proceedings of the 13th Annual Forum,* edited by Robert G. Cope. Association for Institutional Research, 1973.

Hyatt, James A. *A Cost Accounting Handbook for Colleges and Universities.* Washington, DC: National Association of College and University Business Officers, 1983.

————. "Using National Financial Data for Comparative Analysis." In *Successful Responses to Financial Difficulty,* edited by Carol Frances, pp. 95–98. New Directions for Higher Education, no. 38. San Francisco: Jossey-Bass, Inc., 1982.

Jenkins, Robin, and James Topping. "Costing for Policy Analysis." *Business Officer,* vol. 13, no. 12 (June 1980), pp. 25–27.

Jenny, Hans H., with Geoffrey C. Hughes and Richard D. Devine. *Hang-Gliding, or Looking for an Updraft: A Study of College and University Finance in the 1980s—The Capital Margin.* Wooster, OH, and Boulder, CO: The College of Wooster and John Minter Associates, 1981.

Kramer, Martin. "What the Indicators Cannot Tell Us." In *Successful Responses to Financial Difficulty,* edited by Carol Frances, pp. 99–110. New Directions for Higher Education, no. 38. San Francisco: Jossey-Bass, Inc., 1982.

Kreinin, Mordechai E. "Point of View: For a University in Financial Trouble, a Faculty 'Buy-Out' Plan Can Save Money and Face." *The Chronicle of Higher Education,* vol. 23, no. 20 (January 27, 1982a), p. 56.

————. "Preserving Tenure Commitments in Hard Times: The Michigan State Experience." *Academe,* vol. 68, no. 2 (March–April 1982b), pp. 37–45.

Lee, Robert D., Jr., and Ronald W. Johnson. *Public Budgeting Systems.* 2nd ed. Baltimore: University Park Press, 1977.

LeLoup, Lance T. "The Myth of Incrementalism: Analytical Choices in Budgetary Theory." *Polity,* vol. 10, no. 4 (Summer 1978), pp. 488–509.

Leslie, Larry L., and James A. Hyatt. *Higher Education Financing Policies: States/Institutions and Their Interaction.* Tucson, AZ: Center for the Study of Higher Education, University of Arizona, 1981.

Lingenfelter, Paul E., and Freeman H. Beets. *Higher Education Costs: Causes and Containment—A Study of 34 Midwestern Colleges and Universities.* Kansas City, MO: U.S. Department of Education Region VII, 1980.

Mason, Thomas R., ed. *Assessing Computer-based Systems Models.* New Directions for Institutional Research, no. 9. San Francisco: Jossey-Bass, Inc., 1976.

McCoy, Marilyn, and D. Kent Halstead. *Higher Education Financing in the Fifty States: Interstate Comparisons, Fiscal Year 1979.* 2nd ed. Boulder, CO: National Center for Higher Education Management Systems, 1982.

————. *Higher Education Financing in the Fifty States: Interstate Comparisons, Fiscal Year 1981.* 3rd ed. Boulder, CO: National Center for Higher Education Management Systems, 1984.

Meisinger, Richard J., Jr. *State Budgeting for Higher Education: The Uses of Formulas.* Berkeley, CA: Center for Research and Development in Higher Education, University of California, Berkeley, 1976.

Mingle, James R. "Redirecting Higher Education in a Time of Budget Reduction." *Issues in Higher Education,* no. 18. Atlanta: Southern Regional Education Board, 1982.

————, ed. *Management Flexibility and State Regulation in Higher Education.* Atlanta: Southern Regional Education Board, 1983.

Mingle, James R., et al. *Challenges of Retrenchment: Strategies for Consolidating Programs, Cutting Costs, and Reallocating Resources.* San Francisco: Jossey-Bass, Inc., 1981.

Mix, Marjorie C. *Tenure and Termination in Financial Exigency.* AAHE/ERIC Higher Education Research Report no. 3. Washington, DC: American Association for Higher Education, 1978.

Morgan, Anthony W. "Flexibility for Whom: The Case of Forced Savings in Budgeting in Higher Education." *Educational Record,* vol. 56, no. 1 (Winter 1975), pp. 42–47.

Mortimer, Kenneth P., and Michael L. Tierney. *The Three "R's" of the Eighties: Reduction, Reallocation and Retrenchment.* AAHE/ERIC Higher Education Research Report no. 4. Washington, DC: American Association for Higher Education, 1979.

Moser, Collette, Roy Matthews, and Marvin Grandstaff. "Buyouts at MSU." *Academe,* vol. 68, no. 5 (September–October 1982), p. 6.

National Association of College and University Business Officers. *College & University Business Administration.* 4th ed. Washington, DC: NACUBO, 1982.

————. *Indirect Cost Rates—Long Form: A Manual for Preparation of Indirect Cost Studies.* Materials revised and updated annually for NACUBO's workshop on indirect cost rates—long form.

————. "Indirect Costs of Sponsored Programs." Chap. 4:7 in *College & University Business Administration.* 4th ed. Washington, DC: NACUBO, 1982.

National Association of College and University Business Officers and the Committee for the Concerns of Women in New England Colleges and Universities. *Conference for Women Administrators: Financial Management of Colleges and Universities.* Washington, DC: NACUBO and The Committee, n.d.

National Center for Education Statistics. *The Condition of Education.* Washington, DC: U.S. Government Printing Office, 1983.

Nevison, Christopher H. "Effects of Tenure and Retirement Policies on the College Faculty: A Case Study Using Computer Simulation." *Journal of Higher Education,* vol. 51, no. 2 (March/April 1980), pp. 150–166.

O'Neil, Robert M. "A President's Perspective." *Academe,* vol. 69, no. 1 (January–February 1983), pp. 17–20.

Palmer, David D., and Carl V. Patton. "Mid-Career Change Options in Academe: Experience and Possibilities." *Journal of Higher Education,* vol. 52, no. 4 (July/August 1981), pp. 378–398.

Patton, Carl V. *Academia in Transition: Mid-Career Change or Early Retirement.* Cambridge, MA: Abt Books, 1979.

————. "Voluntary Alternatives to Forced Termination." *Academe,* vol. 69, no. 1 (January–February 1983), pp. 1a–8a.

Powell, Ray M. *Accounting Procedures for Institutions.* Notre Dame, IN: University of Notre Dame Press, 1978.

————. *Budgetary Control Procedures for Institutions.* Notre Dame, IN: University of Notre Dame Press, 1980.

Purves, Ralph A., and Lyman A. Glenny. *State Budgeting for Higher Education: Information Systems and Technical Analyses.* Berkeley, CA: Center for Research and Development in Higher Education, University of California, Berkeley, 1976.

Robinson, Daniel D., Howard W. Ray, and Frederick J. Turk. "Cost Behavior Analysis for Planning in Higher Education." *NACUBO Professional File,* vol. 9, no. 5 (May 1977).

Rusk, James. J., and Larry L. Leslie. "The Setting of Tuition in Public Higher Education." *Journal of Higher Education,* vol. 49, no. 6 (November/December 1978), pp. 531–547.

Schmidtlein, Frank A., and Lyman A. Glenny. *State Budgeting for Higher Education: The Political Economy of the Process.* Berkeley, CA: Center for Research and Development in Higher Education, University of California, Berkeley, 1977.

Smith, Donald K. "Coping, Improving, and Planning for the Future during Fiscal Decline: A Case Study from the University of Wisconsin Experience." In *The Monday Morning Experience: Report from the Boyer Workshop on State University Systems,* edited by Martin Kaplan, pp. 25–40. New York: Aspen Institute for Humanistic Studies, 1976.

Stampen, Jacob. *The Financing of Public Higher Education.* AAHE/ERIC Higher Education Research Report no. 9. Washington, DC: American Association for Higher Education, 1980.

Stanford University. *Stanford University Operating Budget Guidelines, 1981–82.* Stanford, CA: The University, 1981.

Strohm, Paul. "Faculty Responsibilities and Rights During Retrenchment." In *Challenges of Retrenchment: Strategies for Consolidating Programs, Cutting Costs, and Reallocating Resources,* by James R. Mingle et al., pp. 134–152. San Francisco: Jossey-Bass, Inc., 1981.

Suslow, Sidney. "Benefits of a Coherent Survival Projection Model." In *Applying Analytic Methods to Planning and Management,* edited by David S. P. Hopkins and Roger G. Schroeder, pp. 19–42. New Directions for Institutional Research, no. 13. San Francisco: Jossey-Bass, Inc., 1977.

————. "Induced Course Load Matrix: Conception and Use." In *Assessing Computer-based Systems Models,* edited by Thomas R. Mason, pp. 35–52. New Directions for Institutional Research, no. 9. San Francisco: Jossey-Bass, Inc., 1976.

Train, John. *Dance of the Money Bees: A Professional Speaks Frankly on Investing.* New York: Harper & Row, 1974.

————. *The Money Masters.* New York: Harper & Row, 1980.

The Twentieth Century Fund Task Force on College and University Endowment Policy. *Funds for the Future.* New York: McGraw-Hill, 1975.

U.S. Bureau of the Census. *Current Population Reports.* Series P-25, no. 721. Washington, DC: U.S. Government Printing Office, April 1978a.

————. *Current Population Reports.* Series P-20, no. 329. Washington, DC: U.S. Government Printing Office, September 1978b.

————. *Current Population Reports.* Series P-25, no. 802. Washington, DC: U.S. Government Printing Office, May 1979.

Van Alstyne, William. "Tenure: A Summary, Explanation, and 'Defense.'" *AAUP Bulletin,* vol. 57, no. 2 (June 1971), pp. 328–333.

Viehland, Dennis, Norman Kaufman, and Barbara Krauth. "Indexing Tuition to Cost of Education: Implications for State Policy." In *Higher Education Financing Policies: States/Institutions and Their Interaction,* edited by Larry L. Leslie and James A. Hyatt, pp. 23–34. Tucson, AZ: Center for the Study of Higher Education, University of Arizona, 1981.

Wildavsky, Aaron. *Budgeting: A Comparative Theory of Budgetary Processes.* Boston: Little, Brown & Co., 1975.

————. *The Politics of the Budgetary Process.* 3rd ed. Boston: Little, Brown & Co., 1979.

Wyatt, Joe B., James C. Emery, and Carolyn P. Landis, eds. *Financial Planning Models: Concepts and Case Studies in Colleges and Universities.* Princeton, NJ: EDUCOM, 1979.

Zeckhauser, Sally H. "Models as Planning Tools: The Harvard Experiment." In *Financial Planning Models: Concepts and Case Studies in Colleges and Universities,* edited by Joe B. Wyatt, James C. Emery, and Carolyn P. Landis, pp. 93–114. Princeton, NJ: EDUCOM, 1979.